D1093875

# THE JOURNALS OF LEWIS & CLARK

Meriwether Lewis

# THE
# JOURNALS
## *OF THE EXPEDITION*

UNDER THE COMMAND OF

# Capt.ˢ LEWIS and CLARK

to the *sources* of the MISSOURI, thence *across*

the ROCKY MOUNTAINS and down

the river COLUMBIA to the PACIFIC Ocean,

performed during the YEARS 1804–5–6

by ORDER of the Government of the United States.

EDITED BY

NICHOLAS BIDDLE

*with an introduction by* JOHN BAKELESS

AND ILLUSTRATED WITH WATER COLORS AND DRAWINGS
BY CARL BODMER AND OTHER CONTEMPORARY ARTISTS

## *VOLUME TWO*

## THE HERITAGE PRESS

*New York*

# CONTENTS OF VOLUME TWO

The Route from the Great Divide to the Pacific and Back to St. Louis  xvi

CHAPTER 15  *Crossing the Great Divide*                                233

Affecting interview between the wife of Chaboneau and the chief of the
Shoshonees. Council held with that nation, and favourable result. The
extreme navigable point of the Missouri mentioned. General character of
the river and of the country through which it passes. Captain Clark in
exploring the source of the Columbia falls in company with another
party of Shoshonees. The geographical information acquired from one
of that party. Their manner of catching fish. The party reach Lewis
river. The difficulties which captain Clark had to encounter in his route.
Friendship and hospitality of the Shoshonees. The party with captain
Lewis employed in making saddles, and preparing for the journey.

CHAPTER 16  *Among the Shoshonee Indians*                              248

Contest between Drewyer and a Shoshonee. The fidelity and honour of
that tribe. The party set out on their journey. The conduct of Cameahwait
reproved, and himself reconciled. The easy parturition of the Shoshonee
women. History of this nation. Their terror of the Pawkees. Their government and family economy in their treatment of their women. Their
complaint of Spanish treachery. Description of their weapons of warfare. Their curious mode of making a shield. The caparison of their
horses. The dress of the man and of the women particularly described.
Their mode of acquiring new names.

CHAPTER 17  *Down the Kooskooskee River*                               264

The party, after procuring horses from the Shoshonees, proceed on their
journey through the mountains. The difficulties and dangers of the route.
A council held with another band of the Shoshonees, of whom some account is given. They are reduced to the necessity of killing their horses
for food. Captain Clark with a small party precedes the main body in
quest of food, and is hospitably received by the Pierced-nose Indians. Arrival of the main body amongst this tribe, with whom a council is held.
They resolve to perform the remainder of their journey in canoes. Sickness of the party. They descend the Kooskooskee to its junction with
Lewis river, after passing several dangerous rapids. Short description of
the Pierced-nose Indians. Their manners and dress.

CHAPTER 18  *Down the Snake and Columbia Rivers*                       285

The party proceed in canoes. Description of an Indian sweating bath
and burial place. Many dangerous rapids passed. Narrow escape of one
of the canoes. In the passage down they are visited by several Indians,
all of whom manifest pacific dispositions. Description of the Sokulk tribe.
Their dress, and manner of building houses. Their pacific character.
Their habits of living. Their mode of boiling salmon. Vast quantities of
salmon amongst the Sokulk. Council held with this tribe. The terror and
consternation excited by captain Clark, concerning which an interesting
cause is related. Some account of the Pisquitpaws. Their mode of burying the dead.

CHAPTER 19 *Down the Columbia to the Great Rapids* 300

The party in their passage still visited by the Indians. Lepage's river described. Immense quantities of salmon caught by the Indians. Description of the river Towahnahiooks. Indian mode of stacking fish, and preparing them for market. Description of the great falls. Description of an Indian canoe. Alarm excited by an anticipated attack from the Eheltoots. A very dangerous rapid passed in safety, called by the Indians the Falls. Account of the Indian houses in the neighbourhood. Another dreadful rapid passed without injury. Some account of the Chilluckittequaw Indians. Captain Clark examines the great rapids. Description of an Indian burial place. The rapids passed in safety.

CHAPTER 20 *From Tidewater to the Pacific Ocean* 320

First appearance of tide water in the Columbia river. Description of the Quicksand river. Some account of the Skilloot Indians. The party pass the river Coweliskee. Some account of the Wahkiacum Indians. Arrival on the borders of the Pacific. Disagreeable and critical situation of the party when first encamped. Their distress occasioned by the incessant torrents of rain. Exposed for thirty days to this drenching deluge, during which time their provisions are spoiled, and most of their few articles of merchandise destroyed. Distress of the party. Adventure of Shannon and his danger from the Wahkiacums. Difficulty of finding a place suitable for a permanent encampment. Visited by several Indians of different tribes, on whom medals are bestowed.

CHAPTER 21 *The Establishment of Fort Clatsop* 336

Extravagant passion of the natives for blue beads, which constitute amongst them the circulating medium of the country. The party still in search of a suitable place for winter quarters. Still suffering from the constant deluges of rain. Are visited by the Indians, with whom they traffic but little, on account of the extravagant prices they ask for every article. Return of captain Lewis who reports that he has found a suitable place for winter quarters. The rain still continues. They prepare to form an encampment on a point of high land on the banks of the river Nutel. Captain Clark goes with a party to find a place suitable for the manufacture of salt. He is hospitably entertained by the Clatsops. This tribe addicted to the vice of gambling. Sickness of some of the party, occasioned by the incessant rains. They form, notwithstanding a permanent encampment for their winter quarters.

CHAPTER 22 *At Fort Clatsop* 353

A party, headed by captain Clark, go in quest of a whale driven on the shore of the Pacific to obtain some of the oil. They pass Clatsop river, which is described. The perilous nature of this jaunt, and the grandeur of the scenery described. Indian mode of extracting whale oil. The life of one of captain Clark's party preserved by the kindness of an Indian woman. A short account of the Chinnooks, of the Clatsops, Killamucks, the Lucktons, and an enumeration of several other tribes. The manner of sepulchre among the Chinnooks, Clatsops, &c. Description of their weapons of war and hunting. Their mode of building houses. Their manufactures, and cookery. Their mode of making canoes. Their great dexterity in managing that vehicle.

CHAPTER 23 *Indians of the Vicinity* 367

An account of the Clatsops, Killamucks, Chinnooks and Cathlamahs. Their uniform custom of flattening the forehead. The dress of these savages, and their ornaments, described. The licensed prostitution of the women, married and unmarried, of which a ludicrous instance is given.

The character of their diseases. The common opinion, that the treatment of women is the standard by which the virtues of an Indian may be known, combatted, and disproved by examples. The respect entertained by these Indians for old age, compared with the different conduct of those nations who subsist by the chase. Their mode of government. Their ignorance of ardent spirits, and their fondness for gambling. Their dexterity in traffic. In what articles their traffic consists. Their extraordinary attachment to blue beads, which forms their circulating medium.

CHAPTER 24   *Botany and Zoology*                              379

A general description of the beasts, birds, and plants, &c. found by the party in this expedition.


CHAPTER 25   *Homeward Bound*                                 410

Difficulty of procuring means of subsistence for the party. They determine to resume their journey to the mountains. They leave in the hands of the Indians a written memorandum, importing their having penetrated to the Pacific, through the route of the Missouri and Columbia, and through the Rocky mountains. The party commence their return route. Dexterity of the Cathlamah Indians in carving. Description of the Coweliskee river. They experience much hospitality from the natives. An instance of the extreme voracity of the vulture. The party are visited by many strange Indians, all of whom are kind and hospitable. Scarcity of game, and embarrassments of the party on that account. Captain Clark discovers a tribe not seen in the descent down the Columbia. Singular adventure to obtain provisions from them. Particular description of the Multnomah village and river. Description of mount Jefferson. Some account by captain Clark of the Neerchokio tribe, and of their architecture. Their sufferings by the small-pox.


CHAPTER 26   *Up the Columbia to the Dalles*                  422

Description of Wappatoo island, and the mode in which the nations gather wappatoo. The character of the soil and its productions. The numerous tribes residing in its vicinity. The probability that they were all of the tribe of the Multnomahs originally, inferred from similarity of dress, manners, language, &c. Description of their dress, weapons of war, their mode of burying the dead. Description of another village, called the Wahclellah village. Their mode of architecture. Extraordinary height of Beacon rock. Unfriendly character of the Indians at that place. The party, alarmed for their safety, resolve to inflict summary vengeance, in case the Wahclellah tribe persist in their outrages and insults. Interview with the chief of that tribe, and confidence restored. Difficulty of drawing the canoes over the rapids. Visited by a party of the Yehugh tribe. Short notice of the Weocksockwillackum tribe. Curious phenomenon observed in the Columbia, from the rapids to the Chilluckittequaws.


CHAPTER 27   *From the Dalles to Walla Walla River*           434

Captain Clark procures four horses for the transportation of the baggage. Some further account of the Skilloot tribe. Their joy at the first appearance of salmon in the Columbia. Their thievish propensities. The party arrive at the village of the Eneeshurs, where the natives are found alike unfriendly. The party now provided with horses. The party prevented from the exercise of hostility against this nation by a friendly adjustment. The scarcity of timber so great that they are compelled to buy wood to cook their provisions. Arrive at the Wahhowpum village. Dance of the natives. Their ingenuity in declining to purchase the canoes, on the supposition that the party would be compelled to leave them behind defeated. The party having obtained a complement of horses, proceed by land. Arrive at the Pishquitpah village, and some account of that people. Their frank and hospitable treatment from the Wollawollahs. Their mode of dancing described. Their mode of making fish-weirs. Their amiable character, and their unusual affection for the whites.

CHAPTER 28   *From the Walla Walla to Commearp Creek*                446

The party still pursue their route towards the Kooskooskee on horseback with Wollawollah guides. Character of the country. The quamash and other flowering shrubs in bloom. The party reach the Kinnooenim creek. They meet with an old acquaintance called the Bighorn Indian. They arrive at the mouth of the Kooskooskee. Singular custom among the Chopunnish women. Difficulty of purchasing provisions from the natives, and the new resort of the party to obtain them. The Chopunnish style of architecture. Captain Clark turns physician, and performs several experiments with success upon the natives, which they reward. An instance of their honesty. The distress of the Indians for want of provisions during the winter. The party finally meet the Twistedhair, to whom was entrusted their horses during their journey down. The quarrel between that chief and another of his nation, on the subject of his horses. The causes of this controversy stated at large. The two chiefs reconciled by the interference of the party, and the horses restored. Extraordinary instance of Indian hospitality towards strangers. A council held with the Chopunnish, and the object of the expedition explained in a very circuitous route of explanation. The party again perform medical cures. The answer of the Chopunnish to the speech delivered at the council, confirmed by a singular ceremony of acquiescence. They promise faithfully to follow the advice of their visitors.


CHAPTER 29   *Encamped on the Upper Kooskooskee*                458

The party encamp amongst the Chopunnish, and receive further evidences of their hospitality. The Indian mode of boiling bear-flesh. Of gelding horses. Their mode of decoying the deer within reach of their arrows. Character of the soil and climate in the Rocky mountains. Varieties of climate. Character of the natives. Their dress and ornaments. Mode of burying the dead. The party administer medical relief to the natives. One of the natives restored to the use of his limbs by sweating, and the curious process by which perspiration was excited. Another proof of Chopunnish hospitality. Success of their sweating prescription on the Indian chief. Description of the horned lizard, and a variety of insects. The attachment of the friends of a dying Indian to a tomahawk which he had stolen from the party, and which they desired to bury with the body. Description of the river Tommanamah. The Indians return an answer to a proposition made by the party.


CHAPTER 30   *In the Bitter Root Mountains Again*                471

The party mingle in the diversions of the Willetpos Indians, a tribe hitherto unnoticed. Their joy on the prospect of a return. Description of the vegetables growing on the Rocky mountains. Various preparations made to resume their journey. The party set out, and arrive at Hungry creek. The serious and desponding difficulties that obstructed their progress. They are compelled to return and wait for a guide across the mountains. Their distress for want of provisions. They resolve to return to the Quamash flats. They are at last so fortunate as to procure Indian guides, with whom they resume their journey to the falls of the Missouri. The danger of the route described. Their scarcity of provisions, and the danger of their journey. Their course lying along the ridges of mountains. Description of the warm springs, where the party encamp. The fondness of the Indians for bathing in them.

CHAPTER 31 *Captain Lewis Seeks a Short-Cut*                    482

The party proceed on their journey with their Indian guides, and at length agree to divide, to take several routes, and to meet again at the mouth of Yellowstone river. The route of captain Lewis is to pursue the most direct road to the falls of the Missouri, then to ascend Maria's river, explore the country, and to descend that river to its mouth. Captain Lewis, accordingly, with nine men proceed up the eastern branch of Clark's river, and take leave of their Indian guides. Description of that branch, and character of the surrounding country. Description of the Cokalahishkit river. They arrive at the ridge dividing the Missouri from the Columbia rivers. Meet once more with the buffalo and brown bear. Immense herds of buffalo discovered on the borders of Medicine river. The party encamp on Whitebear islands. Singular adventure that befel M'Neil. Captain Lewis, with three of his party proceed to explore the source of Maria's river. Tansy river described. He reaches the dividing line of these two streams. General character of the surrounding country.


CHAPTER 32 *Lewis Completes His Separate Exploration*          493

Captain Lewis and his party still proceed on the route mentioned in the last chapter, and arrive at the forks of Maria's river; of which river a particular description is given. Alarmed by the evidence that they are in the neighbourhood of unfriendly Indians, and much distressed for want of provisions, the weather proving unfavourable, they are compelled to return. The face of the country described. Interview with the unfriendly Indians, called Minnetarees of Fort de Prairie. Mutual consternation. Resolution of captain Lewis. They encamp together for the night, apparently with amicable dispositions. The conversation that ensued between these new visitants. The conflict occasioned by the Indians attempting to seize the rifles and horses of the party, in which one is mortally wounded. Captain Lewis kills another Indian, and his narrow escape. Having taken four horses belonging to the Indians, they hastened with all expedition to join the party attached to captain Clark. Arriving near the Missouri they are alarmed by the sound of rifles, which proves fortunately to be from the party of their friends, under the command of sergeant Ordway. The two detachments thus fortunately united, leave their horses, and descend the Missouri in canoes. They continue their route down the river to form a junction with captain Clark. Vast quantities of game found in their passage down the river. Captain Lewis accidentally wounded by one of his own party. They proceed down the Missouri, and at length join captain Clark.


CHAPTER 33 *Captain Clark Explores the Yellowstone*           505

The party commanded by captain Clark, previous to his being joined by captain Lewis, proceed along Clark's river, in pursuance of the route mentioned in a preceding chapter. Their sorry commemoration of our national anniversary. An instance of Sacajawea's strength of memory. Description of the river and of the surrounding country as the party proceed. Several of the horses belonging to the party supposed to be stolen by their Indian neighbours. They reach Wisdom river. Extraordinary heat of a spring. The strong attachment of the party for tobacco, which they find on opening a cache. Sergeant Ordway recovers the horses. Captain Clark divides his party, one detachment of which was to descend the river: they reach Gallatin and Jefferson rivers, of which a description is given. Arrive at the Yellowstone river. Some account of Otter and Beaver rivers. An example of Indian fortification. One of the party seriously and accidentally wounded. Engaged in the construction of canoes. Twenty-four horses stolen, probably by the Indians, in one night.

CHAPTER 34  *Down the Yellowstone; Reunion of the Parties*        516

Captain Clark proceeds with his party down the river. Description of an Indian lodge. Sergeant Pryor arrives with the horses left by the party when they embarked in their canoes; his difficulty in bringing them on. Remarkable rock discovered by captain Clark, and the beauty of the prospect from the summit. They continue their route down the river, of which a particular description is given, as well as of the surrounding country. Yellowstone and Bighorn rivers compared. Great quantities of game found on the banks of the rivers. Immense herds of buffalo. Fierceness of the white bear. Encamp at the junction of the Yellowstone and Missouri. A general outline given of Yellowstone river, comprehending the shoals; its entrance recommended for the formation of a trading establishment. The sufferings of the party from the mosquitoes. Sergeant Pryor, who, with a detachment of the party, was to have brought on the horses, arrives and reports that they were all stolen by the Indians; deprived of these animals, they form for themselves Indian canoes of the skins of beasts, and of curious structure, with which they descend the river over the most difficult shoals and dangerous rapids. Meet with two white men unexpectedly, from whom they procure intelligence of the Indians formerly visited by the party.

CHAPTER 35  *Down the Missouri to White River*        527

The party, while descending the river in their skin canoes, are overtaken by the detachment under captain Lewis, and the whole party, now once more happily united, descend the Missouri together. They once more visit the Minnetaree Indians, and hold a council with that nation as well as with the Mahahas. Captain Clark endeavours to persuade their chiefs to accompany him to the United States, which invitation they decline, on account of their fears of the Sioux, in their passage down the river. Colter, one of the party, requests and obtains liberty to remain among the Indians, for the purpose of hunting beaver. Friendly deportment of the Mandans; council held by captain Clark with the chiefs of the different villages; the chief named the Bigwhite, with his wife and son, agree to accompany the party to the United States, who takes an affecting farewell of his nation. Chaboneau, with his wife and child, decline visiting the United States, and are left among the Indians. The party at length proceed on their journey, and find that the course of the Missouri has, in some places, changed since their passage up that river. They arrive among the Ricaras. Character of the Chayennes; their dress, habits, &c. Captain Clark offers to the chief of this nation a medal, which he at first refuses, believing it to be medicine, but which he is afterwards prevailed on to accept. The party proceed rapidly down the river. Prepare to defend themselves against the Tetons, but receive no injury from them. Incredible numbers of buffalo seen near White river. They meet, at last, with the Tetons, and refuse their invitations to land. Intrepidity of captain Clark.

CHAPTER 36  *The Expedition Returns in Safety to St. Louis*        539

The party are hailed by a group of Indians and fear an attack, but are relieved to learn that they are friendly Yanktons. A flagstaff that had been erected by the party in September, 1804, opposite Calumet bluff, is found still standing. They meet Mr. James Airs, a trader from Mackinaw, who presents the party with tobacco and flour. Next they meet a party on the way to trade with the Yanktons, and obtain their first whiskey in more than a year. Encounter with Mr. Gravelines, who reports the death of the Ricara chief at Washington. Learn of the opinion in the United States that the expedition had perished. They are met with a great welcome at Lacharette and St. Louis.

Acknowledgments        547

# PORTRAITS & COLOR PLATES

## VOLUME TWO

Meriwether Lewis (*after Charles de St.-Memin*)       PAGE ii

William Clark (*Chester Harding and John J. Douberman*)       iii

Indian Painting of a Combat (*copied by Carl Bodmer*)    FACING PAGE 242

> In the scene painted on a buffalo robe by Mato-Topé, the Mandan chief is depicted fighting a Cheyenne chief, distinguished by the otter skin on his head. Mato-Topé's hand has been cut in seizing the knife with which he is about to stab his enemy.

Indian Utensils and Weapons (*Carl Bodmer*)       274

> Tools, weapons, and apparel of various midwestern Indian tribes: 1. Bone tool for scraping wood. 2. Horn ladle. 3. Horseman's short spear. 4. Gunstock club with spear blade. 5. Feathered bonnet. 6. Shield belonging to Mato-Topé. 7. Roached deertail decorated with rattlesnake rattle. 8. Parfleche—painted rawhide envelope for carrying food. 9. Moccasins (left, man's; right, woman's). 10. Quiver, with two types of bows. 11. Coup stick, used in close fighting to win acclaim as an act of bravery. 12. Pipe with catlinite (red clay) stem, inlaid with slate and lead. 13. Calumet, or ceremonial peace pipe. 14. Woman's game ball. 15. Game hoop and spear. 16. Double bone whistle. 17. Dance drum. 18. Man's moccasin. 19. Bundle of tobacco.

Iowa Warrior (*George Bird King*)       298

> Tah-Ro-Hon, famed from his youth for his combats with the Sioux and Osage. A signer of the treaty of St. Louis, he visited Washington, where his portrait was painted.

Assiniboin and Yanktonai Indians (*Carl Bodmer*)       338

> The Assiniboin's headdress combines antelope horns and a crest of trimmed feathers; a rosette of porcupine quills decorates his breast.

Muskwaki (Fox) Indian (*Carl Bodmer*)       390

> Wakusaase's tribe belonged to the Algonquian group and was allied to the Sacs.

Oto Warrior (*George Bird King*)       430

> The "Ottoes" are described in Chapter 2 as among the first with whom the expedition had contact. This warrior's name, No-Way-Ke-Sug-Ga, means "He who strikes two at once."

Interior of the Hut of a Mandan Chief (*Carl Bodmer*)  462

> Between the four center posts that support the roof are shorter posts forming the wall, which is covered on the outside with matting, hay, and earth. Smoke from the central fire escapes through the roof. These large circular houses were warm and spacious.

Blackfoot Indian on Horseback (*Carl Bodmer*)  494

> It was an armed Indian of this tribe who barely missed killing Captain Lewis in July 1806 (see Chapter 32).

Hunting the Bison (*Carl Bodmer*)  530

> Big-game hunting was an easier task for the Indians after the white men brought horses to the New World. With the introduction of fire-arms, the buffalo herds were reduced almost to extinction.

# VOLUME TWO

*From the Great Divide to the Pacific
and Back to St. Louis*

---

AUGUST 17, 1805 TO SEPTEMBER 23, 1806

# THE ROUTE

Chapters 15, 16, and 17 are devoted largely to explorations of routes of passage across the mountains, investigations of waterways on the Pacific side, and interesting accounts of the Shoshones. From them they procured horses and made their way onward, seeking a water route to the Pacific. Captain Clark took his turn at path-seeking, and in Chapter 16 we find him, on August 21, 1805, passing the junction of the Salmon and Lemhi rivers, where Salmon City, Idaho, now stands. He travelled down the banks of Salmon River for some fifty miles, but found the route impossible for the party and returned. Meantime Lewis was awaiting him at the banks of the Jefferson. It was not until September 20, as related in Chapter 17, that the whole party finally reached the Pacific side of the Great Divide. Continuing their journey on horseback they reached a branch of the Kooskooskee River, now the Clearwater. Near this place is now Pierce City, the county seat of Shoshonee County, Idaho. Their land journey continued for only a few days, and then, encouraged by the assurances of the Indians as to a waterway to the Columbia, and also by the sight of navigable water, they began on September 27 to build canoes.

The latter part of Chapter 17 shows the explorers fairly on their way to the sea. They were descending the Kooskooskee, which they called the Clark, although, as we have seen, it is now the Clearwater.

At the junction of this river with the Kimooeenim near the Snake, described in the latter part of this chapter, they passed the present site of Lewiston, Idaho.

The adventurous journey down the Snake sketched in Chapter 18 carried them from Idaho into Washington and to the Columbia at the meeting point of Franklin, Walla Walla, and Yakima counties. The "western branch of the Columbia," described as the Tapteal, is now called the Yakima. The "conical mountain" (Mt. St. Helen's) is in Cowlitz County, Washington.

Chapter 19 continues the record of the voyage down the Columbia. "Le Page's River" is now John Day's River. "Timm Mountain" is Mt. Hood. Their descent of the "Great Falls," or Dalles and Chutes of the Columbia, is graphically described in this chapter and the next. For a part of the way they were travelling through Skamania County, Washington.

In Chapter 20 they pass the Willamette River without discovering it, and they presently catch a glimpse of Mt. St. Helen's. The Wahkiacum Indians whom they mention have disappeared, but the name has been given to the county of Washington west of Cowlitz. On November 7 the travellers obtained their first glimpse of the sea. They camped for the night near Gray's Bay, in the southwestern part of Wahkiakum County, and on the 15th moved to a camp on Baker's Bay. In Chapter 21 there is a description of their winter camp on the south side of the Columbia, some three miles up the Netul River, which empties into Meriwether's Bay.

The "Killamuck" Indians referred to in Chapter 22 are known as the Tillamooks, and the name has been given to Tillamook County, Oregon. Chapters 23 and 24 contain a detailed account of the Indians and the animals and birds observed by the explorers during the winter that they passed at the mouth of the Columbia.

It was on March 23, 1806, that the explorers started on their return (Chapter 25). They had encountered no white men at the mouth of the Columbia, and the scantiness of their remaining supplies increased the hardships of their journey.

Of the written lists and memoranda which they left with the Clatsops, one copy did reach the United States. In the summer of 1806 Captain Hill of the brig *Lydia* entered the Columbia to trade. He carried one of the explorers' papers to Canton, China, and then sent it to Philadelphia.

The vultures referred to in this chapter were the California condors, now nearly extinct. In this chapter and the next there is an account of the discovery of the Multnomah River, now the Willamette. Portland, Oregon, is near the Indian settlement described here. Wappatoo Inlet is now called Willamette Slough. The name "wappatoo" was the term in the Chinook jargon of the Northwest for the potato. The Multnomah Falls is the most noteworthy of the five cascades on the Oregon side of the river, which the explorers passed before they reached the head of tidewater, on April 9, and began the arduous portage around the Cascades of the Columbia and the Dalles.

On April 23 (Chapter 27) they passed the mouth of Rock River. The "Wollawollahs" encountered as they journeyed along the south or Oregon side of the Columbia are now the Walla Walla Indians, and the Youmalolam River is now the Umatilla. The end of this chapter finds the party travelling on horseback along the Walla Walla River through the county of that name. On May 1 they were between the present towns of Prescott and Waitesburg, in Washington. Their journey east of the Columbia continued along Touchet Creek, and, later, along the Kooskooskee, now the Clearwater, in Nez Percé County, Idaho.

The explorers were well to the eastward of the Bitter Root Mountains when they made the camp described in Chapter 29, to await the melting of the snow. The Quamash Flats of Chapter 30 were named for the camass root which was valued by the Indians. This chapter describes the difficult passage of the Bitter Root Mountains. Traveler's Rest Creek is near the summit of these mountains. The travellers had advanced from Idaho into Montana, but they had not yet passed the Great Divide.

Captain Lewis went ahead (Chapter 31), advancing between the Bitter Root and Rocky Mountain ranges, crossing the Missoula River and camping near the present site of Missoula, Montana. On July 7 they crossed the pass in the Rockies which brought them finally to the eastern side. They continued down the Medicine, now the Sun River, to the rendezvous at the Great Falls of the Missouri. Maria's River, which Lewis starts out to explore in Chapters 31 and 32, flows from near the northern boundary of Montana to the Missouri, near the town of Ophir. In Chapters 33 and 34 we can trace the journey of Captain Clark along Clark's or Bitter Root River to Ross' Hole, across the Rockies through Lewis' Pass, down Wisdom or Big Hole River to the forks of the Jefferson, down to the Missouri, and then up the Gallatin, crossing to the Yellowstone and following it to a meeting with Lewis on the Missouri.

The Divide was crossed on July 6, when Clark passed into Beaverhead County, Montana, travelling west of Bismarck City, Montana. A part of this journey followed the present line of the Northern Pacific Railroad from Gallatin City through Bozeman Pass to Livingston. On July 27 they passed from the Big Horn into the Yellowstone and "took a last look at the Rocky Mountains." It was not until August 12 (Chapter 35) that the party were reunited.

On their return to the Mandan villages, near Bismarck, they parted with the faithful Sacajawea, one of the most interesting figures of this expedition, and she and her husband and child remained behind. The hunter Colter, who turned back here to the wilderness, entered upon a dramatic series of adventures, which in 1807 included a flight from the Blackfeet that led to his discovery of the wonders of the Yellowstone National Park. The Indian chief Big White, who accompanied the explorers from this point, was prevented by the hostile Arikaras from returning the next year, and the Missouri Fur Company was paid $7000 to escort him back in 1809.

The return down the Missouri and Mississippi (Chapter 36) ended at St. Louis on September 23, 1806, closing a journey of 7689 miles. (The westward trip had been 4134 miles, the eastward 3555 miles, as the expedition saved 579 miles on their return by going from Traveler's Rest Creek directly to the Falls of the Missouri.)

SATURDAY, AUGUST 17TH, 1805    Captain Lewis rose very early, and despatched Drewyer and the Indian down the river in quest of the boats. Shields was sent out at the same time to hunt, while M'Neal prepared a breakfast out of the remainder of the meat. Drewyer had been gone about two hours, and the Indians were all anxiously waiting for some news, when an Indian who had straggled a short distance down the river, returned with a report that he had seen the white men, who were only a short distance below, and were coming on. The Indians were all transported with joy, and the chief in the warmth of his satisfaction renewed his embrace to captain Lewis, who was quite as much delighted as the Indians themselves; the report proved most agreeably true.

On setting out at seven o'clock, captain Clark with Chaboneau and his wife walked on shore, but they had not gone more than a mile before captain Clark saw Sacajawea, who was with her husband one hundred yards ahead, begin to dance and show every mark of the most extravagant joy, turning round him and pointing to several Indians, whom he now saw advancing on horseback, sucking her fingers at the same time to indicate that they were of her native tribe. As they advanced captain Clark discovered among them Drewyer dressed like an Indian, from whom he learned the situation of the party. While the boats were performing the circuit, he went towards the forks with the Indians, who as they went along, sang aloud with the greatest appearance of delight.

We soon drew near to the camp, and just as we approached it a woman made her way through the crowd towards Sacajawea, and recognising each other, they embraced with the most tender affection. The meeting of these two young women had in it something peculiarly touching, not only in the ardent manner in which their feelings were expressed, but from the real interest of their situation. They had been companions in childhood, in the war with the Minnetarees they had both been taken prisoners in the same battle, they had shared and softened the rigours of their captivity, till one of them had escaped from the Minnetarees, with scarce a hope of ever seeing her friend relieved from the hands of her enemies. While Sacajawea was renewing among the women the friendships of former days, captain Clark went on, and was received by captain Lewis and the chief, who after the first embraces and salutations were over, conducted him to a sort of circular tent or shade of willows. Here he was seated on a white robe; and the chief immediately tied in his hair six small shells resembling pearls, an ornament highly valued by these people, who procured them in the course of trade from the seacoast. The moccasins of the whole party were then taken off, and after much ceremony the smoking began. After this the conference was to be opened, and glad of an opportunity of being able to converse more intelligibly, Sacajawea was sent for; she came into the tent, sat down, and was beginning to interpret, when in the person of Cameahwait she recognised her brother: she instantly jumped up, and ran and embraced him, throwing over him her blanket and weeping profusely: the chief was himself moved, though not in the same degree. After some conversation between them she resumed her seat, and attempted to interpret for us, but her new situation seemed to overpower her, and she was frequently interrupted by her tears. After the council was finished, the unfortunate woman learnt that all her family were dead except two brothers, one of whom was absent,

233

and a son of her eldest sister, a small boy, who was immediately adopted by her. The canoes arriving soon after, we formed a camp in a meadow on the left side, a little below the forks; took out our baggage, and by means of our sails and willow poles formed a canopy for our Indian visitors. About four o'clock the chiefs and warriors were collected, and after the customary ceremony of taking off the moccasins and smoking a pipe, we explained to them in a long harangue the purposes of our visit, making themselves one conspicuous object of the good wishes of our government, on whose strength as well as its friendly disposition we expatiated. We told them of their dependence on the will of our government for all future supplies of whatever was necessary either for their comfort or defence; that as we were sent to discover the best route by which merchandise could be conveyed to them, and no trade would be begun before our return, it was mutually advantageous that we should proceed with as little delay as possible; that we were under the necessity of requesting them to furnish us with horses to transport our baggage across the mountains, and a guide to show us the route, but that they should be amply remunerated for their horses, as well as for every other service they should render us. In the meantime our first wish was, that they should immediately collect as many horses as were necessary to transport our baggage to their village, where, at our leisure we would trade with them for as many horses as they could spare.

The speech made a favourable impression: the chief in reply thanked us for our expressions of friendship towards himself and his nation, and declared their willingness to render us every service. He lamented that it would be so long before they should be supplied with firearms, but that till then they could subsist as they had heretofore done. He concluded by saying that there were not horses here sufficient to transport our goods, but that he would return to the village to-morrow, and bring all his own horses, and encourage his people to come over with theirs. The conference being ended to our satisfaction, we now enquired of Cameahwait what chiefs were among the party, and he pointed out two of them. We then distributed our presents: to Cameahwait we gave a medal of the small size, with the likeness of President Jefferson, and on the reverse a figure of hands clasped with a pipe and tomahawk: to this was added an uniform coat, a shirt, a pair of scarlet leggings, a carrot of tobacco, and some small articles. Each of the other chiefs received a small medal struck during the presidency of general Washington, a shirt, handkerchief, leggings, a knife, and some tobacco.  Medals of the same sort were also presented to two young warriors, who though not chiefs were promising youths and very much respected in the tribe. These honorary gifts were followed by presents of paint, moccasins, awls, knives, beads and looking-glasses. We also gave them all a plentiful meal of Indian corn, of which the hull is taken off by being boiled in lye; and as this was the first they had ever tasted, they were very much pleased with it. They had indeed abundant sources of surprise in all they saw: the appearance of the men, their arms, their clothing, the canoes, the strange looks of the negro, and the sagacity of our dog, all in turn shared their admiration, which was raised to astonishment by a shot from the airgun: this operation was instantly considered as "a great medicine," by which they as well as the other Indians mean something emanating directly from the Great Spirit, or produced by his invisible and incomprehensible agency. The display of all these riches had been intermixed with inquiries into the geographical situation of their country; for we had learnt by experience, that to keep the savages in good temper their attention should not be wearied with too much business; but that the serious affairs should be enlivened by a mixture of what is new and entertaining. Our hunters brought in very seasonably four deer and an antelope, the last of which we gave to the Indians, who in a very short time devoured it.

After the council was over, we consulted as to our future operations. The game does not promise to last here for a number of days, and this circumstance combined with many others to induce our going on as soon as possible. Our Indian information as to the state of the Columbia is of a very alarming kind, and our first object is of course to ascertain the practicability of descending it, of which the Indians discourage our expectations. It was therefore agreed that captain Clark should set off in the morning with eleven men, furnished, besides their arms, with tools for making canoes; that he should take Chaboneau and his wife to the camp of the Shoshonees, where he was to leave them, in order to hasten the collection of horses; that he was then to lead his men down to the Columbia, and if he found it navigable, and the timber in sufficient quantity, begin to build canoes. As soon as he had decided as to the propriety of proceeding down the Columbia or across the mountains, he was to send back one of the men with information of it to captain Lewis, who by that time would have brought up the whole party, and the rest of the baggage as far as the Shoshonee village.

Preparations were accordingly made this evening for such an arrangement. The sun is excessively hot in the day time, but the nights very cold, and rendered still more unpleasant from the want of any fuel except willow brush. The appearances too of game, for many days' subsistence, are not very favourable.

*Sunday.* In order to relieve the men of captain Clark's party from the heavy weight of their arms, provisions and tools, we exposed a few articles to barter for horses, and soon obtained three very good ones, in exchange for which we gave a uniform coat, a pair of leggings, a few handkerchiefs, three knifes and some other small articles, the whole of which did not in the United States cost more than twenty dollars: a fourth was purchased by the men for an old chequered shirt, a pair of old leggings and a knife. The Indians seemed to be quite as well pleased as ourselves at the bargains they had made. We now found that the two inferior chiefs were somewhat displeased at not having received a present equal to that given to the great chief, who appeared in a dress so much finer than their own. To allay their discontent, we bestowed on them two old coats, and promised them that if they were active in assisting us across the mountains they should have an additional present. This treatment completely reconciled them, and the whole Indian party, except two men and two women, set out in perfect good humour to return home with captain Clark.

After going fifteen miles through a wide level valley with no wood but willows and shrubs, he encamped in the Shoshonee cove near a narrow pass where the highlands approach within two hundred yards of each other, and the river is only ten yards wide. The Indians went on further, except the three chiefs and two young men, who assisted in eating two deer brought in by the hunters. After their departure every thing was prepared for the transportation of the baggage, which was now exposed to the air and dried. Our game was one deer and a beaver, and we saw an abundance of trout in the river for which we fixed a net in the evening.

We have now reached the extreme navigable point of the Missouri, which our observation places in latitude 43° 30′ 43″ north. It is difficult to comprise in any general description the characteristics of a river so extensive, and fed by so many streams which have their sources in a great variety of soils and climates. But the Missouri is still sufficiently powerful to give to all its waters something of a common character, which is of course decided by the nature of the country through which it passes. The bed of the river is chiefly composed of a blue mud from which the water itself derives a deep tinge. From its junction here to the place near which it leaves the mountains, its course is embarrassed by rapids and rocks which the hills on each side have thrown into its channel. From that place, its current, with the exception of the falls, is not difficult of navigation, nor is there much variation in its appearance till the mouth of the Platte. That powerful river throws out vast quantities of coarse sand which contribute to give a new face to the Missouri, which is now much more impeded by islands. The sand, as it is drifted down, adheres in time to some of the projecting points from the shore, and forms a barrier to the mud, which at length fills to the same height with the sandbar itself: as soon as it has acquired a consistency, the willow grows there the first year, and by its roots assists the solidity of the whole: as the mud and sand accumulate the cottonwood tree next appears; till the gradual excretion of soils raises the surface of the point above the highest freshets. Thus stopped in its course the water seeks a passage elsewhere, and as the soil on each side is light and yielding, what was only a peninsula, becomes gradually an island, and the river indemnifies itself for the usurpation by encroaching on the adjacent shore. In this way the Missouri like the Mississippi is constantly cutting off the projections of the shore, and leaving its ancient channel, which is then marked by the mud it has deposited and a few stagnant ponds.

The general appearance of the country as it presents itself on ascending may be thus described: From its mouth to the two Charletons, a ridge of highlands borders the river at a small distance, leaving between them fine rich meadows. From the mouth of the two Charletons the hills recede from the river, giving greater extent to the low grounds, but they again approach the river for a short distance near Grand river, and again at Snake creek. From that point they retire, nor do they come again to the neighbourhood of the river till above the Sauk prairie, where they are comparatively low and small. Thence they diverge and reappear at the Charaton Searty, after which they are scarcely if at all discernible, till they advance to the Missouri nearly opposite to the Kanzas.

The same ridge of hills extends on the south side, in almost one unbroken chain, from the mouth of the Missouri to the Kanzas, though decreasing in height beyond the Osage. As they are nearer the river than the hills on the opposite sides, the intermediate low grounds are of course narrower, but the general character of the soil is common to both sides.

In the meadows and along the shore, the tree most common is the cottonwood, which with the willow forms almost the exclusive growth of the Missouri. The hills or rather high grounds, for they do not rise higher than from one hundred and fifty to two hundred feet, are composed of a good rich black soil, which is perfectly susceptible of cultivation, though it becomes richer on the hills beyond the Platte, and are in general thinly covered with timber. Beyond these hills the country extends into high open plains, which are on both sides sufficiently fertile, but the south has the advantage of better streams of water, and may therefore be considered as preferable for settlements. The lands, however, become much better and the timber more abundant between the Osage and the Kanzas.

From the Kanzas to the Nadawa the hills continue at nearly an equal distance, varying from four to eight miles from each other, except that from the little Platte to nearly opposite the ancient Kanzas village, the hills are more remote, and the meadows of course wider on the north side of the river. From the Nadawa the northern hills disappear, except at occasional intervals, where they are seen at a distance, till they return about twenty-seven miles above the Platte near the ancient village of the Ayoways. On the south the hills continue close to the river from the ancient village of the Kanzas up to Council bluff, fifty miles beyond the Platte; forming high prairie lands. On both sides the lands are good, and perhaps this distance from the Osage to the Platte may be recommended as among the best districts on the Missouri for the purposes of settlers.

From the Ayoway village the northern hills again retire from the river, to which they do not return till three hundred and twenty miles above, at Floyd's river. The hills on the south also leave the river at Council bluffs, and reappear at the Mahar village, two hundred miles up the Missouri. The country thus abandoned by the hills is more open and the timber in smaller quantities than below the Platte, so that although the plain is rich and covered with high grass, the want of wood renders it less calculated for cultivation than below that river.

The northern hills after remaining near the Missouri for a few miles at Floyd's river, recede from it at the Sioux river, the course of which they follow; and though they again visit the Missouri at Whitestone river, where they are low, yet they do not return to it till beyond James river. The highlands on the south, after continuing near the river at the Mahar villages, again disappear, and do not approach it till the Cobalt bluffs, about forty-four miles from the villages, and then from those bluffs to the Yellowstone river, a distance of about one thousand miles, they follow the banks of the river with scarcely any deviation.

From the James river, the lower grounds are confined within a narrow space by the hills on both sides, which now continue near each other up to the mountains. The space between them however varies from one to three miles as high as the Muscleshell river, from which the hills approach so high as to leave scarcely any low grounds on the river, and near the falls reach the water's edge. Beyond the falls the hills are scattered and low to the first range of mountains.

The soil during the whole length of the Missouri below the Platte is generally speaking very fine, and although the timber is scarce, there is still sufficient for the purposes of settlers. But beyond that river, although the soil is still rich, yet the almost total absence of timber, and particularly the want of good water, of which there is but a small quantity in the creeks, and even that brackish, oppose powerful obstacles to its settlement. The difficulty becomes still greater between the Muscleshell river and the falls, where besides the greater scarcity of timber, the country itself is less fertile.

The elevation of these highlands varies as they pass through this extensive tract of country. From Wood river they are about one hundred and fifty feet above the water, and continue at that height till they rise near the Osage, from which place to the ancient fortification they again diminish in size. Thence they continue higher till the Mandan village, after which they are rather lower till the neighbourhood of Muscleshell river, where they are met by the Northern hills, which have advanced at a more uniform height, varying from one hundred and fifty to two hundred or three hundred feet. From this place to the mountains the height of both is nearly the same, from three hundred to five hundred feet, and the low grounds so narrow that the traveller seems passing through a range of high country. From Maria's river to the falls, the hills descend to the height of about two or three hundred feet.

AUGUST 19TH   *Monday.* The morning was cold, and the grass perfectly whitened by the frost. We were engaged in preparing packs and saddles to load the horses as soon as they should arrive. A beaver was caught in a trap, but we were disappointed in trying to catch trout in our net; we therefore made a seine of willow brush, and by hauling it procured a number of fine trout, and a species of mullet which we had not seen before: it is about sixteen inches long, the scales small; the nose long, obtusely pointed, and exceeding the under jaw; the mouth opens with folds at the sides; it has no teeth, and the tongue and palate is smooth. The colour of its back and sides is a bluish brown while the belly is white: it has the faggot bones, whence we concluded it to be of the mullet species. It is by no means so well flavoured a fish as the trout, which are the same as those we first saw at the falls, larger than the speckled trout of the mountains in the Atlantic states, and equally well flavoured. In the evening the hunters returned with two deer.

Captain Clark, in the meantime, proceeded through a wide level valley, in which the chief pointed out a spot where many of his tribe were killed in battle a year ago. The Indians accompanied him during the day, and as they had nothing to eat, he was obliged to feed them from his own stores, the hunters not being able to kill any thing. Just as he was entering the mountains, he met an Indian with two mules and a Spanish saddle, who was so polite as to offer one of them to him to ride over the hills. Being on foot, captain Clark accepted his offer and gave him a waistcoat as a reward for his civility. He encamped for the night on a small stream, and the next morning, *Tuesday, August 20th,* he set out at six o'clock.

In passing through a continuation of the hilly broken country, he met several parties of Indians. On coming near the camp, which had been removed since we left them two miles higher up the river, Cameahwait requested that the party should halt. This was complied with: a number of Indians came out from the camp, and with great ceremony several pipes were smoked. This being over captain Clark was conducted to a large leathern lodge prepared for his party in the middle of the encampment, the Indians having only shelters of willow bushes. A few dried berries, and one salmon, the only food the whole village could contribute, were then presented to him; after which he proceeded to repeat in council, what had been already told them, the purposes of his visit; urged them to take their horses over and assist in transporting our baggage, and expressed a wish to obtain a guide to examine the river. This was explained and enforced to the whole village by Cameahwait, and an old man was pointed out who was said to know more of their geography to the north than any other person, and whom captain Clark engaged to accompany him. After explaining his views he distributed a few presents, the council was ended, and nearly half the village set out to hunt the antelope, but returned without success.

Captain Clark in the meantime made particular inquiries as to the situation of the country, and the possibility of soon reaching a navigable water. The chief began by drawing on the ground a delineation of the rivers, from which it appeared that his information was very limited. The river on which the camp is he divided into two branches just above us, which, as he indicated by the opening of the mountains, were in view: he next made it discharge itself into a larger river ten miles below, coming from the southwest: the joint stream continued one day's march to the northwest, and then inclined to the westward for two days' march farther. At that place he placed several heaps of sand on each side, which, as he explained them, represented vast mountains of rock always covered with snow, in passing through which the river was so completely hemmed in by the high rocks, that there was no possibility of travelling along the shore; that the bed of the river was obstructed by sharp-pointed rocks, and such its rapidity, that as far as the eye could reach it presented a perfect column of foam. The mountains he said were equally inaccessible, as neither man nor horse could cross them; that such being the state of the country neither he nor any of his nation had ever attempted to go beyond the mountains. Cameahwait said also that he had been informed by the Chopunnish, or Pierced-nose Indians, who reside on this river west of the mountains, that it ran a great way towards the setting sun, and at length lost itself in a great lake of water which was ill-tasted, and where the white men lived.

An Indian belonging to a band of Shoshonees who live to the southwest, and who happened to be at camp, was then brought in, and enquiries made of him as to the situation of the country in that direction: this he described in terms scarcely less terrible than those in which Cameahwait had represented the west. He said that his relations lived at the distance of twenty days' march from this place, on a course a little to the west of south and not far from the whites, with whom they traded for horses, mules, cloth, metal, beads, and the shells here worn as ornaments, and which are those of a species of pearl oyster. In order to reach his country we should be obliged during the first seven days to climb over steep rocky mountains where there was no game, and we should find nothing but roots for subsistence. Even for these however we should be obliged to contend with a fierce warlike people, whom he called the Broken-moccasin, or moccasin with holes, who lived like bears in holes, and fed on roots and the flesh of such horses as they could steal or plunder from those who passed through the mountains. So rough indeed was the passage, that the feet of the horses would be wounded in such a manner that many of them would be unable to proceed. The next part of the route was for ten days through a dry parched desert of sand, inhabited by no animal which would supply us with subsistence, and as the sun had now scorched up the grass and dried up the small pools of water which are sometimes scattered through this desert in the spring, both ourselves and our horses would perish for want of food and water. About the middle of this plain a large river passes from southeast to northwest, which, though navigable, afforded neither timber nor salmon. Three or four days' march beyond this plain his relations lived, in a country tolerably fertile and partially covered with timber, on another large river running in the same direction as the former; that this last discharges itself into a third large river, on which resided many numerous nations, with whom his own were at war, but whether this last emptied itself into the great or stinking lake, as they called the ocean, he did not know; that from his country to the stinking lake was a great distance, and that the route to it, taken by such of his relations as had visited it, was up the river on which they lived, and over to that on which the white people lived, and which they knew discharged itself into the ocean. This route he advised us to take, but added, that we had better defer the journey till spring, when he would himself conduct us.

This account persuaded us that the streams of which he spoke were southern branches of the Columbia, heading with the Rio des Apostolos, and Rio Colorado, and that the route which he mentioned was to the gulf of California: captain Clark therefore told him that this road was too much towards the south for our purpose, and then requested to know if there was no route on the left of the river where we now are, by which we might intercept it below the mountains; but he knew of none except that through the barren plains, which he said joined the mountains on that side, and through which it was impossible to pass at this season, even if we were fortunate enough to escape the Broken-moccasin Indians. Captain Clark recompensed the Indian by a present of a knife, with which he seemed much gratified, and now inquired of Cameahwait by what route the Pierced-nose Indians, who he said lived west of the mountains, crossed over to the Missouri: this he said was towards the north, but that the road was a very bad one; that during the passage he had been told they suffered excessively from hunger, being obliged to subsist for many days on berries alone, there being no game in that part of the mountains, which were broken and rocky, and so thickly covered with timber that they could scarcely pass.

Surrounded by difficulties as all the other routes are, this seems to be the most practicable of all the passages by land, since, if the Indians can pass the mountains with their women and children, no difficulties which they could encounter could be formidable to us; and if the Indians below the mountains are so numerous as they are represented to be, they must have some means of subsistence equally within our power. They tell us indeed that the nations to the westward subsist principally on fish and roots, and that their only game were a few elk, deer, and antelope, there being no buffalo west of the mountain. The first inquiry however was to ascertain the truth of their information relative to the difficulty of descending the river: for this purpose captain Clark set out at three o'clock in the afternoon, accompanied by the guide and all his men, except one whom he left with orders to purchase a horse and join him as soon as possible.

At the distance of four miles he crossed the river, and eight miles from the camp halted for the night at a small stream. The road which he followed was a beaten path through a wide rich meadow, in which were several old lodges. On the route he met a number of men, women, and children, as well as horses, and one of the men who appeared to possess some consideration turned back with him, and observing a woman with three salmon obtained them from her, and presented them to the party. Captain Clark shot a mountain cock or cock of the plains, a dark brown bird larger than the dunghill fowl, with a long and pointed tail, and a fleshy protuberance about the base of the upper chop, something like that of the turkey though without the snout.

*Wednesday.* In the morning he resumed his march early, and at the distance of five miles reached an Indian lodge of brush, inhabited by seven families of Shoshonees. They behaved with great civility, gave the whole party as much boiled salmon as they could eat, and added as a present several dried salmon and a considerable quantity of chokecherries.

After smoking with them all he visited the fish weir, which was about two hundred yards distant; the river was here divided by three small islands, which occasioned the water to pass along four channels. Of these three were narrow, and stopped by means of trees which were stretched across, and supported by willow stakes, sufficiently near each other to prevent the passage of the fish. About the centre of each was placed a basket formed of willows, eighteen or twenty feet in length, of a cylindrical form, and terminating in a conic shape at its lower extremity; this was situated with its mouth upwards, opposite to an aperture in the weir. The main channel of the water was then conducted to this weir, and as the fish entered it they were so entangled with each other that they could not move, and were taken out by untying the small end of the willow basket. The weir in the main channel was formed in a manner somewhat different; there were in fact two distinct weirs formed of poles and willow sticks quite across the river, approaching each other obliquely with an aperture in each side near the angle. This is made by tying a number of poles together at the top, in parcels of three, which were then set up in a triangular form at the base, two of the poles being in the range desired for the weir, and the third down the stream. To these poles two ranges of other poles are next lashed horizontally, with willow bark and withes, and willow sticks joined in with these crosswise, so as to form a kind of wicker-work from the bottom of the river to the height of three or four feet above the surface of the water. This is so thick as to prevent the fish from passing, and even in some parts with the help of a little gravel and some stone enables them to give any direction which they wish to the water. These two weirs being placed near to each other, one for the purpose of catching the fish as they ascend, the other as they go down the river, is provided with two baskets made in the form already described, and which are placed at the apertures of the weir.

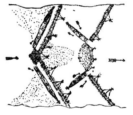

After examining these curious objects, he returned to the lodges, and soon passed the river to the left, where an Indian brought him a tomahawk which he said he had found in the grass, near the lodge where captain Lewis had stayed on his first visit to the village. This was a tomahawk which had been missed at the time, and supposed to be stolen; it was however the only article which had been lost in our intercourse with the nation, and as even that was returned the inference is highly honourable to the integrity of the Shoshonees.

On leaving the lodges captain Clark crossed to the left side of the river, and despatched five men to the forks of it, in search of the man left behind yesterday, who procured a horse and passed by another road as they learnt, to the forks. At the distance of fourteen miles they killed a very large salmon, two and a half feet long, in a creek six miles below the forks: and after travelling about twenty miles through the valley, following the course of the river, which runs nearly northwest, halted in a small meadow on the right side, under a cliff of rocks. Here they were joined by the five men who had gone in quest of Crusatte. They had been to the forks of the river, where the natives resort in great numbers for the purpose of gigging fish, of which they made our men a present of five fresh salmon. In addition to this food, one deer was killed to-day.

The western branch of this river is much larger than the eastern, and after we passed the junction we found the river about one hundred yards in width, rapid and shoaly, but containing only a small quantity of timber. As captain Lewis was the first white man who visited its waters, captain Clark gave it the name of Lewis's river. The low grounds through which he had passed to-day were rich and wide, but at his camp this evening the hills begin to assume a formidable aspect. The cliff under which he lay is of a reddish brown colour, the rocks which have fallen from it are a dark brown flintstone. Near the place are gulleys of white sandstone, and quantities of a fine sand, of a snowy whiteness: the mountains on each side are high and rugged, with some pine trees scattered over them.

AUGUST 22D    *Thursday.* He soon began to perceive that the Indian accounts had not exaggerated: at the distance of a mile he passed a small creek, and the points of four mountains, which were rocky, and so high that it seemed almost impossible to cross them with horses. The road lay over the sharp fragments of rocks which had fallen from the mountains, and were strewed in heaps for miles together, yet the horses altogether unshod, travelled across them as fast as the men, and without detaining them a moment. They passed two bold-running streams, and reached the entrance of a small river, where a few Indian families resided. They had not been previously acquainted with the arrival of the whites, the guide was behind, and the wood so thick that we came upon them unobserved, till at a very short distance. As soon as they saw us, the women and children fled in great consternation; the men offered us every thing they had, the fish on the scaffolds, the dried berries and the collars of elk's tushes worn by the children. We took only a small quantity of the food, and gave them in return some small articles which conduced very much to pacify them. The guide now coming up, explained to them who we were, and the object of our visit, which seemed to relieve the fears, but still a number of the women and children did not recover from their fright, but cried during our stay, which lasted about an hour. The guide, whom we found a very intelligent friendly old man, informed us that up this river there was a road which led over the mountains to the Missouri.

On resuming his route, he went along the steep side of a mountain about three miles, and then reached the river near a small island, at the lower part of which he encamped; he here attempted to gig some fish, but could only obtain one small salmon. The river is here shoal and rapid, with many rocks scattered in various directions through its bed. On the sides of

INDIAN PAINTING OF A COMBAT (copied by Bodmer)

the mountains are some scattered pines, and of those on the left the tops are covered with them; there are however but few in the low grounds through which they passed, indeed they have seen only a single tree fit to make a canoe, and even that was small. The country has an abundant growth of berries, and we met several women and children gathering them who bestowed them upon us with great liberality. Among the woods captain Clark observed a species of woodpecker, the beak and tail of which were white, the wings black, and every other part of the body of a dark brown; its size was that of the robin, and it fed on the seeds of the pine.

*Friday.* Captain Clark set off very early, but as his route lay along the steep side of a mountain, over irregular and broken masses of rocks, which wounded the horses' feet, he was obliged to proceed slowly. At the distance of four miles he reached the river, but the rocks here became so steep, and projected so far into the river, that there was no mode of passing, except through the water. This he did for some distance, though the river was very rapid, and so deep that they were forced to swim their horses. After following the edge of the water for about a mile under this steep cliff, he reached a small meadow, below which the whole current of the river beat against the right shore on which he was, and which was formed of a solid rock perfectly inaccessible to horses. Here too, the little track which he had been pursuing terminated. He therefore resolved to leave the horses and the greater part of the men at this place, and examine the river still further, in order to determine if there were any possibility of descending it in canoes. Having killed nothing except a single goose to-day, and the whole of our provision being consumed last evening, it was by no means advisable to remain any length of time where they were.

He now directed the men to fish and hunt at this place till his return, and then with his guide and three men he proceeded, clambering over immense rocks, and along the sides of lofty precipices which bordered the river, when at about twelve miles distance he reached a small meadow, the first he had seen on the river since he left his party. A little below this meadow, a large creek twelve yards wide, and of some depth, discharges itself from the north. Here were some recent signs of an Indian encampment, and the tracks of a number of horses, who must have come along a plain Indian path, which he now saw following the course of the creek. This stream his guide said led towards a large river running to the north, and was frequented by another nation for the purpose of catching fish. He remained here two hours, and having taken some small fish, made a dinner on them with the addition of a few berries.

From the place where he had left the party, to the mouth of this creek, it presents one continued rapid, in which are five shoals, neither of which could be passed with loaded canoes; and the baggage must therefore be transported for a considerable distance over the steep mountains, where it would be impossible to employ horses for the relief of the men. Even the empty canoes must be let down the rapids by means of cords, and not even in that way without great risk both to the canoes as well as to the men. At one of these shoals, indeed the rocks rise so perpendicularly from the water as to leave no hope of a passage or even a portage without great labour in removing rocks, and in some instances cutting away the earth. To surmount these difficulties would exhaust the strength of the party, and what is equally discouraging would waste our time and consume our provisions, of neither of which have we much to spare. The season is now far advanced, and the Indians tell us we shall shortly have snow: the salmon too have so far declined that the natives themselves are hastening from the country, and not an animal of any kind larger than a pheasant or a squirrel, and of even these a few only will then be seen in this part of the mountains: after which we shall be obliged to rely on our own stock of provisions, which will not support us more than ten days. These circumstances combine to render a passage by water impracticable in our present situation.

To descend the course of the river on horseback is the other alternative, and scarcely a more inviting one. The river is so deep that there are only a few places where it can be forded, and the rocks approach so near the water as to render it impossible to make a route along the water's edge. In crossing the mountains themselves we should have to encounter, besides their steepness, one barren surface of broken masses of rock, down which in certain seasons the torrents sweep vast quantities of stone into the river. These rocks are of a whitish brown, and towards the base of a gray colour, and so hard, that on striking them with steel, they yield a fire like flint. This sombre appearance is in some places scarcely relieved by a single tree, though near the river and on the creeks there is more timber, among which are some tall pine: several of these might be made into canoes, and by lashing two of them together, one of tolerable size might be formed.

After dinner he continued his route, and at the distance of half a mile passed another creek about five yards wide. Here his guide informed him that by ascending the creek for some distance he would have a better road, and cut off a considerable bend of the river towards the south. He therefore pursued a well-beaten Indian track up this creek for about six miles, when leaving the creek to the right he passed over a ridge, and after walking a mile again met the river, where it flows through a meadow of about eighty acres in extent. This they passed and then ascended a high and steep point of a mountain, from which the guide now pointed out where the river broke through the mountains about twenty miles distant. Near the base of the mountains a small river falls in from the south.

This view was terminated by one of the loftiest mountains captain Clark had ever seen, which was perfectly covered with snow. Towards this formidable barrier the river went directly on, and there it was, as the guide observed, that the difficulties and dangers of which he and Cameahwait had spoken commenced. After reaching the mountain, he said, the river continues its course towards the north for many miles, between high perpendicular rocks, which were scattered through its bed: it then penetrated the mountain through a narrow gap, on each side of which arose perpendicularly a rock as high as the top of the mountain before them; that the river then made a bend which concealed its future course from view, and as it was alike impossible to descend the river or clamber over that vast mountain, eternally covered with snow, neither he nor any of his nation had ever been lower than at a place where they could see the gap made by the river on entering the mountain. To that place he said he would conduct captain Clark if he desired it by the next evening. But he was in need of no further evidence to convince him of the utter impracticability of the route before him.

He had already witnessed the difficulties of part of the road, yet after all these dangers his guide, whose intelligence and fidelity he could not doubt, now assured him that the difficulties were only commencing, and what he saw before him too clearly convinced him of the Indian's veracity.

He therefore determined to abandon this route, and returned to the upper part of the last creek we had passed, and reaching it an hour after dark encamped for the night: on this creek he had seen in the morning an Indian road coming in from the north. Disappointed in finding a route by water, captain Clark now questioned his guide more particularly as to the direction of this road which he seemed to understand perfectly. He drew a map on the sand, and represented this road as well as that we passed yesterday on Berry creek as both leading towards two forks of the same great river, where resided a nation called Tushepaws, who having no salmon on their river, came by these roads to the fish weirs on Lewis's river. He had himself been among these Tushepaws, and having once accompanied them on a fishing party to another river he had there seen Indians who had come across the rocky mountains. After a great deal of conversation, or rather signs, and a second and more particular map from his guide, captain Clark felt persuaded that his guide knew of a road from the Shoshonee village they had left, to the great river to the north, without coming so low down as this on a route impracticable for horses.

*Saturday.* He was desirous of hastening his return, and therefore set out AUGUST 24TH early, and after descending the creek to the river, stopped to breakfast on berries in the meadow above the second creek. He then went on, but unfortunately fell from a rock and injured his leg very much; he however walked on as rapidly as he could, and at four in the afternoon rejoined his men. During his absence they had killed one of the mountain cocks, a few pheasants, and some small fish, on which with haws and serviceberries they had subsisted. Captain Clark immediately sent forward a man on horseback with a note to captain Lewis, apprising him of the result of his inquiries, and late in the afternoon set out with the rest of the party and encamped at the distance of two miles. The men were much disheartened at the bad prospect of escaping from the mountains, and having nothing to eat but a few berries which have made several of them sick, they all passed a disagreeable night, which was rendered more uncomfortable by a heavy dew.

*Sunday.* The want of provisions urged captain Clark to return as soon as AUGUST 25TH possible; he therefore set out early, and halted an hour in passing the Indian camp near the fish weirs. These people treated them with great kindness, and though poor and dirty they willingly give what little they possess; they gave the whole party boiled salmon and dried berries, which were not however in sufficient quantities to appease their hunger. They soon resumed their old road, but as the abstinence or strange diet had given one of the men a very severe illness, they were detained very much on his account, and it was not till late in the day they reached the cliff under which they had encamped on the *21st.* They immediately began to fish and hunt, in order to procure a meal. We caught several small fish, and by means of our guide, obtained two salmon from a small party of women and children, who, with one man, were going below to gather berries. This supplied us with about half a meal, but after dark we were regaled with a beaver which one of the hunters brought in. The other game seen in the course of the day were one deer, and a party of elk among the pines on the sides of the mountains.

AUGUST 26TH  *Monday.* The morning was fine, and three men were despatched ahead to hunt, while the rest were detained until nine o'clock, in order to retake some horses which had strayed away during the night. They then proceeded along the route by the forks of the river, till they reached the lower Indian camp where they first were when we met them. The whole camp immediately flocked around him with great appearance of cordiality, but all the spare food of the village did not amount to more than two salmon, which they gave to captain Clark, who distributed them among his men. The hunters had not been able to kill any thing, nor had captain Clark or the greater part of the men any food during the twenty-four hours, till towards evening one of them shot a salmon in the river, and a few small fish were caught, which furnished them with a scanty meal. The only animals they had seen were a few pigeons, some very wild hares, a great number of the large black grasshopper, and a quantity of ground lizards.

AUGUST 27TH  *Tuesday.* The men, who were engaged last night in mending their moccasins, all except one, went out hunting, but no game was to be procured. One of the men however killed a small salmon, and the Indians made a present of another, on which the whole party made a very slight breakfast. These Indians, to whom this life is familiar, seem contented, although they depend for subsistence on the scanty productions of the fishery. But our men who are used to hardships, but have been accustomed to have the first wants of nature regularly supplied, feel very sensibly their wretched situation: their strength is wasting away; they begin to express their apprehensions of being without food in a country perfectly destitute of any means of supporting life, except a few fish. In the course of the day an Indian brought into the camp five salmon, two of which captain Clark bought, and made a supper for the party.

AUGUST 28TH  *Wednesday.* There was a frost again this morning. The Indians gave the party two salmon out of several which they caught in their traps, and having purchased two more, the party was enabled to subsist on them during the day. A camp of about forty Indians from the west fork passed us to-day, on their route to the eastward. Our prospect of provisions is getting worse every day: the hunters who had ranged through the country in every direction where game might be reasonably expected, have seen nothing. The fishery is scarcely more productive, for an Indian who was out all day with his gig killed only one salmon. Besides the four fish procured from the Indians, captain Clark obtained some fishroe in exchange for three small fish-hooks, the use of which he taught them, and which they very readily comprehended. All the men who are not engaged in hunting, are occupied in making pack-saddles for the horses which captain Lewis informed us he had bought.

Two hunters were despatched early in the morning, but they returned without killing any thing, and the only game we procured was a beaver, who was caught last night in a trap which he carried off two miles before he was found. The fur of this animal is as good as any we have ever seen, nor does it in fact appear to be ever out of season on the upper branches of the Missouri. This beaver, with several dozen of fine trout, gave us a plentiful subsistence for the day. The party were occupied chiefly in making pack-saddles, in the manufacture of which we supply the place of nails and boards, by substituting for the first thongs of raw hide, which answer very well; and for boards we use the handles of our oars, and the plank of some boxes, the contents of which we empty into sacks of raw hides made for the purpose. The Indians who visit us behave with the greatest decorum, and the women are busily engaged in making and mending the moccasins of the party. As we had still some superfluous baggage which would be too heavy to carry across the mountains, it became necessary to make a cache or deposit. For this purpose we selected a spot on the bank of the river, three quarters of a mile below the camp, and three men were set to dig it, with a sentinel in the neighbourhood, who was ordered if the natives were to straggle that way, to fire a signal for the workmen to desist and separate. Towards evening the cache was completed without being perceived by the Indians, and the packages prepared for deposit.

AUGUST 20TH

[*Account of Capt. Lewis's party*]

WEDNESDAY, AUGUST 21ST, 1805   The weather was very cold; the water which stood in the vessels exposed to the air being covered with ice a quarter of an inch thick: the ink freezes in the pen, and the low grounds are perfectly whitened with frost: after this the day proved excessively warm. The party were engaged in their usual occupations, and completed twenty saddles with the necessary harness, all prepared to set off as soon as the Indians should arrive. Our two hunters who were despatched early in the morning have not returned, so that we were obliged to encroach on our pork and corn, which we consider as the last resource when our casual supplies of game fail. After dark we carried our baggage to the cache, and deposited what we thought too cumbrous to carry with us: a small assortment of medicines, and all the specimens of plants, seeds, and minerals, collected since leaving the falls of the Missouri.

Late at night Drewyer, one of the hunters, returned with a fawn and a considerable quantity of Indian plunder, which he had taken by way of reprisal. While hunting this morning in the Shoshonee cove, he came suddenly upon an Indian camp, at which were an old man, a young one, three women, and a boy: they showed no surprise at the sight of him, and he therefore rode up to them, and after turning his horse loose to graze sat down and began to converse with them by signs. They had just finished a repast on some roots, and in about twenty minutes one of the women spoke to the rest of the party, who immediately went out, collected their horses and began to saddle them. Having rested himself, Drewyer thought that he would continue his hunt, and rising went to catch his horse who was at a short distance, forgetting at the moment to take up his rifle. He had scarcely gone more than fifty paces when the Indians mounted their horses, the young man snatched up the rifle, and leaving all their baggage, whipped their horses, and set off at full speed towards the passes of the mountains: Drewyer instantly jumped on his horse and pursued them.

After running about ten miles the horses of the women nearly gave out, and the women finding Drewyer gain on them raised dreadful cries, which induced the young man to slacken his pace, and being mounted on a very fleet horse rode round them at a short distance. Drewyer now came up with the women, and by signs persuaded them that he did not mean to hurt them: they then stopped, and as the young man came towards them Drewyer asked him for his rifle, but the only part of the answer which he understood was Pahkee, the name by which they call their enemies, the Minnetarees of fort de Prairie. While they were thus engaged in talking, Drewyer watched his opportunity, and seeing the Indian off his guard, galloped up to him and seized his rifle: the Indian struggled for some time, but finding Drewyer getting too strong for him, had the presence of mind to open the pan and let the priming fall out: he then let go his hold, and giving his horse the whip escaped at full speed, leaving the women to the mercy of the conqueror. Drewyer then returned to where he had first seen them, where he found that their baggage had been left behind, and brought it to camp with him.

AUGUST 22D   *Thursday.* This morning early two men were sent to complete the covering of the cache, which could not be so perfectly done during the night as to elude the search of the Indians. On examining the spoils which Drewyer had obtained, they were found to consist of several dressed and undressed skins; two bags wove with the bark of the silk-grass, each containing a bushel of dried serviceberries, and about the same quantity of roots; an instrument made of bone for manufacturing the flints into heads for arrows; and a number of flints themselves: these were much of the same colour and nearly as transparent as common black glass, and when cut detached itself into flakes, leaving a very sharp edge.

The roots were of three kinds, and folded separate from each in hides of buffalo made into parchment. The first is a fusiform root six inches long, and about the size of a man's finger at the largest end, with radicles larger than is usual in roots of the fusiform sort: the rind is white and thin, the body is also white, mealy, and easily reducible, by pounding, to a substance resembling flour, like which it thickens by boiling, and is of an agreeable flavour: it is eaten frequently in its raw state either green or dried. The second species was much mutilated, but appeared to be fibrous; it is of a cylindrical form about the size of a small quill, hard and brittle. A part of the rind which had not been detached in the preparation was hard and black, but the rest of the root was perfectly white; this the Indians informed us was always boiled before eating; and on making the experiment we found that it became perfectly soft, but had a bitter taste, which was nauseous to our taste, but which the Indians seemed to relish; for on giving the roots to them they were very heartily swallowed.

The third species was a small nut about the size of a nutmeg, of an irregularly rounded form, something like the smallest of the Jerusalem artichokes, which, on boiling, we found them to resemble also in flavour, and is certainly the best root we have seen in use among the Indians. On inquiring of the Indians from what plant these roots were procured, they informed us that none of them grew near this place.

The men were chiefly employed in dressing the skins belonging to the party who accompanied captain Clark. About eleven o'clock Chaboneau and his wife returned with Cameahwait, accompanied by about fifty men with their women and children. After they had encamped near us and turned loose their horses, we called a council of all the chiefs and warriors and addressed them in a speech: additional presents were then distributed, particularly to the two second chiefs, who had agreeably to their promises exerted themselves in our favour. The council was then adjourned, and all the Indians were treated with an abundant meal of boiled Indian corn and beans. The poor wretches, who had no animal food and scarcely any thing but a few fish, had been almost starved, and received this new luxury with great thankfulness. Out of compliment to the chief we gave him a few dried squashes which we had brought from the Mandans, and he declared it was the best food he had ever tasted except sugar, a small lump of which he had received from his sister: he now declared how happy they should all be to live in a country which produced so many good things, and we told him that it would not be long before the white men would put it in their power to live below the mountains, where they might themselves cultivate all these kinds of food instead of wandering in the mountains. He appeared to be much pleased with this information, and the whole party being now in excellent temper after their repast, we began our purchase of horses. We soon obtained five very good ones on very reasonable terms; that is, by giving for each merchandise which cost us originally about six dollars. We have again to admire the perfect decency and propriety of their conduct; for although so numerous, they do not attempt to crowd round our camp or take any thing which they see lying about, and whenever they borrow knives or kettles or any other article from the men, they return them with great fidelity.

Towards evening we formed a drag of bushes, and in about two hours caught five hundred and twenty-eight very good fish most of them large trout. Among them we observed for the first time ten or twelve trout of a white or silvery colour, except on the back and head where they are of a bluish cast: in appearance and shape they resemble exactly the speckled trout, except that they are not quite so large, though the scales are much larger, and the flavour equally good. The greater part of the fish was distributed among the Indians.

AUGUST 23D  *Friday.* Our visitors seem to depend wholly on us for food, and as the state of our provisions obliges us to be careful of our remaining stock of corn and flour, this was an additional reason for urging our departure; but Cameahwait requested us to wait till the arrival of another party of his nation who were expected to-day. Knowing that it would be in vain to oppose his wish, we consented, and two hunters were sent out with orders to go further up the southeast fork than they had hitherto been. At the same time the chief was informed of the low state of our provisions, and advised to send out his young men to hunt. This he recommended them to do, and most of them set out: we then sunk our canoes by means of stones to the bottom of the river, a situation which better than any other secured them against the effects of the high waters, and the frequent fires of the plains; the Indians having promised not to disturb them during our absence, a promise we believe the more readily, as they are almost too lazy to take the trouble of raising them for fire-wood. We were desirous of purchasing some more horses, but they declined selling any until we reached their camp in the mountains.

Soon after starting the Indian hunters discovered a mule buck, and twelve of their horsemen pursued it, for four miles. We saw the chase, which was very entertaining, and at length they rode it down and killed it. This mule buck was the largest deer of any kind we have seen, being nearly as large as a doe elk. Besides this they brought in another deer and three goats; but instead of a general distribution of the meat, and such as we have hitherto seen among all tribes of Indians, we observed that some families had a large share, while others received none. On enquiring of Cameahwait the reason of this custom, he said that meat among them was scarce, that each hunter reserved what he killed for the use of himself and his own family, none of the rest having any claim on what he chose to keep. Our hunters returned soon after with two mule deer and three common deer, three of which we distributed among the families who had received none of the game of their own hunters. About three o'clock the expected party consisting of fifty men, women and children arrived. We now learnt that most of the Indians were on their way down the valley towards the buffalo country, and some anxiety to accompany them appeared to prevail among those who had promised to assist us in crossing the mountains. We ourselves were not without some apprehension that they might leave us, but as they continued to say that they would return with us nothing was said upon the subject. We

were, however, resolved to move early in the morning, and therefore despatched two men to hunt in the cove and leave the game on the route we
should pass to-morrow.

*Saturday.* As the Indians who arrived yesterday had a number of spare
horses, we thought it probable they might be willing to dispose of them, and
desired the chief to speak to them for that purpose. They declined giving
any positive answer, but requested to see the goods which we proposed to
exchange. We then produced some battle-axes which we had made at fort
Mandan, and a quantity of knives; with both of which they appeared very
much pleased; and we were soon able to purchase three horses by giving for
each an axe, a knife, a handkerchief and a little paint. To this we were
obliged to add a second knife, a shirt, a handkerchief and a pair of leggings;
and such is the estimation in which those animals are held, that even at this
price, which was double that for a horse, the fellow who sold him took upon
himself great merit in having given away a mule to us. They now said that
they had no more horses for sale, and as we had now nine of our own, two
hired horses, and a mule, we began loading them as heavily as was prudent,
and placing the rest on the shoulders of the Indian women, left our camp at
twelve o'clock.

We were all on foot, except Sacajawea, for whom her husband had
purchased a horse with some articles which we gave him for that purpose;
an Indian however had the politeness to offer captain Lewis one of his
horses to ride, which he accepted in order better to direct the march of the
party. We crossed the river below the forks, directing our course towards
the cove by the route already passed, and had just reached the lower part of
the cove when an Indian rode up to captain Lewis to inform him that one of
his men was very sick, and unable to come on. The party was immediately
halted at a run which falls into the creek on the left, and captain Lewis rode
back two miles, and found Wiser severely afflicted with the colic: by giving
him some of the essence of peppermint and laudanum, he recovered sufficiently to ride the horse of captain Lewis, who then rejoined the party on
foot. When he arrived he found that the Indians who had been impatiently
expecting his return, at last unloaded their horses and turned them loose,
and had now made their camp for the night. It would have been fruitless to
remonstrate, and not prudent to excite any irritation, and therefore, although the sun was still high, and we had made only six miles, we thought
it best to remain with them: after we had encamped there fell a slight
shower of rain. One of the men caught several fine trout; but Drewyer had
been sent out to hunt without having killed any thing. We therefore gave a
little corn to those of the Indians who were actually engaged in carrying our
baggage, and who had absolutely nothing to eat. We also advised Cameahwait, as we could not supply all his people with provisions, to recommend
to all who were not assisting us, to go on before us to their camp. This he
did: but in the morning, *Sunday 25th*, a few only followed his advice, the
rest accompanying us at some distance on each side.

We set out at sunrise and after going seventeen miles halted for dinner within two miles of the narrow pass in the mountains. The Indians who
were on the sides of our party had started some antelopes, but were obliged
after a pursuit of several hours to abandon the chase: our hunters had in the

meantime brought in three deer, the greater part of which was distributed among the Indians.

Whilst at dinner we learnt by means of Sacajawea, that the young men who left us this morning, carried a request from the chief, that the village would break up its encampment and meet this party to-morrow, when they would all go down the Missouri into the buffalo country. Alarmed at this new caprice of the Indians which, if not counteracted, threatened to leave ourselves and our baggage on the mountains, or even if we reached the waters of the Columbia, prevent our obtaining horses to go on further, captain Lewis immediately called the three chiefs together.

After smoking a pipe he asked them if they were men of their words, and if we can rely on their promises. They readily answered in the affirmative. He then asked if they had not agreed to assist us in carrying our baggage over the mountains. To this they also answered yes. "And why then," said he, "have you requested your people to meet us to-morrow, where it will be impossible for us to trade for horses, as you promised we should? If," he continued, "you had not promised to help us in transporting our goods over the mountains, we should not have attempted it, but have returned down the river, after which no white men would ever have come into your country. If you wish the whites to be your friends, and to bring you arms and protect you from your enemies, you should never promise what you do not mean to perform: when I first met you, you doubted what I said, yet you afterwards saw that I told you the truth. How therefore can you doubt what I now tell you; you see that I have divided amongst you the meat which my hunters kill, and I promise to give all who assist us a share of whatever we have to eat. If therefore you intend to keep your promise, send one of the young men immediately to order the people to remain at the village till we arrive."

The two inferior chiefs then said, that they had wished to keep their words and to assist us; that they had not sent for the people, but on the contrary had disapproved of the measure which was done wholly by the first chief. Cameahwait remained silent for some time: at last he said that he knew he had done wrong, but that seeing his people all in want of provisions, he had wished to hasten their departure for the country where their wants might be supplied. He however now declared, that having passed his word he would never violate it, and counter orders were immediately sent to the village by a young man, to whom we gave a handkerchief in order to ensure despatch and fidelity.

This difficulty being now adjusted, our march was resumed with an unusual degree of alacrity on the part of the Indians. We passed a spot, where six years ago the Shoshonees suffered a very severe defeat from the Minnetarees; and late in the evening we reached the upper part of the cove where the creek enters the mountains. The part of the cove on the northeast side of the creek has lately been burnt, most probably as a signal on some occasion. Here we were joined by our hunters with a single deer, which captain Lewis gave, as a proof of his sincerity, to the women and children, and remained supperless himself. As we came along we observed several large hares, some ducks, and many of the cock of the plains: in the low grounds of the cove were also considerable quantities of wild onions.

*Monday*. The morning was excessively cold, and the ice in our vessels was nearly a quarter of an inch in thickness: we set out at sunrise, and soon reached the fountain of the Missouri, where we halted for a few minutes, and then crossing the dividing ridge reached the fine spring where captain Lewis had slept on the *12th* in his first excursion to the Shoshonee camp. The grass on the hill sides is perfectly dry and parched by the sun, but near the spring was a fine green grass: we therefore halted for dinner and turned our horses to graze. To each of the Indians who were engaged in carrying our baggage was distributed a pint of corn, which they parched, then pounded, and made a sort of soup.

One of the women who had been leading two of our pack horses halted at a rivulet about a mile behind, and sent on the two horses by a female friend: on inquiring of Cameahwait the cause of her detention, he answered with great appearance of unconcern, that she had just stopped to lie in, but would soon overtake us. In fact, we were astonished to see her in about an hour's time come on with her new born infant and pass us on her way to the camp, apparently in perfect health.

This wonderful facility with which the Indian women bring forth their children, seems rather some benevolent gift of nature, in exempting them from pains which their savage state would render doubly grievous, than any result of habit. If, as has been imagined, a pure dry air or a cold and elevated country are obstacles to easy delivery, every difficulty incident to that operation might be expected in this part of the continent: nor can another reason, the habit of carrying heavy burdens during pregnancy, be at all applicable to the Shoshonee women, who rarely carry any burdens, since their nation possesses an abundance of horses. We have indeed been several times informed by those conversant with Indian manners, and who asserted their knowledge of the fact, that Indian women pregnant by white men experience more difficulty in child-birth than when the father is an Indian. If this account be true, it may contribute to strengthen the belief, that the easy delivery of the Indian women is wholly constitutional.

The tops of the high irregular mountains to the westward are still entirely covered with snow; and the coolness which the air acquires in passing them, is a very agreeable relief from the heat, which has dried up the herbage on the sides of the hills. While we stopped, the women were busily employed in collecting the root of a plant with which they feed their children, who like their mothers are nearly half starved and in a wretched condition. It is a species of fennel which grows in the moist grounds; the radix is of the knob kind, of a long ovate form, terminating in a single radicle, the whole being three or four inches long, and the thickest part about the size of a man's little finger: when fresh, it is white, firm, and crisp; and when dried and pounded makes a fine white meal. Its flavour is not unlike that of aniseed, though less pungent. From one to four of these knobbed roots are attached to a single stem which rises to the height of three or four feet, and is jointed, smooth, cylindric, and has several small peduncles, one at each joint above the sheathing leaf. Its colour is a deep green, as is also that of the leaf, which is sheathing, sessile, and *polipartite*, the divisions being long and narrow. The flowers, which are now in bloom, are small and numerous, with white and umbelliferous petals: there are no root leaves. As soon as the seeds have matured, the roots of the present year as well as the stem decline, and are renewed in the succeeding spring from the little knot which unites the roots. The sunflower is also abundant here, and the seeds, which are now ripe, are gathered in considerable quantities, and after being pounded and rubbed between smooth stones, form a kind of meal, which is a favourite dish among the Indians.

After dinner we continued our route and were soon met by a party of young men on horseback, who turned with us and went to the village. As soon as we were within sight of it, Cameahwait requested that we would discharge our guns; the men were therefore drawn up in a single rank, and gave a running fire of two rounds, to the great satisfaction of the Indians. We then proceeded to the encampment where we arrived about six o'clock, and were conducted to the leathern lodge in the centre of thirty-two others made of brush. The baggage was arranged near this tent, which captain Lewis occupied, and surrounded by those of the men so as to secure it from pillage. This camp was in a beautiful smooth meadow near the river, and about three miles above their camp when we first visited the Indians. We here found Colter, who had been sent by captain Clark with a note apprising us that there were no hopes of a passage by water, and that the most practicable route seemed to be that mentioned by his guide, towards the north. Whatever road we meant to take, it was now necessary to provide ourselves with horses; we therefore informed Cameahwait of our intention of going to the great river beyond the mountains, and that we would wish to purchase twenty more horses: he said the Minnetarees had stolen a great number of their horses this spring, but he still hoped they could spare us that number. In order not to lose the present favourable moment, and to keep the Indians as cheerful as possible, the violins were brought out and our men danced to the great diversion of the Indians. This mirth was the more welcome because our situation was not precisely that which would most dispose us for gaiety, for we have only a little parched corn to eat, and our means of subsistence or of success, depend on the wavering temper of the natives, who may change their minds to-morrow.

The Shoshonees are a small tribe of the nation called Snake Indians, a vague denomination, which embraces at once the inhabitants of the southern parts of the Rocky mountains and of the plains on each side. The Shoshonees with whom we now are, amount to about one hundred warriors, and three times that number of women and children. Within their own recollection they formerly lived in the plains, but they have been driven into the mountains by the Pawkees, or the roving Indians of the Sascatchawain, and are now obliged to visit occasionally, and by stealth, the country of their ancestors. Their lives are indeed migratory. From the middle of May to the beginning of September, they reside on the waters of the Columbia, where they consider themselves perfectly secure from the Pawkees who have never yet found their way to that retreat. During this time they subsist chiefly on salmon, and as that fish disappears on the approach of autumn, they are obliged to seek subsistence elsewhere. They then cross the ridge to the waters of the Missouri, down which they proceed slowly and cautiously, till they are joined near the three forks by other bands, either of their own nation or of the Flatheads, with whom they associate against the common enemy. Being now strong in numbers, they venture to hunt buffalo in the plains eastward of the mountains, near which they spend the winter, till the

return of the salmon invites them to the Columbia. But such is their terror
of the Pawkees, that as long as they can obtain the scantiest subsistence,
they do not leave the interior of the mountains; and as soon as they collect a
large stock of dried meat, they again retreat, and thus alternately obtaining
their food at the hazard of their lives, and hiding themselves to consume it.

In this loose and wandering existence they suffer the extremes of
want; for two-thirds of the year they are forced to live in the mountains,
passing whole weeks without meat, and with nothing to eat but a few fish
and roots. Nor can any thing be imagined more wretched than their condition at the present time, when the salmon is fast retiring, when roots are becoming scarce, and they have not yet acquired strength to hazard an encounter with their enemies. So insensible are they however to these calamities,
that the Shoshonees are not only cheerful but even gay; and their character,
which is more interesting than that of any Indians we have seen, has in it
much of the dignity of misfortune. In their intercourse with strangers they
are frank and communicative, in their dealings perfectly fair, nor have we
had during our stay with them, any reason to suspect that the display of all
our new and valuable wealth, has tempted them into a single act of dishon-
esty. While they have generally shared with us the little they possess, they
have always abstained from begging any thing from us. With their liveli-
ness of temper, they are fond of gaudy dresses, and of all sorts of amusements, particularly to games of hazard; and like most Indians fond of boast-
ing of their own warlike exploits, whether real or fictitious.

In their conduct towards ourselves, they were kind and obliging,
and though on one occasion they seemed willing to neglect us, yet we
scarcely knew how to blame the treatment by which we suffered, when we
recollected how few civilised chiefs would have hazarded the comforts or
the subsistence of their people for the sake of a few strangers. This manli-
ness of character may cause or it may be formed by the nature of their government, which is perfectly free from any restraint. Each individual is his
own master, and the only control to which his conduct is subjected, is the advice of a chief supported by his influence over the opinions of the rest of the
tribe. The chief himself is in fact no more than the most confidential person
among the warriors, a rank neither distinguished by any external honor, nor
invested by any ceremony, but gradually acquired from the good wishes of
his companions and by superior merit. Such an officer has therefore strictly
no power; he may recommend or advise or influence, but his commands have
no effect on those who incline to disobey, and who may at any time withdraw
from their voluntary allegiance. His shadowy authority which cannot sur-
vive the confidence which supports it, often decays with the personal vigour
of the chief, or is transferred to some more fortunate or favourite hero.

In their domestic economy, the man is equally sovereign. The man is
the sole proprietor of his wives and daughters, and can barter them away, or
dispose of them in any manner he may think proper. The children are seldom corrected; the boys, particularly, soon become their own masters; they
are never whipped, for they say that it breaks their spirit, and that after being flogged they never recover their independence of mind, even when they
grow to manhood. A plurality of wives is very common; but these are not
generally sisters, as among the Minnetarees and Mandans, but are purchased of different fathers. The infant daughters are often betrothed by the

255

father to men who are grown, either for themselves or for their sons, for whom they are desirous of providing wives. The compensation to the father is usually made in horses or mules; and the girl remains with her parents till the age of puberty, which is thirteen or fourteen, when she is surrendered to her husband. At the same time the father often makes a present to the husband equal to what he had formerly received as the price of his daughter, though this return is optional with her parent. Sacajawea had been contracted in this way before she was taken prisoner, and when we brought her back, her betrothed was still living. Although he was double the age of Sacajawea, and had two other wives, he claimed her, but on finding that she had a child by her new husband, Chaboneau, he relinquished his pretensions and said he did not want her.

The chastity of the women does not appear to be held in much estimation. The husband will for a trifling present lend his wife for a night to a stranger, and the loan may be protracted by increasing the value of the present. Yet strange as it may seem, notwithstanding this facility, any connection of this kind not authorised by the husband, is considered highly offensive and quite as disgraceful to his character as the same licentiousness in civilised societies. The Shoshonees are not so importunate in volunteering the services of their wives as we found the Sioux were; and indeed we observed among them some women who appeared to be held in more respect than those of any nation we had seen. But the mass of the females are condemned, as among all savage nations, to the lowest and most laborious drudgery. When the tribe is stationary, they collect the roots, and cook; they build the huts, dress the skins and make clothing; collect the wood, and assist in taking care of the horses on the route; they load the horses and have the charge of all the baggage. The only business of the man is to fight; he therefore takes on himself the care of his horse, the companion of his warfare; but he will descend to no other labour than to hunt and to fish. He would consider himself degraded by being compelled to walk any distance; and were he so poor as to possess only two horses, he would ride the best of them, and leave the other for his wives and children and their baggage; and if he has too many wives or too much baggage for the horse, the wives have no alternative but to follow him on foot; they are not however often reduced to those extremities, for their stock of horses is very ample.

Notwithstanding their losses this spring they still have at least seven hundred, among which are about forty colts, and half that number of mules. There are no horses here which can be considered as wild; we have seen two only on this side of the Muscleshell river which were without owners, and even those although shy, showed every mark of having been once in the possession of man. The original stock was procured from the Spaniards, but they now raise their own. The horses are generally very fine, of a good size, vigorous and patient of fatigue as well as hunger. Each warrior has one or two tied to a stake near his hut both day and night, so as to be always prepared for action. The mules are obtained in the course of trade from the Spaniards, with whose brands several of them are marked, or stolen from them by the frontier Indians. They are the finest animals of that kind we have ever seen, and at this distance from the Spanish colonies are very highly valued. The worst are considered as worth the price of two horses, and a good mule cannot be obtained for less than three and sometimes four horses. We also saw a bridle bit, stirrups and several other articles which, like the mules, came from the Spanish colonies. The Shoshonees say that they can reach those settlements in ten days' march by the route of the Yellowstone river; but we readily perceive that the Spaniards are by no means favourites. They complain that the Spaniards refuse to let them have fire arms under pretence that these dangerous weapons will only induce them to kill each other. In the meantime, say the Shoshonees, they are left to the mercy of the Minnetarees, who having arms, plunder them of their horses, and put them to death without mercy. "But this should not be," said Cameahwait fiercely, "if we had guns, instead of hiding ourselves in the mountains and living like the bears on roots and berries, we would then go down and live in the buffalo country in spite of our enemies, whom we never fear when we meet on equal terms."

*Knife scabbard.*

As war is the chief occupation, bravery is the first virtue among the Shoshonees. None can hope to be distinguished without having given proofs of it, nor can there be any preferment, or influence among the nation, without some warlike achievement. Those important events which give reputation to a warrior, and which entitle him to a new name, are killing a white bear, stealing individually the horses of the enemy, leading out a party who happen to be successful either in plundering horses or destroying the enemy, and lastly scalping a warrior. These acts seem of nearly equal dignity, but the last, that of taking an enemy's scalp, is an honour quite independent of the act of vanquishing him. To kill your adversary is of no importance unless the scalp is brought from the field of battle, and were a warrior to slay any number of his enemies in action, and others were to obtain the scalps or first touch the dead, they would have all the honours, since they have borne off the trophy.

Although thus oppressed by the Minnetarees, the Shoshonees are still a very military people. Their cold and rugged country inures them to fatigue; their long abstinence makes them support the dangers of mountain warfare, and worn down as we saw them, by want of sustenance, have a look of fierce and adventurous courage. The Shoshonee warrior always fights on horseback; he possesses a few bad guns, which are reserved exclusively for war, but his common arms are the bow and arrow, a shield, a lance and a weapon called by the Chippeways, by whom it was formerly used, the poggamoggon.

The bow is made of cedar or pine covered on the outer side with sinews and glue. It is about two and a half feet long, and does not differ in shape from those used by the Sioux, Mandans and Minnetarees. Sometimes, however, the bow is made of a single piece of the horn of an elk, covered on the back like those of wood with sinews and glue, and occasionally ornamented by a strand wrought of porcupine quills and sinews, which is wrapped round the horn near its two ends. The bows made of the horns of the bighorn, are still more prized, and are formed by cementing with glue flat pieces of the horn together, covering the back with sinews and glue, and loading the whole with an unusual quantity of ornaments. The arrows resemble those of the other Indians except in being more slender than any we have seen. They are contained, with the implements for striking fire, in a narrow quiver formed of different kinds of skin, though that of the otter seems to be preferred. It is just long enough to protect the arrows from the

257

weather, and is worn on the back by means of a strap passing over the right shoulder and under the left arm. The shield is a circular piece of buffalo hide about two feet four or five inches in diameter, ornamented with feathers, and a fringe round it of dressed leather, and adorned or deformed with paintings of strange figures. The buffalo hide is perfectly proof against any arrow, but in the minds of the Shoshonees, its power to protect them is chiefly derived from the virtues which are communicated to it by the old men and jugglers.

To make a shield is indeed one of their most important ceremonies: it begins by a feast to which all the warriors, old men and jugglers are invited. After the repast a hole is dug in the ground about eighteen inches in depth and of the same diameter as the intended shield: into this hole red hot stones are thrown and water poured over them, till they emit a very strong hot steam. The buffalo skin, which must be the entire hide of a male two years old, and never suffered to dry since it was taken from the animal, is now laid across the hole, with the fleshy side to the ground, and stretched in every direction by as many as can take hold of it. As the skin becomes heated, the hair separates and is taken off by the hand; till at last the skin is contracted into the compass designed for the shield. It is then taken off and placed on a hide prepared into parchment, and then pounded during the rest of the festival by the bare heels of those who are invited to it. This operation sometimes continues for several days, after which it is delivered to the proprietor, and declared by the old men and jugglers to be a security against arrows; and provided the feast has been satisfactory, against even the bullets of their enemies. Such is the delusion, that many of the Indians implicitly believe that this ceremony has given to the shield supernatural powers, and that they have no longer to fear any weapons of their enemies.

The poggamoggon is an instrument, consisting of a handle twenty-two inches long, made of wood, covered with dressed leather about the size of a whip-handle: at one end is a thong of two inches in length, which is tied to a round stone weighing two pounds and held in a cover of leather: at the other end is a loop of the same material, which is passed round the wrist so as to secure the hold of the instrument, with which they strike a very severe blow.

Besides these, they have a kind of armour something like a coat of mail, which is formed by a great many folds of dressed antelope skins, united by means of a mixture of glue and sand. With this they cover their own bodies and those of their horses, and find it impervious to the arrow.

The caparison of their horses is a halter and a saddle: the first is either a rope of six or seven strands of buffalo hair plaited or twisted together, about the size of a man's finger and of great strength; or merely a thong of raw hide, made pliant by pounding and rubbing; though the first kind is much preferred. The halter is very long, and is never taken from the neck of the horse when in constant use. One end of it is first tied round the neck in a knot and then brought down to the under jaw, round which it is formed into a simple noose, passing through the mouth: it is then drawn up on the right side and held by the rider in his left hand, while the rest trails after him to some distance. At other times the knot is formed at a little distance from one of the ends, so as to let that end serve as a bridle, while the other trails on the ground. With these cords dangling along side of them the

258

horse is put to his full speed without fear of falling, and when he is turned to graze the noose is merely taken from his mouth. The saddle is formed like the pack-saddles used by the French and Spaniards, of two flat thin boards which fit the sides of the horse, and are kept together by two cross pieces, one before and the other behind, which rise to a considerable height, ending sometimes in a flat point extending outwards, and always making the saddle deep and narrow. Under this a piece of buffalo skin, with the hair on, is placed so as to prevent the rubbing of the boards, and when they mount they throw a piece of skin or robe over the saddle, which has no permanent cover. When stirrups are used, they consist of wood covered with leather; but stirrups and saddles are conveniences reserved for old men and women.

The young warriors rarely use any thing except a small leather pad stuffed with hair, and secured by a girth made of a leathern thong. In this way they ride with great expertness, and they have a particular dexterity in catching the horse when he is running at large. If he will not immediately submit when they wish to take him, they make a noose in the rope, and although the horse may be at a distance, or even running, rarely fail to fix it on his neck; and such is the docility of the animal, that however unruly he may seem, he surrenders as soon as he feels the rope on him. This cord is so useful in this way that it is never dispensed with, even when they use the Spanish bridle, which they prefer, and always procure when they have it in their power. The horse becomes almost an object of attachment: a favourite is frequently painted and his ears cut into various shapes: the mane and tail, which are never drawn nor trimmed, are decorated with feathers of birds, and sometimes a warrior suspends at the breast of his horse the finest ornaments he possesses.

Thus armed and mounted the Shoshonee is a formidable enemy, even with the feeble weapons which he is still obliged to use. When they attack at full speed they bend forward and cover their bodies with the shield, while with the right hand they shoot under the horse's neck.

The only articles of metal which the Shoshonees possess are a few bad knives, some brass kettles, some bracelets or armbands of iron and brass, a few buttons worn as ornaments in their hair, one or two spears about a foot in length, and some heads for arrows made of iron and brass. All these they had obtained in trading with the Crow or Rocky mountain Indians, who live on the Yellowstone. The few bridle-bits and stirrups they procured from the Spanish colonies.

The instrument which supplies the place of a knife among them, is a piece of flint with no regular form, and the sharp part of it not more than one or two inches long: the edge of this is renewed, and the flint itself is formed into heads for arrows, by means of the point of a deer or elk horn, an instrument which they use with great art and ingenuity. There are no axes or hatchets; all the wood being cut with flint or elk-horn, the latter of which is always used as a wedge in splitting wood. Their utensils consist, besides the brass kettles, of pots in the form of a jar, made either of earth, or of a stone found in the hills between Madison and Jefferson rivers, which, though soft and white in its natural state, becomes very hard and black after exposure to the fire. The horns of the buffalo and the bighorn supply them with spoons.

The fire is always kindled by means of a blunt arrow, and a piece of well-seasoned wood of a soft spongy kind, such as the willow or cottonwood.

The Shoshonees are of a diminutive stature, with thick flat feet and ankles, crooked legs, and are, generally speaking, worse formed than any nation of Indians we have seen. Their complexion resembles that of the Sioux, and is darker than that of the Minnetarees, Mandans, or Shawnees. The hair in both sexes is suffered to fall loosely over the face and down the shoulders: some men, however, divide it by means of thongs of dressed leather or otter skin into two equal queues, which hang over the ears and are drawn in front of the body; but at the present moment, when the nation is afflicted by the loss of so many relations killed in war, most of them have the hair cut quite short in the neck, and Cameahwait has the hair cut short all over his head, this being the customary mourning for a deceased kindred.

The dress of the men consists of a robe, a tippet, a shirt, long leggings and moccasins. The robe is formed most commonly of the skins of antelope, bighorn, or deer, though when it can be procured, the buffalo hide is preferred. Sometimes too they are made of beaver, moonax [monax, or marmot], and small wolves, and frequently during the summer of elk skin. These are dressed with the hair on, and reach about as low as the middle of the leg. They are worn loosely over the shoulders, the sides being at pleasure either left open or drawn together by the hand, and in cold weather kept close by a girdle round the waist. This robe answers the purpose of a cloak during the day, and at night is their only covering.

The tippet is the most elegant article of Indian dress we have ever seen. The neck or collar of it is a strip about four or five inches wide, cut from the back of the otter skin, the nose and eyes forming one extremity, and the tail another. This being dressed with the fur on, they attach to one edge of it from one hundred to two hundred and fifty little rolls of ermine skin, beginning at the ear, and proceeding towards the tail. These ermine skins are the same kind of narrow strips from the back of that animal, which are sewed round a small cord of twisted silkgrass thick enough to make the skin taper towards the tail which hangs from the end, and are generally about the size of a large quill. These are tied at the head into little bundles, of two, three or more according to the caprice of the wearer, and then suspended from the collar, and a broad fringe of ermine skin is fixed so as to cover the parts where they unite, which might have a coarse appearance. Little tassels of fringe of the same materials are also fastened to the extremities of the tail, so as to show its black colour to greater advantage. The centre of the collar is further ornamented with the shells of the pearl oyster. Thus adorned, the collar is worn close round the neck, and the little rolls fall down over the shoulders nearly to the waist, so as to form a sort of short cloak, which has a very handsome appearance. These tippets are very highly esteemed, and are given or disposed of on important occasions only. The ermine is the fur known to the northwest traders by the name of the white weasel, but is the genuine ermine; and by encouraging the Indians to take them, might no doubt be rendered a valuable branch of trade. These animals must be very abundant, for the tippets are in great numbers, and the construction of each requires at least one hundred skins.

The shirt is a covering of dressed skin without the hair, and formed of the hide of the antelope, deer, bighorn, or elk, though the last is more rarely used than any other for this purpose. It fits the body loosely, and reaches half way down the thigh. The aperture at the top is wide enough to admit the head, and has no collar, but is either left square, or most frequently terminates in the tail of the animal, which is left entire, so as to fold outwards, though sometimes the edges are cut into a fringe, and ornamented with quills of the porcupine. The seams of the shirt are on the sides, and are richly fringed and adorned with porcupine quills, till within five or six inches of the sleeve, where it is left open, as is also the under side of the sleeve from the shoulder to the elbow, where it fits closely round the arm as low as the wrist, and has no fringe like the sides, and the under part of the sleeve above the elbow. It is kept up by wide shoulder straps, on which the manufacturer displays his taste by the variety of figures wrought with porcupine quills of different colours, and sometimes by beads when they can be obtained. The lower end of the shirt retains the natural shape of the fore legs and neck of the skin, with the addition of a slight fringe; the hair too is left on the tail and near the hoofs, part of which last is retained and split into a fringe.

The leggings are generally made of antelope skins, dressed without the hair, and with the legs, tail and neck hanging to them. Each legging is formed of a skin nearly entire, and reaches from the ankle to the upper part of the thigh, and the legs of the skin are tucked before and behind under a girdle round the waist. It fits closely to the leg, the tail being worn upwards, and the neck highly ornamented with fringe and porcupine quills, drags on the ground behind the heels. As the legs of the animal are tied round the girdle, the wide part of the skin is drawn so high as to conceal the parts usually kept from view, in which respect their dress is much more decent than that of any nation of Indians on the Missouri. The seams of the leggings down the sides, are also fringed and ornamented, and occasionally decorated with tufts of hair taken from enemies whom they have slain. In making all these dresses, their only thread is the sinew taken from the backs and loins of deer, elk, buffalo, or any other animal.

The moccasin is of the deer, elk, or buffalo skin, dressed without the hair, though in winter they use the buffalo skin with the hairy side inward, as do most of the Indians who inhabit the buffalo country. Like the Mandan moccasin, it is made with a single seam on the outer edge, and sewed up behind, a hole being left at the instep to admit the foot. It is variously ornamented with figures wrought with porcupine quills, and sometimes the young men most fond of dress cover it with the skin of a polecat, and trail at their heels the tail of the animal.

The dress of the women consists of the same articles as that of their husbands. The robe though smaller is worn in the same way: the moccasins are precisely similar. The shirt or chemise reaches half way down the leg, is in the same form, except that there is no shoulder-strap, the seam coming quite up to the shoulder; though for women who give suck both sides are open, almost down to the waist. It is also ornamented in the same way with the addition of little patches of red cloth, edged round with beads at the skirts. The chief ornament is over the breast, where there are curious figures made with the usual luxury of porcupine quills. Like the men they have a girdle round the waist, and when either sex wishes to disengage the arm, it is drawn up through the hole near the shoulder, and the lower part of the sleeve thrown behind the body.

Children alone wear beads round their necks; grown persons of both

261

sexes prefer them suspended in little bunches from the ear, and sometimes intermixed with triangular pieces of the shell of the pearl oyster. Sometimes the men tie them in the same way to the hair of the forepart of the head, and increase the beauty of it by adding the wings and tails of birds, and particularly the feathers of the great eagle or calumet bird, of which they are extremely fond. The collars are formed either of sea shells procured from their relations to the southwest, or of the sweet-scented grass which grows in the neighbourhood, and which they twist or plait together, to the thickness of a man's finger, and then cover with porcupine quills of various colours. The first of these is worn indiscriminately by both sexes, the second principally confined to the men, while a string of elk's tusks is a collar almost peculiar to the women and children. Another collar worn by the men is a string of round bones like the joints of a fish's back, but the collar most preferred, because most honourable, is one of the claws of the brown bear. To kill one of these animals is as distinguished an achievement as to have put to death an enemy, and in fact with their weapons is a more dangerous trial of courage. These claws are suspended on a thong of dressed leather, and being ornamented with beads, are worn round the neck by the warriors with great pride. The men also frequently wear the skin of a fox, or a strip of otter skin round the head in the form of a bandeau.

In short, the dress of the Shoshonees is as convenient and decent as that of any Indians we have seen.

They have many more children than might have been expected, considering their precarious means of support and their wandering life. This inconvenience is however balanced by the wonderful facility with which their females undergo the operations of child-birth. In the most advanced state of pregnancy they continue their usual occupations, which are scarcely interrupted longer than the mere time of bringing the child into the world.

The old men are few in number, and do not appear to be treated with much tenderness or respect.

The tobacco used by the Shoshonees is not cultivated among them, but obtained from the Indians of the Rocky mountains, and from some of the bands of their own nation who live south of them: it is the same plant which is in use among the Minnetarees, Mandans, and Ricaras.

Their chief intercourse with other nations seems to consist in their association with other Snake Indians, and with the Flatheads when they go eastward to hunt buffalo, and in the occasional visits made by the Flatheads to the waters of the Columbia for the purpose of fishing. Their intercourse with the Spaniards is much more rare, and it furnishes them with a few articles, such as mules, and some bridles, and other ornaments for horses, which, as well as some of their kitchen utensils, are also furnished by the bands of Snake Indians from the Yellowstone. The pearl ornaments which they esteem so highly come from other bands, whom they represent as their friends and relations, living to the southwest beyond the barren plains on the other side of the mountains: these relations they say inhabit a good country, abounding with elk, deer, bear, and antelope, where horses and mules are much more abundant than they are here, or to use their own expression, as numerous as the grass of the plains.

The names of the Indians varies in the course of their life: originally given in childhood, from the mere necessity of distinguishing objects, or

from some accidental resemblance to external objects, the young warrior is
impatient to change it by some achievement of his own. Any important event, the stealing of horses, the scalping an enemy, or killing a brown bear, entitles him at once to a new name which he then selects for himself, and it is confirmed by the nation. Sometimes the two names subsist together: thus, the chief Cameahwait, which means, "one who never walks," has the war name of Tooettecone, or "black gun," which he acquired when he first signalised himself. As each new action gives a warrior a right to change his name, many of them have had several in the course of their lives. To give to a friend his own name is an act of high courtesy, and a pledge like that of pulling off the moccasin of sincerity and hospitality. The chief in this way gave his name to captain Clark when he first arrived, and he was afterwards known among the Shoshonees by the name of Cameahwait.

The diseases incident to this state of life may be supposed to be few, and chiefly the result of accidents. We were particularly anxious to ascertain whether they had any knowledge of the venereal disorder. After inquiring by means of the interpreter and his wife, we learnt that they sometimes suffered from it, and that they most usually die with it; nor could we discover what was their remedy. It is possible that this disease may have reached them in their circuitous communications with the whites through the intermediate Indians; but the situation of the Shoshonees is so insulated, that it is not probable that it could have reached them in that way, and the existence of such a disorder among the Rocky mountains [Indians] seems rather a proof of its being aboriginal.

## Chapter 17

DOWN THE
KOOSKOOSKEE
RIVER

*TUESDAY, AUGUST 27TH, 1805*   We were now occupied in determining our route and procuring horses from the Indians. The old guide who had been sent on by captain Clark, now confirmed, by means of our interpreter, what he had already asserted, of a road up Berry creek which would lead to Indian establishments on another branch of the Columbia: his reports however were contradicted by all the Shoshonees. This representation we ascribed to a wish on their part to keep us with them during the winter, as well for the protection we might afford against their enemies, as for the purpose of consuming our merchandise amongst them; and as the old man promised to conduct us himself, that route seemed to be the most eligible. We were able to procure some horses, though not enough for all our purposes. This traffic, and our inquiries and councils with the Indians, consumed the remainder of the day.

AUGUST 28TH

[*End of separate account of Capt. Lewis's party*]

The purchase of horses was resumed, and our stock raised to twenty-two. Having now crossed more than once the country which separates the head waters of the Missouri from those of the Columbia, we can designate the easiest and most expeditious route for a portage: it is as follows:

From the forks of the [Jefferson] river north 60° west, five miles to the point of a hill on the right: then south 80° west, ten miles to a spot where the creek is ten miles [yards] wide, and the highlands approach within two hundred yards; southwest five miles to a narrow part of the bottom; then turning south 70° west, two miles to a creek on the right: thence south 80° west, three miles to a rocky point opposite to a thicket of pines on the left: from that place west, three miles to the gap where is the fountain of the Missouri: on leaving this fountain south 80° west, six miles across the dividing ridge, to a run from the right passing several small streams north 80° west, four miles over hilly ground to the east fork of Lewis's river, which is here forty yards wide.

AUGUST 29TH

*Thursday.* Captain Clark joined us this morning, and we continued our bargains for horses. The late misfortunes of the Shoshonees make the price higher than common, so that one horse cost a pistol, one hundred balls, some powder and a knife; another was changed for a musket, and in this way we obtained twenty-nine. The horses themselves are young and vigorous, but they are very poor, and most of them have sore backs in consequence of the roughness of the Shoshonee saddle. We are therefore afraid of loading them too heavily and are anxious to obtain one at least for each man, to carry the baggage, or the man himself, or in the last resource to serve as food; but with all our exertions we could not provide all our men with horses. We have, however, been fortunate in obtaining for the last three days a sufficient supply of flesh, our hunters having killed two or three deer every day.

AUGUST 30TH

*Friday.* The weather was fine, and having now made all our purchases, we loaded our horses, and prepared to start. The greater part of the band who had delayed their journey on our account, were also ready to depart. We then took our leave of the Shoshonees, who set out on their visit to the Missouri at the same time that we accompanied by the old guide, his four sons, and another Indian, began the descent of the river, along the same road which captain Clark had previously pursued. After riding twelve miles we encamped on the south bank of the river, and as the hunters had brought in three deer early in the morning we did not feel the want of provisions.

*Saturday.* At sunrise we resumed our journey, and halted for three hours on Salmon creek to let the horses graze. We then proceeded to the stream called Berry creek eighteen miles from the camp of last night: as we passed along, the valleys and prairies were on fire in several places, in order to collect the bands of the Shoshonees and the Flatheads, for their journey to the Missouri. The weather was warm and sultry, but the only inconvenience which we apprehend is a dearth of food, of which we had to-day an abundance, having procured a deer, a goose, one duck, and a prairie fowl. On reaching Tower creek we left the former track of captain Clark, and began to explore the new route, which is our last hope of getting out of the mountains. For four miles the road, which is tolerably plain, led us along Berry creek to some old Indian lodges where we encamped for the night; the next day, *Sunday, September 1st, 1805,* we followed the same road which here left the creek and turned to the northwest across the hills. During all day we were riding over these hills, from which are many drains and small streams running into the river to the left, and at the distance of eighteen miles, came to a large creek called Fish creek emptying into the Columbia which is about six miles from us. It had rained in the course of the day, and commenced raining again towards evening. We therefore determined not to leave the low grounds to-night, and after going up Fish creek four miles formed our encampment. The country over which we passed is well watered, but poor and rugged or stony, except the bottoms of Fish creek, and even these are narrow. Two men were sent to purchase fish of the Indians at the mouth of the creek, and with the dried fish which they obtained, and a deer and a few salmon killed by the party, we were still well supplied. Two bear also were wounded but we could procure neither of them.

*Monday.* This morning all the Indians left us, except the old guide, who now conducted us up Fish creek: at one mile and a half we passed a branch of the river coming in through a low ground covered with pine on the left, and two and a half miles further is a second branch from the right; after continuing our route along the hills covered with pine, and a low ground of the same growth, we arrived at the distance of three and a half miles at the forks of the creek. The road which we were following now turned up the east side of these forks, and as our guide informed us led to the Missouri. We were therefore left without any track; but as no time was to be lost we began to cut our road up the west branch of the creek. This we effected with much difficulty; the thickets of trees and brush through which we were obliged to cut our way required great labour; the road itself was over the steep and rocky sides of the hills where the horses could not move without danger of slipping down, while their feet were bruised by the rocks and stumps of trees. Accustomed as these animals were to this kind of life they suffered severely, several of them fell to some distance down the sides of the hills, some turned over with the baggage, one was crippled, and two gave out exhausted with fatigue. After crossing the creek several times we at last made five miles, with great fatigue and labour, and encamped on the left side of the creek in a small stony low ground. It was not, however, till after dark that the whole party was collected, and then, as it rained, and we killed nothing, we passed an uncomfortable night. The party had been too busily occupied with the horses to make any hunting excursion, and though as we came along Fish creek we saw many beaver dams we saw none of the animals themselves.

SEPTEMBER 3D In the morning the horses were very stiff and weary. We sent back two men for the load of the horse which had been crippled yesterday, and which we had been forced to leave two miles behind. On their return we set out at eight o'clock, and proceeded up the creek, making a passage through the brush and timber along its borders. The country is generally supplied with pine, and in the low grounds is a great abundance of fir trees, and under bushes. The mountains are high and rugged, and those to the east of us, covered with snow. With all our precautions the horses were very much injured in passing over the ridges and steep points of the hills, and to add to the difficulty, at the distance of eleven miles, the high mountains closed the creek, so that we were obliged to leave the creek to the right, and cross the mountain abruptly. The ascent was here so steep, that several of the horses slipped and hurt themselves, but at last we succeeded in crossing the mountain, and encamped on a small branch of Fish creek. We had now made fourteen miles in a direction nearly north from the river; but this distance, though short, was very fatiguing, and rendered still more disagreeable by the rain which began at three o'clock. At dusk it commenced snowing, and continued till the ground was covered to the depth of two inches, when it changed into a sleet. We here met with a serious misfortune the last of our thermometers being broken by accident. After making a scanty supper on a little corn and a few pheasants killed in the course of the day, we laid down to sleep, and next morning, *Wednesday 4th*, found every thing frozen, and the ground covered with snow. We were obliged to wait some time in order to thaw the covers of the baggage, after which we began our journey at eight o'clock. We crossed a high mountain forming the dividing ridge between the waters of the creek we had been ascending, and those running to the north and west. We had not gone more than six miles over the snow, when we reached the head of a stream from the right, which directed its course more to the westward. We descended the steep sides of the hills along its border, and at the distance of three miles found a small branch coming in from the eastward. We saw several of the argalia [bighorns], but they were too shy to be killed, and we therefore made a dinner from a deer shot by one of the hunters. Then we pursued the course of the stream for three miles, till it emptied itself into a river from the east. In the wide valley at their junction, we discovered a large encampment of Indians: when we had reached them and alighted from our horses, we were received with great cordiality. A council was immediately assembled, white robes were thrown over our shoulders, and the pipe of peace introduced. After this ceremony, as it was too late to go any further, we encamped, and continued smoking and conversing with the chiefs till a late hour.

SEPTEMBER 5TH The next morning we assembled the chiefs and warriors, and informed them who we were, and the purpose for which we visited their country. All this was however conveyed to them through so many different languages, that it was not comprehended without difficulty. We therefore proceeded to the more intelligible language of presents, and made four chiefs by giving a medal and a small quantity of tobacco to each. We received in turn from the principal chief, a present consisting of the skins of a braro, an otter, and two antelopes, and were treated by the women to some dried roots and berries. We then began to traffic for horses, and succeeded in exchanging seven, purchasing eleven, for which we gave a few articles of merchandise.

This encampment consists of thirty-three tents, in which were about four hundred souls, among whom eighty were men. They are called Ootlashoots, and represent themselves as one band of a nation called Tushepaws, a numerous people of four hundred and fifty tents, residing on the heads of the Missouri and Columbia rivers, and some of them lower down the latter river. In person these Indians are stout, and their complexion lighter than that common among Indians. The hair of the men is worn in queues of otter skin, falling in front over the shoulders. A shirt of dressed skin covers the body to the knee, and on this is worn occasionally a robe. To these were added leggings and moccasins. The women suffer their hair to fall in disorder over the face and shoulders, and their chief article of covering is a long shirt of skin, reaching down to the ankles, and tied round the waist. In other respects, as also in the few ornaments which they possess, their appearance is similar to that of the Shoshonees.

There is however a difference between the language of these people which is still farther increased by the very extraordinary pronunciation of the Ootlashoots. Their words have all a remarkably guttural sound, and there is nothing which seems to represent the tone of their speaking more exactly than the clucking of a fowl, or the noise of a parrot. This peculiarity renders their voices scarcely audible, except at a short distance, and when many of them are talking, forms a strange confusion of sounds. The common conversation we overheard, consisted of low guttural sounds occasionally broken by a loud word or two, after which it would relapse and scarcely be distinguished. They seem kind and friendly and willingly shared with us berries and roots, which formed their only stock of provisions. Their only wealth is their horses, which are very fine, and so numerous that this party had with them at least five hundred.

*Friday.* We continued this morning with the Ootlashoots, from whom we purchased two more horses, and procured a vocabulary of their language. The Ootlashoots set off about two o'clock to join the different bands who were collecting at the three forks of the Missouri. We ourselves proceeded at the same time, and taking a direction N. 30 W. crossed within the distance of one mile and a half, a small river from the right, and a creek coming in from the north. This river is the main stream, and when it reaches the end of the valley, where the mountains close in upon it, is joined by the river on which we encamped last evening, as well as by the creek just mentioned. To the river thus formed we gave the name of captain Clark, he being the first white man who had ever visited its waters. At the end of five miles on this course we had crossed the valley, and reached the top of a mountain covered with pine; this we descended along the steep sides and ravines for a mile and a half, when we came to a spot on the river, where the Ootlashoots had encamped a few days before. We then followed the course of the river, which is from twenty-five to thirty yards wide, shallow, stony, and the low grounds on its borders narrow. Within the distance of three and a half miles, we crossed it several times, and after passing a run on each side, encamped on its right bank, after making ten miles during the afternoon. The horses were turned out to graze, but those we had lately bought were secured and watched, lest they should escape, or be stolen by their former owners. Our stock of flour was now exhausted, and we had but little corn, and as our hunters had killed nothing except two pheasants, our supper consisted chiefly of berries.

SEPTEMBER 7TH *Saturday.* The greater part of the day the weather was dark and rainy: we continued through the narrow low grounds along the river, till at the distance of six miles we came to a large creek from the left, after which the bottoms widen. Four miles lower is another creek on the same side, and the valley now extends from one to three miles, the mountains on the left being high and bald, with snow on the summits, while the country to the right is open and hilly. Four miles beyond this is a creek running from the snow-top'd mountains, and several runs on both sides of the river. Two miles from this last is another creek on the left. The afternoon was now far advanced, but not being able to find a fit place to encamp we continued six miles further till after dark, when we halted for the night. The river here is still shallow and stony, but is increased to the width of fifty yards. The valley through which we passed is of a poor soil, and its fertility injured by the quantity of stone scattered over it. We met two horses which had strayed from the Indians and were now quite wild. No fish was to be seen in the river, but we obtained a very agreeable supply of two deer, two cranes, and two pheasants.

SEPTEMBER 8TH *Sunday.* We set out early: the snow-top'd hills on the left approach the river near our camp, but we soon reached a valley four or five miles wide, through which we followed the course of the river in a direction due north. We passed three creeks on the right, and several runs emptying themselves into the opposite side of the river. At the distance of eleven miles the river turned more towards the west: we pursued it for twelve miles, and encamped near a large creek coming in from the right, which, from its being divided into four different channels, we called Scattering creek. The valley continues to be a poor stony land, with scarcely any timber, except some pine trees along the waters and partially scattered on the hills to the right, which, as well as those on the left, have snow on them. The plant which forces itself most on our attention is a species of prickly pear very common on this part of the river: it grows in clusters, in an oval form about the size of a pigeon's egg, and its thorns are so strong and bearded, that when it penetrates our feet it brings away the pear itself. We saw two mares and a colt, which, like the horses seen yesterday, seemed to have lost themselves and become wild. Our game to-day consisted of two deer, an elk, and a prairie fowl.

SEPTEMBER 9TH *Monday.* We resumed our journey through the valley, and leaving the road on our right crossed the Scattering creek, and halted at the distance of twelve miles on a small run from the east, where we breakfasted on the remains of yesterday's hunt: we here took a meridian altitude, which gave the

268

latitude of 46° 41′ 38.9″: we then continued, and at the distance of four miles passed over to the left bank of the river, where we found a large road through the valley. At this place is a handsome stream of very clear water, a hundred yards wide with low banks, and a bed formed entirely of gravel: it has every appearance of being navigable, but as it contains no salmon, we presume there must be some fall below which obstructs their passage. Our guide could not inform us where this river discharged its waters; he said that as far as he knew its course it ran along the mountains to the north, and that not far from our present position it was joined by another stream nearly as large as itself, which rises in the mountains to the east near the Missouri, and flows through an extensive valley or open prairie. Through this prairie is the great Indian road to the waters of the Missouri; and so direct is the route, that in four days' journey from this place we might reach the Missouri about thirty miles above what we called the Gates of the Rocky mountains, or the spot where the valley of that river widens into an extensive plain on entering the chain of mountains.

At ten miles from our camp is a small creek falling in from the eastward, five miles below which we halted at a large stream which empties itself on the west side of the river. It is a fine bold creek of clear water about twenty yards wide, and we called it *Traveller's-rest* creek; for as our guide told us that we should here leave the river, we determined to remain for the purpose of making celestial observations and collecting some food, as the country through which we are to pass has no game for a great distance.

The valley of the river through which we have been passing is generally a prairie from five to six miles in width, and with a cold gravelly white soil. The timber which it possesses is almost exclusively pine, chiefly of the long-leafed kind, with some spruce, and a species of fir resembling the Scotch fir: near the water courses are also seen a few narrow-leafed cottonwood trees, and the only underbrush is the redwood, honeysuckle, and rosebushes. Our game was four deer, three geese, four ducks, and three prairie fowls: one of the hunters brought in a red-headed woodpecker of the large kind common in the United States, but the first of the kind we have seen since leaving the Illinois.

*Tuesday.* The morning being fair all the hunters were sent out, and the rest SEPTEMBER 10TH of the party employed in repairing their clothes: two of them were sent to the junction of the river from the east, along which the Indians go to the Missouri: it is about seven miles below Traveller's-rest creek; the country at the forks is seven or eight miles wide, level and open, but with little timber: its course is to the north, and we incline to believe that this is the river which the Minnetarees had described to us as running from south to north along the west side of the Rocky mountains, not far from the sources of Medicine river: there is moreover reason to suppose, that after going as far northward as the head-waters of that river it turns to the westward and joins the Tacootchetessee.

Towards evening one of the hunters returned with three Indians, whom he had met in his excursion up Traveller's-rest creek: as soon as they saw him they prepared to attack him with arrows, but he quieted them by laying down his gun and advancing towards them, and soon persuaded them to come to the camp. Our Shoshonee guide could not speak the language of these people, but by the universal language of signs and gesticulations, which is perfectly intelligible among the Indians, he found that these were three Tushepaw Flatheads in pursuit of two men, supposed to be Shoshonees, who had stolen twenty-three of their horses: we gave them some boiled venison and a few presents; such as a fishhook, a steel to strike fire, and a little powder; but they seemed better pleased with a piece of ribbon which we tied in the hair of each of them. They were however in such haste, lest their horses should be carried off, that two of them set off after sunset in quest of the robbers: the third however was persuaded to remain with us and conduct us to his relations: these he said were numerous, and resided on the Columbia in the plain below the mountains. From that place he added, the river was navigable to the ocean; that some of his relations had been there last fall and seen an old white man who resided there by himself, and who gave them some handkerchiefs like those we have. The distance from this place is five sleeps or days' journey. When our hunters had all joined us we found our provisions consisted of four deer, a beaver, and three grouse. The observation of to-day gave 46° 48' 28" as the latitude of Traveller's-rest creek.

SEPTEMBER 11TH  *Wednesday.* Two of our horses having strayed away we were detained all the morning before they were caught. In the meantime our Tushepaw Indian became impatient of the delay, and set out to return home alone. As usual we had despatched four of our best hunters ahead, and as we hoped with their aid and our present stock of provisions to subsist on the route, we proceeded at three o'clock up the right side of the creek, and encamped under some old Indian huts at the distance of seven miles. The road was plain and good: the valley is however narrower than that which we left and bordered by high and rugged hills to the right, while the mountains on the left were covered with snow. The day was fair and warm, the wind from the northwest.

SEPTEMBER 12TH  *Thursday.* There was a white frost this morning. We proceeded at seven o'clock and soon passed a stream falling in on the right, near which was an old Indian camp with a bath or sweating-house covered with earth. At two miles distance we ascended a high, and thence continued through a hilly and thickly timbered country for nine miles, when we came to the forks of the creek, where the road branches up each fork. We followed the western route, and finding that the creek made a considerable bend at the distance of four miles, crossed a high mountain in order to avoid the circuit. The road had been very bad during the first part of the day, but the passage of the mountain, which was eight miles across, was very painful to the horses, as we were obliged to go over steep stony sides of hills and along the hollows and ravines, rendered more disagreeable by the fallen timber, chiefly pine, spruce pine and fir. We at length reached the creek, having made twenty-three miles of a route so difficult that some of the party did not join us before ten o'clock. We found the account of the scantiness of game but too true, as we were not able to procure any thing during the whole of yesterday, and to-day we killed only a single pheasant. Along the road we observed many of the pine trees peeled off, which is done by the Indians to procure the inner bark for food in the spring.

*Friday.* Two of the horses strayed away during the night, and one of them being captain Lewis's, he remained with four men to search for them while we proceeded up the creek: at the distance of two miles we came to several springs issuing from large rocks of a course hard grit, and nearly boiling hot. These seem to be much frequented as there are several paths made by elk, deer and other animals, and near one of the springs a hole or Indian bath, and roads leading in different directions. These embarrassed our guide, who mistaking the road took us three miles out of the proper course over an exceedingly bad route. We then fell into the right road, and proceeded on very well, when having made five miles we stopped to refresh the horses. Captain Lewis here joined us, but not having been able to find his horse, two men were sent back to continue the search. We then proceeded along the same kind of country which we passed yesterday, and after crossing a mountain and leaving the sources of the Traveller's-rest creek on the left, reached after five miles riding a small creek which also came in from the left hand, passing through open glades, some of which were half a mile wide. The road which had been as usual rugged and stony, became firm, plain and level after quitting the head of Traveller's-rest. We followed the course of this new creek for two miles and encamped at a spot where the mountains close on each side. Other mountains covered with snow are in view to the southeast and southwest. We were somewhat more fortunate today in killing a deer and several pheasants which were of the common species, except that the tail was black.

*Saturday.* The day was very cloudy with rain and hail in the valleys, while on the top of the mountains some snow fell. We proceeded early, and continuing along the right side of Glade creek crossed a high mountain, and at the distance of six miles reached the place where it is joined by another branch of equal size from the right. Near the forks the Tushepaws have had an encampment which is but recently abandoned, for the grass is entirely destroyed by horses, and two fish weirs across the creek are still remaining; no fish were however to be seen. We here passed over to the left side of the creek and began the ascent of a very high and steep mountain nine miles across. On reaching the other side we found a large branch from the left, which seems to rise in the snowy mountains to the south and southeast. We continued along the creek two miles further, when night coming on we encamped opposite a small island at the mouth of a branch on the right side of the river. The mountains which we crossed to-day were much more difficult than those of yesterday; the last was particularly fatiguing, being steep and stony, broken by fallen timber, and thickly overgrown by pine, spruce, fir, hackmatack and tamarack. Although we had made only seventeen miles we were all very weary. The whole stock of animal food was now exhausted, and we therefore killed a colt, on which we made a hearty supper. From this incident we called the last creek we had passed from the south Colt-killed creek. The river itself is eighty yards wide, with a swift current, and a stony channel. Its Indian name is Kooskooskee.

*Sunday.* At an early hour we proceeded along the right side of the Koos- kooskee over steep rocky points of land, till at the distance of four miles we reached an old Indian fishing place: the road here turned to the right of the water, and began to ascend a mountain: but the fire and wind had prostrated or dried almost all the timber on the south side, and the ascents were so steep that we were forced to wind in every direction round the high knobs which constantly impeded our progress. Several of the horses lost their foothold and slipped: one of them which was loaded with a desk and small trunk, rolled over and over for forty yards, till his fall was stopped by a tree. The desk was broken; but the poor animal escaped without much injury. After clambering in this way for four miles, we came to a high snowy part of the mountain where was a spring of water, at which we halted two hours to refresh our horses.

On leaving the spring the road continued as bad as it was below, and the timber more abundant. At four miles we reached the top of the mountain, and foreseeing no chance of meeting with water, we encamped on the northern side of the mountain, near an old bank of snow, three feet deep. Some of this we melted, and supped on the remains of the colt killed yesterday. Our only game to-day was two pheasants, and the horses on which we calculated as a last resource begin to fail us, for two of them were so poor, and worn out with fatigue, that we were obliged to leave them behind. All around us are high rugged mountains, among which is a lofty range from southeast to northwest, whose tops are without timber, and in some places covered with snow. The night was cloudy and very cold, and three hours before daybreak, *Monday 16th*, it began to snow, and continued all day, so that by evening it was six or eight inches deep.

This covered the track so completely, that we were obliged constantly to halt and examine, lest we should lose the route. In many places we had nothing to guide us except the branches of the trees which, being low, have been rubbed by the burdens of the Indian horses. The road was, like that of yesterday, along steep hill sides, obstructed with fallen timber, and a growth of eight different species of pine, so thickly strewed that the snow falls from them as we pass, and keeps us continually wet to the skin, and so cold, that we are anxious lest our feet should be frozen, as we have only thin moccasins to defend them.

At noon we halted to let the horses feed on some long grass on the south side of the mountains, and endeavoured by making fires to keep ourselves warm. As soon as the horses were refreshed, captain Clark went ahead with one man, and at the distance of six miles reached a stream from the right, and prepared fires by the time of our arrival at dusk. We here encamped in a piece of low ground, thickly timbered, but scarcely large enough to permit us to lie level. We had now made thirteen miles. We were all very wet, cold, and hungry: but although before setting out this morning, we had seen four deer, yet we could not procure any of them, and were obliged to kill a second colt for our supper.

SEPTEMBER 17TH  *Tuesday*. Our horses became so much scattered during the night, that we were detained till one o'clock before they were all collected. We then continued our route over high rough knobs, and several drains and springs, and along a ridge of country separating the waters of two small rivers. The road was still difficult, and several of the horses fell and injured themselves very much, so that we were unable to advance more than ten miles to a small stream, on which we encamped.

We had killed a few pheasants, but these being insufficient for our subsistence, we killed another of the colts. This want of provisions, and the extreme fatigue to which we were subjected, and the dreary prospects before us, began to dispirit the men. It was therefore agreed that captain Clark should go on ahead with six hunters, and endeavour to kill something for the support of the party.

He therefore set out *Wednesday 18th*, early in the morning in hopes of finding a level country from which he might send back some game. His route lay S. 85° W. along the same high dividing ridge, and the road was still very bad; but he moved on rapidly, and at the distance of twenty miles was rejoiced on discovering far off an extensive plain towards the west and southwest, bounded by a high mountain. He halted an hour to let the horses eat a little grass on the hill sides, and then went on twelve and a half miles till he reached a bold creek, running to the left, on which he encamped. To this stream he gave the very appropriate name of Hungry creek; for having procured no game, they had nothing to eat.

In the meantime we were detained till after eight o'clock by the loss of one of our horses which had strayed away and could not be found. We then proceeded, but having soon finished the remainder of the colt killed yesterday, felt the want of provisions, which was more sensible from our meeting with no water, till towards nightfall we found some in a ravine among the hills. By pushing on our horses almost to their utmost strength, we made eighteen miles.

We then melted some snow, and supped on a little portable soup, a few canisters of which, with about twenty weight of bear's oil, are our only remaining means of subsistence. Our guns are scarcely of any service, for there is no living creature in these mountains, except a few small pheasants, a small species of gray squirrel, and a blue bird of the vulture kind about the size of a turtle dove or jay, and even these are difficult to shoot.

*Thursday.* Captain Clark proceeded up the creek, along which the road was more steep and stony than any he had yet passed. At six miles distance he reached a small plain, in which he fortunately found a horse, on which he breakfasted, and hung the rest on a tree for the party in the rear. Two miles beyond this he left the creek, and crossed three high mountains, rendered almost impassable from the steepness of the ascent and the quantity of fallen timber. After clambering over these ridges and mountains, and passing the heads of some branches of Hungry creek, he came to a large creek running westward. This he followed for four miles, then turned to the right down the mountain, till he came to a small creek to the left. Here he halted, having made twenty-two miles on his course, south eighty degrees west, though the winding route over the mountains almost doubled the distance. On descending the last mountain, the heat became much more sensible after the extreme cold he had experienced for several days past. Besides the breakfast in the morning, two pheasants were their only food during the day, and the only kinds of birds they saw were the blue jay, a small white-headed hawk, a larger hawk, crows, and ravens.

We followed soon after sunrise. At six miles the ridge terminated and we had before us the cheering prospect of the large plain to the southwest. On leaving the ridge we again ascended and went down several mountains, and six miles further came to Hungry creek where it was fifteen yards wide, and received the waters of a branch from the north. We went up it on a course nearly due west, and at three miles crossed a second branch flowing from the same quarter. The country is thickly covered with pine timber, of which we have enumerated eight distinct species. Three miles beyond this last branch of Hungry creek we encamped, after a fatiguing route of eighteen miles. The road along the creek is a narrow rocky path near the edges of very high precipices, from which a fall seems almost inevitable destruction. One of our horses slipped and rolling over with his load down the hill side, which was nearly perpendicular and strewed with large irregular rocks, nearly a hundred yards, and did not stop till he fell into the creek: we all expected he was killed, but to our astonishment, on taking off his load, he rose, and seemed but little injured, and in twenty minutes proceeded with his load. Having no other provision we took some portable soup, our only refreshment during the day. This abstinence, joined with fatigue, has a visible effect on our health. The men are growing weak and losing their flesh very fast: several are afflicted with the dysentery, and eruptions of the skin are very common.

september 20th    *Friday.* Captain Clark went on through a country as rugged as usual, till on passing a low mountain he came at the distance of four miles to the forks of a large creek. Down this he kept on a course south 60° west for two miles, then turning to the right, continued over a dividing ridge where were the heads of several little streams, and at twelve miles distance descended the last of the rocky mountains and reached the level country. A beautiful open plain partially supplied with pine now presented itself. He continued for five miles when he discovered three Indian boys, who, on observing the party, ran off and hid themselves in the grass. Captain Clark immediately alighted, and giving his horse and gun to one of the men went after the boys. He soon relieved their apprehensions and sent them forward to the village about a mile off with presents of small pieces of ribbon.

Soon after the boys had reached home, a man came out to meet the party, with great caution, but he conducted them to a large tent in the village, and all the inhabitants gathered round to view with a mixture of fear and pleasure these wonderful strangers. The conductor now informed captain Clark by signs, that the spacious tent was the residence of the great chief, who had set out three days ago with all the warriors to attack some of their enemies towards the southwest; that he would not return before fifteen or eighteen days, and that in the meantime there were only a few men left to guard the women and children. They now set before them a small piece of buffalo meat, some dried salmon, berries, and several kinds of roots. Among these last is one which is round and much like an onion in appearance and sweet to the taste: it is called quamash, and is eaten either in its natural state, or boiled into a kind of soup or made into a cake, which is then called pasheco. After the long abstinence this was a sumptuous treat; we returned the kindness of the people by a few small presents, and then went on in company with one of the chiefs to a second village in the same plain, at the distance of two miles. Here the party was treated with great kindness and passed the night. The hunters were sent out, but though they saw some tracks of deer were not able to procure any thing.

INDIAN UTENSILS AND WEAPONS (Bodmer)

We were detained till ten o'clock before we could collect our scattered horses; we then proceeded for two miles, when to our great joy we found the horse which captain Clark had killed, and a note apprising us of his intention of going to the plains towards the southwest, and collect provisions by the time we reached him. At one o'clock we halted on a small stream, and made a hearty meal of horse flesh. On examination it now appeared that one of the horses was missing, and the man in whose charge he had been, was directed to return and search for him. He came back in about two hours without having been able to find the horse; but as the load was too valuable to be lost, two of the best woodsmen were directed to continue the search while we proceeded. Our general course was south 25° west through a thick forest of large pine, which has fallen in many places, and very much obstructs the road. After making about fifteen miles we encamped on a ridge where we could find but little grass and no water. We succeeded, however, in procuring a little from a distance, and supped on the remainder of the horse.

On descending the heights of the mountains the soil becomes gradually more fertile, and the land through which we passed this evening, is of an excellent quality. It has a dark gray soil, though very broken, and with large masses of gray freestone above the ground in many places. Among the vegetable productions we distinguished the alder, honeysuckle, and huckleberry, common in the United States, and a species of honeysuckle, known only westward of the Rocky mountains, which rises to the height of about four feet, and bears a white berry. There is also a plant resembling the chokecherry, which grows in thick clumps eight or ten feet high, and bears a black berry with a single stone of a sweetish taste. The arbor vitae, too, is very common, and grows to a great size, being from two to six feet in diameter.

*Saturday.* The free use of food, to which he had not been accustomed, made captain Clark very sick both yesterday evening and during the whole of today. He therefore sent out all the hunters and remained himself at the village, as well on account of his sickness as for the purpose of avoiding suspicion and collecting information from the Indians as to the route.

The two villages consist of about thirty double tents, and the inhabitants call themselves Chopunnish or Pierced-nose [Nez-Percé]. The chief drew a chart of the river, and explained, that a greater chief than himself, who governed this village and was called the Twisted-hair, was now fishing at the distance of half a day's ride down the river: his chart made the Kooskooskee fork a little below his camp, a second fork below, still further on a large branch flowed in on each side, below which the river passed the mountains: here was a great fall of water, near which lived white people, from whom were procured the white beads and brass ornaments worn by the women.

A chief of another band made a visit this morning, and smoked with captain Clark. The hunters returned without having been able to kill any thing; captain Clark purchased as much dried salmon, roots and berries as he could, with the few articles he chanced to have in his pockets, and having sent them by one of the men and a hired Indian back to captain Lewis, he went on towards the camp of the Twisted-hair. It was four o'clock before he set out, and the night soon came on; but having met an Indian coming from the river, they engaged him by a present of a neck-cloth, to guide them to the Twisted-hair's camp. For twelve miles they proceeded through the plain before they reached the river hills, which are very high and steep. The whole valley from these hills to the Rocky mountain is a beautiful level country, with a rich soil covered with grass: there is however, but little timber, and the ground is badly watered: the plain is so much lower than the surrounding hills, or so much sheltered by them, that the weather is quite warm, while the cold of the mountains was extreme. From the top of the river hills they proceeded down for three miles till they reached the water side, between eleven and twelve o'clock at night: here we found a small camp of five squaws and three children, the chief himself being encamped, with two others, on a small island in the river: the guide called to him and he soon came over. Captain Clark gave him a medal, and they smoked together till one o'clock.

We could not set out till eleven o'clock, because being obliged in the evening to loosen our horses to enable them to find subsistence, it is always difficult to collect them in the morning. At that hour we continued along the ridge on which we had slept, and at a mile and a half reached a large creek running to our left, just above its junction with one of its branches. We proceeded down the low grounds of this creek, which are level, wide, and heavily timbered, but turned to the right at the distance of two and a half miles, and began to pass the broken and hilly country; but the thick timber had fallen in so many places that we could scarcely make our way. After going five miles we passed the creek on which captain Clark had encamped during the night of the *19th*, and continued five miles further over the same kind of road, till we came to the forks of a large creek. We crossed the northern branch of this stream, and proceeded down it on the west side for a mile: here we found a small plain where there was tolerable grass for the horses, and therefore remained during the night, having made fifteen miles on a course S. 30° W.

The arbor vitae increases in size and quantity as we advance: some of the trees we passed to-day being capable of forming periogues at least forty-five feet in length. We were so fortunate also as to kill a few pheasants and a prairie wolf, which, with the remainder of the horse, supplied us with one meal, the last of our provisions, our food for the morrow being wholly dependent on the chance of our guns.

SEPTEMBER 22D    *Sunday*. Captain Clark passed over to the island with the Twisted-hair, who seemed to be cheerful and sincere in his conduct. The river at this place is about one hundred and sixty yards wide, but interrupted by shoals, and the low grounds on its borders are narrow. The hunters brought in three deer; after which captain Clark left his party, and accompanied by the Twisted-hair and his son, rode back to the village, where he arrived about sunset: they then walked up together to the second village, where we had just arrived. We had intended to set out early, but one of the men having neglected to hobble his horse he strayed away, and we were obliged to wait till nearly twelve o'clock. We then proceeded on a western course for two and a half miles, when we met the hunters sent by captain Clark from the village, seven and a half miles distant, with provisions. This supply was most sea-

276

sonable, as we had tasted nothing since last night, and the fish, and roots, and berries, in addition to a crow which we killed on the route, completely satisfied our hunger. After this refreshment we proceeded in much better spirits, and at a few miles were overtaken by the two men who had been sent back after a horse on the *20th*. They were perfectly exhausted with the fatigue of walking and the want of food; but as we had two spare horses they were mounted and brought on to the village.

They had set out about three o'clock in the afternoon of the *20th* with one horse between them: after crossing the mountain they came to the place where we had eaten the horse. Here they encamped, and having no food made a fire and roasted the head of the horse, which even our appetites had spared, and supped on the ears, skin, lips, &c. of the animal. The next morning, *21st*, they found the track of the horse, and pursuing it recovered the saddle-bags, and at length about eleven o'clock, the horse himself. Being now both mounted, they set out to return and slept at a small stream: during the day they had nothing at all except two pheasants, which were so torn to pieces by the shot, that the head and legs were the only parts fit for food. In this situation they found the next morning, *22d*, that during the night their horses had run away from them or been stolen by the Indians. They searched for them until nine o'clock, when seeing that they could not recover them and fearful of starving if they remained where they were, they set out on foot to join us, carrying the saddle-bags alternately. They walked as fast as they could during the day, till they reached us in a deplorable state of weakness and inanition.

As we approached the village, most of the women, though apprised of our being expected, fled with their children into the neighbouring woods. The men, however, received us without any apprehension, and gave us a plentiful supply of provisions. The plains were now crowded with Indians, who came to see the persons of the whites, and the strange things they brought with them: but as our guide was perfectly a stranger to their language we could converse by signs only. Our inquiries were chiefly directed to the situation of the country, the courses of the rivers, and the Indian villages, of all which we received information from several of the Indians, and as their accounts varied but little from each other, we were induced to place confidence in them. Among others, the Twisted-hair drew a chart of the river on a white elk skin. According to this, the Kooskooskee forks a few miles from this place; two days towards the south is another and larger fork on which the Shoshonee or Snake Indians fish: five days' journey further is a large river from the northwest into which Clark's river empties itself: from the mouth of that river to the falls is five days' journey further: on all the forks as well as on the main river great numbers of Indians reside, and at the falls are establishments of whites. This was the story of the Twisted-hair.

*Monday.* The chiefs and warriors were all assembled this morning, and we explained to them where we came from, the objects of our visiting them, and our pacific intentions towards all the Indians. This being conveyed by signs, might not have been perfectly comprehended, but appeared to give perfect satisfaction. We now gave a medal to two of the chiefs, a shirt in addition to the medal already received by the Twisted-hair, and delivered a flag and a handkerchief for the grand chief on his return. To these were added a knife, a handkerchief and a small piece of tobacco for each chief. The inhabitants did not give us any provisions gratuitously. We therefore purchased a quantity of fish, berries (chiefly red haws) and roots; and in the afternoon went on to the second village. The Twisted-hair introduced us into his own tent, which consisted however of nothing more than pine bushes and bark, and gave us some dried salmon boiled. We continued our purchases, and obtained as much provision as our horses could carry in their present weak condition as far as the river. The men exchanged a few old canisters for dressed elk skins, of which they made shirts: great crowds of the natives are round us all night, but we have not yet missed any thing except a knife and a few other articles stolen yesterday from a shot pouch. At dark we had a hard wind from the southwest accompanied with rain which lasted half an hour, but in the morning, *Tuesday, 24th*, the weather was fair. We sent back Colter in search of the horses lost in the mountains, and having collected the rest set out at ten o'clock along the same route already passed by captain Clark towards the river.

All round the village the women are busily employed in gathering and dressing the pasheco root, of which large quantities are heaped up in piles over the plain. We now felt severely the consequence of eating heartily after our late privations: captain Lewis and two of the men were taken very ill last evening, and to-day he could scarcely sit on his horse, while others were obliged to be put on horseback, and some from extreme weakness and pain, were forced to lie down along side of the road for some time. At sunset we reached the island where the hunters had been left on the *22d*. They had been unsuccessful, having killed only two deer since that time, and two of them are very sick. A little below this island is a larger one on which we encamped, and administered Rush's pills to the sick.

SEPTEMBER 25TH    *Wednesday.* The weather was very hot, and oppressive to the party, most of whom are now complaining of sickness. Our situation indeed, rendered it necessary to husband our remaining strength, and it was determined to proceed down the river in canoes. Captain Clark therefore set out with the Twisted-hair and two young men, in quest of timber for canoes. As he went down the river he crossed at the distance of a mile a creek from the right, which from the rocks that obstructed its passage, he called Rockdam river. The hills along the river are high and steep: the low grounds are narrow, and the navigation of the river embarrassed by two rapids. At the distance of three miles further he reached two nearly equal forks of the river, one of which flowed in from the north. Here he rested for an hour, and cooked a few salmon which one of the Indians caught with a gig. Here too, he was joined by two canoes of Indians from below: they were long, steady, and loaded with the furniture and provisions of two families. He now crossed the south fork, and returned to the camp on the south side, through a narrow pine bottom the greater part of the way, in which was found much fine timber for canoes. One of the Indian boats with two men, set out at the same time, and such was their dexterity in managing the pole, that they reached camp within fifteen minutes after him, although they had to drag the canoe over three rapids. He found captain Lewis, and several of the men still very sick; and distributed to such as were in need of it, salts and tartar emetic.

*Thursday.* Having resolved to go down to some spot calculated for building canoes, we set out early this morning and proceeded five miles, and encamped on low ground on the south, opposite the forks of the river. But so weak were the men that several were taken sick in coming down; the weather being oppressively hot. Two chiefs and their families followed us, and encamped with a great number of horses near us: and soon after our arrival we were joined by two Indians, who came down the north fork on a raft. We purchased some fresh salmon, and having distributed axes, and portioned off the labour of the party, began, *Friday 27th*, at an early hour, the preparations for making five canoes. But few of the men, however, were able to work, and of these several were soon taken ill, as the day proved very hot. The hunters too, returned without any game, and seriously indisposed, so that nearly the whole party was now ill. We procured some fresh salmon; and Colter, who now returned with one of the horses, brought half a deer, which was very nourishing to the invalids: several Indians from a camp below, came up to see us.

*Saturday.* The men continue ill, though some of those first attacked are re- covering. Their general complaint is a heaviness at the stomach, and a lax, which is rendered more painful by the heat of the weather, and the diet of fish and roots, to which they are confined, as no game is to be procured. A number of Indians collect about us in the course of the day to gaze at the strange appearance of every thing belonging to us.

*Sunday.* The morning was cool, the wind from the southwest; but in the aft- ernoon the heat returned. The men continue ill; but all those who are able to work are occupied at the canoes. The spirits of the party were much recruited by three deer brought in by the hunters; and the next day, *Monday 30th*, the sick began to recruit their strength, the morning being fair and pleasant. The Indians pass in great numbers up and down the river, and we observe large quantities of small duck going down this morning.

## Tuesday, October 1st, 1805

The morning was cool, the wind easterly, but the latter part of the day was warm. We were visited by several Indians from the tribes below, and others from the main south fork. To two of the most distinguished men we made presents of a ring and brooch, and to five others a piece of ribbon, a little tobacco, and the fifth part of a neckcloth. We now dried our clothes and other articles, and selected some articles such as the Indians admire, in order to purchase some provisions, as we have nothing left except a little dried fish, which operates as a complete purgative.

*Wednesday.* The day is very warm. Two men were sent to the village with a quantity of these articles to purchase food. We are now reduced to roots, which produce violent pains in the stomach. Our work continued as usual, and many of the party are convalescent. The hunters returned in the afternoon with nothing but a small prairie-wolf, so that our provisions being exhausted, we killed one of the horses to eat, and provide soup for the sick.

OCTOBER 3D    *Thursday.* The fine cool morning and easterly wind had an agreeable effect upon the party, most of whom are now able to work. The Indians from below left us, and we were visited by others from different quarters.

OCTOBER 4TH    *Friday.* Again we had a cool east wind from the mountains. The men were now much better, and captain Lewis himself so far recovered as to walk about a little. Three Indians arrived to-day from the Great river to the south. The two men also returned from the village with roots and fish, and as the flesh of the horse killed yesterday was exhausted, we were confined to that diet, though unwholesome as well as unpleasant. The afternoon was warm.

OCTOBER 5TH    *Saturday.* The wind easterly, and the weather cool. The canoes being nearly finished it became necessary to dispose of our horses. They were therefore collected to the number of thirty-eight, and being branded and marked were delivered to three Indians, the two brothers and the son of a chief, who promises to accompany us down the river. To each of these men we gave a knife and some small articles, and they agreed to take good care of the horses till our return. The hunters with all their diligence are unable to kill any thing, the hills being high and rugged, and the woods too dry to hunt deer, which is the only game in the country. We therefore continue to eat dried fish and roots, which are purchased from the squaws, by means of small presents, but chiefly white beads, of which they are extravagantly fond. Some of these roots seem to possess very active properties, for after supping on them this evening, we were swelled to such a degree as to be scarcely able to breathe for several hours. Towards night we launched two canoes which proved to be very good.

OCTOBER 6TH    *Sunday.* This morning is again cool, and the wind easterly. The general course of the winds seems to resemble that which we observed on the east side of the mountain. While on the head waters of the Missouri, we had every morning a cool wind from the west. At this place a cool breeze springs up during the latter part of the night, or near daybreak, and continues till seven or eight o'clock, when it subsides, and the latter part of the day is warm. Captain Lewis is not so well as he was, and captain Clark was also taken ill. We had all our saddles buried in a cache near the river, about half a mile below, and deposited at the same time a canister of powder, and a bag of balls. The time which could be spared from our labours on the canoes, was devoted to some astronomical observations. The latitude of our camp as deduced from the mean of two observations is 46° 34′ 56.3″ north.

OCTOBER 7TH    *Monday.* This morning all the canoes were put in the water and loaded, the oars fixed, and every preparation made for setting out, but when we were all ready, the two chiefs who had promised to accompany us, were not to be found, and at the same time we missed a pipe tomahawk. We therefore proceeded without them. Below the forks this river is called the Kooskooskee, and is a clear rapid stream, with a number of shoals and difficult places. For some miles the hills are steep, the low grounds narrow, but then succeeds an open country with a few trees scattered along the river. At the distance of nine miles is a small creek on the left. We passed in the course of the day ten rapids, in descending which, one of the canoes struck a rock, and sprung a leak: we however continued for nineteen miles, and encamped on the left side of the river, opposite to the mouth of a small run. Here the canoe was unloaded and repaired, and two lead canisters of powder deposited; several camps of Indians were on the sides of the river, but we had little intercourse with any of them.

*Tuesday.* We set out at nine o'clock. At eight and a half miles we passed an island: four and a half miles lower a second island, opposite a small creek on the left side of the river. Five miles lower is another island on the left: a mile and a half below which is a fourth. At a short distance from this is a large creek from the right, to which we gave the name of Colter's creek, from Colter one of the men. We had left this creek about a mile and a half, and were passing the last of fifteen rapids which we had been fortunate enough to escape, when one of the canoes struck, and a hole being made in her side, she immediately filled and sunk. The men, several of whom could not swim, clung to the boat till one of our canoes could be unloaded, and with the assistance of an Indian boat, they were all brought to shore. All the goods were so much wet, that we were obliged to halt for the night, and spread them out to dry. While all this was exhibited, it was necessary to place two sentinels over the merchandise, for we found that the Indians, though kind and disposed to give us every aid during our distress, could not resist the temptation of pilfering some of the small articles. We passed during our route of twenty miles to-day, several encampments of Indians on the islands, and near the rapids, which places are chosen as most convenient for taking salmon. At one of these camps we found our two chiefs, who after promising to descend the river with us, had left us; they however willingly came on board after we had gone through the ceremony of smoking.

*Wednesday.* The morning was as usual, cool; but as the weather both yesterday and to-day was cloudy, our merchandise dried but slowly. The boat, though much injured, was repaired by ten o'clock so as to be perfectly fit for service; but we were obliged to remain during the day till the articles were sufficiently dry to be reloaded: the interval we employed in purchasing fish for the voyage and conversing with the Indians. In the afternoon we were surprised at hearing that our old Shoshonee guide and his son had left us, and been seen running up the river several miles above. As he had never given any notice of his intention, nor had even received his pay for guiding us, we could not imagine the cause of his desertion, nor did he ever return to explain his conduct. We requested the chief to send a horseman after him to request that he would return and receive what we owed him. From this however he dissuaded us, and said very frankly, that his nation, the Chopunnish, would take from the old man any presents that he might have on passing their camp.

     The Indians came about our camp at night, and were very gay and good-humoured with the men. Among other exhibitions was that of a squaw who appeared to be crazy: she sang in a wild incoherent manner, and would offer to the spectators all the little articles she possessed, scarifying herself in a horrid manner if any one refused her present: she seemed to be an object of pity among the Indians, who suffered her to do as she pleased without interruption.

*Thursday.* A fine morning. We loaded the canoes and set off at seven o'clock. At the distance of two and a half miles we had passed three islands, the last of which is opposite to a small stream on the right. Within the following three and a half miles is another island and a creek on the left, with wide low grounds, containing willow and cottonwood trees, on which were three tents of Indians. Two miles lower is the head of a large island, and six and a half miles further we halted at an encampment of eight lodges on the left, in order to view a rapid before us: we had already passed eight, and some of them difficult; but this was worse than any of them, being a very hazardous ripple strewed with rocks: we here purchased roots and dined with the Indians. Among them was a man from the falls, who says that he saw white people at that place, and is very desirous of going down with us; an offer which however we declined. Just above this camp we had passed a tent, near which was an Indian bathing himself in a small pond or hole of water, warmed by throwing in hot stones.

After finishing our meal we descended the rapid with no injury, except to one of our boats which ran against a rock, but in the course of an hour was brought off with only a small split in her side. This ripple, from its appearance and difficulty, we named the Rugged rapid. We went on over five other rapids of a less dangerous kind, and at the distance of five miles reached a large fork of the river from the south; and after coming twenty miles, halted below the junction on the right side of the river.

Our arrival soon attracted the attention of the Indians, who flocked in all directions to see us. In the evening the Indian from the falls, whom we had seen at the Rugged rapid, joined us with his son in a small canoe, and insisted on accompanying us to the falls. Being again reduced to fish and roots we made an experiment to vary our food by purchasing a few dogs, and after having been accustomed to horse-flesh, felt no disrelish to this new dish. The Chopunnish have great numbers of dogs which they employ for domestic purposes, but never eat; and our using the flesh of that animal soon brought us into ridicule as dog-eaters.

The country at the junction of the two rivers is an open plain on all sides, broken towards the left by a distant ridge of highland, thinly covered with timber: this is the only body of timber which the country possesses; for at the forks there is not a tree to be seen, and during almost the whole descent of sixty miles down the Kooskooskee from its forks there are very few. This southern branch is in fact the main stream of Lewis's river on which we encamped when among the Shoshonees. The Indians inform us that it is navigable for sixty miles; that not far from its mouth it receives a branch from the south; and a second and larger branch, two days' march up, and nearly parallel to the first Chopunnish villages, we met near the mountains. This branch is called Pawnashte, and is the residence of a chief, who, according to their expression, has more horses than he can count. The river has many rapids, near which are situated many fishing camps; there being ten establishments of this before reaching the first southern branch; one on that stream, five between that and the Pawnashte; one on that river, and two above it; besides many other Indians who reside high up on the more distant waters of this river. All these Indians belong to the Chopunnish nation, and live in tents of an oblong form, covered with flat roofs.

At its mouth Lewis's river is about two hundred and fifty yards

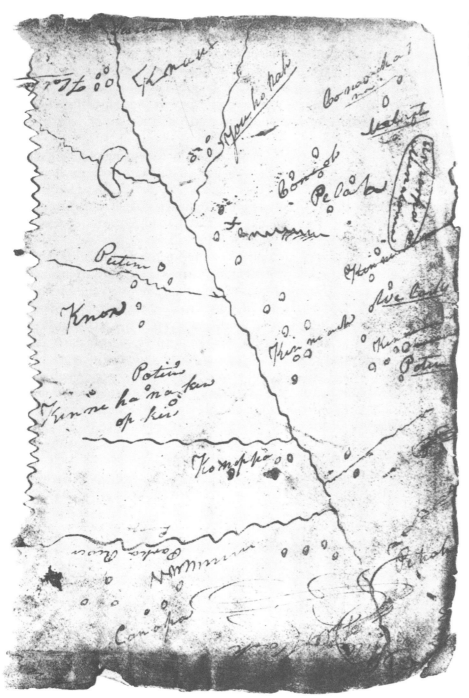

*Map locating Indian tribes, from a page of Captain Clark's field book.*

wide, and its water is of a greenish blue colour. The Kooskooskee, whose waters are clear as crystal, one hundred and fifty yards in width, and after the union the river enlarges to the space of three hundred yards: at the point of the union is an Indian cabin, and in Lewis's river a small island.

The Chopunnish or Pierced-nose nation, who reside on the Kooskooskee and Lewis's rivers, are in person stout, portly, well-looking men: the women are small, with good features, and generally handsome, though the complexion of both sexes is darker than that of the Tushepaws. In dress they resemble that nation, being fond of displaying their ornaments. The buffalo or elk-skin robe decorated with beads, sea-shells, chiefly mother-of-pearl, attached to an otter-skin collar and hung in the hair, which falls in front in two queues; feathers, paints of different kinds, principally white, green, and light blue, all of which they find in their own country: these are the chief ornaments they use. In the winter they wear a short shirt of dressed skins, long painted leggings and moccasins, and a plait of twisted grass round the neck.

The dress of the women is more simple, consisting of a long shirt of argalia or ibex skin, reaching down to the ankles without a girdle: to this are tied little pieces of brass and shells and other small articles; but the head is not at all ornamented. The dress of the female is indeed more modest, and more studiously so than any we have observed, though the other sex is careless of the indelicacy of exposure.

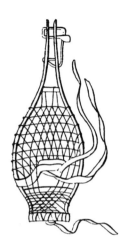

The Chopunnish have very few amusements, for their life is painful and laborious; and all their exertions are necessary to earn even their precarious subsistence. During the summer and autumn they are busily occupied in fishing for salmon, and collecting their winter store of roots. In the winter they hunt the deer on snow shoes over the plains, and towards spring cross the mountains to the Missouri for the purpose of trafficking for buffalo robes. The inconveniences of that comfortless life are increased by frequent encounters with their enemies from the west, who drive them over the mountains with the loss of their horses, and sometimes the lives of many of the nation. Though originally the same people, their dialect varies very perceptibly from that of the Tushepaws: their treatment to us differed much from the kind and disinterested services of the Shoshonees: they are indeed selfish and avaricious; they part very reluctantly with every article of food or clothing; and while they expect a recompense for every service however small, do not concern themselves about reciprocating any presents we may give them.

They are generally healthy—the only disorders which we have had occasion to remark being of a scrofulous kind, and for these, as well as for the amusement of those who are in good health, hot and cold bathing is very commonly used.

The soil of these prairies is of a light yellow clay intermixed with small smooth grass: it is barren, and produces little more than a bearded grass about three inches high, and a prickly pear, of which we now found three species: the first is of the broad-leafed kind, common to the Missouri. The second has the leaf of a globular form, and is also frequent on the upper part of the Missouri, particularly after it enters the Rocky mountains. The third is peculiar to this country, and is much more inconvenient than the other two: it consists of small thick leaves of a circular form, which grow from the margin of each other as in the broad-leafed pear of the Missouri: these leaves are armed with a greater number of thorns, which are stronger, and appear to be barbed; and as the leaf itself is very slightly attached to the stem, as soon as one thorn touches the moccasin it adheres and brings with it the leaf, which is accompanied by a reinforcement of thorns.

FRIDAY, OCTOBER 11TH, 1805  This morning the wind was from the east, and the weather cloudy. We set out early, and at the distance of a mile and a half reached a point of rocks in a bend of the river towards the left, near to which was an old Indian house, and a meadow on the opposite bank. Here the hills came down towards the water, and formed by the rocks, which have fallen from their sides, a rapid over which we dragged the canoes. We passed, a mile and a half further, two Indian lodges in a bend towards the right, and at six miles from our camp of last evening reached the mouth of a brook on the left. Just above this stream we stopped for breakfast at a large encampment of Indians on the same side; we soon began to trade with them for a stock of provisions, and were so fortunate as to purchase seven dogs and all the fish they would spare.

While this traffic was going on, we observed a vapour bath or sweating house in a different form from that used on the frontiers of the United States, or in the Rocky mountains. It was a hollow square of six or eight feet deep, formed in the river bank by damming up with mud the other three sides, and covering the whole completely except an aperture about two feet wide at the top. The bathers descend by this hole, taking with them a number of heated stones, and jugs of water; and after being seated round the room, throw the water on the stones till the steam becomes of a temperature sufficiently high for their purposes. The baths of the Indians in the Rocky mountains is of different sizes, the most common being made of mud and sticks like an oven, but the mode of raising the steam is exactly the same. Among both these nations it is very uncommon for a man to bathe alone, he is generally accompanied by one or sometimes several of his acquaintances; indeed it is so essentially a social amusement, that to decline going in to bathe when invited by a friend is one of the highest indignities which can be offered to him. The Indians on the frontiers generally use a bath which will accommodate only one person, and is formed of a wickered work of willows about four feet high, arched at the top, and covered with skins. In this the patient sits till by means of the heated stones and water he has perspired sufficiently. Almost universally these baths are in the neighbourhood of running water, into which the Indians plunge immediately on coming out of the vapour bath, and sometimes return again, and subject themselves to a second perspiration. This practice is, however, less frequent among our neighbouring nations than those to the westward. This bath is employed either for pleasure or for health, and is used indiscriminately for rheumatism, venereal, or in short for all kinds of diseases.

On leaving this encampment we passed two more rapids, and some swift water, and at the distance of four and a half miles reached one which was much more difficult to pass. Three miles beyond this rapid, are three huts of Indians on the right, where we stopped and obtained in exchange for a few trifles some pasheco roots, five dogs and a small quantity of dried fish. We made our dinner of part of each of these articles, and then proceeded on without any obstruction, till after making twelve and a half miles we came to a stony island on the right side of the river, opposite to which is a rapid, and a second at its lower point. About three and a half miles beyond the island is a small brook which empties itself into a bend on the right, where we encamped at two Indian huts, which are now inhabited. Here we met two Indians belonging to a nation who reside at the mouth of this river. We had made thirty-one miles to-day, although the weather was warm, and we found the current obstructed by nine different rapids, more or less difficult to pass.

All these rapids are fishing places of great resort in the season, and as we passed we observed near them slabs and pieces of split timber raised from the ground, and some entire houses which are vacant at present, but will be occupied as soon as the Indians return from the plains on both sides of the river, where our chief informs us they are now hunting the antelope. Near each of these houses is a small collection of graves, the burial places of those who frequent these establishments. The dead are wrapped up in robes of skins, and deposited in graves, which are covered over with earth and marked or secured by little pickets or pieces of wood, stuck promiscuously over and around it. The country on both sides, after mounting a steep ascent of about two hundred feet, becomes an open, level and fertile plain, which is, however, as well as the borders of the river itself, perfectly destitute of any kind of timber; and the chief growth which we observed consisted of a few low blackberries. We killed some geese and ducks. The wind in the after part of the day changed to the southwest and became high, but in the morning, *Saturday 12th*, it shifted to the east, and we had a fair cool morning.

After purchasing all the provisions these Indians would spare, which amounted to only three dogs and a few fish, we proceeded. We soon reached a small island, and in the course of three miles passed three other islands nearly opposite to each other, and a bad rapid on the left in the neighbourhood of them. Within the following seven miles we passed a small rapid, and an island on the left, another stony island and a rapid on the right, just below which a brook comes in on the same side, and came to a bend towards the right opposite to a small island. From this place we saw some Indians on the hills, but they were too far off for us to have any intercourse, and showed no disposition to approach us. After going on two miles to a bend towards the left, we found the plains, which till now had formed rugged cliffs over the river, leaving small and narrow bottoms, become much lower on both sides, and the river itself widens to the space of four hundred yards, and continues for the same width, the country rising by a gentle ascent towards the high plains. At two and a half miles is a small creek on the left opposite to an island. For the three following miles, the country is low and open on both sides, after which it gradually rises till we reached a bend of the river towards the right, three and a half miles further, in the course of which we passed a rapid and an island. The wind now changed to the southwest, and became violent. We passed an island at the distance of four miles, another one mile beyond it, where the water was swift and shallow, and two miles further, a rapid at the upper point of a small stony island. We went along this island by the mouth of a brook on the right, and encamped on the same side opposite to a small island close under the left shore.

Our day's journey had been thirty miles, and we might have gone still further, but as the evening was coming on we halted at the head of a rapid, which the Indians represented as dangerous to pass, for the purpose of examining it before we set out in the morning. The country has much the same appearance as that we passed yesterday, consisting of open plains, which when they approach the water are faced with a dark-coloured rugged stone. The river is as usual much obstructed by islands and rapids, some of which are difficult to pass. Neither the plains nor the borders of the river possess any timber, except a few hackberry bushes and willows, and as there is not much driftwood, fuel is very scarce.

*Sunday*. The morning was windy and dark, and the rain which began before daylight, continued till near twelve o'clock. Having viewed very accurately the whole of this rapid we set out, the Indians going on before us to pilot the canoes. We found it, as had been reported, a very dangerous rapid, about two miles in length, and strewed with rocks in every direction, so as to require great dexterity to avoid running against them. We however passed through the channel, which is towards the left, and about the centre of the rapid, without meeting with any accident. Two miles below it we had another bad rapid, a mile beyond which is a large creek in a bend to the left. This we called Kimooenim creek. OCTOBER 13TH

On leaving it the river soon became crowded with rough black rocks, till at the distance of a mile it forms a rapid which continues for four miles, and during the latter part of it for a mile and a half, the whole river is compressed into a narrow channel, not more than twenty-five yards wide. The water happened to be low as we passed, but during the high waters, the navigation must be very difficult. Immediately at the end of this rapid, is a large stream in a bend to the right, which we called Drewyer's river, after George Drewyer one of the party. A little below the mouth of this river is a large fishing establishment, where there are the scaffolds and timbers of several houses piled up against each other, and the meadow adjoining contains a number of holes, which seem to have been used as places of deposits for fish for a great length of time. There were no entire houses standing, and we saw only two Indians who had visited the narrows, but we were overtaken by two others, who accompanied us on horseback down the river, informing us that they meant to proceed by land down to the great river. Nine and a half miles below Drewyer's river, we passed another rapid, and three and a half miles farther reached some high cliffs in a bend to the left. Here after passing the timbers of a house, which were preserved on forks, we encamped on the right side, near a collection of graves, such as we had seen above. The country was still an open plain without timber, and our day's journey had no variety, except the fishing houses which are scattered near the situations convenient for fishing, but are now empty. Our two Indian companions spent the night with us.

*Monday*. The wind was high from the southwest during the evening, and this morning it changed to the west, and the weather became very cold until about twelve o'clock, when it shifted to the southwest, and continued in that quarter during the rest of the day. We set out early, and after passing some swift water, reached at two and a half miles a rock of a very singular appearance. It was situated on a point to the left, at some distance from the ascending country, very high and large, and resembling in its shape the hull of a ship. At five miles we passed a rapid; at eight another rapid, and a small island on the right, and at ten and a half a small island on the right. We halted a mile and a half below for the purpose of examining a much larger and more dangerous rapid than those we had yet passed. It is three miles in length, and very difficult to navigate. We had scarcely set out, when three OCTOBER 14TH of the canoes stuck fast in endeavouring to avoid the rocks in the channel; soon after in passing two small rocky islands, one of the canoes struck a rock, but was prevented from upsetting, and fortunately we all arrived safe at the lower end of the rapid. Here we dined, and then proceeded, and soon reached another rapid on both sides of the river, which was divided by an island.

As we were descending it one of the boats was driven crosswise against a rock in the middle of the current. The crew attempted to get her off, but the waves dashed over her, and she soon filled; they got out on the rock and held her above water with great exertion, till another canoe was unloaded and sent to her relief; but they could not prevent a great deal of her baggage from floating down the stream. As soon as she was lightened, she was hurried down the channel leaving the crew on the rock. They were brought off by the rest of the party, and the canoe itself, and nearly all that had been washed overboard was recovered. The chief loss was the bedding of two of the men, a tomahawk, and some small articles. But all the rest were wet, and though by drying we were able to save the powder, all the loose packages of which were in this boat, yet we lost all the roots and other provisions, which are spoilt by the water. In order to diminish the loss as far as was in our power, we halted for the night on an island, and exposed every thing to dry.

On landing we found some split timber for houses which the Indians had very securely covered with stone, and also a place where they had deposited their fish. We have hitherto abstained scrupulously from taking any thing belonging to the Indians; but on this occasion we were compelled to depart from this rule; and as there was no other timber to be found in any direction for firewood, and no owner appeared from whom it could be purchased, we used a part of these split planks, bearing in mind our obligation to repay the proprietor whenever we should discover him. The only game which we observed were geese and ducks, of the latter we killed some, and a few of the blue-winged teal. Our journey was fifteen miles in length.

OCTOBER 15TH    *Tuesday.* The morning was fair, and being obliged to remain for the purpose of drying the baggage, we sent out the hunters to the plains, but they returned at ten o'clock, without having seen even the tracks of any large game, but brought in three geese and two ducks. The plains are waving, and as we walked in them, we could plainly discover a range of mountains bearing southeast and northwest, becoming higher as they advanced towards the north, the nearest point bearing south about sixty miles from us. Our stores being sufficiently dry to be reloaded, and as we shall be obliged to stop for the purpose of making some celestial observations at the mouth of the river, which cannot be at a great distance, we concluded to embark and complete the drying at that place: we therefore set out at two o'clock.

For the first four miles we passed three islands, at the lower points of which were the same number of rapids, besides a fourth at a distance from them. During the next ten miles we passed eight islands and three more rapids, and reached a point of rocks on the left side. The islands were of various sizes, but were all composed of round stone and sand: the rapids were in many places difficult and dangerous to pass. About this place the country becomes lower than usual, the ground over the river not being higher than ninety or a hundred feet, and extending back into a waving plain. Soon after leaving this point of rocks, we entered a narrow channel formed by the projecting cliffs of the bank, which rise nearly perpendicular from the water. The river is not however rapid, but gentle and smooth during its confinement, which lasts for three miles, when it falls, or rather widens into a kind of basin nearly round, and without any perceptible current.

After passing through this basin, we were joined by the three Indians who had piloted us through the rapids since we left the forks, and who in company with our two chiefs had gone before us. They had now halted here to warn us of a dangerous rapid, which begins at the lower point of the basin. As the day was too far spent to descend it, we determined to examine before we attempted it, and therefore landed near an island at the head of the rapid, and studied particularly all its narrow and difficult parts. The spot where we landed was an old fishing establishment, of which there yet remained the timbers of a house carefully raised on scaffolds to protect them against the spring tide. Not being able to procure any other fuel, and the night being cold, we were again obliged to use the property of the Indians, who still remain in the plains hunting the antelope. Our progress was only twenty miles in consequence of the difficulty of passing the rapids. Our game consisted of two teal.

*Wednesday.* Having examined the rapids, which we found more difficult OCTOBER 16TH than the report of the Indians had induced us to believe, we set out early, and putting our Indian guide in front, our smallest canoe next, and the rest in succession, began the descent: the passage proved to be very disagreeable; as there is a continuation of shoals extending from bank to bank for the distance of three miles, during which the channel is narrow and crooked, and obstructed by large rocks in every direction, so as to require great dexterity to avoid being dashed on them. We got through the rapids with no injury to any of the boats except the hindmost, which ran on a rock; but by the assistance of the other boats, and of the Indians who were very alert, she escaped, though the baggage she contained was wet. Within three miles after leaving the rapid we passed three small islands, on one of which were the parts of a house put on scaffolds as usual, and soon after came to a rapid at the lower extremity of three small islands; and a second at the distance of a mile and a half below them; reaching six miles below the great rapid a point of rocks at a rapid opposite to the upper point of a small island on the left. Three miles further is another rapid; and two miles beyond this a very bad rapid, or rather a fall of the river: this, on examination, proved so difficult to pass, that we thought it imprudent to attempt, and therefore unloaded the canoes and made a portage of three quarters of a mile. The rapid, which is of about the same extent, is much broken by rocks and shoals, and has a small island in it on the right side.

After crossing by land we halted for dinner, and whilst we were eating were visited by five Indians, who came up the river on foot in great haste: we received them kindly, smoked with them, and gave them a piece of tobacco to smoke with their tribe: on receiving the present they set out to return, and continued running as fast as they could while they remained in sight. Their curiosity had been excited by the accounts of our two chiefs, who had gone on in order to apprise the tribes of our approach and of our

*Captain Clark's
sketch-map of the
junction of Lewis's
River with the
Columbia.*

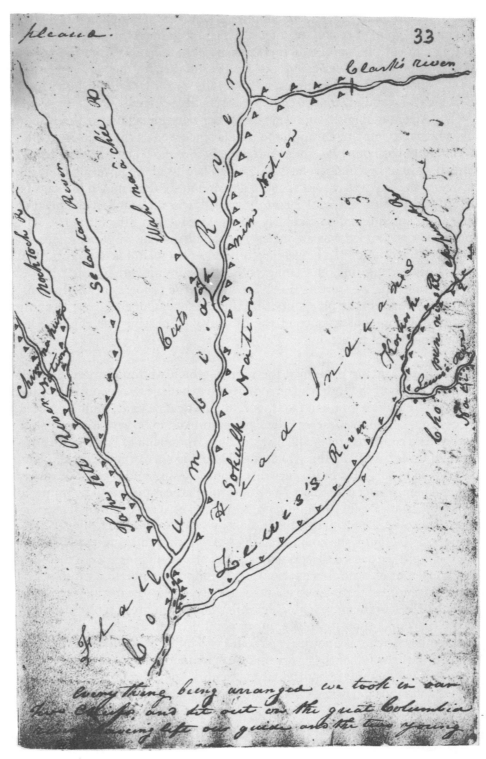

friendly dispositions towards them. After dinner we reloaded the canoes
and proceeded: we soon passed a rapid opposite to the upper point of a sandy
island on the left, which has a smaller island near it. At three miles is a gravelly bar in the river: four miles beyond this the Kimooenim empties itself
into the Columbia, and at its mouth has an island just below a small rapid.

We halted above the point of junction on the Kimooenim to confer with the Indians, who had collected in great numbers to receive us. On landing we were met by our two chiefs, to whose good offices we were indebted for this reception, and also the two Indians who had passed us a few days since on horseback; one of whom appeared to be a man of influence, and harangued the Indians on our arrival. After smoking with the Indians, we formed a camp at the point where the two rivers unite, near to which we found some driftwood, and were supplied by our two old chiefs with the stalks of willows and some small bushes for fuel.

We had scarcely fixed the camp and got the fires prepared, when a chief came from the Indian camp about a quarter of a mile up the Columbia, at the head of nearly two hundred men: they formed a regular procession, keeping time to the noise, rather the music of their drums, which they accompanied with their voices. As they advanced they formed a semicircle round us, and continued singing for some time: we then smoked with them all, and communicated, as well as we could by signs, our friendly intentions towards all nations, and our joy at finding ourselves surrounded by our children: we then proceeded to distribute presents to them, giving the principal chief a large medal, a shirt and handkerchief; to the second chief, a medal of a smaller size, and to a third chief who came down from some of the upper villages, a small medal and a handkerchief. This ceremony being concluded they left us; but in the course of the afternoon several of them returned and remained with us till a late hour. After they had dispersed we proceeded to purchase provisions, and were enabled to collect seven dogs, to which some of the Indians added small presents of fish, and one of them gave us twenty pounds of fat dried horseflesh.

*Thursday.* The day being fair we were occupied in making the necessary observations for determining our longitude, and obtained a meridian altitude, from which it appeared that we were in latitude 46° 15' 13.9". We also measured the two rivers by angles, and found that at the junction the Columbia is nine hundred and sixty yards wide, and Lewis's river five hundred and seventy-five; but soon after they unite, the former widens to the space of from one to three miles, including the islands. From the point of junction the country is a continued plain, which is low near the water, from which it rises gradually, and the only elevation to be seen is a range of high country running from the northeast towards the southwest, where it joins a range of mountains from the southwest, and is on the opposite side about two miles from the Columbia. There is through this plain no tree and scarcely any shrub, except a few willow bushes; and even of smaller plants there is not much more than the prickly pear, which is in great abundance, and is even more thorny and troublesome than any we have yet seen. During this time the principal chief came down with several of his warriors and smoked with us: we were also visited by several men and women, who offered dogs and fish for sale, but as the fish was out of season, and at present abundant in the river, we contented ourselves with purchasing all the dogs we could obtain.

The nation among which we now are call themselves Sokulks; and with them are united a few of another nation, who reside on a western branch, emptying itself into the Columbia a few miles above the mouth of the latter river, and whose name is Chimnapum. The language of both these nations, of each of which we obtained a vocabulary, differs but little from

291

each other, or from that of the Chopunnish who inhabit the Kooskooskee and Lewis's river. In their dress and general appearance also they resemble much those nations; the men wearing a robe of deer or antelope skin, under which a few of them have a short leathern shirt. The most striking difference between them is among the females, the Sokulk women being more inclined to corpulency than any we have yet seen: their stature is low, their faces broad, and their heads flattened in such a manner that the forehead is in a straight line from the nose to the crown of the head: their eyes are of a dirty sable, their hair too is coarse and black, and braided as above without ornament of any kind: instead of wearing, as do the Chopunnish, long leathern shirts, highly decorated with beads and shells, the Sokulk females have no other covering but a truss or piece of leather tied round the hips and then drawn tight between the legs. The ornaments usually worn by both sexes are large blue or white beads, either pendent from their ears, or round the necks, wrists, and arms: they have likewise bracelets of brass, copper, and horn, and some trinkets of shells, fish bones, and curious feathers.

The houses of the Sokulks are made of large mats of rushes, and are generally of a square or oblong form, varying in length from fifteen to sixty feet, and supported in the inside by poles or forks about six feet high: the top is covered with mats, leaving a space of twelve or fifteen inches the whole length of the house, for the purpose of admitting the light and suffering the smoke to pass through: the roof is nearly flat, which seems to indicate that rains are not common in this open country, and the house is not divided into apartments, the fire being in the middle of the large room, and immediately under the hole in the roof: the rooms are ornamented with their nets, gigs, and other fishing tackle, as well as the bow for each inhabitant, and a large quiver of arrows, which are headed with flint stones.

The Sokulks seem to be of a mild and peaceable disposition, and live in a state of comparative happiness. The men like those on the Kimooenim, are said to content themselves with a single wife, with whom we observe the husband shares the labours of procuring subsistence much more than is usual among savages. What may be considered as an unequivocal proof of their good disposition, is the great respect which was shown to old age. Among other marks of it, we observed in one of the houses an old woman perfectly blind, and who we were informed had lived more than a hundred winters. In this state of decrepitude, she occupied the best position in the house, seemed to be treated with great kindness, and whatever she said was listened to with much attention. They are by no means intrusive, and as their fisheries supply them with a competent, if not an abundant subsistence, although they receive thankfully whatever we choose to give, they do not importune us by begging. The fish is, indeed, their chief food, except the roots, and the casual supplies of the antelope, which to those who have only bows and arrows, must be very scanty. This diet may be the direct or the remote cause of the chief disorder which prevails among them, as well as among the Flatheads, on the Kooskooskee and Lewis's river. With all these Indians a bad soreness of the eyes is a very common disorder, which is suffered to ripen by neglect, till many are deprived of one of their eyes, and some have totally lost the use of both. This dreadful calamity may reasonably, we think, be imputed to the constant reflection of the sun on the waters where they are constantly fishing in the spring, summer and fall, and during the rest of the year on the snows of a country which affords no object to relieve the sight.

Among the Sokulks too, and indeed among all the tribes whose chief subsistence is fish, we have observed that bad teeth are very general: some have the teeth, particularly those of the upper jaw, worn down to the gums, and many of both sexes, and even of middle age, have lost them almost entirely. This decay of the teeth is a circumstance very unusual among the Indians, either of the mountains or the plains, and seems peculiar to the inhabitants of the Columbia. We cannot avoid regarding as one principal cause of it, the manner in which they eat their food. The roots are swallowed as they are dug from the ground, frequently nearly covered with a gritty sand: so little idea have they that this is offensive, that all the roots they offer us for sale are in the same condition. A second and a principal cause may be their great use of the dried salmon, the bad effects of which are most probably increased by their mode of cooking it, which is simply to warm, and then swallow the rind, scales and flesh without any preparation. The Sokulks possess but few horses, the greater part of their labours being performed in canoes. Their amusements are similar to those of the Missouri Indians.

In the course of the day captain Clark, in a small canoe with two men, ascended the Columbia. At the distance of five miles he passed an island in the middle of the river, at the head of which is a small and not a dangerous rapid. On the left bank of the river opposite to this river is a fishing place, consisting of three mat houses. Here were great quantities of salmon drying on scaffolds: and indeed from the mouth of the river upwards he saw immense numbers of dead salmon strewed along the shore or floating on the surface of the water, which is so clear that the salmon may be seen swimming in the water at the depth of fifteen or twenty feet. The Indians who had collected on the banks to view him, now joined him in eighteen canoes, and accompanied him up the river. A mile above the rapids he came to the lower point of an island where the course of the river, which had been from its mouth north 83° west, now became due west. He proceeded in that direction, when observing three houses of mats at a short distance he landed to visit them.

On entering one of the houses he found it crowded with men, women and children, who immediately provided a mat for him to sit on, and one of the party undertook to prepare something to eat. He began by bringing in a piece of pine wood that had drifted down the river, which he split into small pieces, with a wedge made of the elks' horn, by means of a mallet of stone curiously carved. The pieces were then laid on the fire, and several round stones placed upon them: one of the squaws now brought a bucket of water, in which was a large salmon about half dried, and as the stones became heated, they were put into the bucket till the salmon was sufficiently boiled for use. It was then taken out, put on a platter of rushes neatly made, and laid before captain Clark, and another was boiled for each of his men. During these preparations he smoked with those about him who would accept of tobacco, but very few were desirous of smoking, a custom which is not general among them, and chiefly used as a matter of form in great ceremonies.

After eating the fish, which was of an excellent flavour, captain Clark set out, and at the distance of four miles from the last island, came to the lower point of another near the left shore, where he halted at two large mat houses. Here as at the three houses below, the inhabitants were occupied in splitting and drying salmon. The multitudes of this fish are almost inconceivable. The water is so clear that they can readily be seen at the depth of fifteen or twenty feet, but at this season they float in such quantities down the stream, and are drifted ashore, that the Indians have only to collect, split and dry them on the scaffolds. Where they procure the timber of which these scaffolds are composed he could not learn, but as there are nothing but willow bushes to be seen for a great distance from the place, it rendered very probable, what the Indians assured him by signs, that they often used dried fish as fuel for the common occasions of cooking.

From this island they showed him the entrance of a western branch of the Columbia, called the *Tapteal*, which as far as could be seen bears nearly west, and empties itself about eight miles above into the Columbia; the general course of which is northwest: towards the southwest a range of highland runs parallel to the river, at the distance of two miles on the left, while on the right side the country is low and covered with the prickly pear, and a weed or plant two or three feet high resembling whins. To the eastward is a range of mountains about fifty or sixty miles distant, which bear north and south; but neither in the low grounds, nor in the highlands is any timber to be seen.

The evening coming on, he determined not to proceed further than the island, and therefore returned to camp, accompanied by three canoes, which contained twenty Indians. In the course of his excursion he shot several grouse and ducks, and received some presents of fish, for which he gave in return small pieces of ribbon. He also killed a prairie cock [sage-grouse], an animal of the pheasant kind, but about the size of a small turkey. It measured from the beak to the end of the toe two feet six inches and three-quarters, from the extremity of the wings three feet six inches, and the feathers of the tail were thirteen inches long. This bird we have seen nowhere except on this river. Its chief food is the grasshopper, and the seed of the wild plant which is peculiar to this river and the upper parts of the Missouri.

The men availed themselves of this day's rest to mend their clothes, dressing skins, and putting their arms in complete order, an object always of primary concern, but particularly at a moment when we are surrounded by so many strangers.

OCTOBER 18TH   *Friday.* We were visited this morning by several canoes of Indians, who joined those who were already with us, and soon opened a numerous council. We informed them as we had done all the other Indian nations of our friendship for them, and of our desire to promote peace among all our red children in this country. This was conveyed by signs through the means of our two chiefs, and seemed to be perfectly understood. We then made a second chief, and gave to all the chiefs a string of wampum, in remembrance of what we had said. Whilst the conference was going on four men came in a canoe from a large encampment on an island about eight miles below, but after staying a few minutes returned without saying a word to us. We now procured from the principal chief and one of the Cuimnapum nation a sketch of the Columbia, and the tribes of his nation living along its banks and those of the Tapteet. They drew it with a piece of coal on a robe, and as we afterwards transferred to paper, it exhibited a valuable specimen of Indian delineation.

Having completed the purposes of our stay, we now began to lay in our stores, and fish being out of season, purchased forty dogs, for which we gave small articles, such as bells, thimbles, knitting-needles, brass wire, and a few beads, an exchange with which they all seemed perfectly satisfied. These dogs, with six prairie cocks killed this morning, formed a plentiful supply for the present. We here left our guide and the two young men who had accompanied him, two of the three not being willing to go any further, and the third could be of no use as he was not acquainted with the river below. We therefore took no Indians but our two chiefs, and resumed our journey in the presence of many of the Sokulks, who came to witness our departure. The morning was cool and fair, and the wind from the southeast.

Soon after proceeding, we passed the island in the mouth of Lewis river, and at eight miles reached a larger island, which extends three miles in length. On going down by this island there is another on the right, which commences about the middle of it, and continues for three and a half miles. While they continue parallel to each other, they occasion a rapid near the lower extremity of the first island, opposite to which on the second island are nine lodges built of mats, and intended for the accommodation of the fishermen, of whom we saw great numbers, and vast quantities of dried fish on their scaffolds.

On reaching the lower point of the island, we landed to examine a bad rapid, and then undertook the passage which is very difficult, as the channel lies between two small islands, with two others still smaller near the left side of the river. Here are two Indian houses, the inhabitants of which were as usual drying fish. We passed the rapid without injury, and fourteen and a half miles from the mouth of Lewis's river, came to an island near the right shore, on which were two other houses of Indians, pursuing the customary occupation. One mile and a half beyond this place, is a mouth of a small brook under a high hill on the left. It seems to run during its whole course through the high country, which at this place begins, and rising to the height of two hundred feet forms cliffs of rugged black rocks which project a considerable distance into the river. At this place too we observed a mountain to the S. W. [Mount St. Helens] the form of which is conical, and its top covered with snow. We followed the river as it entered these highlands, and at the distance of two miles reached three islands, one on each side of the river, and a third in the middle, on which were two houses, where the Indians were drying fish opposite a small rapid. Near these a fourth island begins, close to the right shore, where were nine lodges of Indians, all employed with their fish. As we passed they called to us to land, but as night was coming on, and there was no appearance of wood in the neighbourhood, we went on about a mile further, till observing a log that had drifted down the river, we landed near it on the left side, and formed our camp under a high hill, after having made twenty miles to-day.

Directly opposite to us are five houses of Indians, who were drying fish on the same island where we had passed the nine lodges, and on the other side of the river we saw a number of horses feeding. Soon after landing, we were informed by our chiefs that the large camp of nine houses, belonged to the first chief of all the tribes in this quarter, and that he had called to request us to land and pass the night with him as he had plenty of wood for us. This intelligence would have been very acceptable if it had been explained sooner, for we were obliged to use dried willows for fuel to cook with, not being able to burn the drift-log which had tempted us to land. We now sent the two chiefs along the left side of the river to invite the great chief down to spend the night with us. He came at a late hour, accompanied by twenty men, bringing a basket of mashed berries which he left as a present for us, and formed a camp at a short distance from us.

OCTOBER 19TH The next morning the great chief with two of his inferior chiefs, and a third belonging to a band on the river below, made us a visit at a very early hour. The first of these is called *Yelleppit*, a handsome well proportioned man, about five feet eight inches high, and thirty-five years of age, with a bold and dignified countenance; the rest were not distinguished in their appearance. We smoked with them, and after making a speech gave a medal, a handkerchief, and a string of wampum to Yelleppit, and a string of wampum only to the inferior chiefs. He requested us to remain till the middle of the day, in order that all his nation might come and see us, but we excused ourselves by telling him that on our return we would spend two or three days with him. This conference detained us till nine o'clock, by which time great numbers of the Indians had come down to visit us. On leaving them, we went on for eight miles, when we came to an island near the left shore which continued six miles in length. At the lower extremity of it is a small island on which are five houses, at present vacant, though the scaffolds of fish are as usual abundant. A short distance below, are two more islands, one of them near the middle of the river. On this there were seven houses; but as soon as the Indians, who were drying fish, saw us, they fled to their houses, and not one of them appeared till we had passed, when they came out in greater numbers than is usual for houses of that size, which induced us to think that the inhabitants of the five lodges had been alarmed at our approach and taken refuge with them. We were very desirous of landing in order to relieve their apprehensions, but as there was a bad rapid along the island, all our care was necessary to prevent injury to the canoes. At the foot of this rapid is a rock, on the left shore, which is fourteen miles from our camp of last night, and resembles a hat in its shape.

Four miles beyond this island we came to a rapid, from the appearance of which it was judged prudent to examine it. After landing for that purpose on the left side, we began to enter the channel which is close under the opposite shore. It is a very dangerous rapid, strewed with high rocks and rocky islands, and in many places obstructed by shoals, over which the canoes were to be hauled, so that we were more than two hours in passing through the rapids, which extend for the same number of miles. The rapid has several small islands, and banks of muscleshells are spread along the river in several places.

In order to lighten the boats, captain Clark, with the two chiefs, the interpreter, and his wife, had walked across the low grounds on the left to the foot of the rapids. On the way, captain Clark ascended a cliff about two hundred feet above the water, from which he saw that the country on both sides of the river immediately from its cliffs, was low, and spreads itself into a level plain, extending for a great distance on all sides. To the west at the distance of about one hundred and fifty miles, is a very high mountain covered with snow, and from its direction and appearance, he supposed to be the mount St. Helens, laid down by Vancouver, as visible from the mouth of the Columbia: there is also another mountain [Mount Hood] of a conical form, whose top is covered with snow, in a southwest direction.

As captain Clark arrived at the lower end of the rapid before any, except one of the small canoes, he sat down on a rock to wait for them, and seeing a crane fly across the river, shot it, and it fell near him. Several Indians had been before this passing on the opposite side towards the rapids, and some few who had been nearly in front of him, being either alarmed at his appearance or the report of the gun, fled to their houses. Captain Clark was afraid that these people had not yet heard that white men were coming, and therefore, in order to allay their uneasiness before the whole party should arrive, he got into the small canoe with three men and rowed over towards the houses, and while crossing, shot a duck, which fell into the water. As he approached, no person was to be seen except three men in the plains, and they too fled as he came near the shore. He landed before five houses close to each other, but no one appeared, and the doors, which were of mat, were closed. He went towards one of them with a pipe in his hand, and pushing aside the mat entered the lodge, where he found thirty-two persons, chiefly men and women, with a few children, all in the greatest consternation; some hanging down their heads, others crying and wringing their hands. He went up to them all and shook hands with them in the most friendly manner; but their apprehensions, which had for a moment subsided, revived on his taking out a burning-glass, as there was no roof to the house, and lighting his pipe: he then offered it to several of the men, and distributed among the women and children some small trinkets which he carried about with him, and gradually restored some tranquillity among them. He then left this house, and directing each of the men to go into a house, went himself to a second: here he found the inhabitants more terrified than those he had first seen; but he succeeded in pacifying them, and then visited the other houses, where the men had been equally successful.

After leaving the houses he went out to sit on a rock, and beckoned to some of the men to come and smoke with him; but none of them ventured to join him till the canoes arrived with the two chiefs, who immediately explained our pacific intentions towards them. Soon after the interpreter's wife landed, and her presence dissipated all doubts of our being well-disposed, since in this country, no woman ever accompanies a war party: they therefore all came out and seemed perfectly reconciled; nor could we indeed blame them for their terrors, which were perfectly natural. They told the two chiefs that they knew we were not men, for they had seen us fall from the clouds: in fact, unperceived by them, captain Clark had shot the white crane, which they had seen fall just before he appeared to their eyes: the duck which he had killed also fell close by him, and as there were a few clouds flying over at the moment, they connected the fall of the birds and his sudden appearance, and believed that he had himself dropped from the clouds; the noise of the rifle, which they had never heard before, being considered merely as the sound to announce so extraordinary an event. This belief was strengthened, when on entering the room he brought down fire from the heavens by means of his burning-glass: we soon convinced them satisfactorily that we were only mortals, and after one of our chiefs had explained our history and objects, we all smoked together in great harmony.

These people do not speak precisely the same language as the Indians above, but understand them in conversation. In a short time we were joined by many of the inhabitants from below, several of them on horseback, and all pleased to see us, and to exchange their fish and berries for a few trinkets.

We remained here to dine, and then proceeded. At half a mile the hilly country on the right side of the river ceased: at eleven miles we found a small rapid, and a mile further came to a small island on the left, where there are some willows. Since we had left the five lodges, we passed twenty more, dispersed along the river at different parts of the valley on the right; but as they were now apprised of our coming they showed no signs of alarm. On leaving the island we passed three miles further along a country which is low on both sides of the river, and encamped under some willow trees on the left, having made thirty-six miles to-day.

Immediately opposite to us is an island close to the left shore, and another in the middle of the river, on which are twenty-four houses of Indians, all engaged in drying fish. We had scarcely landed before about a hundred of them came over in their boats to visit us, bringing with them a present of some wood, which was very acceptable: we received them in as kind a manner as we could—smoked with all of them, and gave the principal chief a string of wampum; but the highest satisfaction they enjoyed was the music of two of our violins, with which they seemed much delighted: they remained all night at our fires.

This tribe is a branch of the nation called Pishquitpaws, and can raise about three hundred and fifty men. In dress they resemble the Indians near the forks of the Columbia, except that their robes are smaller and do not reach lower than the waist; indeed, three-fourths of them have scarcely any robes at all. The dress of the females is equally scanty; for they wear only a small piece of a robe which covers their shoulders and neck, and reaches down the back to the waist, where it is attached by a piece of leather tied tight round the body: their breasts, which are thus exposed to view, are large, ill-shaped, and are suffered to hang down very low: their cheekbones high, their heads flattened, and their persons in general adorned with scarcely any ornaments. Both sexes are employed in curing fish, of which they have great quantities on their scaffolds.

OCTOBER 20TH   *Sunday.* The morning was cool, the wind from the southwest. Our appearance had excited the curiosity of the neighbourhood so much, that before we set out about two hundred Indians had collected to see us, and as we were desirous of conciliating their friendship, we remained to smoke and confer with them till breakfast. We then took our repast, which consisted wholly of dog-flesh, and proceeded. We passed three vacant houses near our camp, and at six miles reached the head of a rapid, on descending which we soon came to another, very difficult and dangerous. It is formed by a chain of large black rocks, stretching from the right side of the river, and with several small islands on the left, nearly choking the channel of the river. To this place we gave the name of the Pelican rapid, from seeing a number of pelicans and black cormorants about it. Just below it is a small island near the right shore, where are four houses of Indians, all busy in drying fish. At sixteen miles from our camp we reached a bend to the left

IOWA WARRIOR (King)

opposite to a large island, and at one o'clock halted for dinner on the lower point of an island on the right side of the channel. Close to this was a larger island on the same side, and on the left bank of the river a small one, a little below.

We landed near some Indian huts, and counted on this cluster of three islands, seventeen of their houses filled with inhabitants, resembling in every respect those higher up the river; like the inhabitants, they were busy in preparing fish. We purchased of them some dried fish, which were not good, and a few berries, on which we dined, and then walked to the head of the island for the purpose of examining a vault, which we had marked in coming along.

This place, in which the dead are deposited, is a building about sixty feet long and twelve feet wide, and is formed by placing in the ground poles or forks six feet high, across which a long pole is extended the whole length of the structure. Against this ridge-pole are placed broad boards, and pieces of canoes, in a slanting direction, so as to form a shed. It stands east and west, and neither of the extremities are closed. On entering the western end we observed a number of bodies wrapped carefully in leather robes, and arranged in rows on boards, which were then covered with a mat. This was the part destined for those who had recently died: a little farther on, the bones half decayed were scattered about, and in the centre of the building was a large pile of them heaped promiscuously on each other. At the eastern extremity was a mat, on which twenty-one skulls were placed in a circular form, the mode of interment being first to wrap the body in robes, and as it decays the bones are thrown into the heap, and the sculls placed together. From the different boards and pieces of canoes which form the vault, were suspended on the inside fishing-nets, baskets, wooden-bowls, robes, skins, trenchers, and trinkets of various kinds, obviously intended as offerings of affection to deceased relatives. On the outside of the vault were the skeletons of several horses, and great quantities of bones in the neighbourhood, which induced us to believe that these animals were most probably sacrificed at the funeral rites of their masters.

Having dined we proceeded past a small island, where were four huts of Indians, and at the lower extremity a bad rapid. Half a mile beyond this, and at the distance of twenty-four from our camp, we came to the commencement of the highlands on the right, which are the first we have seen on that side since near the Muscleshell rapids, leaving a valley forty miles in extent. Eight miles lower we passed a large island in the middle of the river, below which are eleven small islands, five on the right, the same number on the left and one in the middle of the stream. A brook falls in on the right side, and a small rivulet empties itself behind one of the islands. The country on the right consists of high and rugged hills; the left is a low plain with no timber on either side, except a few small willow-bushes along the banks; though a few miles after leaving these islands the country on the left rises to the same height with that opposite to it, and becomes an undulating plain. Two miles after passing a small rapid we reached a point of highland in a bend towards the right, and encamped for the evening, after a journey of forty-two miles. The river has been about a quarter of a mile in width, with a current much more uniform than it was during the last two days. We killed two speckled gulls, and several ducks of a delicious flavour.

MONDAY, OCTOBER 21ST, 1805    The morning was cool, and the wind from the southwest. At five and a half miles we passed a small island, and one mile and a half further, another in the middle of the river, which has some rapid water near its head, and opposite to its lower extremity are eight cabins of Indians on the right side. We landed near them to breakfast; but such is the scarcity of wood, that last evening we had not been able to collect any thing except dry willows, and of these not more than barely sufficient to cook our supper, and this morning we could not find enough even to prepare breakfast. The Indians received us with great kindness, and examined every thing they saw with much attention. In their appearance and employments,

*Map from Captain Clark's field book indicating the course and the camping-place of October 21, 1805.*

as well as in their language, they do not differ from those higher up the river. The dress too is nearly the same; that of the men consisting of nothing but a short robe of deer or goat skin; while the women wear only a piece of dressed skin, falling from the neck so as to cover the front of the body as low as the waist; a bandage tied round the body and passing between the legs; and over this a short robe of deer and antelope skin is occasionally thrown. Here we saw two blankets of scarlet, and one of blue cloth, and also a sailor's round jacket; but we obtained only a few pounded roots, and some fish, for which we of course paid them. Among other things we observed some acorns, the fruit of the white oak. These they use as food either raw or roasted, and on enquiry informed us that they were procured from the Indians who live near the great falls. This place they designate by a name very commonly applied to it by the Indians, and highly expressive, the word *Timm*, which they pronounce so as to make it perfectly represent the sound of a distant cataract.

After breakfast we resumed our journey, and in the course of three miles passed a rapid where large rocks were strewed across the river, and at the head of which on the right shore were two huts of Indians. We stopped here for the purpose of examining it, as we always do whenever any danger is to be apprehended, and send round by land all those who cannot swim. Five miles further is another rapid, formed by large rocks projecting from each side, above which were five huts of Indians on the right side, occupied like those we had already seen, in drying fish. One mile below this is the lower point of an island close to the right side, opposite to which on that shore, are two Indian huts.

On the left side of the river at this place, are immense piles of rocks, which seem to have slipped from the cliffs under which they lie; they continue till spreading still farther into the river, at the distance of a mile from the island, they occasion a very dangerous rapid; a little below which on the right side are five huts. For many miles the river is now narrow and obstructed with very large rocks thrown into its channel; the hills continue high and covered, as is very rarely the case, with a few low pine trees on their tops. Between three and four miles below the last rapid occurs a second, which is also difficult, and three miles below it is a small river, which seems to rise in the open plains to the southeast, and falls in on the left. It is forty yards wide at its mouth; but discharges only a small quantity of water at present: we gave it the name of Lepage's river from Lepage one of our company. Near this little river and immediately below it, we had to encounter a new rapid. The river is crowded in every direction, with large rocks and small rocky islands; the passage crooked and difficult, and for two miles we were obliged to wind with great care along the narrow channels and between the huge rocks. At the end of this rapid are four huts of Indians on the right, and two miles below five more huts on the same side. Here we landed and passed the night, after making thirty-three miles.

The inhabitants of these huts explained to us that they were the relations of those who live at the great falls. They appear to be of the same nation with those we have seen above, whom, indeed, they resemble in every thing except that their language, although the same, has some words different. They have all pierced noses, and the men when in full dress wear a long tapering piece of shell or bead put through the nose. These people did not, however, receive us with the same cordiality to which we have been accustomed. They are poor; but we were able to purchase from them some wood to make a fire for supper, of which they have but little, and which they say they bring from the great falls. The hills in this neighbourhood are high and rugged, and a few scattered trees, either small pine or scrubby white oak, are occasionally seen on them. From the last rapids we also observed the conical mountain towards the southwest, which the Indians say is not far to the left of the great falls. From its vicinity to that place we called it the Timm or Falls mountain. The country through which we passed is furnished with several fine springs, which rise either high up the sides of the hills or else in the river meadows, and discharge themselves into the Columbia.

We could not help remarking that almost universally the fishing establishments of the Indians, both on the Columbia and the waters of Lewis's river, are on the right bank. On enquiry we were led to believe that the reason may be found in their fear of the Snake Indians; between whom and themselves, considering the warlike temper of that people, and the peaceful habits of the river tribes, it is very natural that the latter should be anxious to interpose so good a barrier. These Indians are described as residing on a great river to the south, and always at war with the people of this neighbourhood. One of our chiefs pointed out to-day a spot on the left where, not many years ago, a great battle was fought, in which numbers of both nations were killed.

We were agreeably surprised this evening by a present of some very good beer, made out of the remains of the bread, composed of the Pashecoquamash, part of the stores we had laid in at the head of the Kooskooskee, and which by frequent exposure becomes sour and moulded.

OCTOBER 22D  *Tuesday.* The morning was fair and calm. We left our camp at nine o'clock, and after going on for six miles came to the head of an island, and a very bad rapid, where the rocks are scattered nearly across the river. Just above this and on the right side are six huts of Indians. At the distance of two miles below, are five more huts; the inhabitants of which are all engaged in drying fish, and some of them in their canoes killing fish with gigs; opposite to this establishment is a small island in a bend towards the right, on which there were such quantities of fish that we counted twenty stacks of dried and pounded salmon. This small island is at the upper point of one much larger, the sides of which are high uneven rocks, jutting over the water: here there is a bad rapid. The island continues for four miles, and at the middle of it is a large river, which appears to come from the southeast, and empties itself on the left.

We landed just above its mouth in order to examine it, and soon found the route intercepted by a deep, narrow channel, running into the Columbia above the large entrance, so as to form a dry and rich island about 400 yards wide and eight hundred long. Here as along the grounds of the river, the natives had been digging large quantities of roots, as the soil was turned up in many places. We reached the river about a quarter of a mile above its mouth, at a place where a large body of water is compressed within a channel of about two hundred yards in width, where it foams over rocks, many of which are above the surface of the water. These narrows are the end of a rapid which extends two miles back, where the river is closely confined between two high hills, below which it is divided by numbers of large rocks and small islands, covered with a low growth of timber. This river, which is called by the Indians Towahnahiooks, is two hundred yards wide at its mouth, has a very rapid current, and contributes about one fourth as much water as the Columbia possesses before the junction. Immediately at the entrance are three sand islands, and near it the head of an island which runs parallel to the large rocky island.

We now returned to our boats, and passing the mouth of the Towahnahiooks went between the islands. At the distance of two miles we reached the lower end of this rocky island, where were eight huts of Indians. Here too, we saw some large logs of wood, which were most probably rafted down the Towahnahiooks; and a mile below, on the right bank, were sixteen lodges of Indians, with whom we stopped to smoke. Then at the distance of about a mile passed six more huts on the same side, nearly opposite the lower extremity of the island, which has its upper end in the mouth of the Towahnahiooks. Two miles below we came to seventeen huts on the right side of the river, situated at the commencement of the pitch which includes the great falls. Here we halted, and immediately on landing walked down, accompanied by an old Indian from the huts, in order to examine the falls, and ascertain on which side we could make a portage most easily.

We soon discovered that the nearest route was on the right side, and therefore dropped down to the head of the rapid, unloaded the canoes and took all the baggage over by land to the foot of the rapid. The distance is twelve hundred yards. On setting out we crossed a solid rock, about one third of the whole distance; then reached a space of two hundred yards wide, which forms a hollow, where the loose sand from the low grounds has been driven by the winds, and is steep and loose, and therefore disagreeable to pass; the rest of the route is over firm and solid ground. The labour of crossing would have been very inconvenient, if the Indians had not assisted us in carrying some of the heavy articles on their horses; but for this service they repaid themselves so adroitly, that on reaching the foot of the ravine we formed a camp in a position which might secure us from the pilfering of the natives, which we apprehend much more than we do their hostilities.

Near our camp are five large huts of Indians engaged in drying fish and preparing it for the market. The manner of doing this, is by first opening the fish and exposing it to the sun on their scaffolds. When it is sufficiently dried it is pounded fine between two stones till it is pulverised, and is then placed in a basket about two feet long and one in diameter, neatly made of grass and rushes, and lined with the skin of a salmon stretched and dried for the purpose. Here they are pressed down as hard as possible, and the top covered with skins of fish which are secured by cords through the holes of the basket. These baskets are then placed in some dry situation, the corded part upwards, seven being usually placed as close as they can be put together, and five on the top of them. The whole is then wrapped up in mats, and made fast by cords, over which mats are again thrown. Twelve of these baskets, each of which contains from ninety to a hundred pounds, form a stack, which is now left exposed till it is sent to market; the fish thus preserved are kept sound and sweet for several years, and great quantities of it, they inform us, are sent to the Indians who live below the falls, whence it finds its way to the whites who visit the mouth of the Columbia. We observe both near the lodges and on the rocks in the river, great numbers of stacks of these pounded fish.

Besides fish, these people supplied us with filberts and berries, and we purchased a dog for supper; but it was with much difficulty that we were able to buy wood enough to cook it. In the course of the day we were visited by many Indians, from whom we learnt that the principal chiefs of the bands, residing in this neighbourhood, are now hunting in the mountains towards the southwest. On that side of the river none of the Indians have any permanent habitations, and on enquiry we were confirmed in our belief that it was for fear of attacks from the Snake Indians with whom they are at war. This nation they represent as very numerous, and residing in a great number of villages on the Towahnahiooks, where they live principally on salmon. That river they add is not obstructed by rapids above its mouth, but there becomes large and reaches to a considerable distance: the first villages of the Snake Indians on that river being twelve days' journey on a course about southeast from this place.

OCTOBER 23D  *Wednesday*. Having ascertained from the Indians, and by actual examination, the best mode of bringing down the canoes, it was found necessary, as the river was divided into several narrow channels, by rocks and islands, to follow the route adopted by the Indians themselves. This operation captain Clark began this morning, and after crossing to the other side of the river, hauled the canoes over a point of land, so as to avoid a perpendicular fall of twenty feet. At the distance of four hundred and fifty-seven yards we reached the water, and embarked at a place where a long rocky island compresses the channel of the river within the space of a hundred and fifty yards, so as to form nearly a semicircle. On leaving this rocky island the channel is somewhat wider, but a second and much larger island of hard black rock, still divides it from the main stream, while on the left shore it is closely bordered by perpendicular rocks. Having descended in this way for a mile, we reached a pitch of the river, which being divided by two large rocks, descends with great rapidity down a fall eight feet in height: as the boats could not be navigated down this steep descent, we were obliged to land and let them down as slowly as possible by strong ropes of elk skin, which we had prepared for the purpose. They all passed in safety except one, which being loosed by the breaking of the ropes, was driven down, but was recovered by the Indians below. With this rapid ends the first pitch of the great falls, which is not great in point of height, and remarkable only for the singular manner in which the rocks have divided its channel. From the marks every where perceivable at the falls, it is obvious that in high floods, which must be in the spring, the water below the falls rises nearly to a level with that above them. Of this rise, which is occasioned by some obstructions which we do not as yet know, the salmon must avail themselves to pass up the river in such multitudes, that that fish is almost the only one caught in great abundance above the falls; but below that place, we observe the salmon trout, and the heads of a species of trout smaller than the salmon trout, which is in great quantities, and which they are now burying to be used as their winter food. A hole of any size being dug, the sides and bottom are lined with straw, over which skins are laid: on these the fish, after being well dried, is laid, covered with other skins, and the hole closed with a layer of earth twelve or fifteen inches deep.

About three o'clock we reached the lower camp, but our joy at having accomplished this object was somewhat diminished, by the persecution of a new acquaintance. On reaching the upper point of the portage, we found that the Indians had been encamped there not long since, and had left behind them multitudes of fleas. These sagacious animals were so pleased to exchange the straw and fish skins, in which they had been living, for some better residence, that we were soon covered with them, and during the portage the men were obliged to strip to the skin, in order to brush them from their bodies. They were not, however, so easily dislodged from our clothes, and accompanied us in great numbers to our camp.

We saw no game except a sea otter, which was shot in the narrow channel as we came down, but we could not get it. Having therefore scarcely any provisions, we purchased eight small fat dogs, a food to which we are now compelled to have recourse, for the Indians are very unwilling to sell us any of their good fish, which they reserve for the market below. Fortunately, however, the habit of using this animal has completely overcome the repugnance which we felt at first, and the dog, if not a favourite dish, is always an acceptable one. The meridian altitude of to-day gives $45^\circ 42' 57\frac{3}{10}''$ north, as the latitude of our camp.

On the beach near the Indian huts, we observed two canoes of a different shape and size from any which we had hitherto seen: one of these we got in exchange for our smallest canoe, giving a hatchet and a few trinkets to the owner, who said he had purchased it from a white man below the falls, by giving him a horse. These canoes are very beautifully made; they are wide in the middle and tapering towards each end, with curious figures carved on the bow. They are thin, but being strengthened by cross bars, about an inch in diameter, which are tied with strong pieces of bark through holes in the sides, are able to bear very heavy burdens, and seem calculated to live in the roughest water.

A great number of Indians both from above and below the falls visited us to-day, and towards evening we were informed by one of the chiefs who had accompanied us, that he had overheard that the Indians below intended to attack us as we went down the river: being at all times ready for any attempt of that sort, we were not under greater apprehensions than usual at this intelligence: we, therefore, only reexamined our arms and increased the ammunition to one hundred rounds. Our chiefs, who had not the same motives of confidence, were by no means so much at their ease, and when at night they saw the Indians leave us earlier than usual, their suspicions of an intended attack were confirmed, and they were very much alarmed.

The next morning, *Thursday*, the Indians approached us with apparent caution, and behaved with more than usual reserve. Our two chiefs, by whom these circumstances were not unobserved, now told us that they wished to return home; that they could be no longer of any service to us, and they could not understand the language of the people below the falls; that those people formed a different nation from their own; that the two people had been at war with each other, and as the Indians had expressed a resolu-  OCTOBER 24TH tion to attack us, they would certainly kill them. We endeavoured to quiet their fears, and requested them to stay two nights longer, in which time we would see the Indians below, and make a peace between the two nations.

They replied that they were anxious to return and see their horses; we however insisted on their remaining with us, not only in hopes of bringing about an accommodation between them and their enemies, but because they might be able to detect any hostile designs against us, and also assist us in passing the next falls, which are not far off, and represented as very difficult: they at length, agreed to stay with us two nights longer.

About nine o'clock we proceeded, and on leaving our camp near the lower fall, found the river about four hundred yards wide, with a current more rapid than usual, though with no perceptible descent. At the distance of two and a half miles, the river widened into a large bend or basin on the right, at the beginning of which are three huts of Indians. At the extremity of this basin stands a high black rock, which, rising perpendicularly from the right shore, seems to run wholly across the river; so totally indeed does it appear to stop the passage, that we could not see where the water escaped, except that the current appeared to be drawn with more than usual velocity to the left of the rock, where was a great roaring. We landed at the huts of the Indians, who went with us to the top of this rock, from which we saw all the difficulties of the channel. We were no longer at a loss to account for the rising of the river at the falls, for this tremendous rock stretches across the river, to meet the high hills of the left shore, leaving a channel of only forty-five yards wide, through which the whole body of the Columbia must press its way. The water thus forced into so narrow a channel, is thrown into whirls, and swells and boils in every part with the wildest agitation. But the alternative of carrying the boats over this high rock was almost impossible in our present situation, and as the chief danger seemed to be not from any rocks in the channel, but from the great waves and whirlpools, we resolved to try the passage in our boats, in hopes of being able by dexterous steering to escape. This we attempted, and with great care were able to get through, to the astonishment of all the Indians of the huts we had just passed, who now collected to see us from the top of the rock. The channel continues thus confined within a space of about half a mile, when the rock ceased. We passed a single Indian hut at the foot of it, where the river again enlarges itself to the width of two hundred yards, and at the distance of a mile and a half stopped to view a very bad rapid; this is formed by two rocky islands which divide the channel, the lower and larger of which is in the middle of the river. The appearance of this place was so unpromising, that we unloaded all the most valuable articles, such as guns, ammunition, our papers, &c. and sent them by land with all the men that could not swim to the extremity of the rapids. We then descended with the canoes two at a time, and though the canoes took in some water, we all went through safely; after which we made two miles, and stopped in a deep bend of the river towards the right, and encamped a little above a large village of twenty-one houses. Here we landed, and as it was late before all the canoes joined us, we were obliged to remain here this evening, the difficulties of the navigation having permitted us to make only six miles.

This village is situated at the extremity of a deep bend towards the right, and immediately above a ledge of high rocks, twenty feet above the

marks of the highest flood, but broken in several places, so as to form channels which are at present dry, extending nearly across the river; this forms
the second fall, or the place most probably which the Indians indicate by the
word *Timm*. While the canoes were coming on, captain Clark walked with
two men down to examine these channels. On these rocks the Indians are
accustomed to dry fish, and as the season for that purpose is now over, the
poles which they use are tied up very securely in bundles, and placed on the
scaffolds. The stock of fish dried and pounded were so abundant that he
counted one hundred and seven of them making more than ten thousand
pounds of that provision. After examining the narrows as well as the lateness of the hour would permit, he returned to the village through a rocky
open country, infested with polecats.

This village, the residence of a tribe called the Echeloots, consists
of twenty-one houses, scattered promiscuously over an elevated situation,
near a mound about thirty feet above the common level, which has some remains of houses on it, and bears every appearance of being artificial. The
houses, which are the first wooden buildings we have seen since leaving the
Illinois country, are nearly equal in size, and exhibit a very singular appearance. A large hole, twenty feet wide and thirty in length, is dug to the depth
of six feet. The sides are then lined with split pieces of timber, rising just
above the surface of the ground, which are smoothed to the same width by
burning, or shaved with small iron axes. These timbers are secured in their
erect position by a pole, stretched along the side of the building near the
eaves, and supported on a strong post fixed at each corner. The timbers at
the gable ends rise gradually higher, the middle pieces being the broadest.
At the top of these is a sort of semicircle, made to receive a ridge-pole, the
whole length of the house, propped by an additional post in the middle, and
forming the top of the roof. From this ridge-pole to the eaves of the house,
are placed a number of small poles or rafters, secured at each end by fibres
of the cedar. On these poles, which are connected by small transverse bars
of wood, is laid a covering of the white cedar, or arbor vitae, kept on by the
strands of the cedar fibres: but a small distance along the whole length of
the ridge-pole is left uncovered for the purpose of light, and permitting the
smoke to pass through. The roof thus formed has a descent about equal to
that common amongst us, and near the eaves is perforated with a number of
small holes, made most probably to discharge their arrows in case of an attack. The only entrance is by a small door at the gable end, cut out of the
middle piece of timber, twenty-nine and a half inches high, and fourteen
inches broad, and reaching only eighteen inches above the earth. Before this
hole is hung a mat, and on pushing it aside and crawling through, the descent is by a small wooden ladder, made in the form of those used amongst
us. One half of the inside is used as a place of deposit for their dried fish, of
which there are large quantities stored away, and with a few baskets of berries form the only family provisions; the other half adjoining the door, remains for the accommodation of the family. On each side are arranged near
the walls, small beds of mats placed on little scaffolds or bedsteads, raised
from eighteen inches to three feet from the ground, and in the middle of the
vacant space is the fire, or sometimes two or three fires, when, as is indeed
usually the case, the house contains three families.

The inhabitants received us with great kindness—invited us to their houses, and in the evening, after our camp had been formed, came in great numbers to see us: accompanying them was a principal chief, and several of the warriors of the nation below the great narrows. We made use of this opportunity to attempt a reconciliation between them and our two chiefs, and to put an end to the war which had disturbed the two nations. By representing to the chiefs the evils which the war inflicted on them, and the wants and privations to which it subjects them, they soon became disposed to conciliate with each other, and we had some reason to be satisfied with the sincerity of the mutual professions that the war should no longer continue, and that in future they would live in peace with each other. On concluding this negotiation we proceeded to invest the chief with the insignia of command, a medal and some small articles of clothing; after which the violin was produced, and our men danced to the great delight of the Indians, who remained with us till a late hour.

OCTOBER 25TH   *Friday.* We walked down with several of the Indians to view the part of the narrows which they represented as most dangerous: we found it very difficult, but, as with our large canoes the portage was impracticable, we concluded on carrying our most valuable articles by land, and then hazarding the passage. We therefore returned to the village, and after sending some of the party with our best stores to make a portage, and fixed others on the rock to assist with ropes the canoes that might meet with any difficulty, we began the descent, in the presence of great numbers of Indians who had collected to witness this exploit. The channel for three miles is worn through a hard rough black rock from fifty to one hundred yards wide, in which the water swells and boils in a tremendous manner. The three first canoes escaped very well; the fourth, however, had nearly filled with water; the fifth passed through with only a small quantity of water over her. At half a mile we had got through the worst part, and having reloaded our canoes went on very well for two and a half miles, except that one of the boats was nearly lost by running against a rock. At the end of this channel of three miles, in which the Indians inform us they catch as many salmon as they wish, we reached a deep basin or bend of the river towards the right, near the entrance of which are two rocks. We crossed the basin, which has a quiet and gentle current, and at the distance of a mile from its commencement, and a little below where the river resumes its channel, reached a rock which divides it.

At this place we met our old chiefs, who, when we began the portage, had walked down to a village below to smoke a pipe of friendship on the renewal of peace. Just after our meeting we saw a chief of the village above, with a party who had been out hunting, and were then crossing the river with their horses on their way home. We landed to smoke with this chief, whom we found a bold looking man of a pleasing appearance, about fifty years of age, and dressed in a war jacket, a cap, leggings and moccasins: we presented him with a medal and other small articles, and he gave us some meat, of which he had been able to procure but little; for on his route he had met with a war party of Indians from the Towahnahiooks, between whom there was a battle. We here smoked a parting pipe with our two faithful friends, the chiefs, who had accompanied us from the heads of the river, and who now had each bought a horse, intending to go home by land.

308

On leaving this rock the river is gentle, but strewed with a great number of rocks for a few miles, when it becomes a beautiful still stream about half a mile wide. At five miles from the large bend we came to the mouth of a creek twenty yards wide, heading in the range of mountains which run S. S. W. and S. W. for a long distance, and discharging a considerable quantity of water: it is called by the Indians Quenett. We halted below it under a high point of rocks on the left; and as it was necessary to make some celestial observations, we formed a camp on the top of these rocks. This situation is perfectly well calculated for defence in case the Indians should incline to attack us, for the rocks form a sort of natural fortification with the aid of the river and creek, and is convenient to hunt along the foot of the mountains to the west and southwest, where there are several species of timber which form fine coverts for game. From this rock, the pinnacle of the round mountain covered with snow, which we had seen a short distance below the forks of the Columbia, and which we had called the Falls or Timm mountain, is south 43° west, and about thirty-seven miles distant. The face of the country on both sides of the river above and below the falls is steep, rugged, and rocky, with a very small proportion of herbage, and no timber, except a few bushes: the hills, however, to the west, have some scattered pine, white oak and other kinds of trees. All the timber used by the people at the upper falls is rafted down the Towahnahiooks; and those who live at the head of the narrows we have just passed, bring their wood in the same way from this creek to the lower part of the narrows, from which it is carried three miles by land to their habitations.

Both above and below, as well as in the narrows, we saw a great number of sea-otter or seals, and this evening one deer was killed, and great signs of that animal seen near the camp. In the creek we shot a goose, and saw much appearance of beaver, and one of the party also saw a fish, which he took to be a drum-fish. Among the willows we found several snares, set by the natives for the purpose of catching wolves.

*Saturday.* The morning was fine: we sent six men to hunt and to collect resin to pitch the canoes, which, by being frequently hauled over rocks, have become very leaky. The canoes were also brought out to dry, and on examination it was found that many of the articles had become spoiled by being repeatedly wet. We were occupied with the observations necessary to determine our longitude, and with conferences among the Indians, many of whom came on horseback to the opposite shore in the forepart of the day, and showed some anxiety to cross over to us: we did not however think it proper to send for them, but towards evening two chiefs with fifteen men came over in a small canoe: they proved to be the two principal chiefs of the tribes at and above the falls, who had been absent on a hunting excursion as we passed their residence: each of them on their arrival made us a present of deer's flesh, and small white cakes made of roots. Being anxious to ingratiate ourselves in their favour so as to ensure a friendly reception on our return, we treated them with all the kindness we could show: we acknowledged the chiefs, gave a medal of the small size, a red silk handkerchief, an arm-band, a knife, and a piece of paint to each chief, and small presents to several of the party, and half a deer: these attentions were not lost on the Indians, who appeared very well pleased with them. At night a fire was

OCTOBER 26TH

309

made in the middle of our camp, and as the Indians sat round it our men danced to the music of the violin, which so delighted them that several resolved to remain with us all night: the rest crossed the river. All the tribes in this neighbourhood are at war with the Snake Indians, whom they all describe as living on the Towahnahiooks, and whose nearest town is said to be four days' march from this place, and in a direction nearly southwest: there has lately been a battle between these tribes, but we could not ascertain the loss on either side.

The water rose to-day eight inches, a rise which we could only ascribe to the circumstance of the wind's having been up the river for the last twenty-four hours, since the influence of the tide cannot be sensible here on account of the falls below. The hunters returned in the evening; they had seen the tracks of elk and bear in the mountains, and killed five deer, four very large gray squirrels, and a grouse: they inform us that the country off the river is broken, stony, and thinly timbered with pine and white oak; besides these delicacies one of the men killed with a gig a salmon trout, which, being fried in some bear's oil, which had been given to us by the chief whom we had met this morning below the narrows, furnished a dish of a very delightful flavour. A number of white cranes were also seen flying in different directions, but at such a height that we could not procure any of them.

The fleas, with whom we had contracted an intimacy at the falls, are so unwilling to leave us, that the men are obliged to throw off all their clothes, in order to relieve themselves from their persecution.

OCTOBER 27TH   *Sunday.* The wind was high from the westward during last night and this morning, but the weather being fair we continued our celestial observations. The two chiefs who remained with us, were joined by seven Indians, who came in a canoe from below. To these men we were very particular in our attentions; we smoked and eat with them; but some of them who were tempted by the sight of our goods exposed to dry, wished to take liberties with them; to which we were under the necessity of putting an immediate check; this restraint displeased them so much, that they returned down the river in a very ill humour. The two chiefs however remained with us till the evening, when they crossed the river to their party.

Before they went we procured from them a vocabulary of the Echeloot, their native language, and on comparison were surprised at its difference from that of the Eneeshur tongue. In fact although the Echeloots, who live at the great narrows, are not more than six miles from the Eneeshurs or residents at and above the great falls, the two people are separated by a broad distinction of language. The Eneeshurs are understood by all the tribes residing on the Columbia, above the falls; but at that place they meet with the unintelligible language of the Echeloots, which then descends the river to a considerable distance. Yet the variation may possibly be rather a deep shade of dialect than a radical difference, since among both many words are the same, and the identity cannot be accounted for by supposing that their neighbourhood has interwoven them into their daily conversations, because the same words are equally familiar among all the Flathead bands which we have passed. To all these tribes too the strange clucking or guttural noise which first struck us is common. They also flatten the heads of the children in nearly the same manner, but we now begin to observe that the heads of the males, as well as of the other sex, are subjected to this operation, whereas among the mountains the custom has confined it almost to the females. The hunters brought home four deer, one grouse, and a squirrel.

*Monday*. The morning was again cool and windy. Having dried our goods, we were about setting out, when three canoes came from above to visit us, and at the same time two others from below arrived for the same purpose. Among these last was an Indian who wore his hair in a queue, and had on a round hat and a sailor's jacket, which he said he had obtained from the people below the great rapids, who bought them from the whites. This interview detained us till nine o'clock, when we proceeded down the river, which is now bordered with cliffs of loose dark coloured rocks about ninety feet high, with a thin covering of pine and other small trees. At the distance of four miles we reached a small village of eight houses under some high rocks on the right, with a small creek on the opposite side of the river.

We landed and found the houses similar to those we had seen at the great narrows: on entering one of them we saw a British musket, a cutlass, and several brass teakettles, of which they seemed to be very fond. There were figures of men, birds, and different animals, which were cut and painted on the boards which form the sides of the room, and though the workmanship of these uncouth figures was very rough, they were as highly esteemed by the Indians as the finest frescoes of more civilised people. This tribe is called the Chilluckittequaw, and their language although somewhat different from that of the Echeloots, has many of the same words, and is sufficiently intelligible to the neighbouring Indians. We procured from them a vocabulary, and then after buying five small dogs, some dried berries, and a white bread or cake made of roots, we left them. The wind however rose so high, that we were obliged after going one mile to land on the left side opposite to a rocky island, and pass the day there. We formed our camp in a niche above a point of high rocks, and as it was the only safe harbour we could find, submitted to the inconvenience of lying on the sand, exposed to the wind and rain during all the evening. The high wind, which obliged us to consult the safety of our boats by not venturing further, did not at all prevent the Indians from navigating the river.

We had not been long on shore, before a canoe with a man, his wife and two children, came from below through the high waves with a few roots to sell; and soon after we were visited by many Indians from the village above, with whom we smoked and conversed. The canoes used by these people are like those already described, built of white cedar or pine, very light, wide in the middle, and tapering towards the ends, the bow being raised and ornamented with carvings of the heads of animals. As the canoe is the vehicle of transportation, the Indians have acquired great dexterity in the management of it, and guide it safely over the highest waves. They have among their utensils bowls and baskets very neatly made of small bark and grass, in which they boil their provisions. The only game seen to-day were two deer, of which only one was killed, the other was wounded but escaped.

*Tuesday*. The morning was still cloudy, and the wind from the west, but as it had abated its violence, we set out at daylight. At the distance of four miles we passed a creek on the right, one mile below which is a village of seven houses on the same side. This is the residence of the principal chief of the Chilluckittequaw nation, whom we now found to be the same between whom and our two chiefs we had made a peace at the Echeloot village. He received us very kindly, and set before us pounded fish, filberts, nuts, the berries of the Sacacommis, and white bread made of roots. We gave in return a bracelet of ribbon to each of the women of the house, with which they were very much pleased. The chief had several articles, such as scarlet and blue cloth, a sword, a jacket and hat, which must have been procured from the whites, and on one side of the room were two wide split boards placed together, so as to make space for a rude figure of a man cut and painted on them. On pointing to this and asking them what it meant, he said something, of which all we understood was "good," and then stepped to the image and brought out his bow and quiver, which, with some other warlike instruments, were kept behind it.

The chief then directed his wife to hand him his medicine-bag, from which he brought out fourteen fore-fingers, which he told us had once belonged to the same number of his enemies, whom he had killed in fighting with the nations to the southeast, to which place he pointed, alluding no doubt to the Snake Indians, the common enemy of the nations on the Columbia. This bag is about two feet in length, containing roots, pounded dirt, &c. which the Indians only know how to appreciate. It is suspended in the middle of the lodge, and it is supposed to be a species of sacrilege to be touched by any but the owner. It is an object of religious fear, and it is from its sanctity the safest place to deposit their medals and their more valuable articles. The Indians have likewise small bags which they preserve in their great medicine-bag, from whence they are taken and worn around their waists and necks as amulets against any real or imaginary evils. This was the first time we had ever known the Indians to carry from the field any other trophy except the scalp. They were shown with great exultation, and after an harangue which we were left to presume was in praise of his exploits, the fingers were carefully replaced among the valuable contents of the red medicine-bag.

This village being part of the same nation with the village we passed above, the language of the two is the same, and their houses of similar form and materials, and calculated to contain about thirty souls. The inhabitants were unusually hospitable and good-humoured, so that we gave to the place the name of the Friendly village.

We breakfasted here, and after purchasing twelve dogs, four sacks of fish, and a few dried berries, proceeded on our journey. The hills as we passed are high with steep and rocky sides, and some pine and white oak, and an undergrowth of shrubs scattered over them. Four miles below this village is a small river on the right side; immediately below is a village of Chilluckittequaws, consisting of eleven houses. Here we landed and smoked a pipe with the inhabitants, who were very cheerful and friendly. They as well as the people of the last village inform us, that this river comes a considerable distance from the N. N. E., that it has a great number of falls, which prevent the salmon from passing up, and that there are ten nations residing on it who subsist on berries, or such game as they can procure with their bows and arrows. At its mouth the river is sixty yards wide, and has a deep and very rapid channel. From the number of falls of which the Indians spoke, we gave it the name of Cataract river. We purchased four dogs, and then proceeded.

The country as we advance is more rocky and broken, and the pine and low white oak on the hills increase in great quantity. Three miles below Cataract river we passed three large rocks in the river; that in the middle is large and longer than the rest, and from the circumstance of its having several square vaults on it, obtained the name of Sepulchre island. A short distance below are two huts of Indians on the right: the river now widens, and in three miles we came to two more houses on the right; one mile beyond which is a rocky island in a bend of the river towards the left. Within the next six miles we passed fourteen huts of Indians, scattered on the right bank, and then reached the entrance of a river on the left, which we called Labieshe's river, after Labieshe one of our party. Just above this river is a low ground more thickly timbered than usual, and in front are four huts of Indians on the bank, which are the first we have seen on that side of the Columbia. The exception may be occasioned by this spot's being more than usually protected from the approach of their enemies, by the creek, and the thick wood behind.

We again embarked, and at the distance of a mile passed the mouth of a rapid creek on the right eighteen yards wide: in this creek the Indians whom we left take their fish, and from the number of canoes which were in it, we called it Canoe creek. Opposite to this creek is a large sandbar, which continues for four miles along the left side of the river. Just below this a beautiful cascade falls in on the left over a precipice of rock one hundred feet in height. One mile further are four Indian huts in the low ground on the left: and two miles beyond this a point of land on the right, where the mountains become high on both sides, and possess more timber and greater varieties of it than hitherto, and those on the left are covered with snow. One mile from this point we halted for the night at three Indian huts on the right, having made thirty-two miles.

On our first arrival they seemed surprised, but not alarmed at our appearance, and we soon became intimate by means of smoking and our favourite entertainment for the Indians, the violin. They gave us fruit, some roots, and root-bread, and we purchased from them three dogs. The houses of these people are similar to those of the Indians above, and their language the same: their dress also, consisting of robes or skins of wolves, deer, elk, and wild-cat, is made nearly after the same model: their hair is worn in plaits down each shoulder, and round their neck is put a strip of some skin with the tail of the animal hanging down over the breast: like the Indians above they are fond of otter skins, and give a great price for them. We here saw the skin of a mountain sheep [goat], which they say live among the rocks in the mountains: the skin was covered with white hair, the wool long, thick, and coarse, with long coarse hair on the top of the neck, and the back resembling somewhat the bristles of a goat. Immediately behind the village is a pond, in which were great numbers of small swan.

*Wednesday.* A moderate rain fell during all last night, but the morning was cool, and after taking a scanty breakfast of deer, we proceeded. The river is now about three-quarters of a mile wide, with a current so gentle, that it does not exceed one mile and a half an hour; but its course is obstructed by the projection of large rocks, which seemed to have fallen promiscuously from the mountains into the bed of the river. On the left side four different streams of water empty themselves in cascades from the hills: what is, however, most singular is, that there are stumps of pine trees scattered to some distance in the river, which has the appearance of being dammed below and forced to encroach on the shore: these obstructions continue till at the distance of twelve miles, when we came to the mouth of a river on the right, where we landed: we found it sixty yards wide, and its banks possess two kinds of timber which we had not hitherto seen: one is a very large species of ash; the other resembling in its bark the beech; but the tree itself, as also the leaves, are smaller. We called this stream Crusatte's river, after Crusatte, one of our men: opposite to its mouth the Columbia widens to the distance of a mile, with a large sandbar, and large stones and rocks scattered through the channel. We here saw several of the large buzzards, which are of the size of the largest eagle, with the under part of their wings white: we also shot a deer and three ducks; on part of which we dined, and then continued down the Columbia.

Above Crusatte's river the low grounds are about three quarters of a mile wide, rising gradually to the hills, and with a rich soil covered with grass, fern, and other small undergrowth; but below, the country rises with a steep ascent, and soon the mountains approach to the river with steep rugged sides, covered with a very thick growth of pine, cedar, cottonwood, and oak. The river is still strewed with large rocks. Two and a half miles below Crusatte's river is a large creek on the right, with a small island in the mouth. Just below this creek we passed along the right side of three small islands on the right bank of the river, with a larger island on the opposite side, and landed on an island very near the right shore at the head of the great shoot, and opposite two smaller islands at the fall or shoot itself. Just above the island on which we were encamped is a small village of eight large houses in a bend on the right, where the country, from having been very mountainous, becomes low for a short distance. We had made fifteen miles to-day, during all which time we were kept constantly wet with the rain; but as we were able to get on this island some of the ash which we saw for the first time to-day, and which makes a tolerable fire, we were as comfortable as the moistness of the evening would permit.

As soon as we landed, captain Lewis went with five men to the village, which is situated near the river, with ponds in the low grounds behind: the greater part of the inhabitants were absent collecting roots down the river: the few, however, who were at home, treated him very kindly, and gave him berries, nuts, and fish; and in the house were a gun and several articles which must have been procured from the whites; but not being able to procure any information, he returned to the island. Captain Clark had in the meantime gone down to examine the shoot, and to discover the best route for a portage. He followed an Indian path, which, at the distance of a mile, led to a village on an elevated situation, the houses of which had been large, but built in a different form from any we had yet seen, but which had been lately abandoned, the greater part of the boards being put into a pond near the village: this was most probably for the purpose of drowning the fleas, which were in immense quantities near the houses. After going about three miles the night obliged him to return to camp.

*Thursday.* He resumed his search in the morning, through the rain. At the extremity of the basin, in which is situated the island where we are encamped, several rocks and rocky islands are interspersed through the bed of the river. The rocks on each side have fallen down from the mountains; that on the left being high, and on the right the hill itself, which is lower, slipping into the river; so that the current is here compressed within a space of one hundred and fifty yards. Within this narrow limit it runs for the distance of four hundred yards with great rapidity, swelling over the rocks with a fall of about twenty feet: it then widens to two hundred paces, and the current for a short distance becomes gentle; but at the distance of a mile and a half, and opposite to the old village mentioned yesterday, it is obstructed by a very bad rapid, where the waves are unusually high, the river being confined between large rocks, many of which are at the surface of the water. Captain Clark proceeded along the same path he had taken before, which led him through a thick wood and along a hill side, till two and a half miles below the shoots, he struck the river at the place whence the Indians make their portage to the head of the shoot: he here sent Crusatte, the principal waterman, up the stream, to examine if it were practicable to bring the canoes down the water. In the meantime, he, with Joseph Fields, continued his route down the river, along which the rapids seem to stretch as far as he could see. At half a mile below the end of the portage, he came to a house, the only remnant of a town, which, from its appearance, must have been of great antiquity. The house was uninhabited, and being old and decayed, he felt no disposition to encounter the fleas, which abound in every situation of that kind, and therefore did not enter.

About half a mile below this house, in a very thick part of the woods, is an ancient burial place: it consists of eight vaults made of pine or cedar boards closely connected, about eight feet square and six in height; the top secured, covered with wide boards sloping a little, so as to convey off the rain: the direction of all of them is east and west, the door being on the eastern side, and partially stopped with wide boards decorated with rude pictures of men and other animals. On entering we found in some of them four dead bodies, carefully wrapped in skins, tied with cords of grass and bark, lying on a mat in a direction east and west: the other vaults contained only bones, which were in some of them piled to the height of four feet: on the tops of the vaults, and on poles attached to them, hung brass kettles and frying-pans with holes in their bottoms, baskets, bowls, sea-shells, skins, pieces of cloth, hair, bags of trinkets and small bones, the offerings of friendship or affection, which have been saved by a pious veneration from the ferocity of war, or the more dangerous temptations of individual gain: the whole of the walls as well as the door were decorated with strange figures cut and painted on them; and besides these were several wooden images of men, some of them so old and decayed as to have almost lost their shape, which were all placed against the sides of the vaults. These images, as well as those in the houses we have lately seen, do not appear to be at all the objects of adoration: in this place they were most probably intended as resemblances of those whose decease they indicate; and when we observe them in houses, they occupy the most conspicuous part; but are treated more like ornaments than objects of worship. Near the vaults which are standing, are the remains of others on the ground completely rotted and covered with moss; and as they are formed of the most durable pine and cedar timber, there is every appearance, that for a very long series of years this retired spot has been the depository for the Indians near this place.

After examining this place captain Clark went on, and found the river as before strewed with large rocks, against which the water ran with great rapidity. Just below the vaults the mountain, which is but low on the right side, leaves the river, and is succeeded by an open stony level, which extends down the river, while on the left the mountain is still high and rugged. At two miles distance he came to a village of four houses, which were now vacant and the doors barred up: on looking in he saw the usual quantity of utensils still remaining, from which he concluded that the inhabitants were at no great distance collecting roots or hunting, in order to lay in their supply of food for the winter: he left them and went on three miles to a difficult rocky rapid, which was the last in view. Here, on the right, are the remains of a large and ancient village, which could be plainly traced by the holes for the houses and the deposits for fish: after he had examined these rapids and the neighbouring country he returned to camp by the same route: the only game he had obtained was a sandhill crane.

In the meantime we had been occupied in preparations for making the portage, and in conference with the Indians, who came down from the village to visit us. Towards evening two canoes arrived from the village at the mouth of Cataract river, loaded with fish and bears' grease for the market below: as soon as they landed they unloaded the canoes, turned them upside down on the beach, and encamped under a shelving rock near our camp.

We had an opportunity of seeing to-day the hardihood of the Indians of the neighbouring village: one of the men shot a goose, which fell into the river, and was floating rapidly towards the great shoot, when an Indian observing it plunged in after it: the whole mass of the waters of the Columbia, just preparing to descend its narrow channel, carried the animal down with great rapidity: the Indian followed it fearlessly to within one hundred and fifty feet of the rocks, where he would inevitably have been dashed to pieces; but seizing his prey he turned round and swam ashore with great composure. We very willingly relinquished our right to the bird in favour of the Indian who had thus saved it at the imminent hazard of his life: he immediately set to work, and picked off about half the feathers, and then without opening it ran a stick through it and carried it off to roast.

## Friday, November 1st, 1805

The morning was cool and the wind high from the northeast. The Indians who arrived last night, took their empty canoes on their shoulders and carried them below the great shoot, where they put them in the water and brought them down the rapid, till at the distance of two and a half miles they stopped to take in their loading, which they had been afraid to trust in the last rapid, and had therefore carried by land from the head of the shoot.

After their example we carried our small canoe, and all the baggage across the slippery rocks, to the foot of the shoot. The four large canoes were next brought down, by slipping them along poles, placed from one

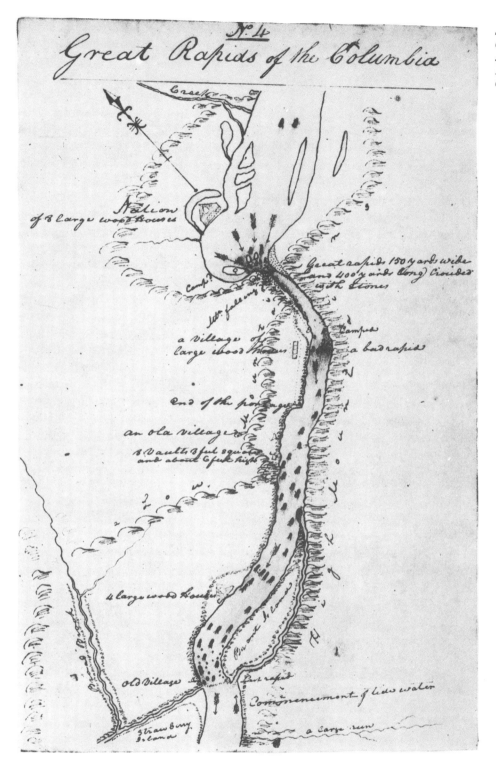

Sketch-map by
Captain Clark to
show the Great
Rapids of the
Columbia.

rock to another, and in some places by using partially streams which escaped along side of the river. We were not, however, able to bring them across without three of them receiving injuries, which obliged us to stop at the end of the shoot to repair them. At this shoot we saw great numbers of sea-otters; but they are so shy that it is difficult to reach them with the musket: one of them that was wounded to-day sunk and was lost. Having by this

317

portage avoided the rapid and shoot of four hundred yards in length, we re-embarked, passed at a mile and a half the bad rapid opposite to the old village on the right, and making our way through the rocks, saw the house just below the end of the portage; the eight vaults near it; and at the distance of four miles from the head of the shoot, reached a high rock, which forms the upper part of an island near the left shore. Between this island and the right shore we proceeded, leaving at the distance of a mile and a half, the village of four houses on our right, and a mile and a half lower came to the head of a rapid near the village on the right. Here we halted for the night, having made only seven miles from the head of the shoot. During the whole of the passage the river is very much obstructed by rocks. The island, which is about three miles long, reaches to the rapid which its lower extremity contributes to form. The meridian altitude of to-day gave us the latitude of 45° 44′ 3″ north.

As we passed the village of four houses, we found that the inhabitants had returned, and stopped to visit them. The houses are similar to those already described, but larger, from thirty-five to fifty feet long, and thirty feet wide, being sunk in the ground about six feet, and raised the same height above. Their beds are raised about four feet and a half above the floor, and the ascent is by a new painted ladder, with which every family is provided, and under them are stored their dried fish, while the space between the part of the bed on which they lie and the wall of the house is occupied by the nuts, roots, berries, and other provisions, which are spread on mats. The fireplace is about eight feet long, and six feet wide, sunk a foot below the floor, secured by a frame, with mats placed around for the family to sit on. In all of the houses are images of men of different shapes, and placed as ornaments in the parts of the house where they are most seen. They gave us nuts, berries, and some dried fish to eat, and we purchased, among other articles, a hat made after their own taste, such as they wear, without a brim. They ask high prices for all that they sell, observing that the whites below, pay dearly for all which they carry there.

We cannot learn precisely the nature of the trade carried on by the Indians with the inhabitants below. But as their knowledge of the whites seems to be very imperfect, and the only articles which they carry to market, such as pounded fish, bear-grass and roots, cannot be an object of much foreign traffic, their intercourse appears to be an intermediate trade with the natives near the mouth of the Columbia: from them these people obtain in exchange for their fish, roots and bear-grass, blue and white beads, copper tea-kettles, brass arm-bands, some scarlet and blue robes, and a few articles of old European clothing. But their great object is to obtain beads, an article which holds the first place in their ideas of relative value, and to procure which they will sacrifice their last article of clothing or the last mouthful of food. Independently of their fondness for them as an ornament, these beads are the medium of trade, by which they obtain from the Indians still higher up the river, robes, skins, chappelel bread, bear-grass, &c. Those Indians in turn, employ them to procure from the Indians in the Rocky mountains, bear-grass, pachico, roots, robes, &c.

These Indians are rather below the common size, with high cheekbones, their noses pierced, and in full dress, ornamented with a tapering piece of white shell or wampum about two inches long. Their eyes are exceedingly sore and weak, many of them have only a single eye, and some perfectly blind. Their teeth prematurely decayed, and in frequent instances, altogether worn away. Their general health, however, seems to be good, the only disorder we have remarked, being tumours in different parts of the body. The women are small and homely in their appearance, their legs and thighs much swelled, and their knees remarkably large; deformities, which are no doubt owing to the manner in which they set on their hams. They go nearly naked, having only a piece of leather tied round the breast, falling thence, nearly as low as the waist; a small robe about three feet square, and a piece of leather, which ill supplies the place of a cover, tied between their legs. Their hair is suffered to hang loose in every direction; and in their persons, as well as in their cookery, they are filthy to a most disgusting degree. We here observe that the women universally have their heads flattened, and in many of the villages, we have lately seen the female children undergo the operation.

SATURDAY, NOVEMBER 2D, 1805   We now examined the rapid below more particularly, and the danger appearing to be too great for the loaded canoes, all those who could not swim were sent with the baggage by land. The canoes then passed safely, and were reloaded; at the foot of the rapid we took a meridian altitude of 59° 45′ 45″. Just as we were setting out seven squaws arrived across the portage loaded with dried fish and bear-grass, neatly packed in bundles, and soon after four Indians came down the rapid in a large canoe. After breakfasting we left our camp at one o'clock, passed the upper point of an island which is separated from the right shore by a narrow channel, through which in high tides the water passes. But at present it contains no running water, and a creek which falls into it from the mountains on the right, is in the same dry condition, though it has the marks of discharging immense torrents at some seasons. The island thus made is three miles in length and about one in width; its situation is high and open, the land rich, and at this time covered with grass and a great number of strawberry vines, from which we gave it the name of Strawberry island. In several places we observed that the Indians had been digging for roots, and indeed the whole island bears every appearance of having been at some period in a state of cultivation. On the left side of the river the low ground is narrow and open: the rapid which we have just passed is the last of all the descents of the Columbia.

At this place the first tide-water commences, and the river in consequence widened immediately below the rapid. As we descended, we reached at the distance of one mile from the rapid a creek under a bluff on the left, at three miles is the lower point of Strawberry island. To this immediately succeed three small islands covered with wood; in the meadow to the right, and at some distance from the hills, stands a high perpendicular rock, about eight hundred feet high, and four hundred yards round the base; this we called the Beacon rock. Just below is an Indian village of nine houses, situated between two small creeks.

At this village the river widens to nearly a mile in extent, the low grounds too become wider, and they as well as the mountains on each side are covered with pine, spruce-pine, cottonwood, a species of ash, and some alder. After being so long accustomed to the dreary nakedness of the country above, the change is as grateful to the eye, as it is useful in supplying us with fuel. Four miles from the village is a point of land on the right, where the hills become lower, but are still thickly timbered. The river is now about two miles wide, the current smooth and gentle, and the effect of the tide has been sensible since leaving the rapid. Six miles lower is a rock rising from the middle of the river to the height of one hundred feet, and about eighty yards at its base. We continued six miles further, and halted for the night under a high projecting rock on the left side of the river opposite the point of a large meadow.

The mountains, which from the great shoot to this place are high, rugged, and thickly covered with timber chiefly of the pine species, here leave the river on each side; the river becomes two and a half miles in width, and the low grounds are extensive and well supplied with wood. The Indians whom we left at the portage passed us, on their way down the river, and seven others who were descending in a canoe for the purpose of trading below, encamped with us. We had made from the foot of the great shoot twenty-nine miles to-day. The ebb-tide rose at our camp about nine inches, the flood must rise much higher. We saw great numbers of water-fowl, such as swan, geese, ducks of various kinds, gulls, plover, and the white and grey brant, of which last we killed eighteen.

*Sunday*. We were detained until ten o'clock by a fog so thick that a man could not be discerned at the distance of fifty steps. As soon as it cleared off we set out in company with our new Indian acquaintances, who came from a village near the great falls. The low grounds along the river are covered so thickly with rushes, vines, and other small growth, that they are almost impassable. At the distance of three miles we reached the mouth of a river on the left, which seemed to lose its waters in a sandbar opposite; the stream itself being only a few inches in depth. But on attempting to wade across, we discovered that the bed was a very bad quicksand, too deep to be passed on foot. We went up a mile and a half to examine this river, and found it to be at this distance a very considerable stream one hundred and twenty yards wide at its narrowest part, with several small islands. Its character resembles very much that of the river Platte. It drives its quicksand over the low grounds with great impetuosity, and such is the quantity of coarse sand which it discharges, that the accumulation has formed a large sandbar or island, three miles long, and a mile and a half wide, which divides the waters of the Quicksand river into two channels. This sand island compresses the Columbia within a space of half a mile, and throws its whole current against the right shore. Opposite to this river, which we call Quicksand river, is a large creek to which we gave the name of Seal river. The first appears to pass through the low country, at the foot of the high range of mountains towards the southeast, while the second as well as all the large creeks on the right side of the Columbia, rise in the same ridge of mountains N. N. E. from this place. The mountain, which we have supposed to be the Mount Hood of Vancouver, bears S. 85° E. about forty-seven miles from the mouth of the Quicksand river.

After dinner we proceeded, and at the distance of three miles reached the lower mouth of Quicksand river. On the opposite side a large creek falls in near the head of an island, which extends for three miles and a half down the river; it is a mile and a half in width, rocky at the upper end, has some timber round its borders, but in the middle is open and has several ponds. Half a mile lower is another island in the middle of the river, to which from its appearance we gave the name of Diamond island. Here we met fifteen Indians ascending the river in two canoes, but the only information we could procure from them was, that they had seen three vessels, which we presume to be European, at the mouth of the Columbia. We went along its right side for three miles, and encamped opposite to it, after making to-day thirteen miles.

A canoe soon after arrived from the village at the foot of the last rapid, with an Indian and his family, consisting of a wife, three children, and a woman who had been taken prisoner from the Snake Indians, living on a river from the south, which we afterwards found to be the Multnomah. Sacajawea was immediately introduced to her, in hopes that being a Snake Indian also, they might understand each other, but their language was not sufficiently intelligible to permit them to converse together. The Indian had

321

a gun with a brass barrel and cock, which he appeared to value very highly.

Below Quicksand river the country is low, rich and thickly wooded on each side of the river: the islands have less timber, but are furnished with a number of ponds near which are vast quantities of fowls, such as swan, geese, brants, cranes, storks, white gulls, cormorants and plover. The river is wide, and contains a great number of sea otters.

In the evening the hunters brought in game for a sumptuous supper, which we shared with the Indians, both parties of whom spent the night with us.

NOVEMBER 4TH *Monday.* The weather was cloudy and cool, and the wind from the west. During the night, the tide rose eighteen inches near our camp. We set out about eight o'clock, and at the distance of three miles came to the lower end of Diamond island. It is six miles long, nearly three in width, and like the other islands, thinly covered with timber, and has a number of ponds or small lakes scattered over its surface. Besides the animals already mentioned we shot a deer on it this morning. Near the end of Diamond island are two others, separated by a narrow channel filled at high tides only, which continue on the right for the distance of three miles, and like the adjacent low grounds, are thickly covered with pine. Just below the last, we landed on the left bank of the river, at a village of twenty-five houses; all of these were thatched with straw, and built of bark, except one which was about fifty feet long, built of boards in the form of those higher up the river, from which it differed however, in being completely above ground, and covered with broad split boards; this village contains about two hundred men of the Skilloot nation, who seem well provided with canoes, of which there were at least fifty-two, and some of them very large, drawn up in front of the village. On landing we found the Indian from above, who had left us this morning, and who now invited us into a lodge of which he appeared to own a part. Here he treated us with a root, round in shape, and about the size of a small Irish potato, which they call wappatoo, it is the common arrowhead or sagittifolia, so much cultivated by the Chinese, and when roasted in the embers till it becomes soft, has an agreeable taste, and is a very good substitute for bread. After purchasing some more of this root, we resumed our journey, and at seven miles distance came to the head of a large island near the left. On the right shore is a fine open prairie for about a mile, back of which the country rises, and is supplied with timber, such as white oak, pine of different kinds, wild crab, and several species of undergrowth, while along the borders of the river, there are only a few cottonwood and ash trees. In this prairie were also signs of deer and elk.

When we landed for dinner, a number of Indians from the last village, came down for the purpose, as we supposed, of paying us a friendly visit, as they had put on their favourite dresses. In addition to their usual covering they had scarlet and blue blankets, sailors' jackets and trowsers, shirts and hats. They had all of them either war axes, spears and bow arrows, or muskets and pistols, with tin powder flasks. We smoked with them and endeavoured to show them every attention, but we soon found them very assuming and disagreeable companions. While we were eating they stole the pipe with which they were smoking, and the great coat of one of the men. We immediately searched them all, and discovered the coat stuffed under the root of a tree near where they were sitting; but the pipe we could not recover. Finding us determined not to suffer any imposition, and discontented with them, they showed their displeasure in the only way which they dared, by returning in an ill humour to their village.

We then proceeded and soon met two canoes with twelve men of the same Skilloot nation, who were on their way from below. The larger of the canoes was ornamented with the figure of a bear in the bow, and a man in the stern, both nearly as large as life, both made of painted wood, and very neatly fixed to the boat. In the same canoe were two Indians finely dressed and with round hats. This circumstance induced us to give the name of Image canoe to the large island, the lower end of which we now passed at the distance of nine miles from its head. We had seen two smaller islands to the right, and three more near its lower extremity. The Indians in the canoe here made signs that there was a village behind those islands, and indeed we presumed there was a channel on that side of the river, for one of the canoes passed in that direction between the small islands, but we were anxious to press forward, and therefore did not stop to examine more minutely. The river was now about a mile and a half in width, with a gentle current, the bottoms extensive and low, but not subject to be overflowed. Three miles below the Image canoe island we came to four large houses on the left side, at which place we had a full view of the mountain which we first saw on the *19th of October*, from the Muscleshell rapid, and which we now find to be the mount St. Helen of Vancouver. It bears north 25° east, about ninety miles distant; it rises in the form of a sugar-loaf to a very great height, and is covered with snow. A mile lower we passed a single house on the left, and another on the right. The Indians had now learnt so much of us, that their curiosity was without any mixture of fear, and their visits became very frequent and troublesome. We therefore continued on till after night, in hopes of getting rid of them; but after passing a village on each side, which on account of the lateness of the hour we saw indistinctly, we found there was no escaping from their importunities. We therefore landed at the distance of seven miles below Image canoe island, and encamped near a single house on the right, having made during the day twenty-nine miles.

The Skilloots whom we passed to-day, speak a language somewhat different from that of the Echeloots or Chilluckittequaws near the long narrows. Their dress is similar, except that the Skilloots possess more articles procured from the white traders; and there is further difference between them, inasmuch as the Skilloots, both males and females, have the head flattened. Their principal food is fish, and wappatoo roots, and some elk and deer, in killing which with their arrows, they seem very expert, for during the short time we remained at the village three deer were brought in. We also observed there a tame brairo.

As soon as we landed we were visited by two canoes loaded with Indians, from whom we purchased a few roots. The grounds along the river continue low and rich, and among the shrubs which cover them is a large quantity of vines resembling the raspberry. On the right the low grounds are terminated at the distance of five miles by a range of high hills covered with tall timber, and running southeast and northwest. The game as usual very abundant, and among other birds we observe some white geese with a part of their wings black.

*Tuesday.* Our choice of a camp had been very unfortunate; for on a sand island opposite to us were immense numbers of geese, swan-ducks, and other wild fowl, who, during the whole night, serenaded us with a confusion of noises which completely prevented our sleeping. During the latter part of the night it rained, and we therefore willingly left our encampment at an early hour. We passed at three miles a small prairie, where the river is only three quarters of a mile in width, and soon after two houses on the left, half a mile distant from each other; from one of which three men came in a canoe merely to look at us, and having done so returned home. At eight miles we came to the lower point of an island, separated from the right side by a narrow channel, on which, a short distance above the end of the island, is situated a large village: it is built more compactly than the generality of the Indian villages, and the front has fourteen houses, which are ranged for a quarter of a mile along the channel. As soon as we were discovered seven canoes came out to see us, and after some traffic, during which they seemed well-disposed and orderly, accompanied us a short distance below. The river here again widens to the space of a mile and a half. As we descended we soon observed, behind a sharp point of rocks, a channel a quarter of a mile wide, which we suppose must be the one taken by the canoes yesterday on leaving Image-canoe island. A mile below the channel are some low cliffs of rocks, near which is a large island on the right side, and two small islands a little further on. Here we met two canoes ascending the river. At this place the shore on the right becomes bold and rocky, and the bank is bordered by a range of high hills covered with a thick growth of pine: on the other side is an extensive low island, separated from the left side by a narrow channel.

Here we stopped to dine, and found the island open, with an abundant growth of grass, and a number of ponds well supplied with fowls; and at the lower extremity are the remains of an old village. We procured a swan, several ducks, and a brant, and saw some deer on the island. Besides this island, the lower extremity of which is seventeen miles from the channel just mentioned, we passed two or three smaller ones in the same distance. Here the hills on the right retire from the river, leaving a high plain, between which, on the left bank, a range of high hills running southeast and covered with pine, forms a bold and rocky shore. At the distance of six miles, however, these hills again return and close the river on both sides.

We proceeded on, and at four miles reached a creek on the right, about twenty yards in width, immediately below which is an old village. Three miles further, and at the distance of thirty-two miles from our camp of last night, we halted under a point of highland, with thick pine trees on the left bank of the river. Before landing we met two canoes, the largest of which had at the bow the image of a bear, and that of a man on the stern: there were twenty-six Indians on board, but they all proceeded upwards, and we were left, for the first time since we reached the waters of the Columbia, without any of the natives with us during the night. Besides the game already mentioned, we killed a grouse much larger than the common size, and observed along the shore a number of striped snakes.

The river is here deep, and about a mile and a half in width. Here too the ridge of low mountains running northwest and southeast, cross the river, and form the western boundary of the plain through which we have just passed. This great plain or valley begins above the mouth of Quicksand river, and is about sixty miles wide in a straight line, while on the right and left it extends to a great distance: it is a fertile and delightful country, shaded by thick groves of tall timber, watered by small ponds, and running on both sides of the river. The soil is rich, and capable of any species of culture; but in the present condition of the Indians, its chief production is the wappatoo root, which grows spontaneously and exclusively in this region. Sheltered as it is on both sides, the temperature is much milder than that of the surrounding country; for even at this season of the year we observe very little appearance of frost. During its whole extent it is inhabited by numerous tribes of Indians, who either reside in it permanently, or visit its waters in quest of fish and wappatoo roots: we gave it the name of the Columbia valley.

*Wednesday.* The morning was cool, wet, and rainy. We proceeded at an early hour between the high hills on both sides of the river, till at the distance of four miles we came to two tents of Indians in a small plain on the left, where the hills on the right recede a few miles from the river, and a long narrow island stretches along the right shore. Behind this island is the mouth of a large river a hundred and fifty yards wide, and called by the Indians, Coweliske. We halted for dinner on the island, but the red wood and green briars are so interwoven with the pine, alder, ash, a species of beech, and other trees, that the woods form a thicket, which our hunters could not penetrate. Below the mouth of the Coweliske a very remarkable knob rises from the water's edge to the height of eighty feet, being two hundred paces round the base; and as it is in a low part of the island, and some distance from the high grounds, the appearance of it is very singular.

On setting out after dinner we overtook two canoes going down to trade: one of the Indians, who spoke a few words of English, mentioned, that the principal person who traded with them was a Mr. Haley, and he showed a bow of iron and several other things which he said Mr. Haley had given him. Nine miles below that river is a creek on the same; and between them three smaller islands; one on the left shore, the other about the middle of the river; and a third near the lower end of the long narrow island, and opposite a high cliff of black rocks on the left, sixteen miles from our camp. Here we were overtaken by the Indians from the two tents we passed in the morning, from whom we now purchased wappatoo roots, salmon, trout, and two beaver skins, for which last we gave five small fishhooks. At these cliffs the mountains, which had continued high and rugged on the left, retired from the river, and as the hills on the other side had left the water at the Coweliske, a beautiful extensive plain now presented itself before us: for a few miles we passed along side of an island a mile in width and three miles long, below which is a smaller island, where the high rugged hills, thickly covered with timber, border the right bank of the river, and terminate the low grounds: these were supplied with common rushes, grass, and nettles; in the moister parts with bullrushes and flags, and along the water's edge some willows. Here also were two ancient villages, now abandoned by their inhabitants, of whom no vestige remains, except two small dogs almost starved, and a prodigious quantity of fleas. After crossing the plain and making five miles, we proceeded through the hills for eight miles. The river is about a mile in width, and the hills so steep that we could not for several miles find a place sufficiently level to suffer us to sleep in a level position: at length, by removing the large stones, we cleared a place fit for our purpose above the reach of the tide, and after a journey of twenty-nine miles slept among the smaller stones under a mountain to the right. The weather was rainy during the whole day; we therefore made large fires to dry our bedding and to kill the fleas, who have accumulated upon us at every old village we have passed.

*Thursday.* The morning was rainy and the fog so thick that we could not see across the river. We observed however, opposite to our camp, the upper point of an island, between which and the steep hills on the right we proceeded for five miles. Three miles lower is the beginning of an island separated from the right shore by a narrow channel; down this we proceeded under the direction of some Indians whom we had just met going up the river, and who returned in order to show us their village. It consists of four houses only, situated on this channel behind several marshy islands formed by two small creeks. On our arrival they gave us some fish, and we afterwards purchased wappatoo roots, fish, three dogs, and two otter skins, for which we gave fishhooks chiefly, that being an article of which they are very fond.

These people seem to be of a different nation from those we have just passed: they are low in stature, ill shaped, and all have their heads flattened. They call themselves Wahkiacum, and their language differs from that of the tribes above, with whom they trade for wappatoo roots. The houses too are built in a different style, being raised entirely above ground, with the eaves about five feet high, and the door at the corner. Near the end opposite to this door is a single fireplace, round which are the beds, raised four feet from the floor of earth; over the fire are hung the fresh fish, and when dried they are stowed away with the wappatoo roots under the beds. The dress of the men is like that of the people above, but the women are clad in a peculiar manner, the robe not reaching lower than the hip, and the body being covered in cold weather by a sort of corset of fur, curiously plaited, and reaching from the arms to the hip; added to this is a sort of petticoat, or rather tissue of white cedar bark, bruised or broken into small strands, and woven into a girdle by several cords of the same material. Being tied round the middle, these strands hang down as low as the knee in front, and to midleg behind, and are of sufficient thickness to answer the purpose of concealment whilst the female stands in an erect position, but in any other attitude is but a very ineffectual defence. Sometimes the tissue is strings of silk grass, twisted and knotted at the end.

After remaining with them about an hour, we proceeded down the channel with an Indian dressed in a sailor's jacket for our pilot, and on reaching the main channel were visited by some Indians who have a temporary residence on a marshy island in the middle of the river, where is a great abundance of water fowl. Here the mountainous country again approaches the river on the left, and a higher mountain is distinguished towards the southwest. At a distance of twenty miles from our camp we halted at a village of Wahkiacums, consisting of seven ill-looking houses, built in the same form with those above, and situated at the foot of the high hills on the

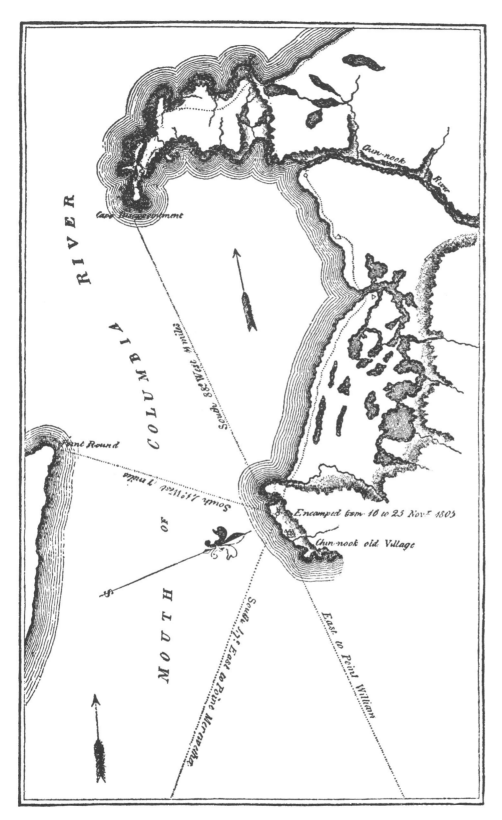

The mouth of the Columbia, where the expedition reached the Pacific Ocean and camped during November 1805, prior to the establishment of Fort Clatsop.

right, behind two small marshy islands. We merely stopped to purchase some food and two beaver skins, and then proceeded. Opposite to these islands the hills on the left retire, and the river widens into a kind of bay crowded with low islands, subject to be overflowed occasionally by the tide.

We had not gone far from this village when the fog cleared off, and we enjoyed the delightful prospect of the ocean; that ocean, the object of all our labours, the reward of all our anxieties. This cheering view exhilarated the spirits of all the party, who were still more delighted on hearing the distant roar of the breakers. We went on with great cheerfulness under the high mountainous country which continued along the right bank; the shore was however so bold and rocky, that we could not, until after going fourteen miles from the last village, find any spot fit for an encampment. At that distance, having made during the day thirty-four miles, we spread our mats on the ground, and passed the night in the rain. Here we were joined by our small canoe, which had been separated from us during the fog this morning. Two Indians from the last village also accompanied us to the camp, but, having detected them in stealing a knife, they were sent off.

NOVEMBER 8TH  *Friday*. It rained this morning; and having changed the clothing which had been wet during yesterday's rain, we did not set out till nine o'clock. Immediately opposite our camp is a rock at the distance of a mile in the river, about twenty feet in diameter and fifty in height, and towards the southwest some high mountains, one of which is covered with snow at the top. We proceeded past several low islands in the bay or bend of the river to the left, which is here five or six miles wide. We were here overtaken by three Indians in a canoe who had salmon to sell. On the right side we passed an old village, and then, at the distance of three miles, entered an inlet or niche about six miles across, and making a deep bend of nearly five miles into the hills on the right shore, where it receives the waters of several creeks. We coasted along this inlet, which, from its little depth, we called Shallow bay, and at the bottom of it halted to dine near the remains of an old village, from which, however, we kept at a cautious distance, as it was occupied by great numbers of fleas. At this place we observed a number of fowl, among which we killed a goose and two ducks, exactly resembling in appearance and flavour the canvassback duck of the Susquehannah. After dinner the three Indians left us, and we then took advantage of the returning tide, to go on about three miles to a point on the right, eight miles distant from our camp; but here the waves ran so high, and dashed about our canoes so much, that several of the men became seasick. It was therefore judged imprudent to go on in the present state of the weather, and we landed at the point. The situation was extremely uncomfortable; the high hills jutted in so closely that there was not room for us to lie level, nor to secure our baggage free from the tide; and the water of the river is too salt to be used; but the waves increasing every moment so much, that we could not move from the spot with safety: we therefore fixed ourselves on the beach left by the ebb-tide, and having raised the baggage on poles, passed a disagreeable night, the rain during the day having wet us completely, as indeed we have been for some days past.

*Saturday.* Fortunately for us, the tide did not rise as high as our camp during the night; but being accompanied by high winds from the south, the canoes, which we could not place beyond its reach, were filled with water, and were saved with much difficulty: our position was very uncomfortable, but as it was impossible to move from it, we waited for a change of weather. It rained, however, during the whole day, and at two o'clock in the afternoon, the flood tide set in, accompanied by a high wind from the south, which, about four o'clock, shifted to the southwest, and blew almost a gale directly from the sea. The immense waves now broke over the place where we were encamped, and the large trees, some of them five or six feet thick, which had lodged at the point, were drifted over our camp, and the utmost vigilance of every man could scarcely save our canoes from being crushed to pieces. We remained in the water and drenched with rain during the rest of the day; our only food being some dried fish, and some rain-water which we caught. Yet, though wet and cold, and some of them sick from using the salt-water, the men are cheerful, and full of anxiety to see more of the ocean. The rain continued all night.

*Sunday.* The following morning, the wind, however, lulled, and the waves not being so high, we loaded our canoes and proceeded. The mountains on the right are high, covered with timber, chiefly pine, and descend in a bold and rocky shore to the water. We went through a deep niche and several inlets on the right, while on the opposite side is a large bay, above which the hills are close on the river. At the distance of ten miles the wind rose from the northwest and the waves became so high that we were forced to return for two miles to a place where we could with safety unload. Here we landed at the mouth of a small run, and having placed our baggage on a pile of drifted logs waited until low water. The river then appeared more calm: we therefore started, but after going a mile found the waves too high for our canoes and were obliged to put to shore. We unloaded the canoes, and having placed the baggage on a rock above the reach of the tide, encamped on some drift logs which formed the only place where we could lie, the hills rising steep over our heads to the height of five hundred feet. All our baggage as well as ourselves were thoroughly wet with the rain, which did not cease during the day; it continued violently during the night, in the course of which the tide reached the logs on which we lay, and set them afloat.

*Monday.* The wind was still high from the southwest, and drove the waves against the shore with great fury: the rain too fell in torrents, and not only drenched us to the skin, but loosened the stones on the hill sides, which then came rolling down upon us. In this comfortless situation we remained all day wet, cold, with nothing but dried fish to satisfy our hunger; the canoes in one place at the mercy of the waves; the baggage in another, and all the men scattered on floating logs, or sheltering themselves in the crevices of the rocks and hill sides. A hunter was despatched in hopes of finding some fresh meat, but the hills were so steep, and covered with undergrowth and fallen timber, that he could not penetrate them, and he was forced to return. About twelve o'clock we were visited by five Indians in a canoe: they came from above this place on the opposite side of the river, and their language much resembles that of the Wahkiacum: they called themselves

*Cathlamahs*. In person they are small, ill made, and badly clothed; though one of them had on a sailor's round jacket and pantaloons, which, as he explained by signs, he had received from the whites below the point: we purchased from them thirteen red char, a fish which we found very excellent. After some time they went on board the boat, and crossed the river, which is here five miles wide, through a very heavy sea.

NOVEMBER 12TH    *Tuesday.* About three o'clock a tremendous gale of wind arose, accompanied with lightning, thunder, and hail: at six it became light for a short time, but a violent rain soon began and lasted during the day. During this storm one of our boats, secured by being sunk with great quantities of stone, got loose, but drifting against a rock, was recovered without having received much injury. Our situation became now much more dangerous, for the waves were driven with fury against the rocks and trees, which till now had afforded us refuge: we therefore took advantage of a low tide, and moved about half a mile round a point to a small brook, which we had not observed till now on account of the thick bushes and driftwood which concealed its mouth. Here we were more safe; but still cold and wet, our clothes and bedding rotten as well as wet, our baggage at a distance, and the canoes, our only means of escape from this place, at the mercy of the waves: we were, however, fortunate enough to enjoy good health, and even had the luxury of getting some fresh salmon and three salmon trout in the brook. Three of the men attempted to go round a point in our small Indian canoe, but the high waves rendered her quite unmanageable; these boats requiring the seamanship of the natives themselves to make them live in so rough a sea.

NOVEMBER 13TH    *Wednesday.* During the night we had short intervals of fair weather, but it began to rain in the morning, and continued through the day. In order to obtain a view of the country below, captain Clark followed up the course of the brook, and with much fatigue, and after walking three miles, ascended the first spur of the mountains. The whole lower country was covered with almost impenetrable thickets of small pine, with which is mixed a species of plant resembling arrowwood, twelve or fifteen feet high, with a thorny stem, almost interwoven with each other, and scattered among the fern and fallen timber: there is also a red berry, somewhat like the solomon's seal, which is called by the natives, solme, and used as an article of diet. This thick growth rendered travelling almost impossible, and it was rendered more fatiguing by the steepness of the mountain, which was so great as to oblige him to draw himself up by means of the bushes. The timber on the hills is chiefly of a large tall species of pine, many of them eight or ten feet in diameter at the stump, and rising sometimes more than one hundred feet in height. The hail which fell two nights since is still to be seen on the mountains: there was no game, and no traces of any, except some old signs of elk: the cloudy weather prevented his seeing to any distance, and he therefore returned to camp, and sent three men in the Indian canoe to try if they could double the point and find some safer harbour for our canoes. At every flood-tide the seas break in great swells against the rocks, and drift the trees among our establishment, so as to render it very insecure. We were confined as usual to dried fish, which is our last resource.

*Thursday.* It rained without intermission during last night and to-day: the wind too is very high, and one of our canoes much injured by being dashed against rocks. Five Indians from below came to us in a canoe, and three of them having landed, informed us that they had seen the men sent down yesterday. At this moment one of them arrived, and informed us that these Indians had stolen his gig and basket: we therefore ordered the two women who remained in the canoe, to restore them; but this they refused, till we threatened to shoot, when they gave back the articles, and we then ordered them to leave us. They were of the Wahkiacum nation. The man now informed us that they had gone round the point as far as the high sea would suffer them in the canoe, and then landed, and that in the night he had separated from his companions, who had gone further down: that at no great distance from where we are is a beautiful sand beach and a good harbour. Captain Lewis concluded to examine more minutely the lower part of the bay, and taking one of the large canoes was landed at the point, whence he proceeded by land with four men, and the canoe returned nearly filled with water.

*Friday.* It continued raining all night, but in the morning the weather be- came calm and fair: we therefore began to prepare for setting out, but before we were ready a high wind sprang up from the southeast, and obliged us to remain. The sun shone until one o'clock, and we were thus enabled to dry our bedding and examine our baggage. The rain, which has continued for the last ten days without an interval of more than two hours, has completely wet all our merchandise, and spoiled some of our fish, destroyed the robes, and rotted nearly one half of our few remaining articles of clothing, particularly the leather dresses. About three o'clock the wind fell, and we instantly loaded the canoes, and left the miserable spot to which we have been confined the last six days. On turning the point we came to the sand beach, through which runs a small stream from the hills; at the mouth of which is an ancient village of thirty-six houses, which has at present no inhabitants except fleas.

Here we met Shannon, who had been sent back to meet us by captain Lewis. The day Shannon left us in the canoe, he and Willard proceeded on till they met a party of twenty Indians, who never having heard of us, did not know where they came from: they however behaved with so much civility, and seemed so anxious that the men should go with them towards the sea, that their suspicions were excited, and they declined going on: the Indians, however, would not leave them, and the men being confirmed in their suspicions, and fearful if they went into the woods to sleep they would be cut to pieces in the night, thought it best to pass the night in the midst of the Indians; they therefore made a fire, and after talking with them to a late hour, laid down with their rifles under their heads. As they awoke this morning they found that the Indians had stolen and concealed their guns; having demanded them in vain, Shannon seized a club, and was about assaulting one of the Indians whom he suspected as a thief, when another Indian began to load a fowling piece, with an intention of shooting him. He therefore stopped and explained by signs, that if they did not give up the guns, a large party would come down the river before the sun rose to such a height, and put every one of them to death. Fortunately, captain Lewis and his party appeared at this time, and the terrified Indians immediately brought the guns, and five of them came on with Shannon. To these men we declared, that if ever any of their nation stole any thing from us he should be instantly shot. They reside to the north of this place, and speak a language different from that of the people higher up the river.

It was now apparent that the sea was at all times too rough for us to proceed further down the bay by water; we therefore landed, and having chosen the best spot we could select, made our camp of boards from the old village. We were now situated comfortably, and being visited by four Wah-kiacums with wappatoo roots, were enabled to make an agreeable addition to our food.

NOVEMBER 16TH    *Saturday*. The morning was clear and beautiful. We therefore, put out all our baggage to dry, and sent several of the party to hunt. Our camp is in full view of the ocean, on the bay laid down by Vancouver, which we distinguish by the name of Haley's bay, from a trader who visits the Indians here, and is a great favourite among them. The meridian altitude of this day gave 46° 19′ 11$\frac{7}{10}$″ as the latitude of our camp. The wind was strong from the southwest, and the waves very high, yet the Indians were passing up and down the bay in canoes, and several of them encamped near us. We smoked with them, but after our recent experience of their thievish disposition, treated them with caution. Though so much exposed to the bad weather, none of the party have suffered, except one, who has a violent cold, in consequence of sleeping for several nights in wet leather. The hunters brought in two deer, a crane, some geese and ducks, and several brant, three of which were white, except a black part of the wing, and much larger than the grey brant, which is itself a size beyond the duck.

NOVEMBER 17TH    *Sunday*. A fair cool morning and easterly wind. The tide rises at this place eight feet six inches in height, and rolls over the beach in great waves.

About one o'clock captain Lewis returned, after having coasted down Haley's bay to cape Disappointment, and some distance to the north along the sea coast. He was followed by several Chinnooks, among whom were the principal chief and his family. They made us a present of a boiled root, very much like the common liquorice in taste and size, and called cul-whamo; in return we gave double the value of their present, and now learnt the danger of accepting any thing from them, since no return, even if ten times the value of their gift, can satisfy them. We were chiefly occupied in hunting, and were able to procure three deer, four brant and two ducks, and also saw some signs of elk.

Captain Clark now prepared for an excursion down the bay, and accordingly started, *Monday 18th* at daylight, accompanied by eleven men. He proceeded along the beach one mile to a point of rocks about forty feet high, where the hills retire, leaving a wide beach, and a number of ponds covered with water-fowl, between which and the mountain is a narrow bottom of alder and small balsam trees. Seven miles from the rocks is the entrance of a creek, or rather drain from the ponds and hills, where is a cabin of Chinnooks. The cabin contained some children, and four women, one of whom was in a most miserable state, covered with ulcers, proceeding as we imagine, from the veneral disease, with which several of the Chinnooks we have seen appear to be afflicted. We were taken across in a canoe by two squaws, to each of whom we gave a fishhook, and then coasting along the bay, passed at two miles the low bluff of a small hill, below which are the ruins of some old huts, and close to it the remains of a whale. The country is low, open and marshy; interspersed with some high pine and a thick under-growth. Five miles from the creek, we came to a stream forty yards wide at low water, which we called Chinnook river. The hills up this river and towards the bay are not high, but very thickly covered with large pine of several species: in many places pine trees, three or four feet in thickness, are seen growing on the bodies of large trees, which though fallen and covered with moss, were in part sound.

Here we dined on some brant and plover, killed as we came along, and after crossing in a boat lying in the sand near some old houses, pro-ceeded along a bluff of yellow clay and soft stone to a little bay or harbour, into which a drain from some ponds empties: at this harbour the land is low, but as we went on it rose to hills of eighty or ninety feet above the water. At the distance of one mile is a second bay, and a mile beyond it, a small rocky island in a deep bend, which seems to afford a very good harbour, and where the natives inform us European vessels anchor for the purpose of trading. We went on round another bay, in which is a second small island of rocks, and crossed a small stream, which rises in a pond near the sea coast, and after running through a low isthmus empties into the bay. This narrow low ground, about two or three hundred yards wide, separates from the main hills a kind of peninsula, the extremity of which is two miles from the an-choring place; and this spot, which was called cape Disappointment, is an elevated, circular knob, rising with a steep ascent one hundred and fifty or one hundred and sixty feet above the water, formed like the whole shore of the bay, as well as of the seacoast, and covered with thick timber on the in-ner side, but open and grassy in the exposure next the sea.

From this cape a high point of land bears south 20° west, about twenty-five miles distant. In the range between these two eminences, is the opposite point of the bay, a very low ground, which has been variously called cape Rond by Lapeyrouse, and point Adams by Vancouver. The wa-ter for a great distance off the mouth of the river, appears very shallow, and within the mouth nearest to point Adams, is a large sandbar, almost covered at high tide. We could not ascertain the direction of the deepest channel, for the waves break with tremendous force the whole distance across the bay, but the Indians point nearer to the opposite side as the best passage. After remaining for some time on this elevation, we descended across the low isth-mus, and reached the ocean at the foot of a high hill, about a mile in circum-ference, and projecting into the sea. We crossed this hill, which is open and has a growth of high coarse grass, and encamped on the north side of it, hav-ing made nineteen miles. Besides the pounded fish and brant, we had for supper a flounder, which we picked up on the beach.

*Tuesday.* In the night it began to rain, and continued till eleven o'clock. Two hunters were sent on to kill something for breakfast, and the rest of the party after drying their blankets soon followed. At three miles we overtook the hunters, and breakfasted on a small deer, which they had been fortunate enough to kill. This, like all those we have seen on this coast, are much

333

darker than our common deer. Their bodies too, are deeper, their legs shorter, and their eyes larger. The branches of the horns are similar, but the upper part of the tail is black, from the root to the end, and they do not leap, but jump like a sheep frightened.

We then continued over rugged hills and steep hollows, near the sea, on a course about north 20° west, in a direct line from the cape, till at the distance of five miles, we reached a point of high land, below which a sandy beach extends, in a direction north 10° west, to another high point about twenty miles distant. This eminence we distinguished by the name of point Lewis. It is there that the highlands, which at the commencement of the sandy beach, recede towards Chinnook river, again approach the ocean. The intermediate country is low, with many small ponds, crowded with birds, and watered by the Chinnook, on the borders of which resides the nation of the same name. We went four miles along the sandy beach to a small pine tree, on which captain Clark marked his name, with the year and day, and then returned to the foot of the hills, passing on the shore a sturgeon ten feet long, and several joints of the back bone of a whale, both which seem to have been thrown ashore and foundered. After dining on the remains of the small deer, we crossed in a southeastern direction to the bay, where we arrived at the distance of two miles, then continued along the bay, crossed Chinnook river, and encamped on its upper side, in a sandy bottom.

NOVEMBER 20TH  *Wednesday.* It rained in the course of the night. A hunter despatched early to kill some food, returned with eight ducks, on which we breakfasted, and then followed the course of the bay to the creek or outlet of the ponds. It was now high tide, the stream three hundred yards wide, and no person in the cabin to take us across. We therefore made a small raft, on which one of the men passed and brought a canoe to carry us over. As we went along the beach we were overtaken by several Indians, who gave us dried sturgeon and wappatoo roots, and soon met several parties of Chinnooks returning from the camp. When we arrived there we found many Chinnooks, and two of them being chiefs, we went through the ceremony of giving to each a medal, and to the most distinguished a flag. Their names were Comcommoly and Chillahlawil. One of the Indians had a robe made of two sea-otter skins, the fur of which was the most beautiful we had ever seen; the owner resisted every temptation to part with it, but at length could not resist the offer of a belt of blue beads which Chaboneau's wife wore round her waist. During our absence the camp had been visited by many Indians, and the men who had been employed in hunting killed several deer, and a variety of wild fowls.

NOVEMBER 21ST  *Thursday.* The morning was cloudy, and from noon till night it rained. The wind too was high from the southeast, and the sea so rough that the water reached our camp. Most of the Chinnooks returned home, but we were visited in the course of the day by people of different bands in the neighbourhood, among whom are the Chiltz, a nation residing on the seacoast near point Lewis, and the Clatsops, who live immediately opposite on the south side of the Columbia. A chief from the grand rapid also came to see us, and we gave him a medal. To each of our visitors we made a present of a small piece of ribbon, and purchased some cranberries and some articles of their manufacture, such as mats, and household furniture, for all which we paid high prices. After we had been relieved from these Indians, we were surprised at a visit of a different kind; an old woman who is the wife of a Chinnook chief, came with six young women, her daughters and nieces, and having deliberately encamped near us, proceeded to cultivate an intimacy between our men and her fair wards.

FRIDAY, NOVEMBER 22D, 1805   It rained during the whole night, and about daylight a tremendous gale of wind rose from the S. S. E. and continued during the whole day with great violence. The sea runs so high that the water comes into our camp, which the rain prevents us from leaving. We purchased from the old squaw for armbands and rings, a few wappatoo roots, on which we subsisted. They are nearly equal in flavour to the Irish potato, and afford a very good substitute for bread. The bad weather has driven several Indians to our camp, but they are still under the terrors of the threat which we made on first seeing them, and now behave with the greatest decency.

NOVEMBER 23D   *Saturday.* The rain continued through the night, but the morning was calm and cloudy. The hunters were sent out and killed three deer, four brant, and three ducks. Towards evening seven Clatsops came over in a canoe with two skins of the sea-otter. To this article they attach an extravagant value, and their demands for it were so high that we were fearful of reducing our small stock of merchandise, on which we must depend for subsistence as we return, to venture on purchasing. To ascertain however their ideas as to the value of different objects, we offered for one of the skins a watch, a handkerchief, an American dollar, and a bunch of red beads; but neither the curious mechanism of the watch, nor even the red beads could tempt him; he refused the offer, but asked for tiacomoshack or chief beads, the most common sort of coarse blue-coloured beads, the article beyond all price in their estimation. Of these blue beads we have but few, and therefore reserve them for more necessitous circumstances.

NOVEMBER 24TH   *Sunday.* The morning being fair, we dried our wet articles and sent out the hunters, but they returned with only a single brant. In the evening a chief and several men of the Chinnooks came to see us; we smoked with them, and bought a sea-otter skin for some blue beads. Having now examined the coast, it becomes necessary to decide on the spot for our wintering quarters. The people of the country subsist chiefly on dried fish and roots, but of these there does not seem to be a sufficient quantity for our support, even were we able to purchase, and the extravagant prices as well as our small store of merchandise forbid us to depend on that resource. We must therefore rely for subsistence on our arms, and be guided in the choice of our residence by the abundance of game which any particular spot may offer. The Indians say that the deer is most numerous at some distance above on the river, but that the country on the opposite side of the bay is better supplied with elk, an animal much larger and more easily killed than deer, with a skin better fitted for clothing, and the meat of which is more nutritive during the winter, when they are both poor. The climate too is obviously much milder here than above the first range of mountains, for the Indians are thinly clad, and say they have little snow, indeed since our arrival the weather has been very warm, and sometimes disagreeably so, and dressed as we are altogether in leather, the cold would be very unpleasant if not injurious. The neighbourhood of the sea is moreover recommended by the facility of supplying ourselves with salt, and the hope of meeting some of the trading vessels, who are expected in about three months, and from whom we may procure a fresh supply of trinkets for our route homewards. These considerations induced us to determine on visiting the opposite side of the bay, and if there was an appearance of much game to establish ourselves there during the winter.

Next day, however, the wind was too high to suffer us to cross the river, but as it blew generally from the east southeast, the coast on the north was in some degree sheltered by the highlands. We therefore set out, and keeping near the shore, halted for dinner in the shallow bay, and after dark, reached a spot near a rock, at some distance in the river, and close to our former camp of the 7th inst. On leaving our camp, seven Clatsops accompanied us in a canoe, but after going a few miles crossed the bay through immense high waves, leaving us in admiration, at the dexterity with which they threw aside each wave as it threatened to come over their canoe. The evening was cloudy, and in the morning it rained.

*Tuesday.* We set out with the wind from east northeast, and a short distance above the rock, near our camp, began to cross the river. We passed between some low, marshy islands, which we called the Seal islands, and reached the south side of the Columbia at a bottom three miles below a point, to which we gave the name of point Samuel. After going along the shore for five miles, we entered a channel two hundred yards in width, which separates from the main land a large, but low island. On this channel, and at the foot of some highlands, is a village where we landed. It consists of nine large wooden houses, inhabited by a tribe called Cathlamahs, who seem to differ neither in dress, language, nor manners, from the Chinnooks and Wahkia-cums: like whom they live chiefly on fish and wappatoo roots. We found, however, as we hoped, some elk meat: after dining on some fresh fish and roots, which we purchased from them at an immoderate price, we coasted along a deep bend of the river towards the south, and at night encamped under a high hill; all the way from the village the land is high, and has a thick growth of pine balsam, and other timber; but as it was still raining very hard, it was with difficulty we procured wood enough to make fires. Soon after we landed, three Indians from the Cathlamah village came down with wappatoo roots, some of which we purchased with fish-hooks.

*Wednesday.* At daylight the next morning, eleven more came down with provisions, skins and mats for sale, but the prices were too high for our reduced finances, and we bought nothing. As we were preparing to set out we missed an axe, which was found under the robe of one of the Indians, and they were all prohibited in consequence from following us. We went on in the rain, which had continued through the night, and passing between a number of islands came to a small river, called by the Indians Kekemahke. We afterwards came to a very remarkable knob of land, projecting about a mile and a half towards Shallow bay, and about four miles round, while the neck of land which connects it to the main shore is not more than fifty yards wide. We went round this projection, which we named point William; but the waves then became so high that we could not venture any farther, and we therefore landed on a beautiful shore of pebbles of various colours, and encamped near an old Indian hut on the isthmus. In drawing our canoes in shore, we had the misfortune to make a split two feet long in one of them. This isthmus opposed a formidable barrier to the sea, for we now found that the water below is salt, while that above is fresh and well tasted. It rained hard during the whole day; it continued all night, and in the morning began more violently, attended with a high wind from the southwest.

It was now impossible to proceed on so rough a sea. We therefore sent several men to hunt, and the rest of us remained during the day, in a situation the most cheerless and uncomfortable. On this little neck of land we are exposed with a miserable covering, which does not deserve the name of a shelter to the violence of the winds; all our bedding and stores, as well as our bodies are completely wet, our clothes rotting with constant exposure, and no food except the dried fish brought from the falls, to which we are again reduced. The hunters all returned hungry, and drenched with rain, having seen neither deer nor elk, and the swan and brant too shy to be approached. At noon the wind shifted to the northwest, and blew with such tremendous fury that many trees were blown down near us. This gale lasted with short intervals during the whole night; but towards morning the wind lulled, though the rain continued, and the waves were still high.

NOVEMBER 29TH  *Friday.* Captain Lewis took the Indian canoe, which is better calculated for rough weather, and with five men went down to a small bay below us, where we expect to find elk. Three other men set out at the same time to hunt in different directions, and the rest remained round the smoke of our fires drying leather, in order to make some new clothes. The night brought only a continuation of rain and hail, with short intervals of fair weather, till in the morning it cleared up about nine o'clock, and the sun shone for several hours.

Other hunters were now sent out, and we passed the remainder of the day in drying our merchandise so long exposed. Several of the men complain of disorders in their bowels, which can be ascribed only to their diet of pounded fish mixed with salt-water: and they are therefore directed to use for that purpose, the fresh water above the point. The hunters had seen three elk, but could not obtain any of them: they however brought in three hawks and a few black ducks, of a species common in the United States, living in large flocks, and feeding on grass: they are distinguished by a sharp white beak, toes separated, and by having no craw. Besides these wild fowls, there are in this neighbourhood a large kind of buzzard with white wings, the grey and the bald eagle, the large red-tailed hawk, the blue magpie, and great numbers of ravens and crows. We observe, however, few small birds, the one which has most attracted our attention being a small brown bird, which seems to frequent logs and the roots of trees. Of other animals there is a great abundance. We see great quantities of snakes, lizards, worms, and spiders, as well as small bugs, flies, and insects of different kinds. The vegetable productions are also numerous. The hills along the coast are high and steep, and the general covering is a growth of lofty pines of different species, some of which rise more than two hundred feet, and are ten or twelve feet in diameter near the root. Besides these trees we observe on the point a species of ash, the alder, the laurel, one species of the wild crab, and several kinds of underbrush, among which the rosebushes are conspicuous.

Left, ASSINIBOIN; right, YANKTONAI INDIAN (Bodmer)

# Sunday, December 1st, 1805

Again we had a cloudy day, and the wind so high from the east, that having ventured in a boat with a view to hunt at some distance, we were obliged to return. We resumed our occupation of dressing leather and mending our old clothes, in which we passed the day. The hunters came in with a report of their having seen two herds of elk, but they could kill nothing, and we therefore again fed upon dried fish. At sunset it began to rain violently, and continued all night, and the next day.

*Monday.* This disagreeable food, pounded fish, has occasioned so much sickness among the men that it is now absolutely necessary to vary it. Three hunters therefore set out, and three more were sent up the Keke-mahke creek in search of fish or birds. Towards evening one of them returned: he had observed great appearances of elk, and even seen two herds of them; but it rained so hard that he could with difficulty get a shot: he had, however, at last killed one, at the distance of six miles from the camp, and a canoe was now sent to bring it. The party from Kekemahke creek were less successful: they had seen no fish, and all the birds, in consequence probably of being much hunted by the Indians, were too shy to be approached.

DECEMBER 2D

*Tuesday.* The wind was from the east, and the morning fair; but, as if a whole day of fine weather was not permitted, towards night it began to rain. Even this transient glimpse of sunshine revived the spirits of the party, who were still more pleased, when the elk killed yesterday was brought into camp. This was the first elk we had killed on the west side of the Rocky mountains, and condemned as we have been to the dried fish, forms a most nourishing food. After eating the marrow of the shank-bones, the squaw chopped them fine, and by boiling, extracted a pint of grease, superior to the tallow itself of the animal. A canoe of eight Indians, who were carrying down wappatoo roots to trade with the Clatsops, stopped at our camp: we bought a few roots for small fish-hooks, and they then left us: but accustomed as we are to the sight, we could not but view with admiration the wonderful dexterity with which they guide their canoes over the most boisterous seas; for though the waves were so high, that before they had gone half a mile the canoe was several times out of sight, they proceeded with the greatest calmness and security. Two of the hunters who set out yesterday had lost their way, and did not return till this evening: they had seen in their ramble great signs of elk, and had killed six elk, which they had butchered and left at a great distance.

DECEMBER 3D

*Wednesday.* A party was sent in the morning, to carry the elk to a bay, some distance below, to which place, if the weather permitted, we would all remove our camp this evening; but the rain which had continued during the night lasted all next day, and was accompanied by so high a wind from the southeast and south, that we dared not risk our canoes on the water. It was high water at eleven o'clock, when the spring-tide rose two feet higher than the common flood-tides. We passed the day around our fires, and as we are so situated that the smoke will not immediately leave the camp, we are very

DECEMBER 4TH

much incommoded, and our eyes injured by it. No news has yet been received from captain Lewis, and we begin to have much uneasiness for his safety.

DECEMBER 5TH  *Thursday.* It rained during the whole night, and this morning the rain and high wind compelled us to remain at our camp. Besides the inconvenience of being thus stopped on our route, we now found that all our stores and bedding are again wet with rain. The high water was at twelve o'clock, and rose two inches beyond that of yesterday. In the afternoon we were rejoiced at the return of captain Lewis, who came in a canoe with three of his men, the other two being left to guard six elk and five deer which they had killed. He had examined the coast, and found a river a short distance below, on which we might encamp during the winter, with a sufficiency of elk for our subsistence within reach. This information was very satisfactory, and we decided on going thither as soon as we could move from the point; but all night and the following day, it rained, and the wind blew hard from the southwest, so that the sea was still too rough for us to proceed. The high-tide of to-day rose thirteen inches higher than it did yesterday, and obliged us to move our camp to a high situation. Here we remained waiting for better weather, till about dark the wind shifted to the north, and the sky was clear. We had now some prospect of being able to leave our situation, and indeed although some rain fell in the course of the night, the next morning was fair.

DECEMBER 7TH  *Saturday.* We therefore loaded our canoes, and proceeded. But the tide was against us, and the waves very high, so that we were obliged to proceed slowly and cautiously. We at length turned a point, and found ourselves in a deep bay; here we landed for breakfast, and were joined by the party sent out three days ago to look for the six elk. In seeking for the elk they had missed their way for a day and a half, and when they reached the place, found the elk so much spoiled that they brought the skins only of four of them. After breakfast we coasted round the bay, which is about four miles across, and receives, besides several small creeks, two rivers called by the Indians, the one Kilhowanakel, the other Netul. We called it Meriwether's bay, from the christian name of captain Lewis, who was no doubt the first white man who surveyed it. As we went along the wind was high from the northeast, and in the middle of the day it rained for two hours, and then cleared off. On reaching the south side of the bay, we ascended the Netul for three miles to the first point of highland on its western bank, and formed our camp in a thick grove of lofty pines, about two hundred yards from the water, and thirty feet above the level of the high tides.

DECEMBER 8TH  *Sunday.* This seemed the most eligible spot for our winter establishment. In order therefore to find a place for making salt, and to examine the country further, captain Clark set out with five men, and pursuing a course south, 60° west, over a dividing ridge, through thick pine timber, much of which had fallen, passed the heads of two small brooks. In the neighbourhood of these the land was swampy and overflowed, and we waded knee-deep till we came to an open ridgy prairie, covered with the plant known on our frontier by the name of Sacacommis. Here is a creek about sixty yards wide, and running towards point Adams; they passed it on a small raft. At this place

340

they discovered a large herd of elk, and after pursuing them for three miles over bad swamps and small ponds, we killed one of them. The agility with which the elk crossed the swamps and bogs, seems almost incredible; as we followed their track, the ground for a whole acre would shake at our tread, and sometimes we sunk to our hips without finding any bottom. Over the surface of these bogs is a species of moss, among which are great numbers of cranberries, and occasionally there rise from the swamp steep and small knobs of earth, thickly covered with pine and laurel. On one of these we halted at night, but it was scarcely large enough to suffer us to lie clear of the water, and had very little dry wood. We succeeded however in collecting enough to make a fire, and having stretched the elk skin to keep off the rain, which still continued, slept till morning when we rose, perfectly wet with rain during the night.

Three men were then sent in pursuit of the elk, while with the other three, captain Clark proceeded westward towards the sea. He passed over three swamps, and then arrived at a creek, which was too deep to ford, and there was no wood to make a raft. He therefore proceeded down it for a short distance, till he found that he was between the forks of a creek. One branch of which he had passed yesterday, turns round towards the southwest to meet another of equal size from the south, and together they form a small river, about seventy yards wide. He returned to the place where he had left the raft, and having crossed proceeded down about a mile, when he met three Indians. They were loaded with fresh salmon which they had taken with a gig, and were now returning to their village on the seacoast, where they invited him to accompany them. He agreed, and they brought out a canoe hid along the banks of the creek. In this they passed over the branch which he had just crossed on a raft, and then carried the canoe a quarter of a mile to the other fork, which they crossed and continued down to the mouth of the

DECEMBER 9TH

river. At this place it makes a great bend, where the river is seventy yards wide; just above, or to the south of which is the village.

We crossed over, and found that it consisted of three houses, inhabited by twelve families of Clatsops. They were on the south exposure of a hill, and sunk about four feet deep into the ground; the walls, roof, and gable-ends being formed of split pine boards; the descent through a small door down a ladder. There are two fires in the middle of the room, and the beds disposed round the walls two or three feet from the fall [floor], so as to leave room under them for their bags, baskets and household articles. The floor itself is covered with mats. Captain Clark was received with much attention. As soon as he entered, clean mats were spread, and fish, berries and roots set before him on small neat platters of rushes. After he had eaten, the men of the other houses came and smoked with him. They all appeared much neater in their persons and diet than Indians generally are, and frequently wash their hands and faces, a ceremony by no means frequent elsewhere. While he was conversing with them, a flock of brant lighted on the water, and he with a small rifle shot one of them at a great distance. They immediately jumped in, and brought it on shore, very much astonished at the shot, which contributed to make them increase their attention. Towards evening it began to rain and blow very violently from the southwest; and captain Clark therefore, determined to remain during the night. When they thought his appetite had returned, an old woman presented him in a bowl, made of light coloured horn, a kind of syrup, pleasant to the taste, and made from a species of berry common in this country, about the size of a cherry, and called by the Indians shelwel: of these berries a bread is also prepared, which being boiled with roots forms a soup, which was served in neat wooden trenchers: this, with some cockles, was his repast.

The men of the village now collected, and began to gamble. The most common game, was one in which one of the company was banker, and played against all the rest. He had a piece of bone, about the size of a large bean, and having agreed with any individual as to the value of the stake, would pass the bone from one hand to the other, with great dexterity, singing at the same time, to divert the attention of his adversary; and then holding it in his hands, his antagonist was challenged to guess in which of them the bone was, and lost or won as he pointed to the right or wrong hand. To this game of hazard they abandoned themselves with great ardour; some times every thing they possess is sacrificed to it, and this evening several of the Indians lost all the beads which they had with them. This lasted for three hours, when captain Clark appearing disposed to sleep, the man who had been most attentive, and whose name was Cuskalah, spread two new mats near the fire, and ordering his wife to retire to her own bed, the rest of the company dispersed at the same time. Captain Clark then lay down, but the violence with which the fleas attacked him, did not leave his rest unbroken, and he rose early.

DECEMBER 10TH    *Tuesday.* The morning was cloudy, with some rain: he walked out on the seashore, and observed the Indians walking up and down the creek and examining the shore: he was at a loss to understand their object, till one of them came to him and explained that they were in search of fish which had been thrown on shore and left by the tide, adding in English, "sturgeon is very good." There is indeed, every reason to suppose, that these Clatsops depend for their subsistence during the winter, chiefly on the fish thus casually thrown on the coast. After amusing himself for some time on the beach, he returned towards the village, and shot on his way two brant. As he came near the village, one of the Indians asked him to shoot a duck about thirty steps distant: he did so, and having accidentally shot off its head, the bird was brought to the village by the Indians, all of whom came round in astonishment: they examined the duck, the musket, and the very small bullet, which were a hundred to the pound, and then exclaimed, "Clouch musquet, wake, commatax musquet" (a good musket, do not understand this kind of

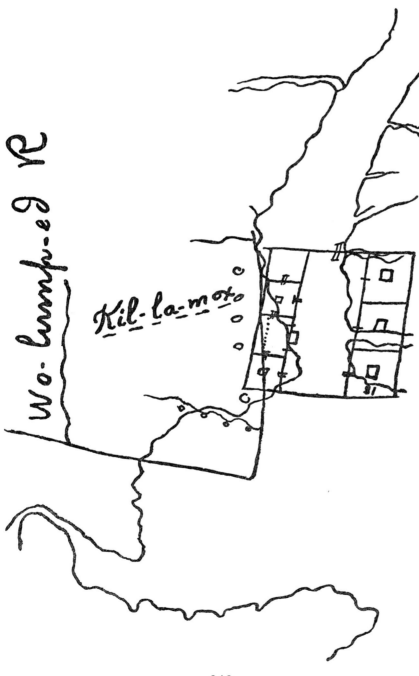

*Captain Clark's plan of Fort Clatsop and vicinity. As can be seen in his sketch of the fort on the next page, the stockade was 50 ft. square. Of the seven rooms, five apparently had their own fireplaces and one had an outside chimney. The gates closing off the 20 x 48 ft. parade ground opened to the south.*

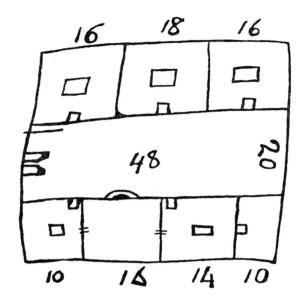

musket). They now placed before him their best roots, fish, and syrup, after which he attempted to purchase a sea-otter skin with some red beads which he happened to have about him; but they declined trading, as they valued none except blue or white beads: he therefore bought nothing but a little berry bread and a few roots in exchange for fish-hooks, and then set out to return by the same route on which he came. He was accompanied by Cuskalah and his brother as far as the third creek, and then proceeded to the camp through a heavy rain. The whole party had been occupied during his absence in cutting down trees to make huts, and in hunting.

DECEMBER 11TH   *Wednesday.* The rain continued last night and the whole of this day. We were, however, all employed in putting up our winter cabins, which we are anxious to finish, as several of the men are beginning to suffer from the excessive dampness: four of them have very violent colds, one has a dysentery, a third has tumours on his legs, and two have been injured by dislocation and straining of their limbs.

DECEMBER 12TH   *Thursday.* We continued to work in the rain at our houses. In the evening there arrived two canoes of Clatsops, among whom was a principal chief, called Comowool. We gave him a medal, and treated his companions with great attention; after which we began to bargain for a small sea-otter skin, some wappatoo roots, and another species of root called shanataque. We readily perceived that they were close dealers, stickled much for trifles, and never closed the bargain until they thought they had the advantage. The wappatoo is dear, as they themselves are obliged to give a high price for it to the Indians above. Blue beads are the articles most in request, the white occupy the next place in their estimation; but they do not value much those of any other colour. We succeeded at last in purchasing their whole cargo for a few fish-hooks and a small sack of Indian tobacco, which we had received from the Shoshonees.

DECEMBER 13TH   The next morning, we treated them to a breakfast on elk meat, of which they seemed very fond, and having purchased from them two skins of the lucervia [loup-cervier, or lynx], and two robes made of the skin of an animal about the size of a cat, they left us. Two hunters returned with the pleasing intelligence of their having killed eighteen elk about six miles off. Our huts begin to rise, for though it rains all day we continue our labours, and are rejoiced to find that the beautiful balsam pine splits into excellent boards, more than two feet in width. In the evening three Indians came in a canoe with provisions and skins for sale, and spent the night with us.

*Saturday.* Again it rained all day, but by working constantly we finished the walls of our huts, and nearly completed a house for our provisions. The constant rains have completely spoiled our last supply of elk; but notwithstanding that scarcely a man has been dry for a great number of days, the sick are recovering. Four men were despatched to guard the elk which were killed yesterday, till a larger party joined them.

*Sunday.* Accordingly, captain Clark with sixteen men set out in three ca- noes, and having rowed for three miles up the river turned up a large creek from the right, and after going three miles further landed about the height of the tide water. The men were then despatched in small parties to bring in the elk, each man returning with a quarter of the animal. In bringing the third and last load, nearly half the men missed their way, and did not return till after night; five of them indeed were not able to find their way at all. It had been cloudy all day, and in the night began to rain, and as we had no cover were obliged to sit up the greater part of the night, for as soon as we lay down the rain would come under us, and compel us to rise.

It was indeed a most uncomfortable situation, but the five men who joined us in the morning had been more unlucky, for in addition to the rain which had poured down upon them all night, they had no fire, and drenched and cold as they were when they reached us, exhibited a most distressing sight. They had left their loads where they slept, and some men were sent after them, while others were despatched after two more elk in another bend of the creek, who after taking these last on board, proceeded to our camp. It rained and hailed during the day, and a high wind from the southeast not only threw down trees as we passed along, but made the river so rough that we proceeded with great risk. We now had the meat house covered, and all our game carefully hung up in small pieces.

*Tuesday.* It rained all night, and this morning there was a high wind, and hail as well as rain fell; and on the top of a mountain about ten miles to the southeast of us we observed some snow. The greater part of our stores is wet, and our leathern tent is so rotten that the slightest touch makes a rent in it, and it will now scarcely shelter a spot large enough for our beds. We were all busy in finishing the inside of the huts. The after part of the day was cool and fair. But this respite was of very short duration, for all night it continued raining and snowing alternately, and in the morning we had snow and hail till twelve o'clock, after which it changed to rain. The air now became cool and disagreeable, the wind high and unsettled, so that being thinly dressed in leather, we were able to do very little on the houses.

*Thursday.* The rain continued all night with short intervals, but the morn- ing was fair and the wind from the southwest. Situated as we are, our only occupation is to work as diligently as we can on our houses, and to watch the changes of the weather, on which so much of our comfort depends. We availed ourselves of this glimpse of sunshine, to send across Meriwether's bay for the boards of an old Indian house; but before the party returned with them, the weather clouded, and we again had hail and rain during the rest of the day. Our only visitors were two Indians who spent a short time with us.

DECEMBER 20TH    *Friday.* A succession of rain and hail during the night. At ten o'clock it cleared off for a short time, but the rain soon recommenced; we now covered in four of our huts; three Indians came in a canoe with mats, roots, and the berries of the sacacommis. These people proceed with a dexterity and finesse in their bargains, which, if they have not learnt from their foreign visitors, it may show how nearly allied is the cunning of savages to the little arts of traffic. They begin by asking double or treble the value of what they have to sell, and lower their demand in proportion to the greater or less degree of ardour or knowledge of the purchaser, who with all his management is not able to procure the article for less than its real value, which the Indians perfectly understand. Our chief medium of trade consists of blue and white beads, files with which they sharpen their tools, fish-hooks, and tobacco: but of all these articles blue beads and tobacco are the most esteemed.

DECEMBER 21ST    *Saturday.* As usual it rained all night and continued without intermission during the day. One of our Indian visitors was detected in stealing a horn spoon, and turned out of the camp. We find that the plant called sacacommis forms an agreeable mixture with tobacco, and we therefore despatched two men to the open lands near the ocean, in order to collect some of it, while the rest continued their work.

DECEMBER 22D    *Sunday.* There was no interval in the rain last night and to-day; so that we cannot go on rapidly with our buildings. Some of the men are indeed quite sick, others have received bruises, and several complain of boils. We discover too, that part of our elk meat is spoiling in consequence of the warmth of the weather, though we have kept a constant smoke under it.

DECEMBER 23D    *Monday.* It continued raining the whole day, with no variation except occasional thunder and hail. Two canoes of Clatsops came to us with various articles for sale; we bought three mats and bags neatly made of flags and rushes, and also the skin of a panther seven feet long, including the tail. For all these we gave six small fish-hooks, a worn-out file, and some pounded fish which had become so soft and mouldy by exposure, that we could not use it: it is, however, highly prized by the Indians of this neighbourhood. Although a very portable and convenient food, the mode of curing seems known, or at least practised only by the Indians near the great falls, and coming from such a distance, has an additional value in the eyes of these people, who are anxious to possess some food less precarious than their ordinary subsistence.

Among these Clatsops was a second chief to whom we gave a medal, and sent some pounded fish to Cuscalah, who could not come to see us, on account of sickness. The next day, however, he came in a canoe with his young brother and two squaws. Having treated captain Clark so kindly at his village we were pleased to see him, and he gave us two mats and a parcel of roots. These we accepted, as it would have been offensive to decline the offer but afterwards two files were demanded in return for the presents, and not being able to spare those articles, we restored the mats and roots. Cuscalah was a little displeased: in the evening however he offered each of us one of the squaws, and even this being declined, Cuscalah as well as the

*Captain Clark's own
journal entry for the
expedition's second
Christmas in the
wilderness.*

*Christmas*
**Wednesday 25th December 1805** 76

at daylight this morning we we awoke by
the discharge of the fire arm of all our party &
a Selute, Shouts and a Song which the whole
party joined in under our windows, after which
they retired to their rooms were Cherefull
all the morning— after brackfast we devid-
ed our tobacco which amounted to 12 carots,
one half of which we gave to the men of the
party who use tobacco, and to those who
doe not use it we make a present of a hand-
-kerchief, The Indians leave us in the evening,
all the party Snugly fixed in their huts— I
recved a present of Capt. L. of a fleece hosrie Shirt
Draws and Socks—, a pr. Mockersons of Whitehouse
a Small Indian basket of Gutherich, two dozen
white weazils tails of the Indian woman, &
Some black root of the Indians before their
Departure— Drewyer informs me that he Saw
a Snake pass across the paarth to day— The
day proved Showery wet and disagreeable.

we would have Spent this day the Nativ-
-ity of Chriet in feasting, had we any thing
either to raise our Spirits or even gratify
our appetites, our Diner Consisted of poor
Elk, So much Spoiled that we eate it thro.
mear necessity, Some Spoiled pounded fish and
a few roots.

whole party of Indians were highly offended: the females particularly
seemed to be much incensed at our indifference about their favours. The
whole stock of meat being now completely spoiled, our pounded fish became again our chief dependence. It had rained constantly all day, but we
still continued working and at last moved into our huts.

*Wednesday.* We were awaked at daylight by a discharge of firearms, which    DECEMBER 25TH
was followed by a song from the men, as a compliment to us on the return

of Christmas, which we have always been accustomed to observe as a day of rejoicing. After breakfast we divided our remaining stock of tobacco, which amounted to twelve carrots, into two parts; one of which we distributed among such of the party as made use of it, making a present of a handkerchief to the others. The remainder of the day was passed in good spirits, though there was nothing in our situation to excite much gaiety. The rain confined us to the house, and our only luxuries in honour of the season, were some poor elk, so much spoiled that we eat it through mere necessity, a few roots, and some spoiled pounded fish.

DECEMBER 26TH   *Thursday.* The next day brought a continuation of rain, accompanied with thunder, and a high wind from the southeast. We were therefore still obliged to remain in our huts, and endeavoured to dry our wet articles before the fire. The fleas which annoyed us near the portage of the great falls, have taken such possession of our clothes, that we are obliged to have a regular search every day through our blankets as a necessary preliminary to sleeping at night. These animals indeed are so numerous, that they are almost a calamity to the Indians of this country. When they have once obtained the mastery of any house it is impossible to expel them, and the Indians have frequently different houses, to which they resort occasionally when the fleas have rendered their permanent residence intolerable; yet in spite of these precautions, every Indian is constantly attended by multitudes of them, and no one comes into our houses without leaving behind him swarms of these tormenting insects.

DECEMBER 27TH   *Friday.* The rain did not cease last night, nor the greater part of the day. In the evening we were visited by Comowool, the chief, and four men of the Clatsop nation, who brought a very timely supply of roots and berries. Among these was one called culwhomo, resembling liquorice in size and taste, and which they roast like a potato; there was also the shanataque, a root of which they are very fond. It is of a black colour, sweet to the taste, and is prepared for eating in a kiln, as the Indians up the Columbia dry the pasheco. These as well as the shellwell berries, they value highly, but were perfectly satisfied with the return we made them, consisting of a small piece of sheepskin, to wear round the chief's head, a pair of earbobs for his son, a small piece of brass, and a little ribbon. In addition to our old enemies the fleas, we observed two mosquitoes, or insects so completely resembling them, that we can perceive no difference in their shape and appearance.

DECEMBER 28TH   *Saturday.* Again it rained during the greater part of last night, and continued all day. Five men were sent out to hunt, and five others despatched to the seaside, each with a large kettle, in order to begin the manufacture of salt. The route to the seacoast is about seven miles in length, in a direction nearly west. Five miles of the distance is through thick wood varied with hills, ravines and swamps, though the land in general possesses a rich black mould. The remaining two miles is formed of open waving prairies of sand, with ridges running parallel to the river, and covered with green grass. The rest of the men were employed in making pickets and gates for our new fort. Although we had no sun, the weather was very warm.

*Sunday.* It rained the whole night, but ceased this morning, and but little rain fell in the course of the day; still the weather was cloudy and the wind high from the southeast. The Clatsop chief and his party left us, after begging for a great number of articles, which, as we could not spare them, we refused except a razor. We were employed all day in picketting the fort: in the evening a young Wahkiacum chief, with four men and two women, arrived with some dressed elk skin and wappatoo for sale. We purchased about a bushel and a half of those roots for some red beads, and small pieces of brass wire and old check. The chief too made us a present of half a bushel more, for which we gave him a medal, and a piece of ribbon, to tie round his hat. These roots are extremely grateful, since our meat has become spoiled, and we were desirous of purchasing the remainder; but the chief would not dispose of any more, as he was on his way to trade with the Clatsops. They remained with us however till the next day, when they were joined by four more of their countrymen, from the Wahkiacum village. These last began by offering us some roots; but as we had now learned that they always expect three or four times as much in return, as the real value of the articles, and are even dissatisfied with that, we declined such dangerous presents.

Towards evening the hunters brought in four elk, and after a long course of abstinence and miserable diet, we had a most sumptuous supper of elk's tongues and marrow. Besides this agreeable repast, the state of the weather had been quite exhilarating. It had rained during the night, but in the morning, though the high wind continued, we enjoyed the fairest and most pleasant weather since our arrival; the sun having shone at intervals, and there being only three showers in the course of the day. By sunset we had completed the fortification, and now announced to the Indians that every day at that hour the gates would be closed, and they must leave the fort and not enter it till sunrise. The Wahkiacums, who had remained with us, and who are very forward in their deportment, complied very reluctantly with this order; but being excluded from our houses, formed a camp near us.

*Tuesday.* As if it were impossible to have twenty-four hours of pleasant weather, the sky last evening clouded, and the rain began and continued through the day. In the morning there came down two canoes, one from the Wahkiacum village, the other contained three men and a squaw of the Skilloot nation. They brought wappatoo, and shanataque roots, dried fish, mats made of flags and rushes, dressed elk skins and tobacco; for which, particularly the skins, they asked a very extravagant price. We purchased some wappatoo, and a little tobacco, very much like that we had seen among the Shoshonees, put up in small neat bags made of rushes. These we obtained in exchange for a few articles, among which fish-hooks are the most esteemed. One of the Skilloots brought a gun which wanted some repair, and having put it in order, we received from him a present of about a peck of wappatoo; we then gave him a piece of sheep skin and blue cloth, to cover the lock, and he very thankfully offered a further present of roots. There is, in fact, an obvious superiority in these Skilloots over the Wahkiacums, who are intrusive, thievish, and impertinent. Our new regulations, however, and the appearance of the sentinel, have improved the behaviour of all our Indian visitors. They left the fort before sunset, even without being ordered.

Besides the fleas, we observe a number of insects in motion to-day. Snakes are yet to be seen; snails too, without covers, are common. On the rivers, and along the shores of Meriwether's bay, are many kinds of large water fowls, but at this period they are excessively wild. The early part of the night was fair.

## Wednesday, January 1st, 1806

We were awaked at an early hour, by a discharge of a volley of small arms, to salute the new year. This is the only mode of doing honour to the day which our situation permits, for though we have reason to be gayer than we were at Christmas, our only dainties are the boiled elk and wappatoo, enlivened by draughts of pure water.

We were visited by a few Clatsops, who came by water, bringing roots and berries for sale. Among this nation we have observed a man about twenty-five years old, of a much lighter complexion than the Indians generally: his face was even freckled, and his hair long, and of a colour inclining to red. He was in habits and manners perfectly Indian; but, though he did not speak a word of English, he seemed to understand more than the others of his party; and, as we could obtain no account of his origin, we concluded that one of his parents, at least, must have been completely white. These Indians stayed with us during the night, and left the fort next morning, having disposed of their cargo for fishing-hooks and other trifling articles.

JANUARY 2D     *Thursday*. The hunters brought in two elk, and we obtained from the traps an otter. This animal, as well as the beaver and the raccoon, are in plenty near the seacoast, and along the small creeks and rivers as high as the grand rapids, and in this country possess an extremely good fur.

The birds which most strike our attention are the large as well as the small or whistling swan, the sandhill crane, the large and small geese, cormorants, brown and white brant, duck and mallard, the canvass and several other species of ducks. There is also a small crow, the blue crested corvus, and the smaller corvus with a white breast, the little brown wren, a large brown sparrow, the bald eagle, and the beautiful buzzard [condor] of the Columbia. All these wild fowl continue with us, though they are not in such numbers as on our first arrival in this neighbourhood.

JANUARY 3D     *Friday*. At eleven o'clock we were visited by our neighbour the Tia, or chief Comowool, who is also called Coone, and six Clatsops. Besides roots, and berries, they brought for sale three dogs and some fresh blubber. Having been so long accustomed to live on the flesh of dogs, the greater part of us have acquired a fondness for it, and our original aversion for it is overcome, by reflecting that while we subsisted on that food we were fatter, stronger, and in general enjoyed better health than at any period since leaving the buffalo country eastward of the mountains. The blubber, which is esteemed by the Indians an excellent food, has been obtained, they tell us, from their neighbours the Killamucks, a nation who live on the seacoast to the southeast, and near one of whose villages a whale had recently been thrown and foundered. Three of the hunters who had been despatched on the *28th*, returned about dark; they had been fifteen miles up the river to the east of us, which falls into Meriwether's bay, and had hunted a considerable distance to the east; but they had not been able to kill more than a single deer, and a few fowls, scarcely sufficient for their subsistence; an incident which teaches us the necessity of keeping out several parties of hunters, in order to procure a supply against any exigency.

*Saturday.* Comowool left us this morning with his party, highly pleased with a present of an old pair of satin breeches. The hunters were all sent in different directions, and we are now becoming more anxious for their success since our store of wappatoo is all exhausted.

*Sunday.* Two of the five men who had been despatched to make salt re- turned. They had carefully examined the coast, but it was not till the fifth day after their departure that they discovered a convenient situation for their manufacture. At length they formed an establishment about fifteen miles southwest of the fort, near some scattered houses of the Clatsop and Killamuck nation, where they erected a comfortable camp, and had killed a stock of provisions. The Indians had treated them very kindly, and made them a present of the blubber of the whale, some of which the men brought home. It was white and not unlike the fat of pork, though of a coarser and more spongy texture, and on being cooked was found to be tender and palatable, and in flavour resembling the beaver. The men also brought with them a gallon of the salt, which was white, fine, and very good, but not so strong as the rock salt common to the western parts of the United States. It proves to be a most agreeable addition to our food, and as the saltmakers can manufacture three or four quarts a day, we have a prospect of a very plentiful supply.

The appearance of the whale seemed to be a matter of importance to all the neighbouring Indians, and as we might be able to procure some of it for ourselves, or at least purchase blubber from the Indians, a small parcel of merchandise was prepared, and a party of the men held in readiness to set out in the morning. As soon as this resolution was known, Chaboneau and his wife requested that they might be permitted to accompany us. The poor woman stated very earnestly that she had travelled a great way with us to see the great water, yet she had never been down to the coast, and now that this monstrous fish was also to be seen, it seemed hard that she should not be permitted to see either the ocean or the whale. So reasonable a request could not be denied; they were therefore suffered to accompany captain Clark, who after an early breakfast set out with twelve men in two canoes.

*Monday.* He proceeded down the Netul into Meriwether bay, intending to go to the Clatsop town, and there procure a guide through the creeks, which there was reason to believe communicated not only with the bay, but with a small river running towards the sea, near where our saltmakers were encamped. Before however he could reach the Clatsop village, the high wind from the northwest compelled him to put into a small creek. He therefore resolved to attempt the passage without a guide, and proceeded up the creek three miles, to some high open land where he found a road. He therefore left the canoes, and followed the path over three deep marshes to a pond about a mile long, and two hundred yards wide. He kept on the left of this pond, and at length came to the creek which he had crossed on a raft, when he had visited Cuscalah's village on the ninth of December. He proceeded down it, till he found a small canoe, fit to hold three persons, in which the whole party crossed the creek. Here they saw a herd of elk, and the men were divided into small parties, and hunted them till after dark, when they met again at the forks of the river. Three of the elk were wounded, but night prevented their taking more than one, which was brought to the camp, and cooked with some sticks of pine which had drifted down the creeks. The weather was beautiful, the sky clear, the moon shone brightly, a circumstance the more agreeable as this is the first fair evening we have enjoyed for two months.

*Two swords, a bludgeon, and a paddle, sketched in Captain*
*Lewis's diary.*

TUESDAY, JANUARY 7TH, 1806   There was a frost this morning. We rose early, and taking eight pounds of flesh, which were all the remains of the elk, proceeded up the south fork of the creek. At the distance of two miles we found a pine tree, which had been felled by one of our saltmakers, and on which we crossed the deepest part of the creek, and waded through the rest. We then went over an open ridgy prairie, three quarters of a mile, to the sea-beach; after following which for three miles, we came to the mouth of a beautiful river, with a bold, rapid current, eighty-five yards wide, and three feet deep, in its shallowest crossings. On its northeast side are the remains of an old village of Clatsops, inhabited by only a single family, who appeared miserably poor and dirty. We gave a man two fish-hooks, to ferry the party over the river, which, from the tribe on its banks, we called Clat-sop river. The creek, which we had passed on a tree, approaches this river within about an hundred yards, and by means of a portage, supplies a communication with the villages near Point Adams. After going on for two miles, we found the saltmakers encamped near four houses of Clatsops and Killamucks, who, though poor, dirty, and covered with fleas, seemed kind and well disposed.

We persuaded a young Indian, by a present of a file, and a promise of some other articles, to guide us to the spot where the whale lay. He led us for two and a half miles over the round slippery stones at the foot of a high hill projecting into the sea, and then suddenly stopping, and uttering the word "peshack" (or bad), explained by signs that we could no longer follow the coast, but must cross the mountain. This promised to be a most laborious undertaking, for the side is nearly perpendicular, and the top lost in clouds. He, however, followed an Indian path which wound along as much as possible, but still the ascent was so steep, that at one place we drew ourselves for about an hundred feet by means of bushes and roots. At length, after two hours' labour, we reached the top of the mountain, where we looked down with astonishment on the prodigious height of ten or twelve hundred feet, which we had ascended. Immediately below us, in the face of this precipice, is a stratum of white earth, used, as our guide informed us, as a paint by the neighbouring Indians. It obviously contains argile, and resembles the earth of which the French porcelain is made, though whether it contains silex or magnesia, or in what proportions, we could not observe. We were here met by fourteen Indians, loaded with oil and blubber, the spoils of the whale, which they were carrying in very heavy burdens, over this rough mountain. On leaving them, we proceeded over a bad road till night, when we encamped on a small run: we were all much fatigued, but the weather was pleasant, and, for the first time since our arrival here, an entire day has passed without rain.

*Wednesday.* In the morning we set out early and proceeded to the top of the mountain, the highest point of which is an open spot facing the ocean. It is situated about thirty miles southeast of cape Disappointment, and projects nearly two and a half miles into the sea. Here one of the most delightful views in nature presents itself. Immediately in front is the ocean, which breaks with fury on the coast, from the rocks of cape Disappointment as far as the eye can discern to the northwest, and against the highlands and irregular piles of rock which diversify the shore to the southeast. To this

Fort Clatsop. 1806.

Diary of the weather for the month of January.

| Day of the month | aspect of the weather at O rise | Wind at O rise | Weather at 4 o'o'k P.M. | Wind at 4 o'k P.M. | Remarks |
|---|---|---|---|---|---|
| 1st | c a r | S. W. | r a c | S. W. | sun visible for a few minutes about 11 A. |
| 2d | c a r | S. W. | r | S. W. | |
| 3d | c a r h | S W | c a r h f | S. W. | the sun visible for a few minutes only |
| 4th | c a r h | S W | r a f o r | S. E | the sun visible about 2 hours |
| 5th | r | S E | r | S. E | |
| 6th | c a r | S E | f | E | the snow about 5 hours this evening & it continued for during the night |
| 7th | f | N. E | c a f | E | it clouded up just about sun set, but but shortly after became fair |
| 8th | f | N. E | c a f | S. E | lost my ? M. obs.t for equal altitude |
| 9th | f | S. W. | c a f | S. W | began to rain at 10 P.M. and continued all night |
| 10th | f. a r | S. W. | c a f | S. W | |
| 11th | c | S. W. | c a r | S. W. | |
| 12th | f a c | N. W | c | N. W | cool this morning but no ice nor frost at midday sand flies and insects in motion |
| 13th | r | S. W. | r | S. W. | |
| 14th | f a r | N. E | c a f | S. | |
| 15th | r a c a | S E | r a r | S. | saw several insects, weather warm ... |
| 16th | r a r | S. W | r a r | S W | rained this morning ... incessantly all night |
| 17th | c a r | S. W | c | S W | rained incessantly all night, insects in motion |
| 18th | r a r | S. W | c a r | S W | rained very hard last night |
| 19th | c a r | S | c a r | S W | rained the greater part of last night |
| 20th | r a r | S. W | r a r | S W | rain greater part of the night wind had |
| 21st | c a r | S. W | c a r | S W | wind hard this morning continued all day |
| 22d | r a r | S W | c a r | S W | wind violent last night & this morning |
| 23d | c a r h | S W | c a f | S. W. | the sun shone about 2 h in the fore noon |
| 24th | c a r | S E | c a r h | E | this morning the snow covered the ground and snow more than anything we have had but no ice |
| 25th | c a r h | N. E | c a r h | N E | the ground covered with snow this morning ... inch deep |
| 26th | c a r h | N. E | c a s | N E | ... this morning the snow more ... deep |
| 27th | f a s | N E | f | N E | |
| 28th | f | N E | f | N E | frost so could water in a vessel exposed during the night freizes 3/4 of an inch only |
| 29th | f | N E | f | N E | |
| 30th | s. a. s | N. | c a s | W | the weather by no means as cold as it has been snow fell about one inch deep |
| 31st | f a c | N E | f | N E | this morning is pleasant ... |

boisterous scene, the Columbia, with its tributary waters, widening into bays as it approaches the ocean, and studded on both sides with the Chinnook and Clatsop villages, forms a charming contrast; while immediately beneath our feet, are stretched the rich prairies, enlivened by three beautiful streams, which conduct the eye to small lakes at the foot of the hills. We stopped to enjoy the romantic view from this place, which we distinguished by the name of Clark's Point of View, and then followed our guide down the mountain. The descent was steep and dangerous: in many places the hill sides, which are formed principally of yellow clay, has been washed by the late rains, and is now slipping into the sea, in large masses of fifty and an hundred acres. In other parts, the path crosses the rugged perpendicular rocks which overhang the sea, into which a false step would have precipitated us. The mountains are covered with a very thick growth of timber, chiefly pine and fir; some of which, near Clark's Point of View, perfectly sound and solid, rise to the height of two hundred and ten feet, and are from eight to twelve in diameter. Intermixed is the white cedar, or arbor vitae, and a small quantity of black alder, two or three feet thick, and sixty or seventy in height.

At length we reached a single house, the remains of an old Killamuck village, situated among some rocks, in a bay immediately on the coast. We then continued for two miles along the sand beach; and after crossing a creek, eighty yards in width, near which are five cabins, reached the place where the waves had thrown the whale on shore. The animal had been placed between two Killamuck villages, and such had been their industry, that there now remained nothing more than the skeleton, which we found to be one hundred and five feet in length. Captain Clark then returned to the village of five huts, on the creek, to which he gave the name of Ecola, or Whale creek. The natives were all busied in boiling the blubber, in a large square trough of wood, by means of heated stones, and preserving the oil, thus extracted, in bladders and the entrails of the whale. The refuse of the blubber, which still contained a portion of oil, are hung up in large flitches, and when wanted for use, are warmed on a wooden spit before the fire, and eaten either alone, or dipped in oil, or with roots of the rush and shanataque. These Killamucks, though they had great quantities, parted with it reluctantly, and at such high prices, that our whole stock of merchandise was exhausted in the purchase of about three hundred pounds of blubber, and a few gallons of oil. With these we set out to return; and having crossed Ecola creek, encamped on its bank, where there was abundance of fine timber.

We were soon joined by the men of the village, with whom we smoked, and who gave us all the information they possessed, relative to their country. These Killamucks are part of a much larger nation of the same name, and they now reside chiefly in four villages, each at the entrance of a creek, all of which fall into a bay on the southwest coast; that at which we now are, being the most northern, and at the distance of about forty-five miles southeast of Point Adams. The rest of the nation are scattered along the coast, and on the banks of a river, which, as we found it in their delineations, we called Killamuck's river, emptying itself in the same direction. During the salmon season they catch great quantities of that fish, in the small creeks, and when they fail, their chief resource was the sturgeon and other fish stranded along the coast. The elk were very numerous in the mountains, but they could not procure many of them with their arrows; and their principal communication with strangers, was by means of the Killamuck river, up which they passed to the Shocatilcum (or Columbia) to trade for wappatoo roots. In their dress, appearance, and indeed every circumstance of life, they differ very little from the Chinnooks, Clatsops, and other nations in the neighbourhood. The chief variation we have observed is in the manner of burying the dead; the bodies being secured in an oblong box of plank, which is placed in an open canoe, lying on the ground, with a paddle, and other small articles of the deceased by his side.

Whilst smoking with the Indians, captain Clark was surprised about ten o'clock by a loud shrill outcry from the opposite village; on hearing which, all the Indians immediately started up to cross the creek, and the guide informed him that some one had been killed. On examination, one of the men was discovered to be absent, and a guard despatched, who met him crossing the creek in great haste. An Indian belonging to another band, and who happened to be with the Killamucks that evening, had treated him with much kindness, and walked arm in arm with him to a tent where our man found a Chinnook squaw, who was an old acquaintance. From the conversation and manner of the stranger, this woman discovered that his object was to murder the white man, for the sake of the few articles on his person, and when he rose, and pressed our man to go to another tent where they would find something better to eat, she held M'Neal by the blanket; not knowing her object, he freed himself from her, and was going on with his pretended friend, when she ran out and gave the shriek which brought the men of the village over, and the stranger ran off before M'Neal knew what had occasioned the alarm.

JANUARY 9TH  *Thursday*. The morning was fine, the wind from the northeast; and having divided our stock of the blubber, we began at sunrise to retread our steps, in order to reach fort Clatsop, at the distance of thirty-five miles. We met several parties of Indians on their way to trade for blubber and oil with the Killamucks; (our route lay across the same mountains which we had already passed) we also overtook a party returning from the village, and could not but regard with astonishment the heavy loads which the women carry over these fatiguing and dangerous paths. As one of the women was descending a steep part of the mountain, her load slipped from her back, and she stood holding it by a strap with one hand, and with the other supporting herself by a bush: captain Clark being near her, undertook to replace the load, and found it almost as much as he could lift, and above one hundred pounds in weight. Loaded as they were, they kept pace with us, till we reached the saltmakers' tents, where we passed the night, while they continued their route.

JANUARY 10TH  *Friday*. We proceeded across Clatsop river, to the place where we had left our canoes; and as the tide was coming in, immediately embarked for the fort, at which place we arrived about ten o'clock at night. During their absence, the men had been occupied in hunting and dressing skins, but in this they were not very successful, as the deer have become scarce, and are, indeed, seen chiefly near the prairies and open grounds, along the coast.

This morning, however, there came to the fort twelve Indians, in a large canoe. They are of the Cathlamah nation, our nearest neighbours above, on the south side of the river. The tia, or chief, whose name was Shahawacap, having been absent on a hunting excursion, as we passed his village, had never yet seen us, and we therefore showed him the honours of our country, as well as our reduced finances would permit. We invested him with a small medal, and received a present of Indian tobacco and a basket of wappatoo in return, for which we gave him a small piece of our tobacco, and thread for a fishing net. They had brought dried salmon, wappatoo, dogs, and mats made of rushes and flags: but we bought only some dogs and wappatoo. These Cathlamahs speak the same language as the Chinnooks and Clatsops, whom they also resemble in dress and manners.

*Saturday*. A party was sent out to bring in some elk killed yesterday, and JANUARY 11TH several were despatched after our Indian canoe, which drifted away last night; but, though the whole neighbourhood was diligently searched, we were unable to find it. This is a serious loss, as she is much superior to our own canoes, and so light that four men can carry her readily without fatigue, though she will carry from ten to twelve hundred pounds, besides a crew of four. In the evening the Cathlamahs left us, on their way to barter their wappatoo with the Clatsops, for some blubber and oil, which these last have procured from the Killamucks, in exchange for beads and other articles.

*Sunday*. Our meat is now becoming scarce; we, therefore, determined to JANUARY 12TH jerk it, and issue it in small quantities, instead of dividing it among the four messes, and leaving to each the care of its own provisions; a plan by which much is lost, in consequence of the improvidence of the men. Two hunters had been despatched in the morning, and one of them, Drewyer, had before evening, killed seven elk. We should scarcely be able to subsist, were it not for the exertions of this most excellent hunter. The game is scarce, and nothing is now to be seen, except elk, which to almost all the men, are very difficult to be procured: but Drewyer, who is the offspring of a Canadian Frenchman, and an Indian woman, has passed his life in the woods, and unites, in a wonderful degree, the dexterous aim of the frontier huntsman, with the intuitive sagacity of the Indian, in pursuing the faintest tracks through the forest. All our men, however, have indeed, become so expert with the rifle, that we are never under apprehensions as to food, since, whenever there is game of any kind, we are almost certain of procuring it.

*Monday*. Captain Lewis took all the men who could be spared, and brought JANUARY 13TH in the seven elk, which they had found untouched by the wolves, of which there are a few in the neighbourhood. The last of the candles which we brought with us being exhausted, we now began to make others of elk tallow.

From all that we have seen and learnt of the Chinnooks, we have been induced to estimate the nation at about twenty-eight houses, and four hundred souls. They reside chiefly along the banks of a river, to which we gave the same name; and which, running parallel to the seacoast, waters a low country with many stagnant ponds, and then empties itself into Haley's bay. The wild fowl of these ponds, and the elk and deer of the neighbourhood, furnish them with occasional luxuries; but their chief subsistence is derived from the salmon and other fish, which are caught in the small streams, by means of nets and gigs, or thrown on shore by the violence of the tide. To these are added some roots, such as the wild liquorice, which is the most common, the shanataque, and the wappatoo, brought down the river by the traders.

The men are low in stature, rather ugly, and ill made: their legs being small and crooked, their feet large, and their heads, like those of the women, flattened in a most disgusting manner. These deformities are in part concealed by robes made of sea-otter, deer, elk, beaver, or fox skins. They also employ in their dress, robes of the skin of a cat peculiar to this country, and of another animal of the same size, which is light and durable, and sold at a high price by the Indians, who bring it from above. In addition to these are worn blankets, wrappers of red, blue, or spotted cloth, and some old sailors' clothes, which were very highly prized. The greater part of the men have guns, powder, and ball.

The women have, in general, handsome faces, but are low and disproportioned, with small feet and large legs and thighs, occasioned, probably, by strands of beads, or various strings, drawn so tight above the ankles, as to prevent the circulation of the blood. Their dress, like that of the Wahkiacums, consists of a short robe, and a tissue of cedar bark. Their hair hangs loosely down the shoulders and back; and their ears, neck, and wrists are ornamented with blue beads. Another decoration which is very highly prized, consists of figures made by puncturing the arms or legs; and on the arm of one of the squaws, we observed the name of J. Bowman, executed in the same way.

In language, habits, and in almost every other particular, they resemble the Clatsops, Cathlamahs, and indeed all the people near the mouth of the Columbia. They, however, seem to be inferior to their neighbours in honesty as well as spirit. No ill treatment or indignity, on our part, seems to excite any feeling, except fear; nor, although better provided than their neighbours with arms, have they enterprise enough to use them advantageously against the animals of the forest, nor offensively against their neighbours; who owe their safety more to the timidity than the forbearance of the Chinnooks. We had heard instances of pilfering whilst we were amongst them, and therefore had a general order, excluding them from our encampment; so that whenever an Indian wished to visit us, he began by calling out "No Chinnook." It may be probable that this first impression left a prejudice against them, since when we were among the Clatsops, and other tribes at the mouth of the Columbia, the Indians had less opportunity of stealing, if they were so disposed.

JANUARY 14TH  *Tuesday*, we were employed in jerking the meat of the elk, and searching for one of the canoes which had been carried off by the tide last night. Having found it, we now had three of them drawn up out of reach of the water, and the other secured by a strong cord, so as to be ready for any emergency.

After many inquiries and much observation, we are at length enabled to obtain a connected view of the nations, who reside along the coast, on both sides of the Columbia. To the south, our personal observation has not extended beyond the Killamucks; but we obtained from those who were acquainted with the seacoast, a list of the Indian tribes, in the order in which they succeed each other, to a considerable distance.

The first nation to the south are the Clatsops, who reside on the southern side of the bay, and along the seacoast, on both sides of Point Adams. They are represented as the remains of a much larger nation; but about four years ago, a disorder, to which till then they were strangers, but which seems, from their description, to have been the small-pox, destroyed four chiefs, and several hundreds of the nation. These are deposited in canoes, a few miles below us on the bay, and the survivors do not number more than fourteen houses, and about two hundred souls.

Next to them along the southeast coast, is a much larger nation, the Killamucks, who number fifty houses, and a thousand souls. Their first establishment are the four huts at the mouth of Ecola creek, thirty-five miles from Point Adams; and two miles below are a few more huts; but the principal town is situated twenty miles lower, at the entrance of a creek, called Nielee, into the bay, which we designate by the name of Killamucks bay. Into the same bay empties a second creek, five miles further, where is a Killamuck village, called Kilherhurst; at two miles a third creek, and a town called Kilherner; and at the same distance a town called *Chishuck*, at the mouth of Killamuck river. Towerquotton and *Chucktin*, are the names of two other towns, situated on creeks which empty into the bottom of the bay, the last of which is seventy miles from Point Adams. The Killamuck river is about one hundred yards wide, and very rapid; but having no perpendicular fall, is the great avenue for trade. There are two small villages of Killamucks settled above its mouth, and the whole trading part of the tribe ascend it, till by a short portage, they carry their canoes over to the Columbian valley, and descend the Multnomah to Wappatoo island. Here they purchase roots, which they carry down the Chockalilum or Columbia; and, after trafficking with the tribes on its banks for the various articles which they require, either return up the Columbia, or cross over through the country of the Clatsops. This trade, however, is obviously little more than a loose and irregular barter, on a very small scale; for the materials for commerce are so extremely scanty and precarious, that the stranding of a whale was an important commercial incident, which interested all the adjoining country. The Killamucks have little peculiar, either in character or manners, and resemble, in almost every particular, the Clatsops and Chinnooks.

Adjoining the Killamucks, and in a direction S. S. E. are the Lucktons, a small tribe inhabiting the seacoast. They speak the same language as the Killamucks, but do not belong to the same nation. The same observation applies to the Kahunkle nation, their immediate neighbours, who are supposed to consist of about four hundred souls, the Lickawis, a still more numerous nation, who have a large town of eight hundred souls; the Youkone nation, who live in very large houses, and number seven hundred souls; the Necketo nation, of the same number of persons; the Ulseah nation, a small town of one hundred and fifty souls; the Youitts, a tribe who live in a small town, containing not more than one hundred and fifty souls; the Shiastuckle nation, who have a large town of nine hundred souls; the Killawats nation of five hundred souls collected into one large town.

With this last nation ends the language of the Killamucks: and the coast, which then turns towards the southwest, is occupied by nations whose languages vary from that of the Killamucks, and from each other. Of these, the first in order are:

The Cookoooose, a large nation of one thousand five hundred souls, inhabiting the shore of the Pacific and the neighbouring mountains. We have seen several of this nation who were taken prisoners by the Clatsops and Killamucks. Their complexion was much fairer than that of the Indians near the mouth of the Columbia, and their heads were not flattened.

Next to these are the Shalalahs, of whom we know nothing, except their numbers, which are computed at twelve hundred souls. Then follow the Luckasos, of about the same number, and the Hannakalals, whom we estimate at six hundred souls.

This is the extent of the Indian information, and judging, as we can do, with considerable accuracy from the number of sleeps, or days journey, the distance which these tribes occupy along the coast, may be estimated at three hundred and sixty miles.

On the north of the Columbia, we have already seen the Chinnooks, of four hundred souls, along the shores of Haley's bay, and the low grounds on Chinnook river. Their nearest neighbours to the northeast are the Killax-thokle, a small nation on the coast, of not more than eight houses, and a hundred souls.

To these succeed the Chilts, who reside above Point Lewis, and who are estimated at seven hundred souls, and thirty-eight houses. Of this nation, we saw, transiently, a few among the Chinnooks, from whom they did not appear to differ. Beyond the Chilts we have seen none of the northwest Indians, and all that we learnt, consisted of an enumeration of their names and numbers.

The nations next to the Chilts, are: the Clamoitomish, of twelve houses, and two hundred and sixty souls; the Potoashees, of ten houses, and two hundred souls; the Pailsk, of ten houses, and two hundred souls; the Quinults, of sixty houses, and one thousand souls; the Chillates, of eight houses, and one hundred and fifty souls; the Calasthorte, of ten houses, and two hundred souls; the Quinnechant, consisting of two thousand souls.

A particular detail of the characters, manners, and habits of the tribes, must be left to some future adventurers, who may have more leisure and a better opportunity than we had to accomplish this object. Those who first visit the ground, can only be expected to furnish sketches rude and imperfect.

JANUARY 15TH    *Wednesday.* Two hunting parties intended setting out this morning, but they were prevented by incessant rain, which confined us all to the fort.

The Chinnooks, Clatsops, and most of the adjoining nations dispose of the dead in canoes. For this purpose a scaffold is erected, by fixing perpendicularly in the ground four long pieces of split timber. These are placed two by two just wide enough apart to admit the canoe, and sufficiently long to support its two extremities. The boards are connected by a bar of wood run through them at the height of six feet, on which is placed a small canoe containing the body of the deceased, carefully wrapped in a robe of dressed skins, with a paddle, and some articles belonging to the deceased, by his side. Over this canoe is placed one of a larger size, reversed, with its gunwale resting on the crossbars, so as to cover the body completely. One or more large mats of rushes or flags are then rolled round the canoes, and the whole secured by cords usually made of the bark of the white cedar. On these crossbars are hung different articles of clothing, or culinary utensils. The method practised by the Killamucks differs somewhat from this; the body being deposited in an oblong box, of plank, which, with the paddle, and other articles, is placed in a canoe, resting on the ground.

With the religious opinions of these people we are but little acquainted, since we understand their language too imperfectly to converse on a subject so abstract; but it is obvious, from the different deposits which they place by their dead, that they believe in a future state of existence. [This fact is much too equivocal to warrant an inference so important. These deposits might have been intended for nothing more than the testimonials of surviving affection. Amongst those savages, where the language was better understood, it does not appear that the Indians intended any thing more by such sacrifices than to testify their reverence for the dead.—*Editor.*]

*Thursday.* To-day we finished curing our meat, and having now a plentiful supply of elk, and salt, and our houses dry and comfortable, we wait patiently for the moment of resuming our journey.

  The implements used in hunting, by the Clatsops, Chinnooks, and other neighbouring nations, are the gun, bow and arrow, deadfall, pits, snares, and spears or gigs. The guns are generally old American or British muskets repaired for this trade; and although there are some good pieces among them, they are constantly out of order, as the Indians have not been sufficiently accustomed to arms to understand the management of them. The powder is kept in small japanned tin flasks, in which the traders sell it; and when the ball or shot fails, they make use of gravel or pieces of metal from their pots, without being sensible of the injury done to their guns. These arms are reserved for hunting elk, and the few deer and bears in this neighbourhood; but as they have no rifles, they are not very successful hunters. The most common weapon is the bow and arrow, with which every man is provided, even though he carries a gun, and which is used in every kind of hunting. The bow is extremely neat, and being very thin and flat, possesses great elasticity. It is made of the heart of the white cedar, about two feet and a half in length, two inches wide at the centre, whence it tapers to the width of half an inch at the extremities; and the back is covered with the sinews of elk, fastened on by means of a glue made from the sturgeon. The string is formed of the same sinews. The arrow generally consists of two parts; the first is about twenty inches long, and formed of light white pine, with the feather at one end, and at the other a circular hole, which receives the second part, formed of some harder wood, and about five inches long, and secured in its place by means of sinews. The barb is either stone, or else of iron or copper, in which latter place, the angle is more obtuse than any we have seen. If, as sometimes happens, the arrow is formed of a single piece, the whole is of a more durable wood, but the form just described is preferred; because, as much of the game consists of wild fowl, on the ponds, it is desirable that they should be constructed so as to float, if they fall into the water. These arrows are kept in a quiver of elk or young bear skin, opening not at the ends, as the common quivers, but at the sides; which, for those who hunt in canoes, is much more convenient. These weapons are not, however, very powerful, for many of the elk we kill have been wounded with them; and, although the barb with the small end of the arrows remain, yet the flesh closes, and the animal suffers no permanent injury. The deadfalls and snares are used in taking the wolf, the raccoon, and the fox, of which there are, however, but few in this country. The spear or gig employed in pursuit of the sea-otter (which they call spuck), the common otter, and

beaver, consists of two points of barbs, and is like those already described, as common among the Indians on the upper part of the Columbia. The pits are chiefly for the elk, and are therefore usually large and deep cubes of twelve or fourteen feet in depth, and are made by the side of some fallen tree lying across the path frequented by the elk. They are covered with slender boughs and moss, and the elk either sinks into it as he approaches the tree, or in leaping over the tree, falls into the pit on the other side.

JANUARY 17TH    *Friday.* Comowool and seven other Clatsops spent the day with us. He made us a present of some roots and berries, and in return we gave him an awl and some thread, which he wanted for the purpose of making a net. We were not able to purchase any more of their provisions, the prices being too high for our exhausted stock of merchandise. One of the Indians was dressed in three very elegant skins of the sea-otter: for these we were very desirous of trafficking; but he refused every exchange except that of blue beads, of which he asked six fathom for each skin, and as we had only four fathom left, he would not accept for the remaining two, either a knife, or any quantity of beads of another sort.

In fishing, the Clatsops, Chinnooks and other nations near this place employ the common straight net, the scooping or dipping net with a long handle, the gig, and the hook and line. The first is of different lengths and depths, and used in taking salmon, char, and trout, in the deep inlets among the marshy grounds, and the mouths of deep creeks. The scooping net is used for small fish in the spring and summer season; and in both kinds the net is formed of silk grass, or the bark of white cedar. The gig is used at all seasons, and for all kinds of fish they can procure with it; so too is the hook and line, of which the line is made of the same material as the net, and the hook generally brought by the traders; though before the whites came, they made hooks out of two small pieces of bone, resembling the European hook, but with a much more acute angle, where the two pieces were joined.

JANUARY 18TH    *Saturday.* We were all occupied in dressing skins, and preparing clothes for our journey homewards.

The houses in this neighbourhood are all large wooden buildings, varying in length from twenty to sixty feet, and from fourteen to twenty in width. They are constructed in the following manner. Two posts of split timber or more, agreeably to the number of partitions, are sunk in the ground, above which they rise to the height of fourteen or eighteen feet. They are hollowed at the top, so as to receive the ends of a round beam or pole, stretching from one to the other, and forming the upper point of the roof for the whole extent of the building. On each side of this range is placed another, which forms the eaves of the house, and is about five feet high; but as the building is often sunk to the depth of four or five feet, the eaves come very near the surface of the earth. Smaller pieces of timber are now extended by pairs, in the form of rafters, from the lower to the upper beam, where they are attached at both ends with cords of cedar bark. On these rafters two or three ranges of small poles are placed horizontally, and se cured in the same way with strings of cedar bark. The sides are now made with a range of wide boards, sunk a small distance into the ground, with the upper ends projecting above the poles at the eaves, to which they are secured by a beam passing outside, parallel with the eave-poles, and tied by cords of cedar bark passing through holes made in the boards at certain distances. The gable ends and partitions are formed in the same way, being fastened by beams on the outside, parallel to the rafters. The roof is then covered with a double range of thin boards, except an aperture of two or three feet in the centre, for the smoke to pass through. The entrance is by a small hole, cut out of the boards, and just large enough to admit the body.

The very largest houses only are divided by partitions, for though three or four families reside in the same room, there is quite space enough for all of them. In the centre of each room is a space six or eight feet square, sunk to the depth of twelve inches below the rest of the floor, and enclosed by four pieces of square timber. Here they make the fire, for which purpose pine bark is generally preferred. Around this fireplace, mats are spread, and serve as seats during the day, and very frequently as beds at night; there is however a more permanent bed made, by fixing, in two or sometimes three sides of the room, posts reaching from the roof down to the ground, and at the distance of four feet from the wall. From these posts to the wall itself, one or two ranges of boards are placed so as to form shelves, on which they either sleep, or where they stow away their various articles of merchandise. The uncured fish is hung in the smoke of their fires, as is also the flesh of the elk, when they are fortunate enough to procure any, which is but rarely.

*Sunday.* This morning we sent out two parties of hunters in different directions. Soon after we were visited by two Clatsop men and a woman, who brought several articles to trade: we purchased a small quantity of train oil for a pair of brass armbands, and succeeded in obtaining a sea-otter skin, for which we gave our only remaining four fathoms of blue beads, the same quantity of white ones, and a knife: we gave a fish-hook also in exchange for one of their hats. These are made of cedar bark and bear-grass, interwoven together in the form of an European hat, with a small brim of about two inches, and a high crown, widening upwards. They are light, ornamented with various colours and figures, and being nearly water-proof, are much more durable than either chip or straw hats. These hats form a small article of traffic with the whites, and the manufacture is one of the best exertions of Indian industry.

They are, however, very dexterous in making a variety of domestic utensils, among which are bowls, spoons, skewers, spits, and baskets. The bowl or trough is of different shapes, sometimes round, semicircular, in the form of a canoe, or cubic, and generally dug out of a single piece of wood, the larger vessels having holes in the sides by way of handle, and all executed with great neatness. In these vessels they boil their food, by throwing hot stones into the water, and extract oil from different animals in the same way. Spoons are not very abundant, nor is there any thing remarkable in their shape, except that they are large and the bowl broad. Meat is roasted on one end of a sharp skewer, placed erect before the fire, with the other fixed in the ground. The spit for fish is split at the top into two parts, between which the fish is placed, cut open, with its sides extended by means of small splinters. The usual plate is a small mat of rushes or flags, on which every thing is served. The instrument with which they dig up roots, is a strong stick, about three feet and a half long, sharpened and a little curved

363

at the lower end, while the upper is inserted into a handle, standing trans-versely, and made of part of an elk or buck's horn.

But the most curious workmanship is that of the basket. It is formed of cedar bark and bear-grass, so closely interwoven, that it is water tight, without the aid of either gum or resin. The form is generally conic, or rather the segment of a cone, of which the smaller end is the bottom of the basket; and being made of all sizes, from that of the smallest cup to the capacity of five or six gallons, answer the double purpose of a covering for the head or to contain water. Some of them are highly ornamented with strands of bear-grass, woven into figures of various colours, which require great labour; yet they are made very expeditiously and sold for a trifle. It is for the construction of these baskets, that the bear-grass forms an article of considerable traffic. It grows only near the snowy region of the high mountains, and the blade, which is two feet long and about three-eighths of an inch wide, is smooth, strong and pliant; the young blades particularly, from their not being exposed to the sun and air, have an appearance of great neatness, and are generally preferred. Other bags and baskets, not water-proof, are made of cedar bark, silk-grass, rushes, flags, and common coarse sedge, for the use of families.

In the manufactures, as well as in the ordinary work of the house, the instrument most in use is a knife, or rather a dagger. The handle of it is small, and has a strong loop of twine for the thumb, to prevent its being wrested from the hand. On each side is a blade, double-edged and pointed; the longer from nine to ten inches, the shorter from four to five. This knife is carried about habitually in the hand, sometimes exposed, but mostly when in company with strangers, put under the robe.

JANUARY 20TH *Monday.* We were visited by three Clatsops, who came merely for the purpose of smoking and conversing with us. We have now only three days' provision, yet so accustomed have the men become to live sparingly, and fast occasionally, that such a circumstance excites no concern, as we all calculate on our dexterity as hunters.

The industry of the Indians is not confined to household utensils: the great proof of their skill is the construction of their canoes. In a country, indeed, where so much of the intercourse between different tribes is carried on by water, the ingenuity of the people would naturally direct itself to the improvement of canoes, which would gradually become, from a mere safe conveyance, an elegant ornament. We have accordingly seen, on the Columbia, canoes of many forms, beginning with the simple boats near the mountains, to those more highly decorated, because more useful nearer the mouth of the Columbia. Below the grand cataract there are four forms of canoes: the first and smallest is about fifteen feet long, and calculated for one or two persons: it is, indeed, by no means remarkable in its structure, and is chiefly employed by the Cathlamahs and Wahkiacums among the marshy islands. The second is from twenty to thirty-five feet long, about two and a half or three feet in the beam, and two feet in the hold. It is chiefly remarkable in having the bowsprit, which rises to some height above the bow, formed by tapering gradually from the sides into a sharp point. Canoes of this shape are common to all the nations below the grand rapids.

But the canoes most used by the Columbia Indians, from the Chilluckittequaws inclusive, to the ocean, are about thirty or thirty-five feet long. The bow, which looks more like the stern of our boats, is higher than the other end, and is ornamented with a sort of comb, an inch in thickness, cut out of the same log which forms the canoe, and extending nine or eleven inches from the bowsprit to the bottom of the boat. The stern is nearly rounded off, and gradually ascends to a point. This canoe is very light and convenient; for though it will contain ten or twelve persons, it may be carried with great ease by four.

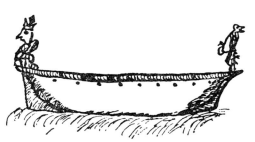

*Two common types of Columbia River canoes: the one at the left, 30–35 ft. long, carried up to a dozen persons; at right is the largest type, used in the tidewater area. Below are sketched two smaller canoes of the area; and a typical paddle, some 5 ft. in length.*

The fourth and largest species of canoe we did not meet till we reached tide-water, near the grand rapids below, in which place they are found among all the nations, especially the Killamucks, and others residing on the seacoast. They are upwards of fifty feet long, and will carry from eight to ten thousand pounds weight, or from twenty to thirty persons. Like all the canoes we have mentioned, they are cut out of a single trunk of a tree, which is generally white cedar, though the fir is sometimes used. The sides are secured by cross-bars, or round sticks, two or three inches in thickness, which are inserted through holes made just below the gunwale, and made fast with cords. The upper edge of the gunwale itself is about five-eighths of an inch thick, and four or five in breadth, and folds outwards, so as to form a kind of rim, which prevents the water from beating into the boat. The bow and stern are about the same height, and each provided with a comb, reaching to the bottom of the boat. At each end, also, are pedestals, formed of the same solid piece, on which are placed strange grotesque figures of men or animals, rising sometimes to the height of five feet, and composed of small pieces of wood, firmly united, with great ingenuity, by inlaying and mortising, without a spike of any kind. The paddle is usually from

four feet and a half to five feet in length; the handle being thick for one third of its length, when it widens, and is hollowed and thinned on each side of the centre, which forms a sort of rib. When they embark, one Indian sits in the stern, and steers with a paddle, the others kneel in pairs in the bottom of the canoe, and sitting on their heels, paddle over the gunwale next to them. In this way they ride with perfect safety the highest waves, and venture without the least concern in seas, where other boats or seamen could not live an instant. They sit quietly and paddle, with no other movement; except, when any large wave throws the boat on her side, and, to the eye of a spectator, she seems lost: the man to windward then steadies her by throwing his body towards the upper side, and sinking his paddle deep into the wave, appears to catch the water and force it under the boat, which the same stroke pushes on with great velocity. In the management of these canoes the women are equally expert with the men; for in the smaller boats, which contain four oarsmen, the helm is generally given to the female. As soon as they land, the canoe is generally hauled on shore, unless she be very heavily laden; but at night the load is universally discharged, and the canoe brought on shore.

Our admiration of their skill in these curious constructions was increased by observing the very inadequate implements with which they are made. These Indians possess very few axes, and the only tool employed in their building, from felling of the tree to the delicate workmanship of the images, is a chisel made of an old file, about an inch or an inch and a half in width. Even of this tool they have not yet learnt the management, for the chisel is sometimes fixed in a large block of wood, and being held in the right hand, the block is pushed with the left without the aid of a mallet. But under all these disadvantages, these canoes, which one would suppose to be the work of years, are made in a few weeks. A canoe, however, is very highly prized: in traffic, it is an article of the greatest value, except a wife, which is of equal consideration; so that a lover generally gives a canoe to the father in exchange for his daughter.

TUESDAY, JANUARY 21ST, 1806    Two of the hunters came back with three elk, which form a timely addition to our stock of provisions. The Indian visitors left us at twelve o'clock.

The Killamucks, Clatsops, Chinnooks, and Cathlamahs, the four neighbouring nations with whom we have had most intercourse, preserve a general resemblance in person, dress, and manners. They are commonly of a diminutive stature, badly shaped, and their appearance by no means prepossessing. They have broad thick flat feet, thick ankles, and crooked legs: the last of which deformities is to be ascribed, in part, to the universal practice of squatting, or sitting on the calves of their legs and heels, and also to the tight bandages of beads and strings worn round the ankles, by the women, which prevent the circulation of the blood, and render the legs, of the females, particularly, ill shaped and swollen. The complexion is the usual copper coloured brown of the North American tribes, though the complexion is rather lighter than that of the Indians of the Missouri, and the frontier of the United States: the mouth is wide and the lips thick; the nose of a moderate size, fleshy, wide at the extremities, with large nostrils, and generally low between the eyes, though there are rare instances of high aquiline noses; the eyes are generally black, though we occasionally see them of a dark yellowish brown, with a black pupil.

But the most distinguishing part of their physiognomy, is the peculiar flatness and width of their forehead, a peculiarity which they owe to one of these customs by which nature is sacrificed to fantastic ideas of beauty. The custom, indeed, of flattening the head by artificial pressure during infancy, prevails among all the nations we have seen west of the Rocky mountains. To the east of that barrier, the fashion is so perfectly unknown, that there the western Indians, with the exception of the Alliatan or Snake nation, are designated by the common name of Flatheads. The singular usage, which nature could scarcely seem to suggest to remote nations, might perhaps incline us to believe in the common and not very ancient origin of all the western nations. Such an opinion might well accommodate itself with the fact, that while on the lower parts of the Columbia, both sexes are universally flatheads, the custom diminishes in receding eastward, from the common centre of the infection, till among the remoter tribes near the mountains, nature recovers her rights, and the wasted folly is confined to a few females. Such opinions, however, are corrected or weakened by considering that the flattening of the head is not, in fact, peculiar to that part of the continent, since it was among the first objects which struck the attention of Columbus.

But wherever it may have begun, the practice is now universal among these nations. Soon after the birth of her child, the mother, anxious to procure for her infant the recommendation of a broad forehead, places it in the compressing machine, where it is kept for ten or twelve months; though the females remain longer than the boys. The operation is so gradual, that it is not attended with pain; but the impression is deep and permanent. The heads of the children, when they are released from the bandage, are not more than two inches thick about the upper edge of the forehead, and still thinner above: nor with all its efforts can nature ever restore its shape; the heads of grown persons being often in a straight line from the nose to the top of the forehead.

The hair of both sexes is parted at the top of the head, and thence falls loosely behind the ears, over the back and shoulders. They use combs, of which they are very fond, and indeed, contrive without the aid of them, to keep their hair in very good order. The dress of the man consists in a small robe, reaching to the middle of the thigh, tied by a string across the breast, with its corners hanging loosely over their arms. These robes are, in general, composed of the skins of a small animal, which we have supposed to be the brown mungo. They have besides, those of the tiger-cat [lynx], deer, panther [cougar], bear, and elk, which last is principally used in war parties. Sometimes they have a blanket woven with the fingers, from the wool of their native sheep; occasionally a mat is thrown over them to keep off rain; but except this robe, they have no other article of clothing during winter or summer, so that every part of the body, but the back and shoulders, is exposed to view. They are very fond of the dress of the whites, whom they call pashisheooks or clothmen; and whenever they can procure any clothes, wear them in our manner: the only article, indeed, which we have not seen among them is the shoe.

The robe of the women is like that worn by the men, except that it does not reach below the waist. Those most esteemed are made of strips of sea-otter skin, which being twisted are interwoven with silk-grass, or the bark of the white cedar, in such a manner that the fur appears equally on both sides, so as to form a soft and warm covering. The skins of the raccoon or beaver are also employed in the same way, though on other occasions these skins are simply dressed in the hair, and worn without further preparation. The garment which covers the body from the waist as low as the knee before and the thigh behind, is the tissue already described, and is made either of the bruised bark of white cedar, the twisted cords of silk-grass, or of flags and rushes. Neither leggings nor moccasins are ever used, the mildness of the climate not requiring them as a security from the weather, and their being so much in the water rendering them an incumbrance. The only covering for the head is a hat made of bear-grass, and the bark of cedar, interwoven in a conic form, with a knob of the same shape at the top. It has no brim, but is held on the head by a string passing under the chin, and tied to a small rim inside of the hat. The colours are generally black and white only, and these are made into squares, triangles, and sometimes rude figures of canoes and seamen harpooning whales. This is all the usual dress of females; but if the weather be unusually severe, they add a vest formed of skins like the robe, tied behind, without any shoulder-straps to keep it up. As this vest covers the body from the armpits to the waist, it conceals the breasts, but on all other occasions they are suffered to remain loose and exposed, and present, in old women especially, a most disgusting appearance.

Sometimes, though not often, they mark their skins by puncturing and introducing some coloured matter: this ornament is chiefly confined to the women, who imprint on their legs and arms, circular or parallel dots. On the arm of one of the squaws we read the name of J. Bowman, apparently a trader who visits the mouth of the Columbia. The favourite decoration however of both sexes, are the common coarse blue or white beads, which are folded very tightly round their wrists and ankles, to the width of three or four inches, and worn in large loose rolls round the neck, or in the shape of

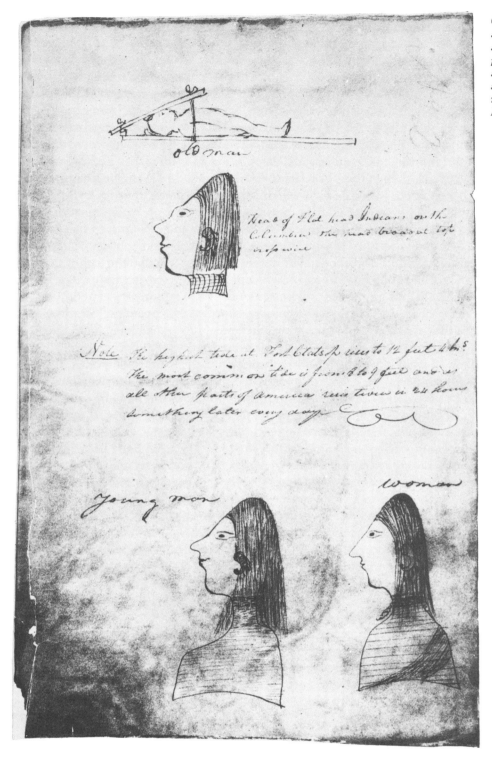

earrings, or hanging from the nose, which last mode is peculiar to the men. There is also a species of wampum very much in use, which seems to be worn in its natural form without any preparation. Its shape is a cone somewhat curved, about the size of a raven's quill at the base, and tapering to a point, its whole length being from one to two and a half inches, and white, smooth, hard and thin. A small thread is passed through it, and the wampum is either suspended from the nose, or passed through the cartilage horizontally, and forms a ring, from which other ornaments hang. This wampum is employed in the same way as the beads, but is the favourite decoration for the noses of the men. The men also use collars made of bears' claws, the women and children those of elks' tusks, and both sexes are adorned with bracelets of copper, iron, or brass, in various forms.

Yet all these decorations are unavailing to conceal the deformities of nature and the extravagance of fashion; nor have we seen any more disgusting object than a Chinnook or Clatsop beauty in full attire. Their broad flat foreheads, their falling breasts, their ill shaped limbs, the awkwardness of their positions, and the filth which intrudes through their finery; all these render a Chinnook or Clatsop beauty in full attire, one of the most disgusting objects in nature. Fortunately this circumstance conspired with the low diet and laborious exercise of our men, to protect them from the persevering gallantry of the fair sex, whose kindness always exceeded the ordinary courtesies of hospitality. Among these people, as indeed among all Indians, the prostitution of unmarried women is so far from being considered criminal or improper, that the females themselves solicit the favours of the other sex, with the entire approbation of their friends and connections. The person is in fact often the only property of a young female, and is therefore the medium of trade, the return for presents, and the reward for services. In most cases, however, the female is so much at the disposal of her husband or parent, that she is farmed out for hire. The Chinnook woman, who brought her six female relations to our camp, had regular prices, proportioned to the beauty of each female; and among all the tribes, a man will lend his wife or daughter for a fish-hook or a strand of beads. To decline an offer of this sort is indeed to disparage the charms of the lady, and therefore gives such offence, that although we had occasionally to treat the Indians with rigour, nothing seemed to irritate both sexes more than our refusal to accept the favours of the females. On one occasion we were amused by a Clatsop, who having been cured of some disorder by our medical skill, brought his sister as a reward for our kindness. The young lady was quite anxious to join in this expression of her brother's gratitude, and mortified that we did not avail ourselves of it, she could not be prevailed on to leave the fort, but remained with Chaboneau's wife, in the next room to ours, for two or three days, declining all the solicitations of the men, till finding, at last, that we did not relent, she went away, regretting that her brother's obligations were unpaid.

The little intercourse which the men have had with these women is, however, sufficient to apprise us of the prevalence of the venereal disease, with which one or two of the party had been so much afflicted, as to render a salivation necessary. The infection in these cases was communicated by the Chinnook women. The others do not appear to be afflicted with it to any extent: indeed, notwithstanding this disorder is certainly known to the Indians on the Columbia, yet the number of infected persons is very inconsiderable. The existence of such a disorder is very easily detected, particularly in the men, in their open style of dress; yet in the whole route down the Columbia, we have not seen more than two or three cases of gonorrhoea, and about double that number of lues venerea. There does not seem to be any simples which are used as specifics in this disorder, nor is any complete cure ever effected. When once a patient is seized, the disorder ends with his life only;

though from the simplicity of their diet, and the use of certain vegetables, they support it for many years with but little inconvenience, and even enjoy tolerable health; yet their life is always abridged by decrepitude or premature old age. The Indians, who are mostly successful in treating this disorder, are the Chippeways. Their specifics are the root of the lobelia, and that of a species of sumac, common to the United States, the neighbourhood of the Rocky mountains, and to the countries westward, and which is readily distinguished by being the smallest of its kind, and by its winged rib, or common footstalk, supporting leaves oppositely pinnate. Decoctions of the roots are used very freely, without any limitation, and are said to soften the violence of the lues, and even to be sovereign in the cure of the gonorrhoea.

The Clatsops and other nations at the mouth of the Columbia, have visited us with great freedom, and we have endeavoured to cultivate their intimacy, as well for the purpose of acquiring information, as to leave behind us impressions favourable to our country. In their intercourse with us they are very loquacious and inquisitive. Having acquired much of their language, we are enabled with the assistance of gestures, to hold conversations with great ease. We find them inquisitive and loquacious, with understandings by no means deficient in acuteness, and with very retentive memories; and though fond of feasts, and generally cheerful, they are never gay. Every thing they see excites their attention and inquiries, but having been accustomed to see the whites, nothing appeared to give them more astonishment than the air-gun. To all our inquiries they answer with great intelligence, and the conversation rarely slackens, since there is a constant discussion of the events, and trade, and politics, in the little but active circle of Killamucks, Clatsops, Cathlamahs, Wahkiacums, and Chinnooks. Among themselves, the conversation generally turns on the subjects of trade, or smoking, or eating, or connection with females, before whom this last is spoken of with a familiarity which would be in the highest degree indecent, if custom had not rendered it inoffensive.

The treatment of women is often considered as the standard by which the moral qualities of savages are to be estimated. Our own observation, however, induced us to think that the importance of the female in savage life, has no necessary relation to the virtues of the men, but is regulated wholly by their capacity to be useful. The Indians whose treatment of the females is mildest, and who pay most deference to their opinions, are by no means the most distinguished for their virtues; nor is this deference attended by any increase of attachment, since they are equally willing with the most brutal husband, to prostitute their wives to strangers. On the other hand, the tribes among whom the women are very much debased, possess the loftiest sense of honour, the greatest liberality, and all the good qualities of which their situation demands the exercise. Where the women can aid in procuring subsistence for the tribe, they are treated with more equality, and their importance is proportioned to the share which they take in that labour; while in countries where subsistence is chiefly procured by the exertions of the men, the women are considered and treated as burdens. Thus, among the Clatsops and Chinnooks, who live upon fish and roots, which the women are equally expert with the men in procuring, the former have a rank and influence very rarely found among Indians. The females are permitted to speak freely before the men, to whom indeed they some-

371

times address themselves in a tone of authority. On many subjects their judgments and opinions are respected, and in matters of trade, their advice is generally asked and pursued. The labours of the family too, are shared almost equally. The men collect wood and make fires, assist in cleansing the fish, make the houses, canoes, and wooden utensils; and whenever strangers are to be entertained, or a great feast prepared, the meats are cooked and served up by the men. The peculiar province of the female is to collect roots, and to manufacture the various articles which are formed of rushes, flags, cedar-bark, and bear-grass; but the management of the canoes, and many of the occupations, which elsewhere devolves wholly on the female, are here common to both sexes.

The observation with regard to the importance of females, applies with equal force to the treatment of old men. Among tribes who subsist by hunting, the labours of the chase, and the wandering existence to which that occupation condemns them, necessarily throws the burden of procuring provisions on the active young men. As soon, therefore, as a man is unable to pursue the chase, he begins to withdraw something from the precarious supplies of the tribe. Still, however, his counsels may compensate his want of activity; but in the next stage of infirmity, when he can no longer travel from camp to camp, as the tribe roams about for subsistence, he is then found to be a heavy burden. In this situation they are abandoned among the Sioux, Assiniboins, and the hunting tribes on the Missouri. As they are setting out for some new excursion, where the old man is unable to follow, his children, or nearest relations, place before him a piece of meat and some water, and telling him that he has lived long enough, that it is now time for him to go home to his relations, who could take better care of him than his friends on earth, leave him, without remorse, to perish, when his little supply is exhausted. The same custom is said to prevail among the Minnetarees, Ahnahawas, and Ricaras, when they are attended by old men on their hunting excursions. Yet, in their villages, we saw no want of kindness to old men. On the contrary, probably because in villages, the means of more abundant subsistence renders such cruelty unnecessary, the old people appeared to be treated with attention, and some of their feasts, particularly the buffalo dances, were intended chiefly as a contribution for the old and infirm.

The dispositions of these people seem mild and inoffensive, and they have uniformly behaved to us with great friendship. They are addicted to begging and pilfering small articles, when it can be done without danger of detection, but do not rob wantonly, nor to any large amount; and some of them having purloined some of our meat, which the hunters had been obliged to leave in the woods, they voluntarily brought some dogs a few days after, by way of compensation. Our force and great superiority in the use of firearms, enable us always to command, and such is the friendly deportment of these people, that the men have been accustomed to treat them with the greatest confidence. It is therefore with difficulty that we can impress on our men a conviction of the necessity of being always on our guard, since we are perfectly acquainted with the treacherous character of Indians in general. We are always prepared for an attack, and uniformly exclude all large parties of Indians from the fort.

Their large houses usually contain several families, consisting of the parents, their sons and daughters-in-law, and grandchildren, among whom the provisions are common, and whose harmony is scarcely ever interrupted by disputes. Although polygamy is permitted by their customs, very few have more than a single wife, and she is brought immediately after the marriage into the husband's family, where she resides until increasing numbers oblige them to seek another house. In this state the old man is not considered as the head of the family, since the active duties, as well as the responsibility, fall on some of the younger members. As these families gradually expand into bands or tribes or nations, the paternal authority is represented by the chief of each association. This chieftain however is not hereditary; his ability to render service to his neighbours, and the popularity which follows it, is at once the foundation and the measure of his authority, the exercise of which does not extend beyond a reprimand for some improper action.

The harmony of their private life is indeed secured by their ignorance of spirituous liquors, the earliest and most dreadful present which civilisation has given to the other natives of the continent. Although they have had so much intercourse with whites, they do not appear to possess any knowledge of those dangerous luxuries; at least they have never inquired after them; which they probably would have done if once they had been introduced among them. Indeed we have not observed any liquor of an intoxicating quality used among these or any Indians west of the Rocky mountains, the universal beverage being pure water. They however sometimes almost intoxicate themselves by smoking tobacco of which they are excessively fond, and the pleasures of which they prolong as much as possible, by retaining vast quantities at a time, till after circulating through the lungs and stomach it issues in volumes from the mouth and nostrils.

But the natural vice of all these people is an attachment for games of hazard which they pursue with a strange and ruinous avidity. The games are of two kinds. In the first, one of the company assumes the office of banker, and plays against the rest. He takes a small stone, about the size of a bean, which he shifts from one hand to the other with great dexterity, repeating at the same time a song adapted to the game, and which serves to divert the attention of the company, till having agreed on the stake, he holds out his hands, and the antagonist wins or loses as he succeeds or fails at guessing in which hand the stone is. After the banker has lost his money, or whenever he is tired, the stone is transferred to another, who in turn challenges the rest of the company. The other game is something like the play of ninepins; two pins are placed on the floor, about the distance of a foot from each other, and a small hole made behind them. The players then go about ten feet from the hole, into which they try to roll a small piece resembling the men used at draughts; if they succeed in putting it into the hole, they win the stake; if the piece rolls between the pins, but does not go into the hole, nothing is won or lost; but the wager is wholly lost if the chequer rolls outside of the pins. Entire days are wasted at these games, which are often continued through the night round the blaze of their fires, till the last article of clothing or even the last blue bead is won from the desperate adventurer.

In traffic they are keen, acute and intelligent, and they employ in all their bargains a dexterity and finesse, which, if it be not learnt from their foreign visitors, may show how nearly the cunning of savages is allied to the little arts of more civilised trade. They begin by asking double or treble the value of their merchandise, and lower the demand in proportion to the ardour or experience in trade of the purchaser; and if he expresses any anxiety, the smallest article, perhaps a handful of roots, will furnish a whole morning's negotiation. Being naturally suspicious, they of course conceive that you are pursuing the same system. They, therefore, invariably refuse the first offer, however high, fearful that they or we have mistaken the value of the merchandise, and therefore cautiously wait to draw us on to larger offers. In this way, after rejecting the most extravagant prices, which we have offered merely for experiment, they have afterwards importuned us for a tenth part of what they had before refused. In this respect, they differ from almost all Indians, who will generally exchange in a thoughtless moment the most valuable article they possess, for any bauble which happens to please their fancy.

These habits of cunning, or prudence, have been formed or increased by their being engaged in a large part of the commerce of the Columbia; of that trade, however, the great emporium is the falls, where all the neighbouring nations assemble. The inhabitants of the Columbian plains, after having passed the winter near the mountains, come down as soon as the snow has left the valleys, and are occupied in collecting and drying roots, till about the month of May. They then crowd to the river, and fixing themselves on its north side, to avoid the incursions of the Snake Indians, continue fishing, till about the first of September, when the salmon are no longer fit for use. They then bury their fish and return to the plains, where they remain gathering quamash, till the snow obliges them to desist. They come back to the Columbia, and taking their store of fish, retire to the foot of the mountains, and along the creeks, which supply timber for houses, and pass the winter in hunting deer or elk, which, with the aid of their fish, enables them to subsist till in the spring they resume the circle of their employments. During their residence on the river, from May to September, or rather before they begin the regular fishery, they go down to the falls, carrying with them skins, mats, silk grass, rushes, and chappelell bread. They are here overtaken by the Chopunnish, and other tribes of the Rocky mountains, who descend the Kooskooskee and Lewis's river for the purpose of selling bear-grass, horses, quamash, and a few skins which they have obtained by hunting, or in exchange for horses, with the Tushepaws.

At the falls, they find the Chilluckittequaws, Eneeshurs, Echeloots, and Skilloots, which last serve as intermediate traders or carriers between the inhabitants above and below the falls. These tribes prepare pounded fish for the market, and the nations below bring wappatoo roots, the fish of the seacoast, berries, and a variety of trinkets and small articles which they have procured from the whites.

The trade then begins. The Chopunnish, and Indians of the Rocky mountains, exchange the articles which they have brought for wappatoo, pounded fish, and beads. The Indians of the plains being their own fishermen, take only wappatoo, horses, beads, and other articles, procured from Europeans. The Indians, however, from Lewis's river to the falls, consume as food or fuel all the fish which they take; so that the whole stock for exportation is prepared by the nations between the Towahnahiooks and the falls, and amounts, as nearly as we could estimate, to about thirty thousand weight, chiefly salmon, above the quantity which they use themselves, or barter with the more eastern Indians. This is now carried down the river by the Indians at the falls, and is consumed among the nations at the mouth of the Columbia, who in return give the fish of the seacoast, and the articles which they obtain from the whites. The neighbouring people catch large quantities of salmon and dry them, but they do not understand or practise the art of drying and pounding it in the manner used at the falls, and being very fond of it, are forced to purchase it at high prices. This article, indeed, and the wappatoo, form the principal subjects of trade with the people of our immediate vicinity. The traffic is wholly carried on by water; there are even no roads or paths through the country, except across the portages which connect the creeks.

But the circumstance which forms the soul of this trade, is the visit of the whites. They arrive generally about the month of April, and either remain until October, or return at that time; during which time, having no establishment on shore, they anchor on the north side of the bay, at the place already described, which is a spacious and commodious harbour, perfectly secure from all except the south and southeast winds; and as they leave it before winter, they do not suffer from these winds, which, during that season, are the most usual and the most violent. This situation is recommended by its neighbourhood to fresh water and wood, as well as to excellent timber for repairs. Here they are immediately visited by the tribes along the seacoast, by the Cathlamahs, and lastly by the Skilloots, that numerous and active people, who skirt the river between the marshy islands and the grand rapids, as well as the Coweliskee, and who carry down the fish prepared by their immediate neighbours the Chilluckittequaws, Eneeshurs, and Echeloots, residing from the grand rapids to the falls, as well as all the articles which they have procured in barter at the market in May. The accumulated trade of the Columbia now consists of dressed and undressed skins of elk, sea-otter, the common otter, beaver, common fox, spuck, and tiger cat. The articles of less importance, are a small quantity of dried or pounded salmon, the biscuits made of the chapelell roots, and some of the manufactures of the neighbourhood.

In return they receive guns (which are principally old British or American muskets), powder, ball and shot, copper and brass kettles, brass tea-kettles, and coffee-pots, blankets, from two to three points, coarse scarlet and blue cloth, plates and strips of sheet copper and brass, large brass wire, knives, tobacco, fish-hooks, buttons, and a considerable quantity of sailors' hats, trousers, coats and shirts. But as we have had occasion to remark more than once, the object of foreign trade which is the most desired, are the common cheap, blue or white beads, of about fifty or seventy to the pennyweight, which are strung on strands a fathom in length, and sold by the yard, or the length of both arms: of these blue beads, which are called tia commashuck, or chief beads, hold the first rank in their ideas of relative value: the most inferior kind, are esteemed beyond the finest wampum, and are temptations which can always seduce them to part with their most valuable effects. Indeed, if the example of civilised life did not completely vindicate their choice, we might wonder at their infatuated attachment to a bauble in itself so worthless. Yet these beads are, perhaps, quite as reasonable objects of research as the precious metals, since they are at once beautiful ornaments for the person, and the great circulating medium of trade with all the nations on the Columbia.

These strangers who visit the Columbia for the purpose of trade or hunting, must be either English or Americans. The Indians inform us that they speak the same language as we do, and indeed the few words which the Indians have learnt from the sailors, such as musket, powder, shot, knife, file, heave the lead, damned rascal, and other phrases of that description, evidently show that the visitors speak the English language. But as the greater part of them annually arrive in April, and either remain till autumn, or revisit them at that time, which we could not clearly understand, the trade cannot be direct from either England or the United States, since the ships could not return thither during the remainder of the year. When the Indians are asked where these traders go on leaving the Columbia, they always point to the southwest, whence we presume that they do not belong to any establishment at Nootka Sound. They do, however, mention a trader by the name of Moore, who sometimes touches at this place, and the last time he came, he had on board three cows; and when he left them, continued along the northwest coast, which renders it probable, that there may be a settlement of whites in that direction. The names and description of all these persons who visit them in the spring and autumn are remembered with great accuracy, and we took down, exactly as they were pronounced, the following list:

The favourite trader is Mr. Haley, who visits them in a vessel with three masts, and continues some time. The others are Youens, who comes also in a three masted vessel, and is a trader; Tallamon, in a three-masted vessel, but he is not a trader; Callalamet in a ship of the same size; he is a trader, and they say has a wooden leg;

| Swipton | three-masted vessel, | trader |
|---|---|---|
| Moore | four- do. | do. |
| Mackey | three- do. | do. |
| Washington | three- do. | do. |
| Mesship | three- do. | do. |
| Davidson | three- do. | does not trade, but hunts elk |
| Jackson | three- do. | trader |
| Bolch | three- do. | do. |

Skelley, also a trader, in a vessel with three masts, but he has been gone for some years. He had only one eye.

It might be difficult to adjust the balance of the advantages or the dangers of this trade to the nations of the Columbia, against the sale of their furs, and the acquisition of a few bad guns and household utensils.

The nations near the mouth of the Columbia enjoy great tranquillity; none of the tribes being engaged in war. Not long since, however, there was a war on the coast to the southwest, in which the Killamucks took several prisoners. These, as far as we could perceive, were treated very well, and though nominally slaves, yet were adopted into the families of their masters, and the young ones placed on the same footing with the children of the purchaser.

# February and March, 1806

The month of February and the greater part of March were passed in the same manner. Every day, parties as large as we could spare them from our other occupations were sent out to hunt, and we were thus enabled to command some days' provision in advance. It consisted chiefly of deer and elk; the first is very lean, and the flesh by no means as good as that of the elk, which, though poor, is getting better: it is indeed our chief dependence. At this time of the year it is in much better order in the prairies near the point, where they feed on grass and rushes, considerable quantities of which are yet green, than in the woody country up the Netul. There, they subsist on huckleberry bushes and fern, but chiefly on evergreen, called shallun, resembling the laurel, which abounds through all the timbered lands, particularly along the broken sides of hills. Toward the latter end of the month [*February*], however, they left the prairies near Point Adams, and retired back to the hills; but fortunately, at the same time the sturgeon and anchovies began to appear, and afforded us a delightful variety of food. In the mean time, the party on the seacoast supplied us with salt: but though the kettles were kept boiling all day and night, the salt was made but slowly; nor was it till the middle of this month that we succeeded in procuring twenty gallons, of which twelve were put in kegs for our journey as far as the deposits on the Missouri.

The neighbouring tribes continued to visit us, for the purpose of trading, or merely to smoke with us. But on the *21st*, a Chinnook chief, whom we had never seen, came over with twenty-five of his men. His name was Tahcum, a man of about fifty years of age, with a larger figure and a better carriage than most of his nation. We received him with the usual ceremonies, gave the party something to eat, smoked most copiously with them all, and presented the chief with a small medal. They were all satisfied with their treatment; and though we were willing to show the chief every civility, could not dispense with our rule of not suffering so many strangers to sleep in the fort. They, therefore, left us at sunset. On the *24th*, Comowool, who is by far the most friendly and decent savage we have seen in this neighbourhood, came with a large party of Clatsops, bringing among other articles, sturgeon and a small fish, which has just begun, within a day or two past, to make their appearance in the Columbia.

From this time, as the elk became scarce and lean, we made use of these fish whenever we could catch them, or purchase them from the Indians. But as we were too poor to indulge very largely in these luxuries, the diet was by no means pleasant, and to the sick, especially, was unwholesome. On the *15th of March* we were visited by Delashilwilt, the Chinnook chief, and his wife, accompanied by the same six damsels, who in the autumn had encamped near us, on the other side of the bay, and whose favours had been so troublesome to several of the men. They formed a camp close to the fort, and began to renew their addresses very assiduously, but we warned the men of the dangers of intercourse with this frail society, and they cautiously abstained from connection with them.

During the greater part of this month, five or six of the men were sick; indeed, we have not had so many complaining since we left Wood river; the general complaint is a bad cold and fever, something in the nature of an influenza, which, joined with a few cases of venereal, and accidental injuries, complete our invalid corps. These disorders may chiefly be imputed to the nature of the climate.

VEGETABLE PRODUCE    The vegetable productions of the country, which furnish a large proportion of the food of the Indians, are the roots of a species of thistle, the fern, the rush, the liquorice, and a small cylindric root, resembling in flavour and consistency the sweet potato.

*1st.* The thistle, called by the natives shanataque, is a plant which grows in a deep, rich, dry loam, with a considerable mixture of sand. The stem is simple, ascending, cylindric, and hispid, and rising to the height of three or four feet. The cauline leaf, which, as well as the stem of the last season is dead, is simple, crenate, and oblong; rather more obtuse at its apex than at its insertion, which is decurrent, and its position declining; whilst the margin is armed with prickles, and its disc is hairy. The flower too is dry and mutilated; but the pericarp seems much like that of the common thistle. The root-leaves, which still possess their verdure, and are about half grown, are of a pale green colour. The root, however, is the only part used. It is from nine to fifteen inches long, about the size of a man's thumb, perpendicular, fusiform, and with from two to four radicles. The rind is of a brown colour, and somewhat rough. When first taken from the earth, it is white, and nearly as crisp as a carrot, and in this state is sometimes eaten without any preparation. But after it is prepared by the same process used for the pasheco quamash, which is the most usual and the best method, it becomes black, and much improved in flavour. Its taste is exactly that of sugar, and it is indeed the sweetest vegetable employed by the Indians. After being baked in the kiln, it is either eaten simply or with train oil; sometimes pounded fine and mixed with cold water, until it is reduced to the consistence of sagamity, or Indian mush, which last method is the most agreeable to our palates.

2. Three species of fern grow in this neighbourhood, but the root of only one is eaten. It is very abundant in those parts of the open lands and prairies which have a deep, loose, rich, black loam, without any sand. There, it attains the height of four or five feet, and is a beautiful plant with a fine green colour in summer. The stem, which is smooth, cylindric, and slightly grooved on one side, rises erectly about half its height, when it divides into two branches, or rather long footstalks, which put forth in pairs from one side only, and near the edges of the groove, declining backwards from the grooved side. These footstalks are themselves grooved and cylindric, and as they gradually taper toward the extremities, put forth others of a smaller size, which are alternate, and have forty or fifty alternate, pinnate, horizontal, and sessile leaves: the leaves are multipartite for half the length of their footstalk, when they assume the tongue-like form altogether; being, moreover, revolute, with the upper disc smooth, and the lower resembling cotton: the top is annual, and therefore dead at present, but it produces no flower or fruit: the root itself is perennial and grows horizontally; sometimes a little diverging, or obliquely descending, and frequently dividing itself as it proceeds, and shooting up a number of stems. It lies about four inches under the surface of the earth, in a cylindrical form, with few or no radicles, and varies from the size of a goose quill to that of a man's finger. The bark is black, thin, brittle, and rather rough, and easily separates in flakes from the part which is eaten: the centre is divided into two parts by a strong, flat, and white ligament, like a piece of thin tape; on each side of which is a white substance, resembling, after the root is roasted, both in ap-

pearance and flavour, the dough of wheat. It has, however, a pungency which is disagreeable, but the natives eat it voraciously, and it seems to be very nutritious.

3. The [horsetail] rush is most commonly used by the Killamucks, and other Indians on the seacoast, along the sands of which it grows in greatest abundance. From each root a single stem rises erectly to the height of three or four feet, somewhat thicker than a large quill, hollow and jointed; about twenty or thirty long, lineal, stellate, or radiate and horizontal leaves surround the stem at each joint, about half an inch above which, its stem is sheathed like the sand rush. When green, it resembles that plant also in appearance, as well as in having a rough stem. It is not branching; nor does it bear, as far as we can discover, either flower or seed. At the bottom of this stem, which is annual, is a small, strong radicle, about an inch long, descending perpendicularly to the root, while just above the junction of the radicle with the stem, the latter is surrounded in the form of a wheel, with six or nine small radicles, descending obliquely: the root attached to this radicle is a perennial solid bulb, about an inch long, and of the thickness of a man's thumb, of an ovate form, depressed on one or two of its sides, and covered with a thin, smooth, black rind: the pulp is white, brittle, and easily masticated. It is commonly roasted, though sometimes eaten raw; but in both states is rather an insipid root.

4. The liquorice of this country does not differ from that common to the United States. It here delights in a deep, loose, sandy soil, and grows very large, and abundantly. It is prepared by roasting in the embers, and pounding it slightly with a small stick, in order to separate the strong ligament in the centre of the root, which is then thrown away, and the rest chewed and swallowed. In this way it has an agreeable flavour, not unlike that of the sweet potato. The root of the cattail, or cooper's flag, is eaten by the Indians. There is also, a species of small, dry, tuberous root, two inches in length, and about the thickness of the finger. They are eaten raw, are crisp, milky, and of an agreeable flavour.

5. Beside the small cylindric root mentioned above, is another of the same form and appearance, which is usually boiled and eaten with train oil. Its taste, however, is disagreeably bitter. But the most valuable of all the Indian roots, is:

6. The wappatoo, or the bulb of the common sagittafolia, or common arrowhead. It does not grow in this neighbourhood, but is in great abundance in the marshy grounds of that beautiful valley, which extends from near Quicksand river for seventy miles westward, and is a principal article of trade between the inhabitants of that valley and those of the seacoast.

The shrub rises to the height of four or five feet; the stem simple and much branched. The bark is of a reddish dark brown; the main stem somewhat rough, while that of the bough is smooth; the leaf is about one-tenth of an inch long, obtuse at the apex, and acute and angular at the insertion of the pedicle. The leaf is three fourths of an inch in length, and three eighths in width, smooth, and of a paler green than evergreens generally are. The fruit is a small deep purple berry, and of a pleasant flavour; the natives eat the berry when ripe, but seldom collect such quantities as to dry for winter use.

The native fruits and berries in use among the Indians, are what they call the shallun; the solme; the cranberry; a berry like the black haw; the scarlet berry, of the plant called sacacommis; a purple berry, like the huckleberry.

*1.* The shallun is an evergreen plant, abounding in this neighbour-hood, and its leaves are the favourite food of the elk. It is a thick growth, cylindrically rising to the height of three, and sometimes five feet, and vary-ing from the size of a goose quill, to that of a man's thumb. The stem is sim-ple, branching, reclining, and partially fluxuose, with a bark which, on the elder part, is of a reddish brown colour, while the younger branches are red where exposed to the sun, and green elsewhere. The leaf is three fourths of an inch in length, and two and a half in breadth; of an oval form; the upper disc of a glossy deep green, the under of a pale green; the fruit is a deep pur-ple berry, about the size of a common black cherry, oval, and rather bluntly pointed; the pericarp is divided into five acute angular points, and envelops a soft pulp, containing a great number of small brown seeds.

*2.* The solme is a small, pale, red berry, the production of a plant, resembling in size and shape that which produces the fruit, called in the United States, Solomon's seal-berry. The berry is attached to the stem in the same manner. It is of a globular form; containing a soft pulp, which envel-ops four seeds about the size of the seed of the common small grape. It grows amongst the woodland moss, and is, to all appearance, an annual plant.

*3.* The cranberry is of the low and viny kind, and grows in the marshes or bogs of this neighbourhood: it is precisely the same as the cran-berry of the United States.

*4.* The fruit which, though rather larger, resembles the black haw, is a light brown berry, the fruit of a tree about the size, shape, and appear-ance in every respect, of that of the United States, called the wild crab-apple. The leaf is also precisely the same, as also the bark in texture and colour. The berries grow in clumps at the end of the small branches; each berry supported by a separate stem, and as many as from three to eighteen or twenty in a clump: the berry is ovate, with one of its extremities attached to a peduncle, where it is to a small degree concave, the wood of which is ex-cessively hard. The natives make their wedges of this wood, in splitting their boards, their firewood, and in hollowing out their canoes; the wedge when driven into solid dry pine, receives not the slightest injury. Our party made use of it likewise for wedges and axe-handles. The fruit is exceedingly acid, and resembles the flavour of the wild crab. The pericarp of the berry contains a soft pulpy substance, divided into four cells, each containing a single seed; the outer coat of the pericarp, is a thin smooth though firm and tough pellicle.

*5.* The plant [bearberry], called sacacommis by the Canadian trad-ers derives its name from this circumstance: that the clerks of the trading companies are generally very fond of smoking its leaves, which they carry about with them in a small bag. It grows generally in an open piny wood-land country, or on its borders. We found this berry in the prairies border-ing on the Rocky mountains, or in the more open woodlands. It is indiscrim-inately the growth of a very rich or a very poor soil, and is found in the same abundance in both. The natives on the western side of the Rocky mountains are very fond of this berry, although to us it was a very tasteless and insipid fruit: the shrub is an evergreen, and retains its verdure in the same perfection the whole season round. However inclement the climate, the root puts forth a great number of stems which separate near the surface of the ground, each stem from the size of a small quill to that of a man's finger: these are much branched, the branches forming an acute angle with the stem, and all more properly procumbent than creeping: although it sometimes puts forth radicles from the stems and branches, which strike obliquely into the ground: these radicles are by no means general or equable in their distances from each other, nor do they appear calculated to furnish nutriment to the plant: the bark is formed of several layers of a smooth, thin, brittle and reddish substance easily separated from the stem: the leaves with respect to their position are scattered, yet closely arranged, and particularly near the extremities of the twigs: the leaf is about three-fourths of an inch in length; oval, pointed and obtuse; of a deep green, slightly grooved; and the footstalk is of proportionable length: the berry is attached in an irregular manner to the small boughs among the leaves, and always supported by separate, small and short peduncles: the insertion produces a slight concavity in the berry, while its opposite side is slightly convex. The outer coat of the pericarp is a thin, firm, tough pellicle: the inner coat consists of a dry, mealy powder, of a yellowish white colour, enveloping from four to six large, light, brown seeds: the colour of the fruit is a fine scarlet: the natives eat these berries without any preparation: the fruit ripens in September, and remains on the bushes all winter unaffected by the frost: they are sometimes gathered and hung in the lodges in bags, where they are dried without further trouble.

6. The deep purple berry, like the huckleberry, terminates bluntly, and has a cap or cover at the end: the berries are attached separately to the sides of the boughs by a short stem, hanging underneath and they often grow very near each other, on the same bough: the berry separates very easily from the stem; the leaves adhere closely: the shrub rises to the height of six or eight feet, and sometimes grows on high lands, but more frequently on low marshy grounds: the shrub is an evergreen, and about ten inches in circumference, divides into many irregular branches, and seldom more than one stem springs from one root, although they associate very thickly: the bark is somewhat rough and of a reddish brown colour: the wood is very hard: the leaves are alternate and attached by a short footstalk to the horizontal sides of the boughs: the form is a long oval, rather more acute towards the apex than at the point of insertion: its margin slightly serrate, its sides collapsing, thick, firm, smooth and glossy: the under surface is of a pale or whitish green, and the upper of a fine deep green. This beautiful shrub retains its verdure throughout the year, and is more peculiarly beautiful in winter. The natives sometimes eat the berries without preparation: sometimes they dry them in the sun, and at others in their sweating kilns: they very frequently pound them, and bake them in large loaves, weighing from ten to fifteen pounds: the bread keeps very well for one season, and retains its juices better by this mode of preparation than any other: this bread when broken is stirred in cold water, until it acquires the consistency of soup, and then eaten.

The trees of a larger growth are very abundant; the whole neighbourhood of the coast is supplied with great quantities of excellent timber. The predominating growth is the fir, of which we have seen several species. There is one singular circumstance attending all the pine of this country, which is, that when consumed it yields not the slightest particle of ashes.

The *first* species grows to an immense size, and is very commonly twenty-seven feet in circumference six feet above the earth's surface: they rise to the height of two hundred and thirty feet, and one hundred and twenty of that height without a limb. We have often found them thirty-six feet in circumference. One of our party measured one, and found it to be forty-two feet in circumference, at a point beyond the reach of an ordinary man. This trunk for the distance of two hundred feet was destitute of limbs: this tree was perfectly sound, and at a moderate calculation, its size may be estimated at three hundred feet. The timber is [sound] throughout, and rives better than any other species; the bark scales off in flakes irregularly round, and of a reddish brown colour, particularly the younger growth: the trunk is simple, branching, and not very proliferous. The leaf is acerose, one tenth of an inch in width, and three fourths in length, firm, stiff, and acuminate. It is triangular, a little declining, thickly scattered on all sides of the bough, and springs from small triangular pedestals of soft, spongy, elastic bark at the junction of the boughs. The bud scales continue to encircle their respective twigs for several years. Captain Lewis has counted as many as the growth of four years beyond their scales; it yields but little resin, and we have never been able to discover the cone, although we have killed several.

The *second* [hemlock-spruce] is a much more common species, and constitutes at least one half of the timber in this neighbourhood. It seems to resemble the spruce, rising from one hundred and sixty to one hundred and eighty feet, and is from four to six in diameter, straight, round, and regularly tapering. The bark is thin, of a dark colour, much divided in small longitudinal interstices: the bark of the boughs and young trees is somewhat smooth, but not equal to the balsam fir: the wood is white, very soft, but difficult to rive: the trunk is a simple, branching, and diffuse stem, not so proliferous as the pines and firs usually are. It puts forth buds from the sides of the small boughs, as well as from their extremities: the stem terminates like the cedar, in a slender pointed top: the leaves are petiolate, the footstalks short, acerose, rather more than half a line in width, and very unequal in length; the greatest length seldom exceeds one inch, while other leaves intermixed on every part of the bough, do not exceed a quarter of an inch. The leaf has a small longitudinal channel on the upper disc, which is of a deep and glossy green, while the under disc is of a whitish green only: it yields but little resin. What is remarkable, the cane is not longer than the end of a man's thumb, it is soft, flexible, of an ovate form, and produced at the ends of the small twigs.

The *third* species resembles in all points, the Canadian balsam fir. It grows from two and a half to four feet in diameter, and rises to the height of eighty or an hundred feet. The stem is simple, branching, and proliferous: its leaves are sessile, acerose, one eighth of an inch in length, and one sixteenth in width, thickly scattered on the twigs, and adhere to the three under sides only; gibbous, a little declining, obtusely pointed, soft, and flexible. The upper disc is longitudinally marked with a slight channel, of a deep glossy-green; the under of a pale green and not glossy. This tree affords in considerable quantities, a fine deep aromatic balsam, resembling the balsam of Canada in taste and appearance. The small pistils filled, rise like a blister on the trunk and the branches. The bark that envelops these pistils, is soft and easily punctured: the general appearance of the bark is dark and smooth; but not so remarkable for that quality as the white pine of our country. The wood is white and soft.

The *fourth* species in size resembles the second. The stem is simple, branching, ascending, and proliferous; the bark is of a reddish dark brown, and thicker than that of the third species, divided by small longitudinal interstices, not so much magnified as in the second species. The relative position of the leaves resembles those of the balsam fir, excepting that they are only two thirds the width, and little more than half the length, and that the upper disc is not so green and glossy. The wood yields no balsam, and but little resin. The wood is white and tough although rather porous.

The *fifth* species [Douglas fir] in size resembles the second, and has a trunk simple, branching, and proliferous. The bark is of a thin dark brown, divided longitudinally by interstices, and scaling off in thin rolling flakes. It yields but little balsam: two-thirds of the diameter of the trunk in the centre, presents a reddish white; the remainder is white, porous, and tough: the twigs are much longer and more slender than in either of the other species; the leaves are acerose, one-twentieth of an inch in width, and one inch in length; sextile, inserted on all sides of the bough, straight, and obliquely pointing towards the extremities. The upper disc has a small longitudinal channel, and is of a deep green, and not so glossy as the balsam fir. The under disc is of a pale green.

We have seen a species of this fir on low marshy grounds, resembling in all points the foregoing, except that it branches more diffusively. This tree is generally thirty feet in height, and two in diameter. The diffusion of its branches may result from its open situation, as it seldom grows in the neighbourhood of another tree. The cone is two and a half inches in length, and three and three-quarters in its greatest circumference. It tapers regularly to a point, and is formed of the imbricated scales, of a bluntly rounded form. A thin leaf is inserted in the pith of the cone, which overlays the centre of, and extends half an inch beyond the point of each scale.

The *sixth* species [giant white pine] does not differ from what is usually denominated the white pine in Virginia. The unusual length of the cone seems to constitute the only difference. It is sometimes sixteen or eighteen inches in length, and is about four in circumference. It grows on the north side of the Columbia, near the ocean.

The *seventh* and last species [spruce] grows in low grounds, and in places frequently overflown by the tide, seldom rising higher than thirty-five feet, and not more than from two and a half to four in diameter: the stem is simple, branching and proliferous: the bark resembles that of the first species, but more rugged: the leaves are acerose, two-tenths of an inch in width, three-fourths in length, firm, stiff, and a little acuminated: they end in short pointed tendrils, gibbous, and thickly scattered on all sides of the branch, though they adhere to the three under sides only: those inserted on the under side incline sidewise, with upward points, presenting the leaf in the shape of a scythe: the others are pointing upwards, sextile and like those of the first species, grow from the small triangular pedestals, of a bark, spongy, soft and elastic. The under disc is of a deep glossy green, the other of a pale whitish green: the boughs retain the leaves of a six years' growth: the bud scales resemble those of the first species: the cone is of an ovate figure, three and a half inches in length, and three in circumference, thickest in the middle, and tapering and terminating in two obtuse points: it is composed of small, flexible scales, imbricated, and of a reddish brown colour. Each of these scales covers two small seeds, and is itself covered in the centre by a small, thin, inferior scale, acutely pointed: these scales proceed from the sides of the bough, as well as from its extremities. It was nowhere seen above the Wappatoo.

The stem of the black alder arrives to a great size. It is simple, branching, and diffuse: the bark is smooth, of a light colour, with white spreading spots, resembling those of the beech: the leaf, fructification, &c. resemble precisely those of the common alder of our country: the shrubs grow separately from different roots, and not in clusters, like those of the United States. The black alder does not cast its leaf until the first of December. It is sometimes found growing to the height of sixty or seventy feet, and is from two to four in diameter.

There is a tree [broad-leaf maple] common to the Columbia river, below the entrance of Cataract river, when divested of its foliage, much resembling the ash. The trunk is simple, branching, and diffuse: the leaf is petiolate, plain, divided by four deep lines, and resembling those of the palm, and considerably lobate: the lobes terminate in from three to five angular points, and their margins are indented with irregular and somewhat circular incisures: the petiolate is cylindrical, smooth, and seven inches long; the leaf itself eight inches in length, and twelve in breadth: this tree is frequently three feet in diameter, and rises from forty to fifty feet: the fruit is a winged seed, somewhat resembling that of the maple.

In the same part of the country there is also another growth [vine maple], resembling the white maple, though much smaller, and is seldom to be seen of more than six or seven inches in diameter. These trees grow in clusters, from fifteen to twenty feet in height, from the same bed of roots, spreading, and leaning outwards: the twigs are long and slender, the stem simple and branching, the bark, in colour, resembling the white maple, the leaf is petiolate, plain, scattered, nearly circular, with acute, angular incisures round the margin, of an inch in length, and from six to eight in number: the acute angular points so formed, are crenate, three inches in length and four in width; the petiole is cylindric, smooth, and an inch and a quarter in length, and the fruit is not known.

The undergrowth consists of honeysuckles, elder, seven bark or nine bark, huckleberry, a shrub like the quillwood, a plant like the mountain-holly, a green briar, the fern.

    SHRUBS

  *1.* The honeysuckle common to the United States we found in this neighbourhood. We first discovered the honeysuckle on the waters of the Kooskooskee, near the Chopunnish nation; also below the grand rapids.

  *2.* The elder which is also common to our country, was found in great abundance in the woodlands, on this side of the Rocky mountains. It differs in the colour of its berry: this being of a pale sky blue, while that of the United States is of a deep purple.

3. The seven bark, or, as it is usually denominated, the nine bark of the United States, is also common to this country.

4. The huckleberry. There is a species of huckleberry, common to the highlands, from the commencement of the Columbian valley to the sea-coast, rising to the height of six or eight feet, branching and diffuse: the trunk is cylindrical, of a dark brown colour; the collateral branches are green, smooth, and square, and put forth a number of alternate branches of the same colour, and from the two horizontal sides only. The fruit is a small deep purple berry, held in much esteem by the natives: the leaf is of a pale green, and small, three-fourths of an inch in length, and three-eighths in width, oval, terminating more acutely at the apex than at the insertion of the footstalk: the base is nearly entire, and but slightly serrate: the footstalks are short; their relative position is alternate, two-ranked, and proceeding from the horizontal sides of the boughs only.

5. There are two species of shrubs, first seen at the grand rapids of the Columbia, and which have since been seen elsewhere; they grow in rich dry grounds, usually in the neighbourhood of some water course: the roots are creeping and cylindrical. The stem of the first species is from a foot to eighteen inches in height, and about as large as an ordinary goose quill: it is simple, unbranched, and erect: its leaves are cauline, compound and spreading: the leaflets are jointed, and oppositely pinnate, three pair, and terminating in one sextile, widest at the base, and tapering to an acuminate point: it is an inch and a quarter in its greatest width, and three inches and a quarter in length: each point of the margin is armed with a subulate thorn, and from thirteen to seventeen in number: are veined, glossy, carinated and wrinkled: their points obliquely tending towards the extremity of the common footstalk.

The stem of the second species is procumbent, about the size of that of the first species, jointed and unbranched: its leaves are cauline, compound, and oppositely pinnate: the rib is from fourteen to sixteen inches in length, cylindric and smooth: the leaflets are two inches and a half long, and one inch wide, and of the greatest width half an inch from the base: this they regularly surround, and from the same point tapering to an acute apex: this is usually terminated with a small subulate thorn: they are jointed and oppositely pinnate, consisting of six pair, and terminating in one: sessile, serrate, and ending in a small subulate spire, from twenty-five to twenty-seven in number: they are smooth, plain, and of a deep green, and all obliquely tending towards the extremity of the footstalk: they retain their green all winter.

The large-leafed thorn, has a leaf about two inches and a half long, which is petiolate, and conjugate: the leaflets are petiolate, acutely pointed, having their margins cut with unequal and irregular incisures: the shrub, which we had once mistaken for the large-leafed thorn, resembled the stem of that shrub, excepting the thorn: it bears a large three-headed leaf.

6. The briar is of the class Polyandria, and order Polygynia: the flowers are single: the peduncle long and cylindrical: the calyx is a perianth, of one leaf, five cleft, and acutely pointed: the perianth is proper, erect, inferior in both petals, and germen [ovary]; the corolla consists of five

acute, pale scarlet petals, inserted in the receptacle with a short and narrow cleft: the corolla is smooth, moderately long, situated at the base of the germen, permanent, and in shape resembling a cup: the stamens and filaments are subulate, inserted into the receptacle, unequal and bent inwards, concealing the pystilium [pistils]; the anther is two-lobed and inflated, situated on the top of the filament of the pystilium: the germ is conical, imbricated, superior, sessile and short: the styles are short, compared with the stamen, capillary smooth and obtuse: they are distributed over the surface of the germ, and deciduous without any perceptible stamen.

7. The green-briar grows most abundantly in rich dry lands, in the vicinity of a water course, and is found in small quantities in piny lands at a distance from the water. In the former situation the stem is frequently of the size of a man's finger, and rises perpendicularly four or five feet: it then descends in an arch, becomes procumbent, or rests on some neighbouring plants: it is simple, unbranched, and cylindric: in the latter situation it grows much smaller, and usually procumbent: the stem is armed with sharped and forked briars: the leaf is petiolate, ternate and resembles in shape and appearance that of the purple raspberry, so common to the Atlantic states: the fruit is a berry resembling the blackberry in all points, and is eaten when ripe by the natives, which they hold in much esteem, although it is not dried for winter consumption. This shrub was first discovered at the entrance of Quicksand river: it grows so abundantly in the fertile valley of Columbia, and the islands, that the country is almost impenetrable: it retains its verdure late in summer.

8. Besides the fern already described, as furnishing a nutritious root, there are two other plants of the same species, which may be divided into the large and the small:

The large fern rises three or four feet: the stem is a common footstalk, proceeding immediately from the radix, somewhat flat, about the size of a man's arm, and covered with innumerable black coarse capillary radicles, issuing from every part of its surface: one of these roots will send forth from twenty to forty of these common footstalks, bending outwards from the common centre: the ribs are cylindric and marked longitudinally their whole length, with a groove on the upper side: on either side of this groove, and a little below its edge the leaflets are inserted: these are shortly petiolate for about two thirds the length of the middle rib, commencing from the bottom, and from thence to the extremity sessile: the rib is terminated by a single undivided lanceolate leaflet: these are from two to four inches in length, and have a small acute angular projection, and obliquely cut at the base: the upper surface is smooth, and of a deep green: the under surface of a pale green and covered with a brown protuberance of a woolly appearance, particularly near the central fibre: the leaflets are alternately pinnate, and in number, from one hundred and ten to one hundred and forty: they are shortest at the two extremities of the common footstalk, largest in the centre, gradually lengthening, and diminishing as they succeed each other.

The small fern rises likewise with a common footstalk from the radix, from four to eight in number: from four to eight inches long: the central rib is marked with a slight longitudinal groove throughout its whole length: the leaflets are oppositely pinnate, about one third of the length of the common footstalk, from the bottom, and thence alternately pinnate: the

footstalk terminates in a simple undivided lanceolate leaflet: these are oblong, obtuse, convex, absolutely entire, and the upper disc is marked with
a slight longitudinal groove: near the upper extremity these leaflets are de-
cursively pinnate, as are all those of the large fern. Both of these species preserve green during the winter.

DOMESTIC
ANIMALS
The quadrupeds of this country from the Rocky mountains to the Pacific
ocean, may be conveniently divided into the domestic and the wild animals.
The first embraces the horse and dog only.

*1*. The horse is confined principally to the nations inhabiting the
great plains of Columbia, extending from latitude 40° to 50° N., and
occupying the tract of territory lying between the Rocky mountains, and a
range of mountains which pass the Columbia river about the great falls
from longitude 16° to 121° W. The Shoshonees, the Chopunnish, Sokulks,
Escheloots, Eneshures, and Chilluckittequaws, all enjoy the benefit of that
docile, noble, and generous animal; and all of them, except the three last,
possess immense numbers.

They appear to be of an excellent race, lofty, elegantly formed, active and durable: many of them appear like fine English coursers; some of
them are pied with large spots of white irregularly scattered, and intermixed with a dark brown bay: the greater part, however, are of an uniform
colour, marked with stars and white feet, and resemble in fleetness and bottom, as well as in form and colour, the best blooded horses of Virginia. The
natives suffer them to run at large in the plains, the grass of which affords
them their only winter subsistence; their masters taking no trouble to lay
in a winter's store for them: notwithstanding, they will, unless much exercised, fatten on the dry grass afforded by the plains during the winter. The
plains are rarely if ever moistened by rain, and the grass is consequently
short and thin. The natives, excepting those of the Rocky mountains, appear
to take no pains in selecting their male horses for breed; and indeed, those
of that class appear much the most indifferent. Whether the horse was originally a native of this country or not, the soil and climate appear to be perfectly well adapted to the nature of this animal. Horses are said to be found
wild in many parts of this extensive country. The several tribes of Shoshonees who reside towards Mexico, on the waters of the Mutlomah river, and
particularly one of them, called Shaboboah, have also a great number of
mules, which the Indians prize more highly than horses. An elegant horse
may be purchased of the natives for a few beads or other paltry trinkets,
which in the United States, would not cost more than one or two dollars.
The abundance and cheapness of horses, will be extremely advantageous to
those who may hereafter attempt the fur trade to the East Indies, by the way
of Columbia river, and the Pacific ocean.

*2*. The dog is unusually small, about the size of an ordinary cur: he
is usually parti-coloured, amongst which, the black, white, brown, and
brindle are the colours most predominant: the head is long, the nose pointed,
the eyes small, the ears erect and pointed, like those of the wolf: the hair is
short and smooth, excepting on the tail, where it is long and straight, like
that of the ordinary cur-dog. The natives never eat the flesh of this animal,
and he appears to be in no other way servicable to them than in hunting elk.

The second division comprehends the brown, white, or grisly bear, the black bear; the deer, common red deer, the black-tailed fallow deer, the mule deer, the elk, the wolves, the large brown wolf, the small wolf of the plains, the large wolf of the plains, the tiger-cat, the foxes, the common red fox, the silver fox, the fisher or black fox, the large red fox of the plains, the kit-fox, or small fox of the plains, the antelope, the sheep, beaver, common otter, sea-otter, mink, seal, raccoon, squirrels, large grey squirrel, small grey squirrel, small brown squirrel, ground squirrel, braro, rat, mouse, mole, panther, hare, rabbit, polecat or skunk.

*First*, the brown, white or grisly bear, which seem to be of the same family, with an accidental variation of colour only, inhabit the timbered parts of the Rocky mountains. They are rarely found on the westerly side, and are more commonly below the Rocky mountains, in the plains, or on their borders, amidst copses of brush and underwood, and near the water courses. We are unable to learn that they inhabit at all in the woody country, bordering on the coast, as far in the interior as the range of mountains which pass the Columbia, between the great falls and the rapids of that river.

2. The black bear differs in no respect from those common to the United States. They chiefly inhabit timbered parts of the Rocky mountains, and likewise the borders of the great plains of the Columbia. They are sometimes found in the tract which lies between those plains and the Pacific ocean. One of our hunters saw one of this species, which was the only one we have discovered since our residence in fort Clatsop.

3. The deer are of three kinds: the common red deer, the black-tailed fallow deer, and the mule deer.

(1) The common red deer inhabit the Rocky mountains, in the neighbourhood of the Chopunnish, and about the Columbia, and down the river as low as where the tide water commences. They do not appear to differ essentially from those of the United States, being the same in shape, size, and appearance. The tail is however different, which is of an unusual length, far exceeding that of the common deer. Captain Lewis measured one, and found it to be seventeen inches long.

(2) The black-tailed fallow deer are peculiar to this coast, and are a distinct species, partaking equally of the qualities of the mule and the common deer. Their ears are longer, and their winter coat darker than those of the common deer. The receptacle of the eye more conspicuous, their legs shorter, their bodies thicker and larger. The tail is of the same length with that of the common deer, the hair on the under side white, and on its sides and top of a deep jetty black: the hams resemble in form and colour those of the mule, which it likewise resembles in its gait. The black-tailed deer never runs at full speed, but bounds with every foot from the ground, at the same time, like the mule deer. He sometimes inhabits the woodlands, but more often the prairies and open grounds. It may be generally said, that he is of a size larger than the common deer, and less than the mule deer. The flesh is seldom fat, and in flavour is far inferior to any other of the species.

(3) The mule deer inhabit both the seacoast and the plains of the Missouri, and likewise the borders of the Kooskooskee river, in the neighbourhood of the Rocky mountains. It is not known whether they exist in the interior of the great plains of the Columbia, or on the lower borders, near

the mountains which pass the river above the great falls. The properties of this animal have already been noticed.

4. The elk [wapiti] is of the same species with that which inhabits much the greatest part of North America. They are common to every part of this country, as well the timbered lands as the plains, but are much more abundant in the former than in the latter. In the month of March we discovered several which had not cast their horns, and others where the new horns had grown to the length of six inches. The latter were in much the best order, and from hence we draw the inference that the leanest elk retain their horns the longest.

5. The wolf is either the large brown wolf, or the wolf of the plains, of which last there are two kinds, the large and the small. The large brown wolf inhabits the woody countries on the borders of the Pacific, and the mountains which pass the Columbia river, between the great falls and rapids, and resembles in all points those of the United States. The large and small wolves of the plains, principally inhabit the open country and the woodlands on their borders. They resemble, both in appearance and habit, those of the Missouri plains. They are by no means abundant in the plains of the Columbia, as they meet there but very little game for their subsistence.

6. The tiger-cat [lynx] inhabits the borders of the plains, and the woody country in the neighbourhood of the Pacific. This animal is of a size larger than the wild cat of our country, and much the same in form, agility, and ferocity. The colour of the back, neck, and sides is of a reddish brown, irregularly variegated with small spots of dark brown: the tail is about two inches long, and nearly white, except the extremity, which is black. It terminates abruptly, as if it had been amputated: the belly is white, and beautifully variegated with small black spots: the legs are of the same colour with the sides, and the back legs are marked transversely with black stripes: the ears are black on the outer side, covered with fine, short hair, except at the upper point, which is furnished with a pencil of hair, fine, straight, and black, three-fourths of an inch in length. The hair of this animal is long and fine, far exceeding that of the wild cat of the United States, but inferior in that quality to that of the bear of the northwest. The skin of this animal is in great demand amongst the natives, for of this they form their robes, and it requires four to make up the complement.

7. Of the foxes we have seen several species.

The large red fox of the plains, and the kit-fox or small red fox of the plains, are the same which are found on the banks of the Missouri. They are found almost exclusively in the open plains, or on the tops of brush within the level country: the common red fox of the United States, inhabits the country bordering the coast, nor does this animal appear to have undergone any alteration.

The black fox [sic], or as it is termed in the neighbourhood of Detroit, the fisher, is found in the woody country bordering on the coast. How it should have acquired this appellation it is difficult to imagine, as it certainly does not prey upon fish. These animals are extremely strong and active, and admirably expert in climbing: this they perform with the greatest ease, and bound from tree to tree in pursuit of the squirrel or raccoon, their most usual food. Their colour is of a jetty black, excepting a small white spot upon the breast: the body is long, the legs short, and resembling those

390

MUSKWAKI (FOX) INDIAN (Bodmer)

of the ordinary turnspit dog. The tail is remarkably long, and not differing in other particulars from that of the ordinary fox.

The silver fox is an animal very rare, even in the country he inhabits. We have seen nothing but the skins of this animal, and those in the possession of the natives of the woody country below the Columbia falls, which makes us conjecture it to be an inhabitant of that country exclusively. From the skin it appeared to be of the size of the large red fox of the plains, resembling that animal in form, and particularly in the dimensions of the tail. The legs captain Lewis conjectured to be somewhat larger. It has a long deep lead coloured fur, for foil, intermixed with long hairs, either of a black or white colour at the lower part, and invariably white at the top, forming a most beautiful silver grey. Captain Lewis thought this the most beautiful of the whole species, excepting one which he discovered on the Missouri near the natural walls.

*8.* The antelope [pronghorn] inhabits the great plains of the Columbia, and resembles those found on the banks of the Missouri, and indeed in every part of the untimbered country, but they are by no means so abundant on this as on the other side of the Rocky mountains. The natives in this place make themselves robes of their skins, and preserve the hair entire. In the summer and autumn, when the salmon begin to decline, the majority of the natives leave the sides of the river, and reside in the open plains, to hunt the antelope, which they pursue on horseback, and shoot with their arrows.

*9.* The sheep [mountain goat] is found in many places, but mostly in the timbered parts of the Rocky mountains. They live in greater numbers on the chain of mountains forming the commencement of the woody country on the coast, and passing the Columbia between the falls and rapids. We have only seen the skins of these animals, which the natives dress with the wool, and the blankets which they manufacture from the wool. The animal from this evidence appears to be of the size of our common sheep, of a white colour: the wool is fine on many parts of the body, but in length not equal to that of our domestic sheep. On the back, and particularly on the top of the head, this is intermixed with a considerable proportion of long straight hairs. From the Indian account these animals have erect pointed horns: one of our engagées informed us that he had seen them in the black hills, and that the horns were lunated like those of our domestic sheep. We have nevertheless too many proofs to admit a doubt of their existing, and in considerable numbers on the mountains near the coast.

*10.* The beaver of this country is large and fat: the flesh is very palatable, and at our table was a real luxury. On the *7th of January,* 1806, our hunter found a beaver in his traps, of which he made a bait for taking others: this bait will entice the beaver to the trap, as far as he can smell it, and this may be fairly stated to be at the distance of a mile, as their sense of smelling is very acute. To prepare beaver bait, the castor or bark stone is first gently pressed from the bladder-like bag which contains it, into a vial of four ounces, with a large mouth: five or six of these stones are thus taken, to which must be added a nutmeg, a dozen or fifteen cloves, and thirty grains of cinnamon, finely pulverized and stirred together, and as much ardent spirits added to the composition as will reduce the whole to the consistency of mustard. All this must be carefully corked, as it soon loses its efficacy if exposed to open air. The scent becomes much stronger in four or five days after preparation, and, provided proper precaution is exercised, will preserve its efficacy for months. Any strong aromatic spices will answer; their sole virtue being to give variety and pungency to the scent of the bark stone.

The male beaver has six stones, two of which contain a substance much like finely pulverized bark, of a pale yellow colour, and in smell resembling tanners' ooze; these are called bark stones or castors. Two others, which like the bark stone resemble small bladders, contain pure strong oil, of a strong rank smell, and are called the oil stone, and the other two are the testicles. The bark stones are two inches in length: the others are somewhat smaller, of an oval form, and lie in a bunch together, between the skin and the root of the tail, with which they are closely connected, and seem to communicate. The female brings forth once in a year only, and has sometimes two and sometimes four at a birth, which usually happens in the latter end of May and the beginning of June: at this time she is said to drive the male from the lodge, who would otherwise destroy the young. They propagate like the fowl, by the gut, and the male has no other sexual distinction that we could discover.

11. The common otter has already been described, and this species does not differ from those inhabiting the other parts of America.

12. The sea-otter resides only on the seacoast, or in the neighbourhood of the salt water. When fully grown, he arrives to the size of a large mastiff dog. The ears and eyes, particularly the former, which are not an inch in length, are thick, pointed, fleshy, and covered with short hair: the tail is ten inches long, thick at the point of insertion and partially covered with a deep fur on the upper side: the legs are very short, and the feet, which have five toes each, are broad, large, and webbed: the legs are covered with fur, and the feet with short hair: the body of this animal is long, and of the same thickness throughout: from the extremity of the tail to the nose they measure five feet. The colour is a uniform dark brown, and, when in good order and season, perfectly black. This animal is unrivalled for the beauty, richness, and softness of his fur: the inner part of the fur, when opened, is lighter than the surface in its natural position: there are some black and shining hairs intermixed with the fur, which are rather longer, and add much to its beauty: the fur about the ears, nose and eyes, in some of this species, presents a lighter colour, sometimes a brown: their young are often seen of a cream-coloured white about the nose, eyes and forehead, and which are always much lighter than their other parts: their fur is however much inferior to that of the full grown otter.

13. The mink inhabits the woody country bordering on the coast, and does not differ in any point from those of the United States.

14. The seal are found on this coast in great numbers, and as far up the Columbia river as the Great Falls, and none have been discovered beyond them. The skins of such as captain Lewis examined, were covered with a short, coarse, stiff, and glossy hair, of a reddish brown colour. This animal, when in the water, appeared of a black colour, and sometimes spotted with white. We believe that there are several species of this animal to be found in this country, but we could not procure a sufficient number to make the examination: the skins were precisely of the same kind as our countrymen employ in the manufacture of trunks.

*15*. The raccoon inhabits woody countries bordering on the coast, in considerable numbers, and are caught by the natives with snares or pitfalls: they hold their skins in but little or no estimation, and very seldom make them into robes.

*16*. The squirrels we have seen, are:

The large grey squirrel. This animal appears to be an inhabitant of a narrow tract of country, well covered with whiteoak timber, and situated on the upper side of the mountains just below Columbia falls. This animal we have only found in those tracts which have been covered with timber; for in countries where pine is most abundant, he does not appear: he is much superior in size to the common grey squirrel, and resembles in form, colour and size, the fox squirrel of the Atlantic states: the tail exceeds the whole length of the body and the head: the eyes are dark, the whiskers long and black: the back, sides of the head and tail, and outward part of the legs, are all of a blue-coloured grey: the breast, belly, and inner part of the body, are all of a pure white: the hair is short, like that of the fox squirrel, though much finer, and intermixed with a portion of fur. The natives hold the skin of this animal in high estimation, which they use in forming their robes. He subsists on the acorn and filberts, which last grows in great abundance in the oak country.

The small grey squirrel is common to every part of the Rocky mountains where timber abounds. He differs from the dark brown squirrel in colour only. The back, sides, neck, head, tail and outer side of the legs, are of a brownish lead-coloured grey: the tail is slightly touched with a dark reddish colour, near the extremity of some of the hairs: the throat, breast, belly, and inner parts of the legs, are of the colour of a tanner's ooze, and have a narrow strip of black, commencing behind each shoulder, and entering longitudinally about three inches, between the colours of the sides and belly. Their habits are precisely those of the dark brown squirrel, and like them they are extremely nimble and active.

There is also a species of squirrel, evidently distinct, which we have denominated the burrowing squirrel. He inhabits these plains, and somewhat resembles those found on the Missouri: he measures one foot and five inches in length, of which the tail comprises two and a half inches only: the neck and legs are short; the ears are likewise short, obtusely pointed, and lie close to the head, and the aperture larger than will generally be found among burrowing animals. The eyes are of a moderate size, the pupil black, and the iris of a dark sooty brown: the whiskers are full, long, and black: the teeth, and, indeed, the whole contour, resemble those of the squirrel: each foot has five toes; the two inner ones of the fore feet are remarkably short, and are equipped with blunt nails: the remaining toes on the front feet are long, black, slightly curved, and sharply pointed: the hair of the tail is thickly inserted on the sides only, which gives it a flat appearance, and a long oval form: the tips of the hair forming the outer edges of the tail are white, the other extremity of a fox red: the under part of the tail resembles an iron grey; the upper is of a reddish brown: the lower part of the jaws, the under part of the neck, legs and feet, from the body and belly downwards, are of a light brick red: the nose and eyes are of a darker shade, of the same colour: the upper part of the head, neck and body, are of a curious brown grey, with a slight tinge of brick red: the longer hairs of these parts are of

393

a reddish white colour, at their extremities, and falling together, give this animal a speckled appearance.

These animals form in large companies, like those on the Missouri, occupying with their burrows sometimes two hundred acres of land: the burrows are separate, and each possesses, perhaps, ten or twelve of these inhabitants. There is a little mound in front of the hole, formed of the earth thrown out of the burrow, and frequently there are three or four distinct holes, forming one burrow, with these entrances around the base of these little mounds. These mounds, sometimes about two feet in height and four in diameter, are occupied as watch-towers by the inhabitants of these little communities. The squirrels, one or more, are irregularly distributed on the tract they thus occupy, at the distance of ten, twenty, or sometimes from thirty to forty yards. When any one approaches, they make a shrill whistling sound, somewhat resembling tweet, tweet, tweet, the signal for their party to take the alarm, and to retire into their entrenchments. They feed on the roots of grass, &c.

The small brown squirrel is a beautiful little animal, about the size and form of the red squirrel of the eastern Atlantic states and western lakes. The tail is as long as the body and neck, and formed like that of the red squirrel: the eyes are black, the whiskers long and black but not abundant: the back, sides, head, neck, and outer part of the legs are of a reddish brown: the throat, breast, belly, and inner part of the legs are of a pale red: the tail is a mixture of black and fox-coloured red, in which the black predominates in the middle, and the other on the edges and extremity: the hair of the body is about half an inch long, and so fine and soft it has the appearance of fur: the hair of the tail is coarser and double in length. This animal subsists chiefly on the seeds of various species of pine and is always found in the pine country.

The ground squirrel [chipmunk] is found in every part of this country, as well in the prairies as in the woodlands, and is one of the few animals which we have seen in every part of our journey, and differs in no respect from those of the United States.

There is still another species [prairie-dog], denominated by captain Lewis the barking squirrel, found in the plains of the Missouri. This animal commonly weighs three pounds: the colour is a uniform bright brick red and grey, and the former predominates: the under side of the neck and belly are lighter than the other parts of the body: the legs are short, and the breast and shoulders wide: the head is stout and muscular, and terminates more bluntly, wider, and flatter than that of the common squirrel: the ears are short, and have the appearance of amputation: the jaw is furnished with a pouch to contain his food, but not so large as that of the common squirrel: the nose is armed with whiskers on each side, and a few long hairs are inserted on each jaw, and directly over the eyes: the eye is small and black: each foot has five toes, and the two outer ones are much shorter than those in the centre. The two inner toes of the fore-feet are long, sharp, and well adapted to digging and scratching. From the extremity of the nose to the end of the tail this animal measures one foot and five inches, of which the tail occupies four inches.

Notwithstanding the clumsiness of his form, he is remarkably active, and he burrows in the ground with great rapidity. These animals burrow and reside in their little subterraneous villages like the burrowing squirrel. To these apartments, although six or eight usually associate together, there is but one entrance. They are of great depth, and captain Lewis once pursued one to the depth of ten feet, and did not reach the end of the burrow. They occupy, in this manner, several hundred acres of ground, and when at rest their position is generally erect on their hinder feet and rump: they sit with much confidence, and bark at the intruder as he approaches, with a fretful and harmless intrepidity. The note resembles that of the little toy-dog: the yelps are in quick and angry succession, attended by rapid and convulsive motions, as if they were determined to sally forth in defence of their freehold. They feed on the grass of their village, the limits of which they never venture to exceed. As soon as the frost commences, they shut themselves up in their caverns, and continue until the spring opens. The flesh of this animal is not unpleasant to the taste.

17. Sewellel is a name given by the natives to a small animal found in the timbered country on this coast. It is more abundant in the neighbourhood of the great falls and rapids of the Columbia than on the coast which we inhabit.

The natives make great use of the skins of this animal in forming their robes, which they dress with the fur on, and attach them together with sinews of the elk or deer: the skin, when dressed, is from fourteen to eighteen inches long, and from seven to nine in width: the tail is always separated from the skin by the natives when making their robes. This animal mounts a tree and burrows in the ground precisely like a squirrel: the ears are short, thin, and pointed, and covered with a fine short hair, of a uniform reddish brown: the bottom or the base of the long hairs, which exceed the fur but little in length, as well as the fur itself, are of a dark colour next to the skin for two-thirds of the length of this animal: the fur and hair are very fine, short, thickly set, and silky: the ends of the fur and tip of the hair are of a reddish brown, and that colour predominates in the usual appearance of the animal. Captain Lewis offered considerable rewards to the Indians, but was never able to procure one of these animals alive.

18. The braro [blaireau, or badger], so called from the French engagées, appears to be an animal of the civet species, and much resembles the common badger. These animals inhabit the open plains of the Columbia, sometimes those of the Missouri, and are sometimes found in the woods: they burrow in hard grounds with surprising ease and dexterity, and will cover themselves in a very few moments: they have five long fixed nails on each foot; those on the fore feet are much the longest, and one of those on each hind foot is double, like that of the beaver: they weigh from fourteen to eighteen pounds: the body is long in proportion to its thickness: the fore legs are remarkably large, muscular, and are formed like those of the turnspit dog, and, as well as the hind legs, are short: these animals are broad across the shoulders and breast: the neck is short, the mouth wide, and furnished with sharp, straight teeth, both above and below, with four sharp, straight, pointed tusks, two in the upper, and two in the lower jaw: the eyes are black and small; whiskers are placed in four points on each side near the nose, and on the jaws near the opening of the mouth: the ears are short, wide, and oppressed, as if a part had been amputated: the tail is four inches in length, the hair of which is longest at the point of the junction with the

body, and growing shorter until it ends in an acute point: the hairs of the body are much shorter on the sides and rump than those on any other part, which gives the body an apparent flatness, particularly when the animal rests upon his belly: the hair is upwards of three inches in length, especially on the rump, where it extends so far towards the point of the tail, it conceals the shape of that part, and gives to the whole of the hinder parts of the body the appearance of a right angled triangle, of which the point of the tail forms an acute angle: the small quantity of coarse fur intermixed with the hair is of a reddish pale yellow.

19. The rat which inhabits the Rocky mountains, like those on the borders of the Missouri, in the neighbourhood of the mountains, has the distinguishing traits of possessing a tail covered with hair like the other parts of the body. These animals are probably of the same species with those of the Atlantic states, which have not this characteristic distinction: the ordinary house rat we found on the banks of the Missouri, as far up as the woody country extends, and the rat, such as has been described, captain Lewis found in the state of Georgia, and also in Madison's cave in Virginia.

20. The mouse which inhabits this country is precisely the same with those which inhabit the United States.

21. The mole. This animal differs in no respect from the species so common in the United States.

22. The panther [cougar] is found indifferently, either in the great plains of the Columbia, the western side of the Rocky mountains, or on the coast of the Pacific. He is the same animal so well known on the Atlantic coast, and most commonly found on the frontiers, or unsettled parts of our country. He is very seldom found, and when found, so wary, it is difficult to reach him with a musket.

23. The hare ["jack-rabbit"] on this side of the Rocky mountains inhabits the great plains of the Columbia. On the eastward of those mountains they inhabit the plains of the Missouri. They weigh from seven to eleven pounds: the eye is large and prominent, the pupil of a deep sea-green, occupying one-third of the diameter of the eye; the iris is of a bright yellowish and silver colour; the ears are placed far back, and very near each other, which the animal can, with surprising ease and quickness, dilate, and throw forward, or contract, and hold upon his back at pleasure: the head, neck, back, shoulders, thighs, and outer part of the legs and thighs are of a lead colour: the sides, as they approach the belly, become gradually more white: the belly, breast, and inner part of the legs and thighs are white, with a light shade of lead colour: the tail is round and bluntly pointed, covered with white, soft, fine fur, not quite so long as on the other parts of the body: the body is covered with a deep, fine, soft, close fur. The colours here described are those which the animal assumes from the middle of April to the middle of November; the rest of the year he is of a pure white, except the black and reddish brown of the ears, which never change. A few reddish brown spots are sometimes intermixed with the white, at this season (February 26, 1806) on their heads and the upper part of their necks and shoulders: the body of the animal is smaller and longer in proportion to its height than the rabbit: when he runs he conveys his tail straight behind, in the direction of his body: he appears to run and bound with surprising agility and ease: he is extremely fleet, and never burrows or takes shelter in the

ground when pursued. His teeth are like those of the rabbit, as is also his upper lip, which is divided as high as the nose. His food is grass, herbs, and in winter he feeds much on the bark of several aromatic herbs, growing on the plains. Captain Lewis measured the leaps of this animal, and found them commonly from eighteen to twenty-one feet: they are generally found separate, and are never seen to associate in greater numbers than two or three.

*24.* The rabbit is the same with those of our own country, and are found indifferently, either on the prairies or the woodlands, and are not very abundant.

*25.* The polecat is also fund in every part of this country: they are very abundant on some parts of the Columbia, particularly in the neighbourhood of the Great falls and narrows of that river, where they live in the cliffs along the river, and feed on the offal of the Indian fishing shores. They are of the same species as those found in the other parts of North America.

The birds which we have seen between the Rocky mountains and the Pacific may be divided into two classes, the terrestrial and the aquatic. In the former class are to be arranged:

*1.* The grouse or prairie hen. This is peculiarly the inhabitant of the great plains of the Columbia, and does not differ from those of the upper portion of the Missouri. The tail is pointed, the feathers in the centre, and much longer than those on the sides. This species differs essentially in the formation of the plumage from those of the Illinois, which have their tails composed of feathers of an equal length. In the winter season this bird is booted to the first joint of the toes; the toes are curiously bordered on their lower edges with narrow hard scales, which are placed very close to each other, and extend horizontally about one eighth of an inch on each side of the toes, adding much to the broadness of the feet, a security which bounteous nature has furnished them for passing over the snows with more ease, and what is very remarkable, in the summer season these scales drop from the feet. This bird has four toes on each foot, the colour is a mixture of dark brown, reddish and yellowish brown, with white confusedly mixed. In this assemblage of colours, the reddish brown prevails most on the upper parts of the body, wings, and tail, and the white underneath the belly, and the lower parts of the breast and tail. These birds associate in large flocks in autumn and winter, and even in summer are seen in companies of five or six. They feed on grass, insects, leaves of various shrubs in the plains, and on the seeds of several species of speth [spilt] and wild rye, which grow in richer soils. In winter their food consists of the buds of the willow and cottonwood, and native berries.

*2.* The cock of the plains [sage-grouse] is found on the plains of the Columbia in great abundance, from the entrance of the southeast fork of the Columbia to that of Clark's river. It is about two-thirds the size of our ordinary turkey. The beak is large, short, covered and convex, the upper exceeding the lower chop: the nostrils are large, and the back black. The colour is an uniform mixture of a dark brown, resembling the dove, and a reddish and yellowish brown, with some small black specks. In this mixture the dark brown prevails, and has a slight cast of the dove-colour: the wider side of the large feathers of the wings are of a dark brown only. The tail is com-

posed of nineteen feathers, and that inserted in the centre is the longest, the remaining nine on each side gradually diminish. The tail when folded comes to a very sharp point, and appears proportionably long, when compared with the other parts of the body. In the act of flying, the tail resembles that of the wild pigeon, although the motion of the wings is much like that of the pheasant and grouse. This bird has four toes on each foot, of which the hindmost is the shortest, and the leg is covered with feathers about half the distance between the knee and foot. When the wing is expanded there are wide openings between its feathers, the plumage being too narrow to fill up the vacancy: the wings are short in comparison with those of the grouse or pheasant. The habits of this bird resemble those of the grouse, excepting that his food is that of the leaf and buds of the pulpy-leafed thorn. Captain Lewis did not remember to have seen this bird but in the neighbourhood of that shrub, which they sometimes feed on, the prickly pear. The gizzard is large, and much less compressed and muscular than in most fowls, and perfectly resembles a maw. When this bird flies he utters a cackling sound, not unlike that of the dunghill fowl. The flesh of the cock of the plains is dark, and only tolerable in point of flavour, and is not so palatable either as that of the pheasant or grouse. The feathers about the head are pointed and stiff and short, fine and stiff about the ears; at the base of the beak several hairs are to be seen. This bird is invariably found in the plains.

3. The pheasant, of which we distinguish the large black and white pheasant, the small speckled pheasant, the small brown pheasant:

(1) The large black and white pheasant differs but little from those of the United States; the brown is rather brighter, and has a more reddish tint. This bird has eighteen feathers in the tail, of about six inches in length. He is also booted to the toes: the two tufts of long black feathers on each side of the neck, so common in the male of this species inhabiting the United States, are no less observable in this pheasant: the feathers on the body are of a dark brown, tipped with white and black, in which mixture the black predominates; the white are irregularly intermixed with those of the black and dark brown in every part, but in greater proportion about the neck, breast, and belly: this mixture makes this bird resemble much that kind of dunghill fowl, which the housewives of our country call Domminicker. On the breast of some of these species the white predominates: the tufts on the neck leave a space about two and a half inches long, and one inch in width, where no feathers grow, though concealed by the plumage connected with the higher and under parts of the neck; this space enables them to contract or dilate the feathers on the neck with more ease: the eye is dark, the beak is black, curved, somewhat pointed, and the upper exceeds the under chop: a narrow vermillion stripe runs above each eye, not protuberant but uneven, with a number of minute rounded dots. The bird feeds on wild fruits, particularly the berry of the sacacommis, and exclusively resides in that portion of the Rocky mountains watered by the Columbia.

(2) The small speckled pheasant resides in the same country with the foregoing, and differs only in size and colour. He is half the size of the black and white pheasant, associates in much larger flocks, and is very gentle: the black is more predominant, and the dark brown feathers less frequent in this than in the larger species: the mixture of white is more general on every part. This bird is smaller than our pheasant, and the body more

round: the flesh of both these species is dark, and with our means of cooking, not well flavoured.

(3) The small brown pheasant [ruffed grouse] is an inhabitant of the same country, and is of the same size and shape of the speckled pheasant, which he likewise resembles in his habits. The stripe above the eye in this species is scarcely perceptible, and is, when closely examined, of a yellow or orange colour, instead of the vermillion of the other species: the colour is a uniform mixture of dark yellowish brown, with a slight aspersion of brownish white on the breast, belly, and feathers underneath the tail: the whole appearance has much the resemblance of the common quail: this bird is also booted to the toes: the flesh of this is preferable to the other two.

4. The buzzard [vulture] is, we believe, the largest bird of North America. One which was taken by our hunters was not in good condition, and yet the weight was twenty-five pounds. Between the extremity of the  wings the bird measured nine feet and two inches: from the extremity of the beak to the toe, three feet nine and a half inches; from the hip to the toe, two feet; the circumference of the head was nine and three-quarter inches: that of the neck seven and a half inches; that of the body inclusive of two feet three inches: the diameter of the eye is four and a half tenths of an inch; the iris is of a pale scarlet red, and the pupil of a deep sea-green: the head and part of the neck are uncovered by feathers: the tail is composed of twelve feathers of equal length, each of the length of fourteen inches: the legs are uncovered and not entirely smooth: the toes are four in number, three forward, and that in the centre much the largest; the fourth is short, inserted near the inner of the three other toes, and rather projecting forward: the thigh is covered with feathers as low as the knee, the top or upper part of the toes are imbricated with broad scales, lying transversely: the nails are black, short, and bluntly pointed: the under side of the wing is covered with white down and feathers: a white stripe of about two inches in width marks the outer part of the wing, embracing the lower points of the plumage, covering the joints of the wing: the remainder is of a deep black: the skin of the beak and head to the joining of the neck, is of a pale orange colour; the other part, destitute of plumage, is of a light flesh colour. It is not known that this bird preys upon living animals: we have seen him feeding on the remains of the whale and other fish thrown upon the coast by the violence of the waves. This bird was not seen by any of the party until we had descended Columbia river, below the great falls, and he is believed to be of the vulture genus, although the bird lacks some of the characteristics, particularly the hair on the neck, and the plumage on the legs.

5. The robin is an inhabitant of the Rocky mountains: the beak is smooth, black, and convex; the upper chop exceeds the other in length, and a few small black hairs garnish the sides of its base: the eye is of a uniform deep sea-green colour: the legs, feet, and talons are white, of which the front one is of the same length of the leg, including the talon; these are slightly imbricated, curved, and sharply pointed: the crown, from the beak back to the neck, embracing more than half the circumference of the neck, the back, and tail, are all of a bluish dark brown: the two outer feathers of the tail are dashed with white near their tips, imperceptible when the tail is folded: a fine black forms the ground of their wings; two stripes of the same colour pass on either side of the head, from the base of the beak to the junction, and

embrace the eye to its upper edge: a third stripe of the same colour passes from the sides of the neck to the tips of the wings, across the croup, in the form of a gorget: the throat, neck, breast, and belly, are of a fine brick red, tinged with yellow; a narrow stripe of this colour commences just above the centre of each eye, and extends backwards to the neck till it comes in contact with the black stripe before mentioned, to which it seems to answer as a border: the feathers forming the first and second ranges of the coverts of the two joints of the wing next to the body, are beautifully tipped with this brick red, as is also each large feather of the wing, on the short side of its plumage. This beautiful little bird feeds on berries. The robin is an inhabitant exclusively of the woody country; we have never heard its note, which the coldness of the season may perhaps account for.

6. The crow and raven is exactly the same in appearance and note as that on the Atlantic, except that it is much smaller on the Columbia.

7. The hawks too of this coast do not differ from those of the United States. We here see the large brown hawk, the small or sparrow hawk, and one of an intermediate size, called in the United States, the hen hawk, which has a long tail and blue wings, and is extremely fierce, and rapid in its flight. The hawks, crows, and ravens are common to every part of this country, their nests being scattered in the high cliffs, along the whole course of the Columbia and its southeastern branches.

8. The large blackbird [grackle] is the same with those of our country, and is found every where in this country.

9. The large hooting owl we saw only on the Kooskooskee under the Rocky mountains. It is the same in form and size with the owl of the United States, though its colours, particularly the reddish brown, seem deeper and brighter.

10. The turtle-dove and the robin (except the Columbian robin already described) are the same as those of the United States, and are found in the plains as well as in the common broken country.

11. The magpie is most commonly found in the open country, and resemble those of the Missouri, already described.

12. The large woodpecker or laycock, the lark woodpecker, and the common small white woodpecker, with a red head, are the inhabitants exclusively of the timbered lands, and differ in no respect from birds of the same species in the United States.

13. The lark, which is found in the plains only, and is not unlike what is called in Virginia, the old field lark, is the same with those already described as seen on the Missouri.

14. The flycatcher is of two species:

The first [winter-wren] is of a small body, of a reddish brown colour: the tail and neck short, and the beak pointed: some fine black specks are intermingled with the reddish brown. This is of the same species with that which remains all winter in Virginia, where it is sometimes called the wren.

The second species has recently returned, and emigrates during the winter. The colours of this bird are, a yellowish brown, on the back, head, neck, wing and tail; the breast and belly are of a yellowish white; the tail is in the same proportion as that of the wren, but the bird itself is of a size smaller than the wren: the beak is straight, pointed, convex, rather large at the base, and the chops are of equal length. The first species is smaller, and in fact the smallest bird which captain Lewis had ever seen, excepting the humming bird. Both of this species are found exclusively in the woody country.

*15.* Corvus. The blue-crested, and the small white-breasted corvus, are both natives of the piny country, and are invariably found as well on the Rocky mountains as on this coast. They have already been described.

*16.* The snipe, &c. The common snipe of the marshes, and the common sand snipe, are of the same species as those so well known in the United States. They are by no means found in such abundance here as they are on the coast of the Atlantic.

*17.* The leathern winged bat, so familiar to the natives of the United States, is likewise found on this side of the Rocky mountains.

*18.* The white woodpecker, likewise frequents these regions, and reminds our party of their native country, by his approaches. The head of this bird is of a deep red colour, like that of the United States. We have conjectured that he has lately returned, as he does not abide in this country during the winter. The large woodpecker, and the lark woodpecker, are found in this country, and resemble those of the United States.

*19.* The black woodpecker is found in most parts of the Rocky mountains, as well as in the western and southwestern mountains. He is about the size of the lark woodpecker, or turtle-dove, although his wings are longer than the wings of either of those birds: the beak is one inch in length, black, curved at the base, and sharply pointed: the chops are the same in length; around the base of the beak, including the eye and a small part of the throat, there is a fine crimson red: the neck, as low down as the croup [breast] in front, is of an iron grey: the belly and breast present a curious mixture of white and blood-red, which has much the appearance of paint, where the red predominates: the top of the head, back, sides, and upper surface of the wings and tail, exhibit the appearance of a glossy green, in a certain exposure to the light: the under side of the wings and tail, is of a sooty black: the tail is equipped with ten feathers, sharply pointed, and those in the centre the longest, being about two and a half inches in length: the tongue is barbed and pointed, and of an elastic and cartilaginous substance: the eye is rather large, the pupil black, and the iris of a dark and yellowish brown: the bird in its actions when flying, resembles the small red-headed woodpecker common to the United States, and likewise in its notes: the pointed tail renders essential service when the bird is sitting and retaining his resting position against the perpendicular sides of a tree: the legs and feet are black, and covered with wide imbricated scales: he has four toes on each foot, two in the rear and two in front, the nails of which are much curved and pointed remarkably sharp: he feeds on bugs and a variety of insects.

*20.* The calumet [golden] eagle, sometimes inhabits this side of the Rocky mountains. This information captain Lewis derived from the natives, in whose possession he had seen their plumage. These are of the same species with those of the Missouri, and are the most beautiful of all the family of eagles in America. The colours are black and white, and beautifully variegated. The tail feathers, so highly prized by the natives, are composed of twelve broad feathers of unequal length, which are white, except within two inches of their extremities, where they immediately change to a jetty black: the wings have each a large circular white spot in the middle, which is only visible when they are extended: the body is variously marked with black and white: in form they resemble the bald eagle, but they are rather smaller, and fly with much more rapidity. This bird is feared by all his carnivorous competitors, who, on his approach, leave the carcase instantly, on which they had been feeding. The female breeds in the most inaccessible parts of the mountains, where she makes her summer residence, and descends to the plains only in the fall and winter seasons. The natives are at this season on the watch, and so highly is this plumage prized by the Mandans, the Minnetarees, and the Ricaras, that the tail feathers of two of these eagles will be purchased by the exchange of a good horse or gun, and such accoutrements. Amongst the great and little Osages, and those nations inhabiting the countries where the bird is more rarely seen, the price is even double of that above mentioned. With these feathers the natives decorate the stems of their sacred pipes or calumets, from whence the name of the calumet eagle is derived. The Ricaras have domesticated this bird in many instances, for the purpose of obtaining its plumage. The natives, on every part of the continent, who can procure the feathers, attach them to their own hair, and the manes and tails of their favourite horses, by way of ornament. They also decorate their war caps or bonnets with these feathers.

AQUATIC BIRDS As to the aquatic birds of this country, we have to repeat the remark, that, as we remained near the coast during the winter only, many birds, common both in the summer and autumn, might have retired from the cold, and been lost to our observation. We saw, however, the large blue, and brown heron; the fishing hawk; the blue-crested fisher; several species of gulls; the cormorant; two species of loons; brant of two kinds; geese; swan; and several species of ducks.

1. The large blue and brown herons, or cranes, as they are usually termed in the United States, are found on the Columbia below tide-water. They differ in no respect from the same species of bird in the United States. The same may be observed of

2. The fishing hawk, with the crown of the head white, and the back of a mealy white, and of

3. The blue-crested or king-fisher, both of which are found every where on the Columbia and its tributary waters; though the fishing hawk is not abundant, particularly in the mountains.

4. Of gulls, we have remarked four species on the coast and the river, all common to the United States.

5. The cormorant is, properly speaking, a large black duck that feeds on fish. Captain Lewis could perceive no difference between this bird and those ducks which inhabit the Potomack and other rivers on the Atlantic coast. He never remembered to have seen those inhabiting the Atlantic states, so high up the river as they have been found in this quarter. We first discovered the cormorant on the Kooskooskee, at the entrance of Chopunnish river: they increased in numbers as we descended, and formed much the greatest portion of the water-fowl which we saw until we reached the Columbia at the entrance of the tides. They abound even here, but bear no proportion to the number of other water-fowl seen at this place.

*6.* The loon. There are two species of loons:

The speckled loon, found on every part of the rivers of this country. They are of the same size, colour and form, with those of the Atlantic coast.

The second species [grebe] we found at the falls of Columbia, and from thence downwards to the ocean. This bird is not more than half the size of the speckled loon; the neck is, in front, long, slender and white: the plumage on the body and back of the head and neck are of a dun or ash colour: the breast and belly are white, the beak like that of the speckled loon; and like them, it cannot fly, but flutters along on the surface of the water, or dives for security when pursued.

*7.* The brant are of three kinds; the white, the brown, and the pied.

(*1*) The white brant [snow-goose] are very common on the shores of the Pacific, particularly below the water, where they remain in vast numbers during the winter: they feed like the swan-geese, on the grass, roots, and seeds which grow in the marshes: this bird is about the size of the brown brant, or a third less than the common Canadian wild goose: the head is rather larger, the beak thicker than that of the wild goose, shorter, and of much the same form, being of a yellowish white colour, except the edges of the chops, which are frequently of a dark brown: the legs and feet are of the same form of the goose, and are of a pale flesh colour: the tail is composed of sixteen feathers of equal length as those of the geese and brown brant are, and bears about the same proportion in point of length: the eye is of a dark colour, and nothing remarkable in size: the wings are larger when compared with those of the geese, but not so much so as in the brown brant: the colour of the plumage is a pure uniform white, except the large feathers at the extremity of the wings, which are black: the large feathers at the first joint of the wing next to the body are white: the note of this bird differs essentially from that of the goose; it more resembles that of the brown brant, but is somewhat different; it is like the note of a young domestic goose, that has not perfectly attained its full sound: the flesh of this bird is exceedingly fine, preferable to either the goose or brown brant.

(*2*) The brown brant are much of the same colour, form, and size as the white, only that their wings are considerably longer and more pointed: the plumage of the upper part of the body, neck, head, and tail, are much the colour of the Canadian goose, but somewhat darker, in consequence of some dark feathers irregularly scattered throughout; they have not the same white on the neck and sides of the head as the goose, nor is the neck darker than the body: like the goose, they have some white feathers on the rump at the joining of the tail: the beak is dark, and the legs and feet also dark with a greenish cast: the breast and belly are of a lighter colour than the back, and is also irregularly intermixed with dark brown and black feathers, which give it a pied appearance: the flesh is darker and better than that of the goose: the habits of these birds resemble those of the geese, with this difference, that they do not remain in this climate in such numbers during the winter as the others, and that they set out earlier in the fall season on their return to the south, and arrive later in the spring than the goose. There is no difference between this bird and that called simply the brant, so common on the lakes, on the Ohio and Mississippi. The small goose of this country is rather less than the brant; its head and neck like the brant.

(*3*) The pied brant weigh about eight and a half pounds, differing from the ordinary pied brant in their wings, which are neither so long nor so pointed: the base of the beak is for a little distance white, suddenly succeeded by a narrow line of dark brown: the remainder of the neck, head, back, wings and tail, all except the tips of the feathers, are of a bluish brown of the common wild goose: the breast and belly are white, with an irregular mixture of black feathers, which give those parts a pied appearance. From the legs back underneath the tail and around its junction with the body above, the feathers are white: the tail is composed of eighteen feathers, the longest in the centre, and measures six inches with the barrel of the quill: those on the sides of the tail are something shorter, and bend with the extremities inwards towards the centre of the tail: the extremities of these feathers are white: the beak is of a light flesh colour: the legs and feet, which do not differ in structure from those of the goose or brant of other species, are of an orange colour: the eye is small, the iris of a dark yellowish brown, and pupil black: the note is much that of the common pied brant, from which in fact, they are not to be distinguished at a distance, although they certainly are of a distinct species: the flesh is equally palatable with that of common pied brant. They do not remain here during the winter in such numbers as the bird above mentioned: this bird is here denominated the pied brant, on account of the near resemblance, and for want of another appellation.

8. The geese are either the large or small kind: the large goose resembles our ordinary wild or Canadian goose; the small is rather less than the brant, which it resembles in the head and neck, where it is larger in proportion than that of the goose: the beak is thicker and shorter; the note like that of a tame goose. In all other points it resembles the large goose, with which it associates so frequently, that it was some time before it was discovered to be of a distinct species.

9. The swan are of two kinds, the large and the small: The large swan is the same common to the Atlantic states; the small differs only from the large in size and in note: it is about one fourth less, and its note is entirely different. It cannot be justly imitated by the sound of letters; it begins with a kind of whistling sound, and terminates in a round full note, louder at the end: this note is as loud as that of the large species; whence it might be denominated the whistling swan: its habits, colour, and contour appear to be precisely those of the larger species. These birds were first found below the great narrows of the Columbia, near the Chilluckittequaw nation: they are very abundant in this neighbourhood, and remained with the party all winter, and in number they exceed those of the larger species in the proportion of five to one.

10. Of ducks, we enumerate many kinds: the duckinmallard; the canvass-back duck; the red-headed fishing duck, the black and white duck; the little brown duck; black duck; two species of divers, and blue-winged teal.

(1) The duckinmallard, or common large duck, resembles the domestic duck, are very abundant, and found in every part of the river below the mountains: they remain here all winter, but during this season do not continue much above tide-water.

(2) The canvass-back duck is a most beautiful fowl, and most delicious to the palate: it is found in considerable numbers in this neighbour-

hood. It is of the same species with those of the Delaware, Susquehannah and Potomack, where it is called the canvass-back duck, and in James' river it is known by the name of the shelled drake [sheldrake]. From this last mentioned river, it is said, however, that they have almost totally disappeared. To the epicure of those parts of the United States, where this game is in plenty, nothing need be said in praise of its exquisite flavour, and those on the banks of the Columbia are equally delicious. We saw nothing of them until after we had reached the marshy islands.

(3) The red-headed fishing duck is common to every part of the river, and was likewise found in the Rocky mountains, and was the only duck discovered in the waters of the Columbia within those mountains. They feed chiefly on crawfish, and are the same in every respect as those on the rivers and the mountains bordering on the Atlantic ocean.

(4) The black and white duck is small, and a size larger than the teal. The male is beautifully variegated with black and white: the white occupies the side of the head, breast and back, the tail, feathers of the wings, and two tufts of feathers which cover the upper part of the wings, when folded, and likewise the neck and head: the female is darker. This is believed to be the same species of duck common to the Atlantic coast, and called the butter-box: the beak is wide and short, and, as well as the legs, of a dark colour, and the flesh extremely well flavoured. In form it resembles the duckinmallard, although not more than half the size of that bird. It generally resorts to the grassy marshes, and feeds on grass seeds, as well as roots.

(5) The black duck [coot] is about the size of the blue-winged teal; the colour of a dusky black; the breast and belly somewhat lighter, and of a dusky brown: the legs stand longitudinally with the body, and the bird when on shore, stands very erect: the legs and feet are of a dark brown: it has four toes on each foot, and a short one at the heel: the long toes are in front, unconnected with the web: the webs are attached to each side of the several joints of the toe, and divided by several sinews [sinus] at each joint, the web assuming in the intermediate part an elliptical form: the beak is about two inches long, straight, fluted on the sides, and tapering to a sharp point: the upper chop is the longest, and bears on its base, at its junction with the head, a little conic protuberance of a cartilaginous substance, being of a reddish brown at the point: the beak is of an ivory colour; the eye dark. These ducks usually associate in large flocks, are very noisy, and have a sharp shrill whistle: they are fat and agreeably flavoured; feed principally on moss and vegetable productions of the water: they are not exclusively confined to the water at all seasons, captain Lewis has noticed them on many parts of the rivers Ohio and Mississippi.

(6) The divers [grebes] are the same with those of the United States. The smaller species have some white feathers about the rump, with no perceptible tail, and are very acute and quick in their motion: the body is of a reddish brown; the beak sharp, and somewhat curved, like that of the pheasant: the toes are not connected, but webbed, like those of the black duck. The larger species are about the size of the teal, and can fly a short distance, which the smaller but seldom attempt: they have a short tail; their colour is also a uniform brick reddish-brown: the beak is straight and pointed: the feet are of the same form with the other species: the legs re-

405

markably thin and flat, one edge being in front. The food of both species is fish and flesh: their flesh is unfit for use.

(7) The blue-winged teal is an excellent duck, and in all respects the same as those of the United States.

One of our hunters killed a [scaup] duck which appeared to be a male. It was of a size less than the duckinmallard; the head, the neck as low as the croup, the back, tail, and covert of the wings were all of a deep fine black, with a slight mixture of purple about the head and neck: the belly and breast are white: some long feathers which lie underneath the wings, and cover the thighs, were of a pale dove colour, with fine black specks: the large feathers of the wings are of a dove colour: the legs are dark; the feet are composed of four toes, of which three are in front connected by a web: the fourth is short and flat, and placed high on the heel behind the leg: the tail is composed of fourteen short pointed feathers: the beak of this duck is remarkably wide, and two inches in length: the upper chop exceeds the under one, both in length and width, insomuch, that when the beak is closed, the under chop is entirely concealed by the upper: the tongue indenture on the margin of the chops, is like those of the mallard: the nostrils are large, longitudinal, and connected: a narrow strip of white garnishes the base of the upper chop: this is succeeded by a pale sky-blue colour, occupying about an inch; which again is succeeded by a transverse stripe of white, and the extremity is a fine black: the eye is moderately large, the pupil black, and of a fine orange colour: the feathers on the crown of the head are longer than those on the upper part of the neck and other parts of the head, which give it the appearance of being crested.

FISH  The fish, which we have had an opportunity of seeing, are, the whale, porpoise, skate, flounder, salmon, red char, two species of salmon trout, mountain, or speckled trout, bottlenose, anchovy, and sturgeon.

*1.* The whale is sometimes pursued, harpooned and taken by the Indians, although it is much more frequently killed by running foul of the rocks in violent storms, and thrown on shore by the action of the wind and tide. In either case, the Indians preserve and eat the blubber and oil; the bone they carefully extract and expose to sale.

*2.* The porpoise is common on this coast, and as far up the river as the water is brackish. The Indians sometimes gig them, and always eat their flesh when they can procure it.

*3.* The skate is also common in the salt water: we saw several of them which had perished, and were thrown on shore by the tide.

*4.* The flounder is also well known here, and we have often seen them left on the beach after the departure of the tide. The Indians eat this fish, and think it very fine. These several species of fish are the same with those on the Atlantic coast.

*5.* The common salmon and red char are the inhabitants of both the sea and rivers. The former are usually the largest, and weigh from five to fifteen pounds: they extend themselves into all the rivers and little creeks on this side of the continent, and to them the natives are much indebted for their subsistence: the body of the fish is from two and an half to three feet long, and proportionably broad: it is covered with imbricated scales, of a moderate size, and gills: the eye is large, and the iris of a silvery colour: the

406

pupil is black, the rostrum or nose extends beyond the under jaw, and both jaws are armed with a single series of long teeth, which are subulate and inflected near the extremities of the jaws, where they are also more closely arranged: they have some sharp teeth of smaller size, and some sharp points placed on the tongue, which is thick and fleshy: the fins of the back are two; the first is placed nearer the head than the ventral fins, and has several rays: the second is placed far back, near the tail, and has no rays. The flesh of this fish is, when in order, of a deep flesh-coloured red, and every shade from that to an orange yellow: when very meagre it is almost white: the roes of this fish are in high estimation among the natives, who dry them in the sun, and preserve them for a great length of time: they are of the size of a small pea, nearly transparent, and of a reddish yellow cast; they resemble very much, at a little distance, our common garden currants, but are more yellow. Both the fins and belly of this fish are sometimes red, particularly the male. The red char are rather broader, in proportion to their length, than the common salmon: the scales are also imbricated, but rather larger; the rostrum exceeds the under jaw more, and the teeth are neither so large or so numerous as those of the salmon: some of them are almost entirely red on the belly and sides; others are much more white than the salmon, and none of them are variegated with the dark spots which mark the body of the other: their flesh, roes, and every other particular, with regard to the form, are those of the salmon.

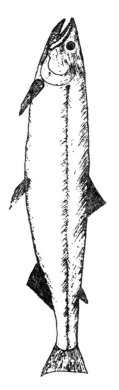

6. Of the salmon trout, we observe two species, differing only in colour; they are seldom more than two feet in length, and narrow in proportion to their length, much more so than the salmon or red char. The jaws [of the silver salmon] are nearly of the same length, and are furnished with a single series of small subulate straight teeth, not so long nor as large as those of the salmon. The mouth is wide, and the tongue is also furnished with some teeth: the fins are placed much like those of the salmon. At the great falls we found this fish of a silvery white colour on the belly and sides, and a bluish light brown on the back and head. The second species [salmon trout] is of a dark colour on its back, and its sides and belly are yellow, with transverse stripes of dark brown; sometimes a little red is intermixed with these colours on the belly and sides towards the head. The eye, flesh, and roe, are like those described of the salmon: the white species found below the falls, were in excellent order, when the salmon were entirely out of season and not fit for use. They associate with the red char, in little rivulets and creeks: the Indians say that the salmon begin to run early in May. The white salmon trout is about two feet and eight inches long, and weighs ten pounds: the eye is moderately large, the pupil black, with a small admixture of yellow, and iris of a silvery white, and a little turbid near its border with a yellowish brown. The fins are small in proportion to the fish; are bony but not pointed, except the tail and back fins, which are pointed a little: the prime back fin and ventral ones contain each ten rays, those of the gills thirteen, that of the tail twelve, and the small fin placed near and above the tail has no bony rays, but is a tough flexible substance, covered with smooth skin. It is thicker in proportion to its width than the salmon: the tongue is thick and firm, beset on each border with small subulate teeth, in a single series: the teeth and the mouth are as before described. Neither this fish nor the salmon are caught with the hook, nor do we know on what they feed.

7. The mountain or speckled trout are found in the waters of the Columbia within the mountains: they are the same with those found in the upper part of the Missouri, but are not so abundant in the Columbia as on that river. We never saw this fish below the mountains, but from the transparency and coldness of the Kooskooskee, we should not doubt of its existence in that stream as low as its junction with the southeast branch of the Columbia.

8. The bottlenose is the same with that before mentioned on the Missouri, and is found exclusively within the mountains.

9. The anchovy, which the natives call olthen, is so delicate a fish that it soon becomes tainted, unless pickled or smoked: the natives run a small stick through the gills and hang it up to dry in the smoke of their lodges, or kindle small fires under it for the purpose of drying: it needs no previous preparation of gutting, and will be cured in twenty-four hours: the natives do not appear to be very scrupulous about eating them when a little foetid.

MOLLUSKS, ETC. Of shell fish we observe the clam, periwinkle, common mussel, the cockle, and a species with a circular flat shell.

The clams [mussels] of this coast are very small; the shell consists of two valves, which open with hinges: the shell is smooth, thin, of an oval form like that of the common mussel, and of sky-blue colour. It is about one and a half inches in length and hangs in clusters to the moss of the rocks: the natives sometimes eat them.

The periwinkles, both of the river and the ocean, are similar to those found in the same situation on the Atlantic coast.

The common mussels of the river are also the same with those on the rivers of the Atlantic coast. The cockle is small, and resembles much that of the Atlantic.

There is also an animal that inhabits a shell perfectly circular, about three inches in diameter, thin and entire on the margin, convex and smooth on the upper side, plain on the under part, and covered with a number of minute capillary fibres, by means of which it attaches itself to the sides of the rocks: the shell is thin, and consists of one valve; a small circular aperture is formed in the centre of the under shell: the animal is soft and boneless.

The pellucid substance and fuci. The pellucid jelly-like substance, called the sea-nettle, is found in great abundance along the strand, where it has been thrown up by the waves and tide.

There are two species of the fuci thrown up in that manner: The first species at one extremity consists of a large vesicle or hollow vessel, which will contain from one to two gallons: it is of a conic form, the base of which forms the extreme end, and is convex and globular, bearing at its centre some short, broad, and angular fibres: the substance is about the consistence of the rind of a citron melon, and three-fourths of an inch thick: the rind is smooth from the small extremity of the cone; a long hollow cylindric and regular tapering tube extends to twenty or thirty feet, and is then terminated with a number of branches, which are flat, half an inch in width, rough, particularly on the edges, where they are furnished with a number of little ovate vesicles or bags of the size of a pigeon's egg: this plant seems to be calculated to float at each extremity, while the little end of the tube, from whence the branches proceed, lie deepest in the water. The other species seen on the coast towards the Killamucks, resembles a large pumpkin; it is solid, and its specific gravity is greater than the water, though sometimes thrown out by the waves: it is of a yellowish brown colour; the rind smooth, and its consistence is harder than that of the pumpkin; but easily cut with a knife: there are some dark brown fibres, rather harder than any other part, which pass longitudinally through the pulp or fleshy substance which forms the interior of this marine production.

The reptiles of this country are the rattlesnake, the gartersnake, lizard, and snail. REPTILES

The gartersnake appears to belong to the same family with the common gartersnakes of the Atlantic coast, and like that snake they inherit no poisonous qualities: they have one hundred and sixty scuta on the abdomen, and seventy on the tail: those on the abdomen near the head and jaws as high as the eye, are of a bluish white, which, as it recedes from the head, becomes of a dark brown: the field of the back and sides black: a narrow stripe of a light yellow runs along the centre of the back; on each side of this stripe there is a range of small transverse, oblong spots, of a pale brick red, diminishing as they recede from the head, and disappear at the commencement of the tail: the pupil of the eye is black, with a narrow ring of white bordering on its edge; the remainder of the iris is of a dark yellowish brown.

The horned lizard, called, and for what reason we never could learn, the prairie buffalo, is a native of these plains, as well as those on the Missouri: they are of the same size, and much the same in appearance as the black lizard: the belly is however broader, the tail shorter, and the action much slower: the colour is generally brown intermixed with yellowish brown spots: the animal is covered with minute scales, interspersed with small horny points, like blunt prickles on the upper surface of the body: the belly and throat resemble those of the frog, and are of a light yellowish brown: the edge of the belly is likewise beset with small horny projections, imparting to those edges a serrate appearance: the eye is small and dark: above and behind the eyes there are several projections of that bone, and their extremities also being armed with a firm black substance, resemble the appearance of horns sprouting from the head: these animals are found in greatest numbers in the sandy open plains, and appear in the greatest abundance after a shower of rain: they are sometimes found basking in the sunshine, but conceal themselves in little holes of the earth in much the greatest proportion of the time: this may account for their appearance in such numbers after the rain, as their holes may thus be rendered untenantable.

Many reasons had determined us to remain at fort Clatsop till the first of April. Besides the want of fuel in the Columbian plains, and the impracticability of passing the mountains before the beginning of June, we were anxious to see some of the foreign traders, from whom, by means of our ample letters of credit, we might have recruited our exhausted stores of merchandise. About the middle of March however, we become seriously alarmed for the want of food: the elk, our chief dependence, had at length deserted their usual haunts in our neighbourhood, and retreated to the mountains. We were too poor to purchase other food from the Indians, so that we were sometimes reduced, notwithstanding all the exertions of our hunters, to a single day's provision in advance. The men too, whom the constant rains and confinement had rendered unhealthy, might we hoped be benefitted by leaving the coast, and resuming the exercise of travelling. We therefore determined to leave fort Clatsop, ascend the river slowly, consume the month of March in the woody country, where we hope to find subsistence, and in this way reach the plains about the first of April, before which time it will be impossible to attempt crossing them: for this purpose we began our preparations.

During the winter we had been very industrious in dressing skins, so that we now had a sufficient quantity of clothing, besides between three and four hundred pair of moccasins. But the whole stock of goods on which we are to depend, either for the purchase of horses or of food, during the long tour of nearly four thousand miles, is so much diminished, that it might all be tied in two handkerchiefs. We have in fact nothing but six blue robes, one of scarlet, a coat and hat of the United States artillery uniform, five robes made of our large flag, and a few old clothes trimmed with ribbon. We therefore feel that our chief dependence must be on our guns, which fortunately for us are all in good order, as we had taken the precaution of bringing a number of extra locks, and one of our men proved to be an excellent artist in that way. The powder had been secured in leaden canisters, and though on many occasions they had been under water, it remained perfectly dry, and we now found ourselves in possession of one hundred and forty pounds of powder, and twice that quantity of lead, a stock quite sufficient for the route homewards.

After much trafficking, we at last succeeded in purchasing a canoe for a uniform coat and half a carrot of tobacco, and took a canoe from the Clatsops, as a reprisal for some elk which some of them had stolen from us in the winter. We were now ready to leave fort Clatsop, but the rain prevented us for several days from caulking the canoes, and we were forced to wait for calm weather, before we could attempt to pass point William. In the meantime we were visited by many of our neighbours, for the purpose of taking leave of us. The Clatsop Commowool has been the most kind and hospitable of all the Indians in this quarter: we therefore gave him a certificate of the kindness and attention which we had received from him, and added a more substantial proof of our gratitude, the gift of all our houses and furniture. To the Chinnook chief Delashelwilt, we gave a certificate of the same kind: we also circulated among the natives several papers, one of which we also posted up in the fort, to the following effect:

"*The object of this last, is, that through the medium of some civilised person, who may see the same, it may be made known to the world, that the party consisting of the persons whose names are hereunto annexed, and who were sent out by the government of the United States to explore the interior of the continent of North America, did penetrate the same by the way of the Missouri and Columbia rivers, to the discharge of the latter into the Pacific ocean, where they arrived on the 14th day of November 1805, and departed the 23d day of March, 1806, on their return to the United States, by the same route by which they had come out.*"

On the back of some of these papers, we sketched the connection of the upper branches of the Missouri and Columbia rivers, with our route, and the track which we intended to follow on our return. This memorandum was all that we deemed it necessary to make; for there seemed but little chance that any detailed report to our government, which we might leave in the hands of the savages, to be delivered to foreign traders, would ever reach the United States. To leave any of our men here, in hopes of their procuring a passage home in some transient vessel, would too much weaken our party, which we must necessarily divide during our route; besides that, we will most probably be there ourselves sooner than any trader, who, after spending the next summer here, might go on some circuitous voyage.

The rains and wind still confined us to the fort; but at last our provisions dwindled down to a single day's stock, and it became absolutely necessary to remove: we therefore sent a few hunters ahead, and stopped the boats as well as we could with mud.

*Sunday.* The next morning the canoes were loaded, and at one o'clock in the afternoon we took a final leave of fort Clatsop. The wind was still high, but the alternative of remaining without provisions was so unpleasant, that we hoped to be able to double point William. We had scarcely left the fort when we met Delashelwilt, and a party of twenty Chinnooks, who understanding that we had been trying to procure a canoe, had brought one for sale. Being, however, already supplied, we left them, and after getting out of Meriwether's bay, began to coast along the south side of the river: we doubled point William without any injury, and at six o'clock reached, at the distance of sixteen miles from fort Clatsop, the mouth of a small creek, where we found our hunters. They had been fortunate enough to kill two elk, but at such a distance that we could not send for them before the next morning, *Monday, March 24th,* when they were brought in for breakfast. We then proceeded. The country is covered with a thick growth of timber: the water however is shallow to the distance of four miles from shore; and although there is a channel deep enough for canoes on the south side, yet as the tide was low, we found some difficulty in passing along. At one o'clock we reached the Cathlamah village, where we halted for about two hours, and purchased some wappatoo and a dog for the invalids. This village we have already described, as situated opposite to the Seal islands: on one of these the Indians have placed their dead in canoes, raised on scaffolds, above the reach of the tide. These people seem to be more fond of carving in wood than their neighbours, and have various specimens of their taste about the houses. The broad pieces supporting the roof and the board through which

411

doors are cut, are the objects on which they chiefly display their ingenuity, and are ornamented with curious figures, sometimes representing persons in a sitting posture supporting a burden.

On resuming our route among the Seal islands, we mistook our way, which an Indian observing, he pursued us and put us into the right channel. He soon, however, embarrassed us, by claiming the canoe we had taken from the Clatsops, and which he declared was his property: we had found it among the Clatsops, and seized it as a reprisal for a theft committed by that nation; but being unwilling to do an act of injustice to this Indian, and having no time to discuss the question of right, we compromised with him for an elk skin, with which he returned perfectly satisfied. We continued our route along the shore, and after making fifteen miles encamped at an old village of nine houses, opposite to the lower village of the Wahkiacums. Here we were overtaken by two Chinnooks, who came to us after dark, and spent the night at our camp. We found plenty of wood for fires, which were quite necessary, as the weather had become cold.

MARCH 25TH     *Tuesday*. This morning proved so disagreeably cold that we did not set out before seven o'clock, when having breakfasted, we continued along the southern side of the river. The wind, however, as well as a strong current was against us, so that we proceeded slowly. On landing for dinner at noon, we were joined by some Clatsops, who had been on a trading voyage to the Skilloots, and were now on their return loaded with dried anchovies, wappatoo, and sturgeon. After dinner we crossed the river to a large island, along the side of which we continued about a mile till we reached a single house, occupied by three men, two women, and the same number of boys, all of the Cathlamah nation. They were engaged in fishing or trolling for sturgeon, of which they had caught about a dozen, but they asked so much for them that we were afraid to purchase. One of the men purchased the skin of a sea-otter, in exchange for a dressed elk skin and a handkerchief. Near adjoining this house was another party of Cathlamahs, who had been up the river on a fishing excursion, and been successful in procuring a large supply, which they were not disposed to sell.

We proceeded on to the head of the island, and then crossed to the north side of the river. Here the coast formed a continued swamp for several miles back, so that it was late in the evening before we were able to reach a spot fit for our camp. At length we discovered the entrance of a small creek, opposite to the place where we were encamped on the sixth of November, and though the ground was low and moist, yet as the spot was sheltered from the wind, we resolved to pass the night there: we had now made fifteen miles. Here we found another party of ten Cathlamahs, who had established a temporary residence here for the purpose of fishing sturgeon and taking seal, in both of which they had been successful. They gave us some of the flesh of the seal, which was a valuable addition to the lean elk. The low grounds which we passed are supplied with cottonwood, and the tree [broad-leaf maple] resembling the ash, except in its leaf, with red willow, broad-leafed willow, seven bark [Douglas hardhack], gooseberry, green briar, and the large-leafed thorn.

The wind was very high towards evening, and continued to blow so violent in the morning, *March 26th*, that we could not set out before eight

412

o'clock. In the meantime finding that one of our neighbours, the Cathla-mahs, by name Wallale, was a person of distinction, we gave him a medal of a small size, with which he was invested with the usual ceremonies. He appeared highly gratified, and requited us with a large sturgeon. The wind having abated, we proceeded to an old village, where we halted for dinner, having met on the way Sahawacap the principal chief of all the Cathlamahs, who was on his return from a trading voyage up the river, with wappatoo and fish, some of which he gave us, and we purchased a little more. At dinner we were overtaken by two Wahkiacums, who have been following us for twenty-four hours, with two dogs, for which they are importuning us to give them some tobacco; but as we have very little of that article left, they were obliged to go off disappointed. We received at the same time an agreeable supply of three eagles and a large goose, brought in by the hunters. After dinner we passed along the north shore opposite to a high fine bottom and dry prairie, at the upper end of which, near a grove of white-oak trees, is an island which we called Fanny's island. There were some deer and elk at a distance in the prairie, but as we could not stay to hunt, we continued till late in the evening, when we encamped on the next island above Fanny's. According to the estimate we made in descending the river, which we begin, however, to think was short, our journey of to-day was eighteen miles. Some Indians came to us, but we were occupied in procuring wood, which we found it difficult to obtain in sufficient quantity for our purposes, and they therefore did not remain long.

*Thursday*. We set out early, and were soon joined by some Skilloots, with fish and roots for sale. At ten o'clock we stopped to breakfast at two houses of the same nation, where we found our hunters, who had not returned to camp last night, but had killed nothing. The inhabitants seemed very kind and hospitable. They gave almost the whole party as much as they could eat of dried anchovies, wappatoo, sturgeon, quamash, and a small white tuberous root, two inches long and as thick as a man's finger, which, when eaten raw, is crisp, milky, and of an agreeable flavour. The Indians also urged us to remain with them all day, and hunt elk and deer, which they said were abundant in the neighbourhood; but as the weather would not permit us to dry and pitch our canoes, we declined their offer and proceeded.

At the distance of two miles we passed the entrance of Coweliskee river. This stream discharges itself on the north side of the Columbia, about three miles above a remarkably high rocky knoll, the south side of which it washes in passing, and which is separated from the northern hills by a wide bottom of several miles in extent. The Coweliskee is one hundred and fifty yards wide, deep and navigable, as the Indians assert, for a considerable distance, and most probably waters the country west and north of the range of mountains which cross the Columbia between the great falls and rapids. On the lower side of this river, a few miles from its entrance into the Columbia, is the principal village of the Skilloots, a numerous people, differing, however, neither in language, dress, nor manners, from the Clatsops, Chinnooks, and other nations at the mouth of the Columbia. With the Chinnooks they have lately been at war, and though hostilities have ceased, yet they have not resumed their usual intercourse, so that the Skilloots do not go as far as the sea, nor do the Chinnooks come higher up than the Seal islands,

413

the trade between them being carried on by the Clatsops, Cathlamahs, and Wahkiacums, their mutual friends. On this same river, above the Skilloots, resides the nation called Hullooetell, of whom we learnt nothing, except that the nation was numerous. Late in the evening we halted at the beginning of the bottom land, below Deer island, after having made twenty miles. Along the low grounds on the river were the cottonwood, sweet-willow, the oak, ash, the broad-leafed ash [maple], and the growth resembling the beech; while the hills are occupied almost exclusively by different species of fir, and the black alder is common to the hills as well as the low grounds. During the day we passed a number of fishing camps, on both sides of the river, and were constantly attended by small parties of the Skilloots, who behaved in the most orderly manner, and from whom we purchased as much fish and roots as we wanted on very moderate terms. The night continued as the day had been, cold, wet, and disagreeable.

MARCH 28TH    *Friday.* We left our camp at an early hour, and by nine o'clock reached an old Indian village on the left side of Deer island. Here we found a party of our men whom we had sent on yesterday to hunt, and who now returned after killing seven deer, in the course of the morning, out of upwards of a hundred which they had seen. They were the common fallow deer with long tails, and though very poor are better than the black-tailed fallow deer of the coast, from which they differ materially. Soon after our arrival the weather became fair, and we therefore immediately hauled the boats on shore, and having dried them by means of large fires, put on the pitch. We also took this opportunity of drying our baggage; and as some of the hunters had not yet returned, it was deemed advisable to pass the night at our present camp. This island, which has received from the Indians the appropriate name of Elalah, or Deer island, is surrounded on the water side by an abundant growth of cottonwood, ash, and willow, while the interior consists chiefly of prairies interspersed with ponds. These afford refuge to great numbers of geese, ducks, large swan, sandhill cranes, a few canvass-backed ducks, and particularly the duckinmallard, the most abundant of all. There are also great numbers of snakes resembling our gartersnakes in appearance, and like them not poisonous. Our hunters brought in three deer, a goose, some ducks, an eagle, and a tiger-cat, but such is the extreme voracity of the vultures, that they had devoured in the space of a few hours, four of the deer killed this morning; and one of our men declared, that they had besides dragged a large buck about thirty yards, skinned it, and broke the backbone. We were visited during the day by a large canoe with ten Indians of the Quathlapotle nation, who reside about seventeen miles above us. We had advanced only five miles to-day.

MARCH 29TH    *Saturday.* At an early hour we proceeded along the side of Deer island, and halted for breakfast at the upper end of it, which is properly the commencement of the great Columbian valley. We were here joined by three men of the Towahnahiook nation, with whom we proceeded, till at the distance of fourteen miles from our camp of last evening we reached a large inlet or arm of the river, about three hundred yards wide, up which they went to their villages. A short distance above this inlet a considerable river empties itself from the north side of the Columbia. Its name is Chawahnahiooks. It is

414

about one hundred and fifty yards wide, and at present discharges a large body of water, though the Indians assure us that at a short distance above its mouth, the navigation is obstructed by falls and rapids. Three miles beyond the inlet is an island near the north shore of the river, behind the lower end of which is a village of Quathlapotles, where we landed, about three o'clock. The village consists of fourteen large wooden houses. The people themselves received us very kindly, and voluntarily spread before us wappatoo and anchovies, but as soon as we had finished enjoying this hospitality, if it deserves that name, they began to ask us for presents. They were, however, perfectly satisfied with the small articles which we distributed according to custom, and equally pleased with our purchasing some wappatoo, twelve dogs and two sea-otter skins. We also gave to the chief a small medal, which he, however, soon transferred to his wife. After remaining some time we embarked, and coasting along this island, which after the nation we called Quathlapotle island, encamped for this night in a small prairie on the north side of the Columbia, having made by estimate nineteen miles. The river is rising fast.

In the course of the day we saw great numbers of geese, ducks, and large and small swans, which last are very abundant in the ponds where the wappatoo grows, as they feed much on that root. We also observed the crested king-fisher, and the large and small blackbird: and this evening heard, without seeing, the large hooting owl. The frogs, which we have not found in the wet marshes near the entrance of the Columbia, are now croaking in the swamps and marshes with precisely the same note common in the United States. The gartersnakes appear in vast quantities, and are scattered through the prairies in large bundles of forty or fifty entwined round each other: among the moss on the rocks we observed a species of small wild onions growing so closely together as to form a perfect turf, and equal in flavour to the chives of our gardens, which they resemble in appearance.

*Sunday.* Soon after our departure we were met by three Clanaminamuns, one of whom we recognised as our companion yesterday. He pressed us very much to visit his countrymen on the inlet, but we had no time to make the circuit, and parted. We had not proceeded far before a party of Claxtars, and Cathlacumups, passed us in two canoes, on their way down the river; and soon after we were met by several other canoes, filled with persons of different tribes on each side of the river. We passed, also, several fishing camps, on Wappatoo island, and then halted for breakfast on the north side of the river, near our camp of the *4th of November.* Here we were visited by several canoes from two villages on Wappatoo island; the first, about two miles above us, is called Clahnaquah, the other a mile above them, has the name of Multnomah. After higgling much in the manner of those on the seacoast, these Indians gave us a sturgeon with some wappatoo and pashequaw in exchange for small fishhooks. As we proceeded we were joined by other Indians, and on coming opposite to the Clahnaquah village, we were shown another village about two miles from the river on the northeast side, and behind a pond running parallel with it. Here they said the tribe called Shotos resided. About four o'clock the Indians all left us. Their chief object in accompanying us appeared to be to gratify curiosity; but though they behaved in the most friendly manner, most of them were prepared with their instruments of war. About sunset we reached a beautiful prairie, opposite the middle of what we had called Image-canoe island, and having made twenty-three miles, encamped for the night. In the prairie is a large pond or lake, and an open grove of oak borders the back part. There are many deer and elk in the neighbourhood, but they are very shy, and the annual fern which is now abundant and dry, makes such a rustling as the hunters pass through it, that they could not come within reach of the game, and we obtained nothing but a single duck.

MARCH 31ST  *Monday*. We set out very early, and at eight o'clock landed on the north side of the river and breakfasted. Directly opposite is a large wooden house, belonging to the Shahala nation, the inhabitants of which came over to see us. We had observed in descending the river last year, that there were at the same place, twenty-four other houses built of wood and covered with straw, all of which are now destroyed: on inquiry the Indians informed us, that their relations whom we saw last fall, usually visit them at that season for the purpose of hunting deer and elk, and collecting wappatoo, but that they had lately returned to their permanent residence at the Rapids, we presume in order to prepare for the salmon season, as that fish will soon begin to run. At ten o'clock we resumed our route along the north side of the river, and having passed Diamond island, and Whitebrant island, halted for the night at the lower point of a handsome prairie. Our camp which is twenty-five miles from that of last night, is situated opposite to the upper entrance of Quicksand river: a little below a stream from the north empties itself into the Columbia, near the head of Whitebrant island. It is about eighty yards wide, and at present discharges a large body of very clear water, which near the Columbia overflows its low banks, and forms several large ponds. The natives inform us that this river is of no great extent, and rises in the mountains near us, and that at a mile from its mouth it is divided into two nearly equal branches, both of which are incapable of being navigated, on account of their numerous falls and rapids. Not being able to learn any Indian name, we called it Seal river, from the abundance of those animals near its mouth. At the same place we saw a summer duck, or a wood duck, as it is sometimes called; it is the same with those of the United States, and the first we had seen since entering the Rocky mountains last summer.

The hunters, who had been obliged to halt below Seal river on account of the waves being too high for their small canoe, returned after dark with the unwelcome news that game was scarce in that quarter.

## Tuesday, April 1st, 1806

Three Indians had followed us yesterday, and encamped near us last night. On putting to them a variety of questions relative to their country, they assured us that Quicksand river, which we had hitherto deemed so considerable, extends no further than the southwest side of mount Hood, which is south 85° east, forty miles distant from this place; that it is moreover navigable for a very short distance only, in consequence of falls and rapids, and that no nation inhabits its borders. Several other persons affirmed that it rose near mount Hood, and sergeant Pryor, who was sent for the purpose of examining it, convinced us of the truth of their statement. He had found the river three hundred yards wide, though the channel was not more than fifty yards, and about six feet deep. The current was rapid, the water turbid, the bed of the river is formed entirely of quicksand, and the banks low and at present overflowed. He passed several islands, and at three and a half miles distance a creek from the south, fifty yards wide; his farthest course was six miles from the mouth of the river, but there it seemed to bend to the east, and he heard the noise of waterfalls. If Quicksand river then does not go beyond mount Hood, it must leave the valley a few miles from its entrance, and run nearly parallel with the Columbia. There must therefore be some other large river, which we have not yet seen, to water the extensive country between the mountains of the coast and Quicksand river: but the Indians could give us no satisfactory information of any such stream.

Whilst we were making these inquiries, a number of canoes came to us, and among the rest a number of families were descending the river. They told us that they lived at the Great rapids, but that a great scarcity of provisions there, had induced them to come down in hopes of finding subsistence in this fertile valley. All those who lived at the rapids, as well as the nations above them, were in much distress for want of food, having consumed their winter store of dried fish, and not expecting the return of the salmon before the next full moon, which will happen on the second of May: this intelligence was disagreeable and embarrassing. From the falls to the Chopunnish nation, the plains afford no deer, elk, or antelope, on which we can rely for subsistence. The horses are very poor at this season, and the dogs must be in the same condition if their food the fish have failed, so that we had calculated entirely on purchasing fish. On the other hand it is obviously inexpedient to wait for the return of the salmon, since in that case we might not reach the Missouri before the ice would prevent our navigating it. We might besides hazard the loss of our horses, for the Chopunnish, with whom we left them, intend crossing the mountains as early as possible, which is about the beginning of May, and they would take our horses with them, or suffer them to disperse, in either of which cases the passage of the mountains will be almost impracticable. We therefore, after much deliberation, decided to remain here till we collect meat enough to last us till we reach the Chopunnish nation, to obtain canoes from the natives as we ascend, either in exchange for our periogues, or by purchasing them with skins and merchandise. These canoes may in turn be exchanged for horses with the natives of the plains, till we obtain enough to travel altogether by land. On reaching the southeast branch of the Columbia, four or five men shall be sent on to the Chopunnish to have our horses in readiness, and thus we shall have a stock of horses sufficient to transport our baggage and to supply us with provisions, for we now perceive that they will form our only certain resource for food.

The hunters returned from the opposite side of the river with some deer and elk, which were abundant there, as were also the tracks of the black bear; while on the north side we could kill nothing.

In the course of our dealings to-day we purchased a canoe from an Indian, for which we gave six fathom of wampum beads. He seemed perfectly satisfied and went away, but returned soon after, cancelled the bargain, and giving back the wampum requested that we would restore him the canoe. To this we consented, as we knew this method of trading to be very common and deemed perfectly fair.

APRIL 2D     *Wednesday.* Being now determined to collect as much meat as possible, two parties, consisting of nine men, were sent over the river to hunt, three were ordered to range the country on this side, while all the rest were employed in cutting and scaffolding the meat which we had already. About eight o'clock several canoes arrived to visit us, and among the rest were two young men, who were pointed out as Cushooks. On inquiry, they said that their nation resided at the falls of a large river, which empties itself into the south side of the Columbia, a few miles below us, and they drew a map of the country, with a coal on a mat. In order to verify this information, captain Clark persuaded one of the young men, by a present of a burning-glass, to accompany him to the river, in search of which he immediately set out with a canoe and seven of our men. After his departure other canoes arrived from above, bringing families of women and children, who confirmed the accounts of a scarcity of provisions. One of these families, consisting of ten or twelve persons, encamped near us, and behaved perfectly well. The hunters on this side of the river, returned with the skins of only two deer, the animals being too poor for use.

APRIL 3D     *Thursday.* A considerable number of Indians crowded us to-day, many of whom came from the upper part of the river. These poor wretches confirm the reports of scarcity among the nations above; which, indeed, their appearance sufficiently prove, for they seem almost starved, and greedily pick the bones and refuse meat thrown away by us.

In the evening captain Clark returned from his excursion. On setting out yesterday at half past eleven o'clock, he directed his course along the south side of the river, where, at the distance of eight miles, he passed a village of the Nechecolee tribe, belonging to the Eloot nation. The village itself is small, and being situated behind Diamond island, was concealed from our view as we passed both times along the northern shore. He continued till three o'clock, when he landed at the single house already mentioned, as the only remains of a village of twenty-four straw huts. Along the shore were great numbers of small canoes for gathering wappatoo, which were left by the Shahalas, who visit the place annually. The present inhabitants of the house are part of the Neerchokioo tribe of the same nation. On entering one of the apartments of the house, captain Clark offered several articles to the Indians, in exchange for wappatoo, but they appeared sullen and ill-humoured, and refused to give him any. He therefore sat down by the fire, opposite to the men, and taking a port-fire match from his pocket, threw a small piece of it into the flame, at the same time took his pocket compass, and by means of a magnet, which happened to be in his inkhorn, made the needle turn round very briskly. The match now took fire, and burned violently, on which, the Indians terrified at this strange exhibition, immediately brought a quantity of wappatoo, and laid it at his feet, begging him to put out the bad fire: while an old woman continued to speak with great vehemence, as if praying and imploring protection. Having received the roots, captain Clark put up the compass, and as the match went out of itself, tranquillity was restored, though the women and children still took refuge

418

in their beds, and behind the men. He now paid them for what he had used, and after lighting his pipe, and smoking with them, he continued down the river.

He now found what we had called Image-canoe island, to consist of three islands, the one in the middle concealing the opening between the other two in such a way, as to present to us on the opposite side of the river, the appearance of a single island. At the lower point of the third, and thirteen miles below the last village, he entered the mouth of a large river which was concealed by three small islands in its mouth, from those who descend or go up the Columbia. This river, which the Indians call Multnomah, from a nation of the same name, residing near it on Wappatoo island, enters the Columbia, one hundred and forty miles from the mouth of the latter river, of which it may justly be considered as forming one fourth, though it had now fallen eighteen inches below its greatest annual height. From its entrance mount Regnier [Rainier] bears nearly north, mount St. Helen's north, with a very high humped mountain a little to the east of it, which seems to lie in the same chain with the conic-pointed mountains before mentioned. Mount Hood bore due east, and captain Clark now discovered to the southeast, a mountain which we had not yet seen, and to which he gave the name of mount Jefferson. Like mount St. Helen's its figure is a regular cone covered with snow, and is probably of equal height with that mountain, though being more distant, so large a portion of it does not appear above the range of mountains which lie between these and this point.

Soon after entering the Multnomah he was met by an old Indian descending the river alone in a canoe. After some conversation with him, the pilot informed captain Clark, that this old man belonged to the Clackamos nation, who reside on a river forty miles up the Multnomah. The current of this latter river, is as gentle as that of the Columbia, its surface is smooth and even, and it appears to possess water enough for the largest ship, since, on sounding with a line of five fathoms, he could find no bottom for at least one-third of the width of the stream. At the distance of seven miles, he passed a sluice or opening, on the right, eighty yards wide, and which separates Wappatoo island from the continent, by emptying itself into the inlet below. Three miles further up, he reached a large wooden house, on the east side, where he intended to sleep, but on entering the rooms he found such swarms of fleas that he preferred lying on the ground in the neighbourhood. The guide informed him that this house is the temporary residence of the Nemalquinner tribe of the Cushook nation, who reside just below the falls of the Multnomah, but come down here occasionally to collect wappatoo: it was thirty feet long, and forty deep; built of broad boards, covered with the bark of white cedar; the floor on a level with the surface of the earth, and the arrangement of the interior like those near the seacoast. The inhabitants had left their canoes, mats, bladders, train-oil, baskets, bowls, and trenchers, lying about the house at the mercy of every visitor; a proof, indeed, of the mutual respect for the property of each other, though we have had very conclusive evidence that the property of white men is not deemed equally sacred. The guide informed him further, that a small distance above were two bayous, on which were a number of small houses belonging to the Cushooks, but that the inhabitants had all gone up to the falls of the Multnomah, for the purpose of fishing.

419

Early the next morning captain Clark proceeded up the river, which during the night, had fallen about five inches. At the distance of two miles he came to the centre of a bend under the highlands on the right side, from which its course, as could be discerned, was to the east of southeast. At this place the Multnomah is five hundred yards wide, and for half that distance across, the cord of five fathoms would not reach the bottom. It appears to be washing away its banks, and has more sandbars and willow points than the Columbia. Its regular gentle current, the depth and smoothness, and uniformity with which it rolls its vast body of water, prove that its supplies are at once distant and regular; nor, judging from its appearance and courses, is it rash to believe that the Multnomah and its tributary streams water the vast extent of country between the western mountains and those of the seacoast, as far perhaps as the waters of the gulf of California. About eleven o'clock he reached the house of the Neerchokioo, which he now found to contain eight families; but they were all so much alarmed at his presence, notwithstanding his visit yesterday, that he remained a very few minutes only. Soon after setting out, he met five canoes filled with the same number of families, belonging to the Shahala nation. They were descending the river in search of subsistence, and seemed very desirous of coming alongside of the boat; but as there were twenty-one men on board, and the guide said that all these Shahalas, as well as their relations at the house which we had just left, were mischievous bad men, they were not suffered to approach. At three o'clock he halted for an hour at the Nechecolee house, where his guide resided.

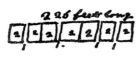

This large building is two hundred and twenty-six feet in front, entirely above ground, and may be considered as a single house, because the whole is under one roof; otherwise it would seem more like a range of buildings, as it is divided into seven distinct apartments, each thirty feet square, by means of broad boards set on end from the floor to the roof. The apartments are separated from each other by a passage or alley four feet wide, extending through the whole depth of the house, and the only entrance is from this alley, through a small hole about twenty-two inches wide, and not more than three feet high. The roof is formed of rafters and round poles laid on them longitudinally. The whole is covered with a double row of the bark of the white cedar, extending from the top eighteen inches over the eaves, and secured as well as smoothed by splinters of dried fir, inserted through it at regular distances. In this manner the roof is made light, strong, and durable. Near this house are the remains of several other large buildings, sunk in the ground and constructed like those we had seen at the great narrows of the Columbia, belonging to the Eloots, with whom these people claim an affinity. In manners and dress these Nechecolees differ but little from the Quathlapotles and others of this neighbourhood; but their language is the same used by the Eloots, and though it has some words in common with the dialects spoken here, yet the whole air of the language is obviously different. The men too are larger, and both sexes better formed than among the nations below; and the females are distinguished by wearing larger and longer robes, which are generally of deer skin dressed in the hair, than the neighbouring women. In the house were several old people of both sexes, who were treated with much respect, and still seemed healthy, though most of them were perfectly blind. On inquiring the cause of the decline of their village, an old man, the father of the guide, and a person of some distinction, brought forward a woman very much marked with the small-pox, and said, that when a girl she was very near dying with the disorder which had left those marks, and that all the inhabitants of the houses now in ruins had fallen victims to the same disease. From the apparent age of the woman, connected with her size at the time of her illness, captain Clark judged that the sickness must have been about thirty years ago, the period about which we have supposed that the small-pox prevailed on the seacoast.

He then entered into a long conversation with regard to all the adjacent country and its inhabitants, which the old man explained with great intelligence, and then drew with his finger in the dust a sketch of the Multnomah, and Wappatoo island. This captain Clark copied and preserved. He now purchased five dogs, and taking leave of the Nechecolee village, returned to camp.

FRIDAY, APRIL 4, 1806 The hunters were still out in every direction. Those from the opposite side of the river returned with the flesh of a bear and some venison, but the flesh of six deer and an elk which they had killed was so meagre and unfit for use, that they had left it in the woods. Two other deer were brought in, but as the game seemed poor, we despatched a large party to some low grounds on the south, six miles above us, to hunt there until our arrival. As usual many of the Indians came to our camp, some descending the rivers with their families, and others from below with no object except to gratify their curiosity.

The visit of captain Clark to the Multnomahs, now enabled us to combine all that we had seen or learnt of the neighbouring countries and nations. Of these the most important spot is Wappatoo island, a large extent of country lying between the Multnomah, and an arm of the Columbia, which we have called Wappatoo inlet, and separated from the main land by a sluice eighty yards wide, which at the distance of seven miles up the Multnomah connects that river with the inlet. The island thus formed is about twenty miles long, and varies in breadth from five to ten miles: the land is high and extremely fertile, and on most parts is supplied with a heavy growth of cottonwood, ash, the large-leafed ash, and sweet-willow, the black alder, common to the coast, having now disappeared.

But the chief wealth of this island consists of the numerous ponds in the interior, abounding with the common arrowhead (sagittaria sagittifolia) to the root of which is attached a bulb growing beneath it in the mud. This bulb, to which the Indians give the name of wappatoo, is the great article of food, and almost the staple article of commerce on the Columbia. It is never out of season; so that at all times of the year, the valley is frequented

by the neighbouring Indians who come to gather it. It is collected chiefly by the women, who employ for the purpose canoes from ten to fourteen feet in length, about two feet wide, and nine inches deep, and tapering from the middle, where they are about twenty inches wide. They are sufficient to contain a single person and several bushels of roots, yet so very light that a woman can carry them with ease; she takes one of these canoes into a pond where the water is as high as the breast, and by means of her toes, separates from the root this bulb, which on being freed from the mud rises immediately to the surface of the water, and is thrown into the canoe. In this manner these patient females remain in the water for several hours even in the depth of winter. This plant is found through the whole extent of the valley in which we now are, but does not grow on the Columbia farther eastward.

This valley is bounded westward by the mountainous country bordering the coast, from which it extends eastward thirty miles in a direct line, till it is closed by the range of mountains crossing the Columbia above the great falls. Its length from north to south we are unable to determine, but we believe that the valley must extend to a great distance: it is in fact the only desirable situation for a settlement on the western side of the Rocky mountains, and being naturally fertile, would, if properly cultivated, afford subsistence for forty or fifty thousand souls. The highlands are generally of a dark rich loam, not much injured by stones, and though waving, by no means too steep for cultivation, and a few miles from the river they widen at least on the north side, into rich extensive prairies. The timber on them is abundant, and consists almost exclusively of the several species of fir already described, and some of which grow to a great height. We measured a fallen tree of that species, and found that including the stump of about six feet, it was three hundred and eighteen feet in length, though its diameter was only three feet. The dogwood is also abundant on the uplands: it differs from that of the United States in having a much smoother bark, and in being much larger, the trunk attaining a diameter of nearly two feet. There is some white cedar of a large size, but no pine of any kind. In the bottom lands are the cotton wood, ash, large-leafed ash, and sweet willow. Interspersed with these are the pashequaw, shanataque, and compound fern, of which the natives use the roots, the red flowering currant abounds on the upland, while along the river bottoms grow luxuriantly the watercress, strawberry, cinquefoil, narrowdock, sandrush, and the flowering pea, which is not yet in bloom.

There is also a species of the bear's-claw now blooming, but the large-leafed thorn has disappeared, nor do we see any longer the huckleberry, the shallun, nor any of the other evergreen shrubs which bear berries, except the species, the leaf of which has a prickly margin.

Among the animals, we observe the martin, small geese, the small speckled woodpecker, with a white back, the blue-crested corvus, ravens, crows, eagles, vultures, and hawks. The mellow bug, long-legged spider, as well as the butterfly and blowingfly, and tick, have already made their appearance, but none of all these are distinguished from animals of the same sort in the United States. The mosquitoes too have resumed their visits, but are not yet troublesome.

The nations who inhabit this fertile neighbourhood are very numerous. The Wappatoo inlet extends three hundred yards wide, for ten or twelve miles to the south, as far as the hills near which it receives the waters of a small creek whose sources are not far from those of the Killamuck river. On that creek resides the Clackstar nation, a numerous people of twelve hundred souls, who subsist on fish and wappatoo, and who trade by means of the Killamuck river, with the nation of that name on the seacoast. Lower down the inlet, towards the Columbia, is the tribe called Cathlacumup. On the sluice which connects the inlet with the Multnomah, are the tribes, Cathlanahquiah, and Cathlacomatup: and on Wappatoo island, the tribes of Clannahminamun, and Clahnaquah. Immediately opposite, near the Towahnahiooks, are the Quathlapotles, and higher up on the side of the Columbia, the Shotos. All these tribes, as well as the Cathlahaws, who live somewhat lower on the river, and have an old village on Deer island, may be considered as parts of the great Multnomah nation, which has its principal residence on Wappatoo island, near the mouth of the large river to which they give their name. Forty miles above its junction with the Columbia, it receives the waters of the Clackamos, a river which may be traced through a woody and fertile country to its sources in mount Jefferson, almost to the foot of which it is navigable for canoes. A nation of the same name resides in eleven villages along its borders: they live chiefly on fish and roots, which abound in the Clackamos and along its banks, though they sometimes descend to the Columbia to gather wappatoo, where they cannot be distinguished by dress or manners, or language from the tribes of Multnomahs. Two days' journey from the Columbia, or about twenty miles beyond the entrance of the Clackamos, are the falls of the Multnomah. At this place are the permanent residences of the Cushooks and Chahcowahs, two tribes who are attracted to that place by the fish, and by the convenience of trading across the mountains and down Killamuck river, with the nation of Killamucks, from whom they procure train oil. These falls were occasioned by the passage of a high range of mountains; beyond which the country stretches into a vast level plain, wholly destitute of timber. As far as the Indians, with whom we conversed, had ever penetrated that country, it was inhabited by a nation called Calahpoewah, a very numerous people whose villages, nearly forty in number, are scattered along each side of the Multnomah, which furnish them with their chief subsistence, fish, and the roots along its banks.

All the tribes in the neighbourhood of Wappatoo island, we have considered as Multnomahs; not because they are in any degree subordinate to that nation; but they all seem to regard the Multnomahs as the most powerful. There is no distinguished chief, except the one at the head of the Multnomahs; and they are moreover linked by a similarity of dress and manners, and houses and language, which much more than the feeble restraints of Indian government contribute to make one people. These circumstances also separate them from nations lower down the river. The Clatsops, Chinnooks, Wahkiacums and Cathlamahs understand each other perfectly; their language varies, however, in some respects from that of the Skilloots; but on reaching the Multnomah Indians, we found, that although many words were the same, and a great number differed only in the mode of accenting them, from those employed by the Indians near the mouth of the Columbia, yet there was a very sensible variation of language.

The natives of the valley are larger and rather better shaped than those of the seacoast: their appearance too is generally healthy, but they are afflicted with the common disease of the Columbia, soreness of the eyes. To whatever this disorder may be imputed it is a great national calamity: at all ages their eyes are sore and weak, and the loss of one eye is by no means uncommon, while in grown persons total blindness is frequent, and almost universal in old age. The dress of the men has nothing different from that used below, but are chiefly remarked by a passion for large brass buttons, which they fix on a sailor's jacket, when they are so fortunate as to obtain one, without regard to any arrangement. The women also wear the short robe already described; but their hair is most commonly braided into two tresses falling over each ear in front of the body, and instead of the tissue of bark, they employ a piece of leather in the shape of a pocket handkerchief tied round the loins. This last is the only and ineffectual defence when the warmth of the weather induces them to throw aside the robe.

The houses are in general on a level with the ground, though some are sunk to the depth of two or three feet into the ground, and like those near the coast adorned or disfigured by carvings or paintings on the posts, doors and beds: they do not possess any peculiar weapon except a kind of broad sword made of iron, from three to four feet long, the blade about four inches wide, very thin and sharp at all its edges, as well as at the point. They have also bludgeons of wood in the same form; and both kinds generally hang at the head of their beds. These are formidable weapons.

Like the natives of the seacoast, they are also very fond of cold, hot, and vapour baths, which are used at all seasons, and for the purpose of health as well as pleasure. They, however, add a species of bath peculiar to themselves, by washing the whole body with urine every morning.

The mode of burying the dead in canoes, is no longer practised by the natives here. The place of deposit is a vault formed of boards, slanting like the roof of a house from a pole supported by two forks. Under this vault the dead are placed horizontally on boards, on the surface of the earth, and carefully covered with mats. Many bodies are here laid on each other, to the height of three or four corpses, and different articles, which were most esteemed by the dead, are placed by their side; their canoes themselves being sometimes broken to strengthen the vault.

The trade of all these inhabitants is in anchovies, sturgeon, but chiefly in wappatoo, to obtain which, the inhabitants both above and below them on the river, come at all seasons, and supply in turn, beads, cloth, and various other articles procured from the Europeans.

*Saturday*. We dried our meat as well as the cloudy weather would permit. In the course of his chase yesterday, one of our men who killed the bear, found a nest of another with three cubs in it. He returned to-day in hopes of finding her, but he brought only the cubs, without being able to see the dam, and on this occasion, Drewyer, our most experienced huntsman, assured us that he had never known a single instance where a female bear, who had once been disturbed by a hunter and obliged to leave her young, returned to them again. The young bears were sold for wappatoo to some of the many Indians who visited us in parties during the day, and behaved very well. APRIL 5TH

Having made our preparations of dried meat, we set out next morning, *Sunday 6th*, by nine o'clock, and continued along the north side of the river for a few miles, and then crossed to the river to look for the hunters, who had been sent forward the day before yesterday. We found them at the upper end of the bottom with some Indians, for we are never freed from the visits of the natives. They had killed three elk, and wounded two others so badly, that it was still possible to get them. We therefore landed, and having prepared scaffolds and secured the five elk, we encamped for the night.

The following morning, the weather having been fair and pleasant, had dried a sufficient quantity of meat to serve us as far as the Chopunnish, with occasional supplies, if we can procure them, of dogs, roots, and horses. In the course of the day several parties of Shahalas, from a village eight miles above us, came to visit us, and behaved themselves very properly, except that we were obliged to turn one of them from the camp for stealing a piece of lead. Every thing was now ready for our departure, but in the morning, *Tuesday 8th*, the wind blew with great violence, and we were obliged to unload our boats, which were soon after filled with water. The same cause prevented our setting out to-day; we therefore despatched several hunters round the neighbourhood, but in the evening they came back with nothing but a duck. They had, however, seen some of the black-tailed, jumping, or fallow deer, like those about fort Clatsop, which are scarce near this place, where the common long-tailed fallow deer are most abundant. They had also observed two black bears, the only kind that we have discovered in this quarter. A party of six Indians encamped at some distance, and late at night the sentinel stopped one of the men, an old man who was creeping into camp APRIL 7TH in order to pilfer: he contented himself with frightening the Indian, and then giving him a few stripes with a switch, turned the fellow out, and he soon afterwards left the place with all his party.

*Wednesday.* The wind having moderated, we reloaded the canoes, and set out by seven o'clock. We stopped to take up two hunters who had left us yesterday, but were unsuccessful in the chase, and then proceeded to the Wahclellah village, situated on the north side of the river, about a mile below Beacon rock. During the whole of the route from our camp, we passed along under high, steep, and rocky sides of the mountains, which now close on each side of the river, forming stupendous precipices, covered with the fir and white cedar. Down these heights frequently descend the most beautiful cascades, one of which, a large creek, throws itself over a perpendicular rock three hundred feet above the water, while other smaller streams precipitate themselves from a still greater elevation, and evaporating in a mist, again collect and form a second cascade before they reach the bottom of the rocks. We stopped to breakfast at this village. We here found the tomahawk which had been stolen from us on the fourth of last November: they assured us they had bought it of the Indians below; but as the latter had already informed us that the Wahclellahs had such an article, which they had stolen, we made no difficulty about retaking our property.

This village appears to be the wintering station of the Wahclellahs and Clahclellahs, two tribes of the Shahala nation. The greater part of the first tribe have lately removed to the falls of the Multnomah, and the second have established themselves a few miles higher up the Columbia, opposite the lower point of Brant island, where they take salmon, that being the commencement of the rapids. They are now in the act of removing, and carrying off with them, not only the furniture and effects, but the bark and most of the boards of their houses. In this way nine have been lately removed. There are still fourteen standing, and in the rear of the village are the traces of ten or twelve others of more ancient date. These houses are either sunk in the ground or on a level with the surface, and are generally built of boards and covered with cedar bark. In the single houses there is generally a division near the door, which is in the end; or in case the house be double, opens on the narrow passage between the two. Like those we had seen below at the Neerchokioo tribe, the women wear longer and larger robes than their neighbours the Multnomahs, and suspend various ornaments from the cartilage of the nose: the hair is, however, worn in the same sort of braid, falling over each ear, and the truss is universal from the Wappatoo island to Lewis's river. The men also form their hair into two queues by means of otter skin thongs, which fall over the ears so as to give that extraordinary width to the face which is here considered so ornamental. These people seemed very unfriendly, and our numbers alone seemed to secure us from ill treatment.

While we were at breakfast the grand chief of the Chilluckittequaws arrived, with two inferior chiefs, and several men and women of his nation. They were returning home, after trading in the Columbian valley, and were loaded with wappatoo and dried anchovies, which, with some beads, they had obtained in exchange for chappelell, bear-grass and other small articles. As these people had been very kind to us as we descended the river, we endeavoured to repay them by every attention in our power. After purchasing, with much difficulty, a few dogs and some wappatoo from the Wahclellahs, we left them at two o'clock, and passing under the Beacon rock, reached in two hours the Clahclellah village.

This Beacon rock, which we now observed more accurately than as we descended, stands on the north side of the river, insulated from the hills. The northern side has a partial growth of fir or pine. To the south it rises in an unbroken precipice to the height of seven hundred feet, where it terminates in a sharp point, and may be seen at the distance of twenty miles below. This rock may be considered as the commencement of tide-water, though the influence of the tide is perceptible here in autumn only, at which time the water is low. What the precise difference at those seasons is, we cannot determine; but on examining a rock which we lately passed, and comparing its appearance now with that which we observed last November, we judge the flood of this spring to be twelve feet above the height of the river at that time. From Beacon rock as low as the marshy islands, the general width of the river is from one to two miles, though in many places it is still greater.

On landing at the Clahclellahs we found them busy in erecting their huts, which seem to be of a temporary kind only, so that most probably they do not remain longer than the salmon season. Like their countrymen, whom we had just left, these people were sulky and ill-humoured, and so much on the alert to pilfer, that we were obliged to keep them at a distance from our baggage. As our large canoes could not ascend the rapids on the north side, we passed to the opposite shore, and entered the narrow channel which separates it from Brant island. The weather was very cold and rainy, and the wind so high, that we were afraid to attempt the rapids this evening, and therefore, finding a safe harbour, we encamped for the night. The wood in this neighbourhood has lately been on fire, and the firs have discharged considerable quantities of pitch, which we collected for some of our boats. We saw to-day some turkey-buzzards, which are the first we have observed on this side of the Rocky mountains.

*Thursday.* Early in the morning we dropped down the channel to the lower end of Brant island, and then drew our boats up the rapid. At the distance of a quarter of a mile we crossed over to a village of Clahclellahs, consisting of six houses, on the opposite side. The river is here about four hundred yards wide, and the current so rapid, that although we employed five oars for each canoe, we were borne down a considerable distance. While we were at breakfast, one of the Indians offered us two sheep-skins for sale, one, which was the skin of a full grown sheep [mountain goat], was as large as that of a common deer: the second was smaller, and the skin of the head, with the horns remaining, was made into a cap, and highly prized as an ornament by the owner. He however sold the cap to us for a knife, and the rest of the skin for those of two elk; but as they observed our anxiety to purchase the other skin, they would not accept the same price for it, and as we hoped to procure more in the neighbourhood, we did not offer a greater. The horns of the animal were black, smooth, and erect, and they rise from the middle of the forehead, a little above the eyes, in a cylindrical form, to the height of four inches, where they are pointed. The Clahclellahs informed us that the sheep are very abundant on the heights, and among the cliffs of the adjacent mountains; and that these two had been lately killed out of a herd of thirty-six, at no great distance from the village.

We were soon joined by our hunters with three black-tailed fallow deer, and having purchased a few white salmon, proceeded on our route. The south side of the river is impassable, and the rapidity of the current as well as the large rocks along the shore, render the navigation of even the north side extremely difficult. During the greater part of the day it was necessary to draw them along the shore, and as we have only a single tow-rope that is strong enough, we are obliged to bring them one after the other. In this tedious and laborious manner, we at length reached the portage on the north side, and carried our baggage to the top of a hill, about two hundred paces distant, where we encamped for the night. The canoes were drawn on shore and secured, but one of them having got loose, drifted down to the last village, the inhabitants of which brought her back to us; an instance of honesty which we rewarded with a present of two knives.

It rained all night and the next morning, *Friday, 11th*, so that the tents, and skins which covered the baggage, were wet. We therefore determined to take the canoes first over the portage, in hopes that by the afternoon the rain would cease, and we might carry our baggage across without injury. This was immediately begun by almost the whole party, who in the course of the day dragged four of the canoes to the head of the rapids, with great difficulty and labour. A guard, consisting of one sick man and three who had been lamed by accidents, remained with captain Lewis to guard the baggage. This precaution was absolutely necessary to protect it from the Wahclellahs, whom we discovered to be great thieves, notwithstanding their apparent honesty in restoring our boat: indeed, so arrogant and intrusive have they become, that nothing but our numbers, we are convinced, saves us from attack. They crowded about us while we were taking up the boats, and one of them had the insolence to throw stones down the bank at two of our men.

We now found it necessary to depart from our mild and pacific course of conduct. On returning to the head of the portage, many of them met our men, and seemed very ill disposed. Shields had stopped to purchase a dog, and being separated from the rest of the party, two Indians pushed him out of the road, and attempted to take the dog from him. He had no weapon but a long knife, with which he immediately attacked them both, hoping to put them to death before they had time to draw their arrows, but as soon as they saw his design, they fled into the woods. Soon afterwards we were told by an Indian who spoke Clatsop, which we had ourselves learnt during the winter, that the Wahclellahs had carried off captain Lewis's dog to their village below. Three men well armed were instantly despatched in pursuit of them, with orders to fire if there was the slightest resistance or hesitation. At the distance of two miles, they came within sight of the thieves, who finding themselves pursued, left the dog and made off. We now ordered all the Indians out of our camp, and explained to them, that whoever stole any of our baggage, or insulted our men, should be instantly shot; a resolution which we were determined to enforce, as it was now our only means of safety.

We were visited during the day by a chief of the Clahclellahs, who seemed mortified at the behaviour of the Indians, and told us that the persons at the head of their outrages were two very bad men, who belonged to the Wahclellah tribe, but that the nation did not by any means wish to displease us. This chief seemed very well disposed, and we had every reason to believe was much respected by the neighbouring Indians. We therefore gave him a small medal, and showed him all the attentions in our power, with which he appeared very much gratified, and we trust his interposition may prevent the necessity of our resorting to force against his countrymen.

Many Indians from the villages above, passed us in the course of the day, on their return from trading with the natives of the valley, and among others, we recognised an Eloot, who with ten or twelve of his nation were on their way home to the long narrows of the Columbia. These people do not, as we are compelled to do, drag their canoes up the rapids, but leave them at the head, as they descend, and carrying their goods across the portage, hire or borrow others from the people below. When the trade is over they return to the foot of the rapids, where they leave these boats and resume their own at the head of the portage. The labour of carrying the goods across is equally shared by the men and women, and we were struck by the contrast between the decent conduct of all the natives from above, and the profligacy and ill manners of the Wahclellahs. About three quarters of a mile below our camp is a burial ground, which seems common to the Wahclellahs, Clahclellahs, and Yehhuhs. It consists of eight sepulchres on the north bank of the river.

*Saturday.* The rain continued all night and this morning. Captain Lewis now took with him all the men fit for duty, and began to drag the remaining periogues over the rapids. This has become much more difficult than when we passed in the autumn; at that time there were in the whole distance of seven miles only three difficult points; but the water is now very considerably higher, and during all that distance the ascent is exceedingly laborious and dangerous, nor would it be practicable to descend, except by letting down the empty boats by means of ropes. The route over this part, from the head to the foot of the portage, is about three miles: the canoes which had been already dragged up were very much injured, by being driven against the rocks, which no precautions could prevent. This morning as we were drawing the fifth canoe round a projecting rock, against which the current sets with great violence, she unfortunately offered too much of her side to the stream. It then drove her with such force, that with all the exertions of the party we were unable to hold her, and were forced to let go the cord, and see her drift down the stream, and be irrecoverably lost. We then began to carry our effects across the portage, but as all those who had short rifles took them in order to repel any attack from the Indians, it was not until five o'clock in the afternoon that the last of the party reached the head of the rapids, accompanied by our new friend the Wahclellah chief. The afternoon being so far advanced, and the weather rainy and cold, we determined to halt for the night, though very desirous of going on, for during the three last days we have not advanced more than seven miles.

The portage is two thousand eight hundred yards, along a narrow road, at all times rough, and now rendered slippery by the rain. About half way is an old village which the Clahclellah chief informs us is the occasional residence of his tribe. These houses are uncommonly large, one of them measured one hundred and sixty by forty feet, and the frames are constructed in the usual manner, except that it is double so as to appear like one house within another. The floors are on a level with the ground, and the roofs have been taken down and sunk in a pond behind the village. We find that our conduct yesterday has made the Indians much more respectful; they do not crowd about us in such numbers, and behave with much more propriety. Among those who visited us were about twenty of the Yehhuhs, a tribe of Shahalas, whom we had found on the north side of river, immediately above the rapids, but who had now emigrated to the opposite shore, where they generally take salmon. Like their relations, the Wahclellahs, they have taken their houses with them, so that only one is now standing where the old village was. We observe generally, that the houses which have the floor on a level with the earth, are smaller, and have more the appearance of being temporary than those which are sunk in the ground, whence we presume that the former are the dwellings during spring and summer, while the latter are reserved for the autumn and winter. Most of the houses are built of boards and covered with bark, though some of the more inferior kind are constructed wholly of cedar bark, kept smooth and flat by small splinters fixed crosswise through the bark, at the distance of twelve or fourteen inches apart. There is but little difference in appearance between these Yehhuhs, Wahclellahs, Clahclellahs, and Neerchokioos, who compose the Shahala nation. On comparing the vocabulary of the Wahclellahs with that of the Chinnooks, we found that the names for numbers were precisely the same, though the other parts of the language were essentially different. The women of all these tribes braid their hair, pierce the nose, and some of them have lines of dots reaching from the ankle as high as the middle of the leg. These Yehhuhs behaved with great propriety, and condemned the treatment we had received from the Wahclellahs. We purchased from one of them the skin of a sheep killed near this place, for which we gave in exchange the skins of a deer and an elk. These animals, he tells us, usually frequent the rocky parts of the mountains, where they are found in great numbers. The bighorn is also an inhabitant of these mountains, and the natives have several robes made of their skins. The mountains near this place are high, steep, and strewed with rocks, which are principally black. Several species of fir, white pine, and white cedar, forms their covering, while near the river we see the cottonwood, sweet-willow, a species of maple, the broad-leafed ash, the purple haw, a small species of cherry, the purple currant, gooseberry, red-willow, the vining and whiteberry honeysuckle, the huckleberry, sacacommis, two kinds of mountain holly, and the common ash.

APRIL 13TH *Sunday.* The loss of our periogue yesterday obliges us to distribute our loading between the two canoes, and the two remaining periogues. This being done, we proceeded along the north side of the river, but soon finding that the increased loading rendered our vessels difficult to manage, if not dangerous in case of high wind, the two periogues only continued on their route, while captain Lewis with the canoes crossed over to the Yehhuh village, with a view of purchasing one or two more canoes. The village now consisted of eleven houses, crowded with inhabitants, and about sixty fighting men. They were very well disposed, and we found no difficulty in procuring

OTO WARRIOR (King)

two small canoes, in exchange for two robes and four elk skins. We also purchased with deer skins, three dogs, an animal which has now become a favourite food, for it is found to be a strong healthy diet, preferable to lean deer or elk, and much superior to horseflesh in any state. With these he proceeded along the south side of the river, and joined us in the evening. We had gone along the north shore as high as Cruzatte's river, to which place we had sent some hunters the day before yesterday, and where we were detained by the high winds. The hunters however did not join us, and we therefore, as soon as the wind had abated, proceeded on for six miles, where we halted for captain Lewis, and in the meantime went out to hunt. We procured two black-tailed fallow deer, which seem to be the only kind inhabiting these mountains. Believing that the hunters were still below us, we despatched a small canoe back for them, and in the morning, *April 14th*, they all joined us with four more deer. After breakfast we resumed our journey, and though the wind was high during the day, yet by keeping along the northern shore, we were able to proceed without danger. At one o'clock we halted for dinner at a large village situated in a narrow bottom, just above the entrance of Canoe creek. The houses are detached from each other, so as to occupy an extent of several miles, though only twenty in number. Those which are inhabited are on the surface of the earth, and built in the same shape as those near the rapids; but there were others at present evacuated, which are completely under ground. They are sunk about eight feet deep, and covered with strong timbers, and several feet of earth in a conical form. On descending by means of a ladder through a hole at the top, which answers the double purpose of a door and a chimney, we found that the house consisted of a single room, nearly circular and about sixteen feet in diameter.

The inhabitants, who call themselves Weocksockwillacum, differ but little from those near the rapids, the chief distinction in dress, being a few leggings and moccasins, which we find here like those worn by the Chopunnish. These people have ten or twelve very good horses, which are the first we have seen since leaving this neighbourhood last autumn. The country below is, indeed, of such a nature, as to prevent the use of this animal, except in the Columbian valley, and there they would [not] be of great service, for the inhabitants reside chiefly on the river side, and the country is too thickly wooded to suffer them to hunt game on horseback. Most of these, they inform us, have been taken in a warlike excursion, which was lately made against the Towahnahiooks, a part of the Snake nation living in the upper part of the Multnomah, to the southeast of this place. Their language is the same with that of the Chilluckittequaws. They seemed inclined to be very civil, and gave us in exchange, some roots, chapelell, filberts, dried berries, and five dogs.

After dinner we proceeded, and passing at the distance of six miles, the high cliffs on the left, encamped at the mouth of a small run on the same side. A little above us is a village, consisting of about one hundred fighting men of a tribe called Smackshops, many of whom passed the evening with us: They do not differ in any respect from the inhabitants of the village below.

APRIL 15TH    In hopes of purchasing horses we did not set out the next morning, *Tuesday*, till after breakfast, and in the meantime exposed our merchandise, and made them various offers; but as they declined bartering, we left them and soon reached the Sepulchre rock, where we halted a few minutes. The rock itself stands near the middle of the river, and contains about two acres of ground above high water. On this surface are scattered thirteen vaults, constructed like those below the Rapids, and some of them more than half filled with dead bodies. After satisfying our curiosity with these venerable remains, we returned to the northern shore, and proceeded to a village at the distance of four miles: on landing, we found that the inhabitants belonged to the same nation we had just left, and as they also had horses, we made a second attempt to purchase a few of them: but with all our dexterity in exhibiting our wares, we could not induce them to sell, as we had none of the only articles which they seemed desirous of procuring, a sort of war hatchet, called by the northwest traders an eye-dog. We therefore purchased two dogs, and taking leave of these Weocksockwillacums, proceeded to another of their villages, just below the entrance of Cataract river. Here too, we tried in vain to purchase some horses, nor did we meet with more success at the two villages of Chilluckittequaws, a few miles farther up the river. At three in the afternoon, we came to the mouth of Quinett creek, which we ascended a short distance and encamped for the night, at the spot we had called Rock fort. Here we were soon visited by some of the people from the great narrows and falls: and on our expressing a wish to purchase horses, they agreed to meet us to-morrow on the north side of the river, where we would open a traffic. They then returned to their villages to collect the horses.

APRIL 16TH    *Wednesday.* In the morning, captain Clark crossed with nine men, and a large part of the merchandise, in order to purchase twelve horses to transport our baggage, and some pounded fish, as a reserve during the passage of the Rocky mountains. The rest of the men were employed in hunting and preparing saddles.

From the rapids [Cascades] to this place, and indeed as far as the commencement of the narrows [Dalles], the Columbia is from half a mile to three quarters in width, and possesses scarcely any current: its bed consists principally of rock, except at the entrance of Labiche river, which takes its rise in mount Hood, from which, like Quicksand river, it brings down vast quantities of sand. During the whole course of the Columbia from the Rapids to the Chilluckittequaws are the trunks of many large pine trees standing erect in water, which is thirty feet deep at present, and never less than ten. These trees could never have grown in their present state, for they are all very much doated [doted, decayed], and none of them vegetate; so that the only reasonable account which can be given of this phenomenon, is, that at some period, which the appearance of the trees induces us to fix within twenty years, the rocks from the hill sides have obstructed the narrow pass at the rapids, and caused the river to spread through the woods. The mountains which border as far as the Sepulchre rock, are high and broken, and its romantic views occasionally enlivened by beautiful cascades rushing from the heights, and forming a deep contrast with the firs, cedars and pines, which darken their sides. From the Sepulchre rock, where the low country begins, the long-leafed pine is the almost exclusive growth of timber; but our present camp is the last spot where a single tree is to be seen on the wide plains, which are now spread before us to the foot of the Rocky mountains. It is, however, covered with a rich verdure of grass and herbs, some inches in height, which forms a delightful and exhilarating prospect, after being confined to the mountains and thick forests on the seacoast. The climate too, though only on the border of the plains, is here very different from that we have lately experienced. The air is drier and more pure, and the ground itself is as free from moisture as if there had been no rain for the last ten days. Around this place are many esculent plants used by the Indians: among which is a currant, now in bloom, with a yellow blossom like that of the yellow currant of the Missouri, from which however it differs specifically. There is also a species of hyacinth growing in the plains, which presents at this time a pretty flower of a pale blue colour, and the bulb of which is boiled or baked, or dried in the sun, and eaten by the Indians. This bulb, of the present year, is white, flat in shape and not quite solid, and it overlays and presses closely that of the last year, which, though much thinner and withered, is equally wide, and sends forth from its sides a number of small radicles.

Our hunters obtained one of the long-tailed deer with the young horns, about two inches, and a large black or dark brown pheasant, such as we had seen on the upper part of the Missouri. They also brought in a large grey squirrel, and two others resembling it in shape, but smaller than the common grey squirrel of the United States, and of a pied grey and yellowish brown colour. In addition to this game, they had seen some antelopes, and the tracks of several black bear, but no appearance of elk. They had seen no birds, but found three eggs of the parti-coloured corvus [magpie]. Though the salmon has not yet appeared, we have seen less scarcity than we apprehended from the reports we had heard below. At the rapids, the natives subsist chiefly on a few white salmon-trout, which they take at this time, and considerable quantities of a small indifferent mullet of an inferior quality. Beyond that place we see none except dried fish of the last season, nor is the sturgeon caught by any of the natives above the Columbia, their whole stores consisting of roots, and fish either dried or pounded.

Captain Clark had, in the meantime, been endeavouring to purchase horses, without success, but they promised to trade with him if he would go up to the Skilloot village, above the long narrows. He therefore sent over to us for more merchandise, and then accompanied them in the evening to that place, where he passed the night.

*Thursday.* The next day he sent to inform us that he was still unable to purchase any horses, but intended going as far as the Eneeshur village to-day, whence he would return to meet us to-morrow at the Skilloot village. In the evening the principal chief of the Chilluckittequaws came to see us, accompanied by twelve of his nation, and hearing that we wanted horses, he promised to meet us at the narrows with some for sale.

APRIL 17TH

FRIDAY, APRIL 18TH, 1806    We set out this morning after an early break-fast, and crossing the river, continued along the north side for four miles, to the foot of the first rapid. Here it was necessary to unload and make a por-tage of seven paces over a rock, round which we then drew the empty boats by means of a cord, and the assistance of setting poles. We then reloaded, and at the distance of five miles, reached the basin at the foot of the long narrows. After unloading and arranging the camp, we went up to the Skil-loot village, where we found captain Clark. He had not been able to procure more than four horses, for which he was obliged to give double the price of those formerly purchased from the Shoshonees and the first tribe of Flat-heads. These, however, we hoped might be sufficient with the aid of the small canoes to convey our baggage as far as the villages near the Muscle-shell rapid, where horses are cheaper and more abundant, and where we may probably exchange the canoes for as many horses as we want. The Skilloots, indeed, have a number of horses, but they are unwilling to part with them, though at last we laid out three parcels of merchandise, for each of which they promised to bring us a horse in the morning. The long nar-rows have a much more formidable appearance than when we passed them in the autumn, so that it would, in fact, be impossible either to descend or go up them in any kind of boat. As we had therefore no further use for the two periogues, we cut them up for fuel.

APRIL 19TH    *Saturday.* Early in the morning, all the party began to carry the merchan-dise over the portage. This we accomplished with the aid of our four horses, by three o'clock in the afternoon, when we formed our camp a little above the Skilloot village. Since we left them in the autumn they have removed their village a few hundred yards lower down the river, and have exchanged the cellars in which we then found them, for more pleasant dwellings on the surface of the ground. These are formed by sticks, and covered with mats and straw, and so large, that each is the residence of several families. They are also much better clad than any of the natives below, or than they were themselves last autumn; the dress of the men consists generally of leggings, moccasins, and large robes, and many of them wear shirts in the same form used by the Chopunnish and Shoshonees, highly ornamented, as well as the leggings and moccasins, with porcupine quills. Their modesty is protected by the skin of a fox or some other animal, drawn under a girdle and hanging in front like a narrow apron. The dress of the women differs but little from that worn near the rapids; and both sexes wear the hair over the forehead as low as the eyebrows, with large locks cut square at the ears, and the rest hanging in two queues in front of the body. The robes are made principally of the skins of deer, elk, bighorn, some wolf and buffalo, while the children use the skins of the large grey squirrel. The buffalo is procured from the na-tions higher up the river, who occasionally visit the Missouri; indeed, the greater proportion of their apparel is brought by the nations to the north-west, who come to trade for pounded fish, copper, and beads. Their chief fuel is straw, southern-wood, and small willows. The bear-grass, the bark of the cedar, and the silk-grass are employed in various articles of manufac-ture.

The whole village was filled with rejoicing to-day, at having caught a single salmon, which was considered as the harbinger of vast quantities in four or five days. In order to hasten their arrival the Indians according to custom, dressed fish and cut it into small pieces, one of which was given to each child in the village. In the good humour excited by this occurrence, they parted, though reluctantly, with four other horses, for which we gave them two kettles, reserving only a single small one for a mess of eight men. Unluckily, however, we lost one of the horses by the negligence of the person to whose charge he was committed. The rest were therefore hobbled and tied; but as the nations here do not understand gelding, all the horses but one were stallions, and this being the season when they are most vicious, we had great difficulty in managing them, and were obliged to keep watch over them all night. In the afternoon captain Clark set out with four men for the Eneeshur village at the grand falls, in order to make further attempts to procure horses.

*Sunday.* As it was obviously our interest to preserve the good will of these people, we passed over several small thefts which they have committed, but this morning we learnt that six tomahawks and a knife had been stolen during the night. We addressed ourselves to the chief, who seemed angry with his people and made a harangue to them, but we did not recover the articles, and soon after, two of our spoons were missing. We therefore ordered them all from our camp, threatening to beat severely any one detected in purloining. This harshness irritated them so much that they left us in an ill-humour, and we therefore kept on our guard against any insult. Besides this knavery, the faithlessness of the people is intolerable, frequently after receiving goods in exchange for a horse, they return in a few hours and insist on revoking the bargain, or receiving some additional value. We discovered too, that the horse which was missing yesterday, had been gambled away by the fellow from whom we had purchased him, to a man of a different nation, who had carried him off. Besides these, we bought two more horses, two dogs, and some chapelell, and also exchanged a couple of elk skins for a gun belonging to the chief. This was all we could obtain, for though they had a great abundance of dried fish, they would not sell it, except at a price too exorbitant for our finances.

We now found that no more horses could be procured, and therefore prepared for setting out to-morrow. One of the canoes, for which the Indians would give us very little, was cut up for fuel, two others, together with some elk skins and pieces of old iron, we bartered for beads, and the remaining two small canoes were despatched early next morning, *Monday, 21st*, with all the baggage which could not be carried on horseback. We had intended setting out at the same time, but one of our horses broke loose during the night, and we were under the necessity of sending several men in search of him.

In the meantime, the Indians, who were always on the alert, stole a tomahawk, which we could not recover, though several of them were searched. Another fellow was detected in carrying off a piece of iron, and kicked out of camp: captain Lewis then, addressing the Indians, declared that he was not afraid to fight them; for if he chose, he might easily put them to death, and burn their village; that he did not wish to treat them ill if they did not steal; and that although if he knew who had the tomahawks he would take away the horses of the thieves, yet he would rather lose the prop-

435

erty altogether than take the horse of an innocent man. The chiefs were present at this harangue, hung their heads and made no reply. At ten o'clock the men returned with the horse, and soon after, an Indian who had promised to go with us as far as the Chopunnish, came with two horses, one of which he politely offered to carry our baggage. We therefore loaded nine horses, and giving the tenth to Bratton, who was still too sick to walk, about ten o'clock left the village of these disagreeable people.

At one o'clock we arrived at the village of the Eneeshurs, where we found captain Clark, who had been completely unsuccessful in his attempts to purchase horses, the Eneeshurs being quite as unfriendly as the Skilloots. Fortunately, however, the fellow who had sold a horse, and afterwards lost him at gambling, belonged to this village, and we insisted on taking the kettle and knife which had been given to him for the horse, if he did not replace it by one of equal value. He preferred the latter, and brought us a very good horse. Being here joined by the canoes and baggage across the portage, we halted half a mile above the town, and took dinner on some dogs, after which we proceeded on about four miles and encamped at a village of Eneeshurs, consisting of nine mat huts, a little below the mouth of the Towahnahiooks. We obtained from these people a couple of dogs and a small quantity of fuel, for which we were obliged to give a higher price than usual. We also bought a horse with a back so much injured, that he can scarcely be of much service to us, but the price was some trifling articles, which in the United States would cost about a dollar and a quarter. The dress, the manners, and the language of the Eneeshurs differ in no respect from those of the Skilloots. Like them too, these Eneeshurs are inhospitable and parsimonious, faithless to their engagements, and in the midst of poverty and filth, retain a degree of pride and arrogance which render our numbers our only protection against insult, pillage, and even murder. We are, however, assured by our Chopunnish guide, who appears to be a very sincere, honest Indian, that the nations above will treat us with much more hospitality.

APRIL 22D  *Tuesday*. Two of our horses broke loose in the night and straggled to some distance, so that we were not able to retake them and begin our march before seven o'clock. We had just reached the top of a hill near the village, when the load of one of the horses turned, and the animal taking fright at a robe which still adhered to him, ran furiously towards the village: just as he came there the robe fell, and an Indian hid it in his hut. Two men went back after the horse which they soon took, but the robe was still missing, and the Indians denied having seen it. These repeated acts of knavery now exhausted our patience, and captain Lewis therefore set out for the village, determined to make them deliver up the robe, or to burn the village to the ground. This disagreeable alternative was rendered unnecessary, for on his way he met one of our men, who had found the robe in an Indian hut hid behind some baggage.

We resumed our route, and soon after halted at a hill, from the top of which we enjoyed a commanding view of the range of mountains in which mount Hood stands, and which continue south as far as the eye can reach, with their tops covered with snow. Mount Hood itself bears south 30° west, and the snowy summit of mount Jefferson south 10° west. Towards the south and at no great distance we discern some woody country, and opposite

436

this point of view is the mouth of the Towahnahiooks. This river receives, at the distance of eighteen or twenty miles, a branch from the right, which takes its rise in mount Hood, while the main stream comes in a course from the southeast, and at ten or fifteen miles is joined by a second branch from mount Jefferson. From this place we proceeded with our baggage in the centre, escorted both before and behind by those of the men who were without the care of horses, and having crossed a plain eight miles in extent, reached a village of Eneeshurs, consisting of six houses. Here we bought some dogs on which we dined near the village, and having purchased another horse, went up the river four miles further, to another Eneeshur village of seven mat houses. Our guide now informed us that the next village was at such a distance that we should not reach it this evening, and as we should be able to procure both dogs and wood at this place, we determined to encamp. We here purchased a horse, and engaged for a second in exchange for one of our canoes, but as they were on the opposite side of the river, and the wind very high, they were not able to cross before sunset, at which time the Indian had returned home to the next village above. This evening, as well as at dinner-time, we were obliged to buy wood to cook our meat, for there is no timber in the country, and all the fuel is brought from a great distance. We obtained as much as answered our purposes on moderate terms, but as we are too poor to afford more than a single fire, and lie without any shelter, we find the nights disagreeably cold, though the weather is warm during the daytime.

*Wednesday.* The next morning two of the horses strayed away in consequence of neglecting to tie them as had been directed. One of them was recovered, but as we had a long ride to make before reaching the next village, we could wait no longer than eleven o'clock for the other. Not being found at that time we set out, and after marching for twelve miles over the sands of a narrow rocky bottom on the north side of the river, came to a village near the Rock rapid, at the mouth of a large creek, which we had not observed in descending. It consisted of twelve temporary huts of mat, inhabited by a tribe called Wahhowpum, who speak a language very similar to that of the Chopunnish, whom they resemble also in dress, both sexes being clad in robes and shirts as well as leggings and moccasins. These people seemed much pleased to see us, and readily gave us four dogs and some chapelell and wood in exchange for small articles, such as pewter-buttons, strips of tin, iron, and brass, and some twisted wire, which we had previously prepared for our journey across the plains. These people, as well as some more living in five huts a little below them, were waiting the return of the salmon. We also found a Chopunnish returning home with his family and a dozen young horses, some of which he wanted us to hire, but this we declined, as in that case we should be obliged to maintain him and his family on the route. After arranging the camp we assembled all the warriors, and having smoked with them, the violins were produced, and some of the men danced. This civility was returned by the Indians in a style of dancing such as we had not yet seen. The spectators formed a circle round the dancers, who with their robes drawn tightly round the shoulders, and divided into parties of five or six men, perform by crossing in a line from one side of the circle to the other. All the parties, performers as well as spectators, sang,

APRIL 23D

437

and after proceeding in this way for some time, the spectators join, and the whole concludes by a promiscuous dance and song. Having finished, the natives retired at our request, after promising to barter horses with us in the morning. The river is by no means so difficult of passage nor obstructed by so many rapids as it was in the autumn, the water being now sufficiently high to cover the rocks in the bed.

APRIL 24TH *Thursday.* In the morning we began early to look for our horses, but they were not collected before one o'clock. In the meantime we prepared saddles for three new horses which we purchased from the Wahhowpums, and agreed to hire three more from the Chopunnish Indian who was to accompany us with his family. The natives also had promised to take our canoes in exchange for horses; but when they found that we were resolved on travelling by land, they refused giving us any thing, in hopes that we would be forced to leave them. Disgusted at this conduct, we determined rather to cut them to pieces than suffer these people to enjoy them, and actually began to split them, on which they gave us several strands of beads for each canoe. We had now a sufficient number of horses to carry our baggage, and therefore proceeded wholly by land. At two o'clock we set out, and passing between the hills and the northern shore of the river, had a difficult and fatiguing march over a road alternately sandy and rocky. At the distance of four miles, we came to four huts of the Metcowwee tribe, two miles further the same number of huts, and after making twelve miles from our last night's camp, halted at a larger village of five huts of Metcowwees.

As we came along many of the natives passed and repassed without making any advances to converse, though they behaved with distant respect. We observed in our route no animals except the killdeer, the brown lizard, and a moonax, which the people had domesticated as a favourite. Most of the men complain of a soreness in their feet and legs, occasioned by walking on rough stones and deep sands, after being accustomed for some months past to a soft soil. We therefore determined to remain here this evening, and for this purpose bought three dogs and some chapelell, which we cooked with dry grass and willow boughs. The want of wood is a serious inconvenience, on account of the coolness of the nights, particularly when the wind sets from mount Hood, or in any western direction: those winds being much colder than the winds from the Rocky mountains. There are no dews in the plains, and from the appearance, we presume, that no rain has fallen for several weeks.

By nine o'clock the following morning, *Friday 25th*, we collected our horses and proceeded eleven miles to a large village of fifty-one mat houses, where we purchased some wood and a few dogs, on which we made our dinner. The village contained about seven hundred persons of a tribe called Pishquitpah, whose residence on the river is only during the spring and summer, the autumn and winter being passed in hunting through the plains, and along the borders of the mountains. The greater part of them were at a distance from the river as we descended, and never having seen white men before, they flocked round us in great numbers; but although they were exceedingly curious they treated us with great respect, and were very urgent that we should spend the night with them. Two principal chiefs were pointed out by our Chopunnish companion, and acknowledged by the tribe, and we therefore invested each of them with a small medal. We were also very desirous of purchasing more horses; but as our principal stock of merchandise consists of a dirk, a sword, and a few old clothes, the Indians could not be induced to traffic with us. The Pishquitpahs are generally of a good stature and proportion, and as the heads of neither males nor females are so much flattened as those lower down the river, their features are rather pleasant. The hair is braided in the manner practised by their western neighbours; but the generality of the men are dressed in a large robe, under which is a shirt reaching to the knees, where it is met by long leggings, and the feet covered with moccasins: others, however, wear only the truss and robe. As they unite the occupations of hunting and fishing life, both sexes ride very dexterously, their caparison being a saddle or pad of dressed skin, stuffed with goats' hair, and from which wooden stirrups are suspended; and a hair rope tied at both ends to the under jaw of the animal. The horses, however, though good, suffer much, as do in fact all Indian horses, from sore backs.

Finding them not disposed to barter with us, we left the Pishquit-pahs at four o'clock, accompanied by eighteen or twenty of their young men on horseback. At the distance of four miles, we passed, without halting, five houses belonging to the Wollawollahs; and five miles further, observing as many willows as would answer the purpose of making fires, availed ourselves of the circumstance, by encamping near them. The country through which we passed bore the same appearance as that of yesterday. The hills on both sides of the river are about two hundred and fifty feet high, generally abrupt and craggy, and in many places presenting a perpendicular face of black, hard, and solid rock. From the top of these hills, the country extends itself in level plains to a very great distance, and though not as fertile as the land near the falls, produces an abundant supply of low grass, which is an excellent food for horses. This grass must indeed be unusually nutritious, for even at this season of the year, after wintering on the dry grass of the plains, and being used with greater severity than is usual among the whites, many of these horses are perfectly fat, nor have we, indeed, seen a single one who was poor. In the course of the day we killed several rattle-snakes, like those of the United States, and saw many of the common as well as the horned-lizard. We also killed six ducks, one of which proved to be of a different species [shoveler duck] from any we had yet seen, being distinguished by yellow legs, and feet webbed like those of the duckinmallard. The Pishquitpahs passed the night with us, and at their request, the violin was played, and some of the men amused themselves with dancing. At the same time we succeeded in obtaining two horses at nearly the same prices which had already been refused in the village.

*Saturday.* In the morning we set out early. At the distance of three miles, the APRIL 26TH river hills become low, and retiring to a great distance, leave a low, level, extensive plain, which on the other side of the river, had begun thirteen miles lower. As we were crossing this plain, we were overtaken by several families travelling up the river with a number of horses, and although their company was inconvenient, for the weather was warm, the roads dusty, and their horses crowded in and broke our line of march, yet we were unwilling to displease the Indians by any act of severity. The plain possesses much grass

439

and a variety of herbaceous plants and shrubs; but after going twelve miles, we were fortunate enough to find a few willows, which enabled us to cook a dinner of jerked elk, and the remainder of the dogs purchased yesterday. We then went on sixteen miles further, and six miles above our camp of the nineteenth of October, encamped in the rain, about a mile below three houses of Wollawollahs. Soon after we halted, an Indian boy took a piece of bone, which he substituted for a fish-hook, and caught several chub, nine inches long.

APRIL 27TH    *Sunday.* We were detained till nine o'clock, before a horse, which broke loose in the night, could be recovered. We then passed, near our camp, a small river, called Youmalolam, proceeded through a continuation, till at the distance of fifteen miles, the abrupt and rocky hills three hundred feet high, return to the river. These we ascended, and then crossed a higher plain for nine miles, when we again came to the water side. We had been induced to make this long march because we had but little provisions, and hoped to find a Wollawollah village, which our guide had told us we should reach when next we met the river. There was, however, no village to be seen, and as both the men and horses were fatigued, we halted, and collecting some dry stalks of weeds and the stems of a plant resembling southern wood, cooked a small quantity of jerked meat for dinner. Soon after we were joined by seven Wollawollahs, among whom we recognised a chief by the name of Yellept, who had visited us on the nineteenth of October, when we gave him a medal with the promise of a larger one on our return. He appeared very much pleased at seeing us again, and invited us to remain at his village three or four days, during which he would supply us with the only food they had, and furnish us with horses for our journey. After the cold, inhospitable treatment we have lately received, this kind offer was peculiarly acceptable, and after a hasty meal, we accompanied him to his village, six miles above, situated on the edge of the low country, and about twelve miles below the mouth of Lewis's river.

Immediately on our arrival, Yellept, who proved to be a man of much influence, not only in his own, but in the neighbouring nations, collected the inhabitants, and after having made an harangue, the purport of which was to induce the nations to treat us hospitably, set them an example, by bringing himself an armful of wood, and a platter containing three roasted mullets. They immediately assented to one part, at least of the recommendation, by furnishing us with an abundance of the only sort of fuel they employ, the stems of shrubs growing in the plains. We then purchased four dogs, on which we supped heartily, having been on short allowance for two days past. When we were disposed to sleep, the Indians retired immediately on our request, and indeed, uniformly conducted themselves with great propriety. These people live on roots, which are very abundant in the plains, and catch a few salmon-trout; but at present they seem to subsist chiefly on a species of mullet, weighing from one to three pounds. They now informed us that opposite to the village, there was a route which led to the mouth of the Kooskooskee, on the south side of Lewis's river, that the road itself was good, and passed over a level country, well supplied with water and grass, and that we should meet with plenty of deer and antelope. We knew that a road in that direction would shorten the distance at least eighty miles, and as the report of our guide was confirmed by Yellept and other Indians, we did not hesitate to adopt that course; they added, however, that there were no houses or permanent residence of Indians on the road, and it was therefore deemed prudent not to trust wholly to our guns, but to lay in a stock of provisions.

*Monday.* In the morning, therefore, we purchased ten dogs. While this trade was carrying on by our men, Yellept brought a fine white horse, and presented him to captain Clark, expressing at the same time, a wish to have a kettle; but on being informed that we had already disposed of the last kettle we could spare, he said he would be content with any present we should make in return. Captain Clark therefore gave his sword, for which the chief had before expressed a desire, adding one hundred balls, some powder, and other small articles, with which he appeared perfectly satisfied. We were now anxious to depart, and requested Yellept to lend us canoes for the purpose of crossing the river. But he would not listen to any proposal of leaving the village. He wished us to remain two or three days; but would not let us go to-day, for he had already sent to invite his neighbours, the Chimnapoos, to come down this evening and join his people in a dance for our amusement. We urged, in vain, that by setting out sooner, we would the earlier return with the articles they desired; for a day, he observed, would make but little difference. We at length mentioned, that as there was no wind, it was now the best time to cross the river, and would merely take the horses over, and return to sleep at their village. To this he assented, and we then crossed with our horses, and having hobbled them, returned to their camp.

Fortunately there was among these Wollawollahs, a prisoner belonging to a tribe of Shoshonee or Snake Indians, residing to the south of the Multnomah, and visiting occasionally the heads of the Wollawollah creek. Our Shoshonee woman, Sacajawea, though she belonged to a tribe near the Missouri, spoke the same language as this prisoner, and by their means we were able to explain ourselves to the Indians, and answer all their inquiries with respect to ourselves and the object of our journey. Our conversation inspired them with much confidence, and they soon brought several sick persons, for whom they requested our assistance. We splintered the broken arm of one, gave some relief to another, whose knee was contracted by rheumatism, and administered what we thought beneficial for ulcers and eruptions of the skin, on various parts of the body, which are very common disorders among them. But our most valuable medicine was eye-water, which we distributed, and which, indeed, they required very much: the complaint of the eyes, occasioned by living on the water, and increased by the fine sand of the plains, being now universal.

A little before sunset, the Chimnapoos, amounting to one hundred men, and a few women, came to the village, and joining the Wollawollahs, who were about the same number of men, formed themselves in a circle round our camp, and waited very patiently till our men were disposed to dance, which they did for about an hour, to the tune of the violin. They then requested to see the Indians dance. With this they readily complied, and the whole assemblage, amounting, with the women and children of the village, to several hundred, stood up, and sang and danced at the same time. The exercise was not, indeed, very violent nor very graceful, for the greater part of them were formed into a solid column, round a kind of hollow square, stood on the same place, and merely jumped up at intervals, to keep time to the music. Some, however, of the more active warriors, entered the square, and danced round it sidewise, and some of our men joined in the dance, to the great satisfaction of the Indians. The dance continued till ten o'clock.

APRIL 29TH  *Tuesday.* The next morning Yellept supplied us with two canoes in which we crossed with all our baggage by eleven o'clock, but the horses having strayed to some distance, we could not collect them in time to reach any fit place to encamp if we began our journey, as night would overtake us before we came to water. We therefore thought it advisable to encamp about a mile from the Columbia, on the mouth of the Wollawollah river. This is a handsome stream, about fifty yards wide, and four and a half feet in depth: its waters, which are clear, roll over a bed composed principally of gravel, intermixed with some sand and mud, and though the banks are low they do not seem to be overflowed. It empties into the Columbia, about twelve or fifteen miles from the entrance of Lewis's [Snake] river, and just above a range of high hills crossing the Columbia. Its sources, like those of the Towahnahiooks, Lapage, Youmalolam, and Wollawollah, come, as the Indians inform us, from the north side of a range of mountains which we see to the east and southeast, and which, commencing to the south of mount Hood, stretch in a northeastern direction to the neighbourhood of a southern branch of Lewis's river, at some distance from the Rocky mountains. Two principal branches however of the Towahnahiooks take their rise in mount Jefferson and mount Hood, which in fact appear to separate the waters of the Multnomah and Columbia. They are now about sixty-five or seventy miles from this place, and although covered with snow, do not seem high. To the south of these mountains the Indian prisoner says there is a river, running towards the northwest, as large as the Columbia at this place, which is nearly a mile. This account may be exaggerated, but it serves to show that the Multnomah must be a very large river, and that with the assistance of a southeastern branch of Lewis's river, passing round the eastern extremity of that chain of mountains in which mounts Hood and Jefferson are so conspicuous, waters the vast tract of country to the south, till its remote sources approach those of the Missouri and Rio del Norde.

Near our camp is a fish-weir, formed of two curtains of small willow switches, matted together with withes of the same plant, and extending across the river in two parallel lines, six feet asunder. These are supported by several parcels of poles, in the manner already described, as in use among the Shoshonees, and are either rolled up or let down at pleasure for a few feet, so as either to suffer the fish to pass or detain them. A seine of fifteen or eighteen feet in length is then dragged down the river by two persons, and the bottom drawn up against the curtain of willows. They also employ a smaller seine like a scooping net, one side of which is confined to a semicircular bow five feet long, and half the size of a man's arm, and the other side is held by a strong rope, which being tied at both ends to the bow, forms the chord to the semicircle. This is used by one person, but the only fish which they can take at this time is a mullet of from four to five pounds in weight, and this is the chief subsistence of a village of twelve houses of Wollawollahs, a little below us on this river, as well as of others on the opposite side of the Columbia.

442

In the course of the day we gave small medals to two inferior chiefs, each of whom made us a present of a fine horse. We were in a poor condition to make an adequate acknowledgment for this kindness, but gave several articles, among which was a pistol, with some hundred rounds of ammunition. We have indeed been treated by these people with an unusual degree of kindness and civility. They seem to have been successful in their hunting during the last winter, for all of them, but particularly the women, are much better clad than when we saw them last; both sexes among the Wollawollahs, as well as the Chimnapoos, being provided with good robes, moccasins, long shirts, and leggings. Their ornaments are similar to those used below, the hair cut in the forehead, and queues falling over the shoulders in front of the body: some have some small plaits at the earlocks, and others tie a bundle of the docked foretop in front of the forehead.

They were anxious that we should repeat our dance of last evening, but as it rained a little and the wind was high, we found the weather too cold for such amusement.

*Wednesday*. Although we had hobbled and secured our new purchases, we found some difficulty in collecting all our horses. In the meantime we purchased several dogs, and two horses, besides exchanging one of our least valuable horses for a very good one belonging to the Chopunnish who is accompanying us with his family. The daughter of this man is now about the age of puberty, and being incommoded by the disorder incident to that age, she is not permitted to associate with the family, but sleeps at a distance from her father's camp, and on the route always follows at some distance alone. This delicacy or affection is common to many nations of Indians, among whom a girl in that state is separated from her family, and forbidden to use any article of the household or kitchen furniture, or to engage in any occupation. We have now twenty-three horses, many of whom are young and excellent animals, but the greater part of them are afflicted with sore backs. The Indians in general are cruel masters; they ride very hard, and as the saddles are so badly constructed that it is almost impossible to avoid wounding the back, yet they continue to ride when the poor creatures are scarified in a dreadful manner.

At eleven o'clock we left these honest, worthy people, accompanied by our guide and the Chopunnish family, and directed our course north 30° east, across an open level sandy plain, unbroken except by large banks of pure sand, which have drifted in many parts of the plain to the height of fifteen or twenty feet. The rest of the plain is poor in point of soil, but throughout is generally short grass interspersed with aromatic shrubs, and a number of plants, the roots of which supply the chief sustenance of the natives. Among these we observe a root something like the sweet potato. At the distance of fourteen miles we reached a branch of Wollawollah river, rising in the same range of mountains, and empties itself six miles above the mouth of the latter. It is a bold deep stream, about ten yards wide, and seems to be navigable for canoes. The hills of this creek are generally abrupt and rocky, but the narrow bottom is very fertile, and both possess twenty times as much timber as the Columbia itself; indeed, we now find, for the first time since leaving Rockfort, an abundance of firewood. The growth consists of cottonwood, birch, the crimson haw, red and sweet willow, chokecherry, yellow currants, gooseberry, the honeysuckle with a white berry, rose-bushes, sevenbark, sumac, together with some corn-grass and rushes. The advantage of a comfortable fire induced us, as the night was come, to halt at this place. We were soon supplied by Drewyer with a beaver and an otter, of which we took only a part of the beaver, and gave the rest to the Indians. The otter is a favourite food, though much inferior, at least in our estimation, to the dog, which they will not eat. The horse too is seldom eaten, and never except when absolute necessity compels them to eat it, as the only alternative to prevent their dying of hunger. This fastidiousness does not, however, seem to proceed so much from any dislike to the food, as from attachment to the animal itself, for many of them eat very heartily of the horse-beef which we give them.

## Thursday, May 1st, 1806

At an early hour in the morning we collected our horses, and after breakfast set out about seven o'clock, and followed the road up the creek. The low grounds and plains presented the same appearance as that of yesterday, except that the latter were less sandy. At the distance of nine miles, the Chopunnish Indian, who was in front, pointed out an old unbeaten road to the left, which he informed us was our shortest route. Before venturing, however, to quit our present road, which was level, and not only led us in the proper direction, but was well supplied with wood and water, we halted to let our horses graze till the arrival of our other guide, who happened to be at some distance behind. On coming up he seemed much displeased with the other Indian, and declared that the road we were pursuing was the proper one; that if we decided on taking the left road, it would be necessary to remain till to-morrow morning, and then make an entire day's march before we could reach either water or wood. To this the Chopunnish assented, but declared that he himself meant to pursue that route, and we therefore gave him some powder and lead which he requested.

Four hunters whom we had sent out in the morning, joined us while we halted, and brought us a beaver for dinner. We then took our leave of the Chopunnish at one o'clock, and pursued our route up the creek, through a country similar to that we had passed in the morning. But at the distance of three miles, the hills on the north side became lower, and the bottoms of the creek widened into a pleasant country, two or three miles in extent. The timber too, is now more abundant, and our guide tells us that we shall not want either wood or game from this place as far as the Kooskooskee. We have already seen a number of deer, of which we killed one, and observed great quantities of the curlew, as well as some cranes, ducks, prairie larks, and several species of sparrow, common to the prairies. There is, in fact, very little difference in the general face of the country here from that of the plains on the Missouri, except that the latter are enlivened by vast herds of buffalo, elk and other animals, which give it an additional interest. Over these wide bottoms we continued on a course north, 75° east, till, at the distance of seventeen miles from where we dined, and twenty-six from our last encampment, we halted for the night.

We had scarcely encamped, when three young men came up from

the Wollawollah village, with a steel trap, which had been left behind inadvertently, and which they had come a whole day's journey in order to restore. This act of integrity was the more pleasing, because, though very rare among Indians, it corresponds perfectly with the general behaviour of the Wollawollahs, among whom we had lost carelessly several knives, which were always returned as soon as found. We may, indeed, justly affirm, that of all the Indians whom we have met since leaving the United States, the Wollawollahs were the most hospitable, honest and sincere.

FRIDAY, MAY 2D, 1806 We despatched two hunters ahead; but the horse we had yesterday purchased from the Chopunnish, although closely hobbled, contrived to break loose in the night, and went back to rejoin his companions. He was however overtaken and brought to us about one o'clock, and we then set forward. For three miles we followed a hilly road on the north side of the creek, opposite to a wide bottom, where a branch falls in from the southwest mountains, which, though covered with snow, are about twenty-five miles distant, and do not appear high. We then entered an extensive level bottom, with about fifty acres of land well covered with pine near the creek, and the long-leafed pine occasionally on the sides of the hills along its banks. After crossing the creek at the distance of seven miles from our camp, we repassed it seven miles further, near the junction of one of its branches from the northeast. The main stream here bears to the south, towards the mountains where it rises, and its bottoms then become narrow, as the hills are higher. We followed the course of this northeast branch in a direction N. 45° E. for eight and three quarter miles, when having made nineteen miles, we halted in a little bottom on the north side. The creek is here about four yards wide, and as far as we can perceive, it comes from the east, but the road here turns from it into the high open plain. The soil of the country seems to improve as we advance, and this afternoon we see, in the bottoms, an abundance of quamash now in bloom. We killed nothing but a duck, though we saw two deer at a distance, as well as many sandhill crows, curlews, and other birds common to the prairies, and there is much sign of both beaver and otter, along the creeks. The three young Wollawollahs continued with us. During the day we observed them eating the inner part of the young succulent stem of a plant very common in the rich lands on the Mississippi, Ohio and its branches. It is a large coarse plant, with a ternate leaf, the leaflets of which are three-lobed, and covered with a woolly pubescence, while the flower and fructification resemble that of the parsnip. On tasting this plant, we found it agreeable, and eat heartily of it without any inconvenience.

MAY 3D *Saturday.* We set out at an early hour, and crossed the high plains, which we found more fertile and less sandy than below; yet, though the grass is taller, there are very few aromatic shrubs. After pursuing a course N. 25° E. for twelve miles, we reached the Kinnooenim. This creek rises in the southwest mountains, and though only twelve yards wide, discharges a considerable body of water into Lewis's river, a few miles above the narrows. Its bed is pebbled, its banks low, and the hills near its sides high and rugged; but in its narrow bottoms are found some cottonwood, willow, and the underbrush, which grows equally on the east branch of the Wollawollah. After dining at the Kinnooenim, we resumed our journey over the high plains, in the direction of N. 45° E. and reached, at the distance of three miles, a small branch of that creek about five yards wide. The lands in its neighbourhood are composed of a dark rich loam; its hill sides, like those of the Kinnooenim, are high, its bottoms narrow, and possess but little timber. It increased however in quantity as we advanced along the north side of the creek for eleven miles.

At that distance we were agreeably surprised by the appearance of Weahkoonut, or the Indian whom we had called the Bighorn, from the circumstance of his wearing a horn of that animal, suspended from his left arm. He had gone down with us last year along Lewis's river, and was highly serviceable in preparing the minds of the natives for our reception. He is, moreover, the first chief of a large band of Chopunnish; and hearing that we were on our return, he had come with ten of his warriors to meet us. He now turned back with us, and we continued up the bottoms of the creek for two miles, till the road began to leave the creek, and cross the hill to the plains. We therefore encamped for the night in a grove of cottonwood, after we had made a disagreeable journey of twenty-eight miles. During the greater part of the day the air was keen and cold, and it alternately rained, hailed and snowed; but, though the wind blew with great violence, it was fortunately from the southwest, and on our backs. We had consumed at dinner the last of our dried meat, and nearly all that was left of the dogs; so that we supped very scantily on the remainder, and had nothing for to-morrow. Weahkoonut, however, assured us that there was a house on the river at no great distance, where we might supply ourselves with provisions. We now missed our guide and the Wollawollahs, who left us abruptly this morning, and never returned.

*Sunday.* After a disagreeable night, we collected our horses at an early hour and proceeded with a continuation of the same weather. We are now nearer to the southwest mountains, which appear to become lower as they advance towards the northeast. We followed the road over the plains, north 60° east, for four miles to a ravine, where was the source of a small creek, down the hilly and rocky sides of which we proceeded for eight miles to its entrance into Lewis's river, about seven miles and a half above the mouth of the Kooskooskee. Near this place we found the house of which Weahkoonut had mentioned, and where we now halted for breakfast. It contained six families, but so miserably poor that all we could obtain from them were two lean dogs and a few large cakes of half cured bread, made of a root resembling the sweet potato, of all which we contrived to form a kind of soup. The soil of the plain is good, but it has no timber. The range of southwest mountains is about fifteen miles above us, but continues to lower, and is still covered with snow to its base. After giving a passage to Lewis's river, near their northeastern extremity, they terminate in a high level plain between that river and the Kooskooskee. The salmon not having yet called them to the rivers, the greater part of the Chopunnish are now dispersed in villages through this plain, for the purpose of collecting quamash and cows, which here grow in great abundance, the soil being extremely fertile, and in many places covered with the long-leafed pine, the larch, and balsam-fir, which contribute to render it less thirsty than the open unsheltered plains.

After our repast we continued our route along the west side of the river, where as well as on the opposite shore, the high hills approach it closely, till at the distance of three miles we halted opposite to two houses: the inhabitants consisted of five families of Chopunnish, among whom were Tetoh, or Sky, the younger of the two chiefs who accompanied us in the autumn to the great falls of the Columbia, and also our old pilot who had conducted us down the river to the Columbia. They both advised us to cross here, and ascend the Kooskooskee on the northeast side, this being the shortest and best route to the forks of that river, where we should find the Twistedhair, in whose charge we left our horses, and to which place they promised to show us the way. We did not hesitate to accept this offer, and therefore crossed with the assistance of three canoes; but as the night was coming on, we purchased a little wood and some roots of cows, and encamped, though we had made only fifteen miles to-day. The evening proved cold and disagreeable, and the natives crowded round our fire in such numbers that we could scarcely cook or even keep ourselves warm.

At these houses of Chopunnish we observed a small hut with a single fire, which we are informed is appropriated for women who are undergoing the operation of the menses; there they are obliged to retreat; the men are not permitted to approach within a certain distance of them, and when any thing is to be conveyed to those deserted females, the person throws it to them forty or fifty paces off, and then retires. It is singular, indeed, that amongst the nations of the wilderness, there should be found customs and rites so nearly resembling those of the Jews. It is scarcely necessary to allude more particularly to the uncleanness of Jewish females and the rites of purification.

MAY 5TH  *Monday.* We collected our horses, and at seven o'clock set forward alone; for Weahkoonut, whose people resided above on the west side of Lewis's river, continued his route homeward when we crossed to the huts. Our road was across the plains for four and a half miles, to the entrance of the Kooskooskee. We then proceeded up that river, and at five miles reached a large mat house, but could not procure any provisions from the inhabitants, but on reaching another three miles beyond, we were surprised at the liberality of an Indian, who gave captain Clark a very elegant grey mare, for which, all he requested was a vial of eye-water.

Last autumn, while we were encamped at the mouth of the Chopunnish river, a man who complained of a pain in his knee and thigh, was brought to us in hopes of receiving relief. The man was to appearance recovered from his disorder, though he had not walked for some time. But that we might not disappoint them, captain Clark, with much ceremony, washed and rubbed his sore limb, and gave him some volatile liniment to continue the operation, which either caused, or rather did not prevent his recovery. The man gratefully circulated our praises, and our fame as physicians was increased by the efficacy of some eye-water which we gave them at the same time. We are by no means displeased at this new resource for obtaining subsistence, as they will give us no provisions without merchandise, and our stock is now very much reduced: we cautiously abstain from giving them any but harmless medicines, and as we cannot possibly do harm, our prescriptions, though unsanctioned by the faculty, may be useful, and are entitled to some remuneration.

Four miles beyond this house we came to another large one, containing ten families, where we halted, and made our dinner on two dogs and a small quantity of roots, which we did not procure without much difficulty. Whilst we were eating, an Indian standing by, and looking with great derision at our eating dogs, threw a poor half-starved puppy almost into captain Lewis's plate, laughing heartily at the humour of it. Captain Lewis took up the animal and flung it with great force into the fellow's face, and seizing his tomahawk, threatened to cut him down if he dared to repeat such insolence.

448

He immediately withdrew, apparently much mortified, and we continued our repast of dog very quietly. Here we met our old Chopunnish guide, with his family, and soon afterwards one of our horses, which had been separated from the rest in the charge of the Twistedhair, and been in this neighbourhood for several weeks, was caught and restored to us.

After dinner we proceeded to the entrance of Colter's creek, at the distance of four miles, and having made twenty and a half miles, encamped on the lower side of it. Colter's creek rises not far from the Rocky mountains, and passing in the greater part of its course through a country well supplied with pine, discharges a large body of water. It is about twenty-five yards wide, with a pebbled bed and low banks. At a little distance from us are two Chopunnish houses, one of which contains eight families, and the other, which is by much the largest we have ever seen, inhabited by at least thirty. It is rather a kind of shed, built like all the other huts, of straw and mats in the form of the roof of a house, one hundred and fifty-six feet long, and about fifteen wide, closed at the ends, and having a number of doors on each side. The vast interior is without partitions, but the fire of each family is kindled in a row along the middle of the building, and about ten feet apart.

This village is the residence of one of the principal chiefs of the nation, who is called Neeshnepahkeook, or *Cutnose*, from the circumstance of having his nose cut from the stroke of a lance in battle with the Snake Indians. We gave him a small medal, but though he is a great chief, his influence among his own people does not seem to be considerable, and his countenance possesses very little intelligence. We arrived very hungry and weary, but could not purchase any provisions, except a small quantity of the roots and bread of the cows. They had, however, heard of our medical skill, and made many applications for assistance, but we refused to do any thing unless they gave us either dogs or horses to eat. We had soon nearly fifty patients. A chief brought his wife with an abscess on her back, and promised to furnish us with a horse to-morrow if we would relieve her. Captain Clark, therefore, opened the abscess, introduced a tent, and dressed it with basilicon. We prepared also, and distributed some doses of the flour of sulphur and cream of tartar, with directions for its use. For these we obtained several dogs, but too poor for use, and we therefore postponed our medical operations till the morning. In the meantime a number of Indians, beside the residents of the village, gathered about us or encamped in the woody bottom of the creek.

In the evening, we learnt by means of a Snake Indian, who happens to be at this place, that one of the old men has been endeavouring to excite prejudices against us, by observing that he thought we were bad men, and came here, most probably, for the purpose of killing them. In order to remove such impressions, we made a speech, in which, by means of the Snake Indian, we told them our country and all the purposes of our visit. While we were engaged in this occupation, we were joined by Weahkoonut, who assisted us in effacing all unfavourable impressions from the minds of the Indians.

*Tuesday.* The following morning our practice became more valuable. The woman declared that she had slept better than at any time since her illness. She was therefore dressed a second time, and her husband, according to promise, brought us a horse, which we immediately killed. Besides this woman, we had crowds of other applicants, chiefly afflicted with sore eyes, and after administering to them for several hours, found ourselves once more in possession of a plentiful meal, for the inhabitants began to be more accommodating, and one of them even gave us a horse for our remedies to his daughter, a little girl, who was afflicted with the rheumatism. We moreover, exchanged one of our horses with Weahkoonut, by the addition of a small flag, which procured us an excellent sorrel horse.

We here found three men, of a nation called Skeetsomish, who reside at the falls of a large river, emptying itself into the north side of the Columbia. This river takes its rise from a large lake in the mountains, at no great distance from the falls where these natives live. We shall designate this river, hereafter, by the name of Clark's river, as we do not know its Indian appellation, and we are the first whites who have ever visited its principal branches; for the Great Lake river mentioned by Mr. Fidler, if at all connected with Clark's river, must be a very inconsiderable branch. To this river, moreover, which we have hitherto called Clark's river, which rises in the southwest mountains, we restored the name of Towahnahiooks, the name by which it is known to the Eneeshurs. In dress and appearance these Skeetsomish were not to be distinguished from the Chopunnish, but their language is entirely different, a circumstance which we did not learn till their departure, when it was too late to procure from them a vocabulary.

About two o'clock we collected our horses and set out, accompanied by Weahkoonut, with ten or twelve men, and a man who said he was the brother of the Twistedhair. At four miles we came to a single house of three families, but we could not procure provisions of any kind; and five miles further we halted for the night near another house, built like the rest, of sticks, mats and dried hay, and containing six families. It was now so difficult to procure any thing to eat that our chief dependence was on the horse which we received yesterday for medicine; but to our great disappointment, he broke the rope by which he was confined, made his escape, and left us supperless in the rain.

MAY 7TH   *Wednesday*. The next morning, Weahkoonut and his party left us, and we proceeded up the river with the brother of the Twistedhair as a guide. The Kooskooskee is now rising fast, the water is clear and cold, and as all the rocks and shoals are now covered, the navigation is safe, notwithstanding the rapidity of the current. The timber begins about the neighbourhood of Colter's creek, and consists chiefly of long-leafed pine. After going four miles, we reached a house of six families, below the entrance of a small creek, where our guide advised us to cross the river, as the route was better, and the game more abundant near the mouth of the Chopunnish. We therefore unloaded, and by means of a single canoe, passed to the south side in about four hours, during which time we dined. An Indian of one of the houses now brought two canisters of powder, which his dog had discovered under ground in a bottom some miles above. We immediately knew them to be the same we had buried last autumn, and as he had kept them safely, and had honesty enough to return them, we rewarded him inadequately, but as well as we could, with a steel for striking fire. We set out at three o'clock, and pursued a difficult and stony road for two miles, when we left the river and ascended the hills on the right, which begin to resemble mountains.

But when we reached the heights, we saw before us a beautiful level country, partially ornamented with the long-leafed pine, and supplied with an excellent pasture of thick grass, and a variety of herbaceous plants, the abundant productions of a dark rich soil. In many parts of the plain, the earth is thrown up into little mounds, by some animal [the pocket-gopher], whose habits most resemble those of the salamander; but although these tracks are scattered over all the plains from the Mississippi to the Pacific, we have never yet been able to obtain a sight of the animal itself.

As we entered the plain Neeshnepahkee, the Cutnose, overtook us, and after accompanying us a few miles, turned to the right to visit some of his people, who were now gathering roots in the plain. Having crossed the plain a little to the south of east, we descended a long steep hill, at the distance of five miles, to a creek six yards wide, which empties itself into the Kooskooskee. We ascended this little stream for a mile, and encamped at an Indian establishment of six houses, which seem to have been recently evacuated. Here we were joined by Neeshnepahkee, and the Shoshonee who had interpreted for us on the fifth.

From the plain we observed that the spurs of the Rocky mountains are still perfectly covered with snow, which the Indians inform us is so deep that we shall not be able to pass before the next full moon, that is, the first of June: though others place the time for crossing at a still greater distance. To us, who are desirous of reaching the plains of the Missouri, if for no other reason, for the purpose of enjoying a good meal, this intelligence was by no means welcome, and gave no relish to the remainder of the horse killed at Colter's creek, which formed our supper, part of which had already been our dinner. Observing, however, some deer, and a great appearance of more, we determined to make an attempt to get some of them.

*Thursday.* Therefore, after a cold night's rest, most of the hunters set out at   MAY 8TH
daylight. By eleven o'clock they all returned, with four deer, and a duck of an uncommon kind, which, with the remains of our horse, formed a stock of provisions such as we had not lately possessed. Without our facilities of procuring subsistence with guns, the natives of this country must often suffer very severely. During last winter they were so much distressed for food, that they were obliged to boil and eat the moss growing on the pine trees. At the same period they cut down nearly all the long-leafed pines, which we observed on the ground, for the purpose of collecting its seed, which resemble in size and shape that of the large sunflower, and when roasted or boiled, is nutritious and not disagreeable to the taste. At the present season they peel this pine tree, and eat the inner and succulent bark. In the creek near us, they also procure trout by means of a falling trap, constructed on the same plan with those common to the United States. We gave Neeshnepahkee and his people some of our game and horse-beef, besides the entrails of the deer, and four fawns which we found inside of two of them. They did not eat any of it perfectly raw, but the entrails had very little cooking, and the fawns were boiled whole, and the hide, hair, and entrails all consumed. The Shoshonee was offended at not having as much venison as he wished, and refused to interpret; but as we took no notice of him, he became very officious in the course of a few hours, and made many efforts to reinstate himself in our favour. The mother [brother] of the Twistedhair, and Neeshnepahkee-

ook now drew a sketch, which we preserved, of all the waters west of the Rocky mountains. They make the main southern branch of Lewis's river, much more extensive than the other, and place a great number of Shoshonee villages on its western side.

Between three and four o'clock in the afternoon we set out, in company with Neeshnepahkeeook and other Indians, the brother of the Twistedhair having left us. Our route was up a high steep hill to a level plain, with little wood, through which we passed in a direction parallel to the river, for four miles, when we met the Twistedhair and six of his people. To this chief we had confided our horses and a part of our saddles, last autumn, and we therefore formed very unfavourable conjectures on finding that he received us with great coldness. Shortly after he began to speak in a very loud, angry manner, and was answered by Neeshnepahkeeook. We now discovered that a violent quarrel had arisen between these chiefs, on the subject, as we afterwards understood, of our horses. But as we could not learn the cause, and were desirous of terminating the dispute, we interposed, and told them we should go on to the first water and encamp. We therefore set out, followed by all the Indians, and having reached, at two miles distance, a small stream, running to the right, we encamped with the two chiefs and their little bands, forming separate camps, at a distance from each other. They all appeared to be in an ill humour, and as we had already heard reports that the Indians had discovered and carried off our saddles, and that the horses were very much scattered, we began to be uneasy, lest there should be too much foundation for the report. We were therefore anxious to reconcile the two chiefs as soon as possible, and desired the Shoshonee to interpret for us, while we attempted a mediation: but he peremptorily refused to speak a word: he observed that it was a quarrel between the two chiefs, and he had therefore no right to interfere; nor could all our representations, that by merely repeating what we said, he could not possibly be considered as meddling between the chiefs, induce him to take any part in it.

Soon afterwards Drewyer returned from hunting, and was sent to invite the Twistedhair to come and smoke with us. He accepted the invitation, and as we were smoking the pipe over our fire, he informed us, that according to his promise, on leaving us at the falls of the Columbia, he had collected our horses and taken charge of them, as soon as he had reached home. But about this time Neeshnepahkeeooks and Tunnachemootoolt (the Brokenarm) who, as we passed, had been on a war-party against the Shoshonees on the south branch of Lewis's river, returned, and becoming jealous of him, because the horses had been confided to his care, were constantly quarrelling with him. At length, being an old man, and unwilling to live in perpetual dispute with the two chiefs, he had given up the care of the horses, which had consequently become very much scattered. The greater part of them were, however, still in this neighbourhood; some in the forks between the Chopunnish and Kooskooskee, and three or four at the village of the Brokenarm, about half a day's march higher up the river. He added, that on the rise of the river in the spring, the earth had fallen from the door of the cache and exposed the saddles, some of which had probably been lost; but as soon as he was acquainted with the situation of them, he had them buried in another deposit, where they now are. He now promised that if we would stay to-morrow at his house, a few miles from this place, he would collect such of the horses as were in the neighbourhood, and send his young men for those in the forks over the Kooskooskee. He moreover advised us to visit the Brokenarm, who was a chief of great eminence, and that he would himself guide us to his dwelling. We told him that we meant to follow his advice in every respect; that we had confided our horses to his charge, and expected that he would deliver them to us, on which we should willingly pay him the two guns and ammunition, as we had promised. With this he seemed very much pleased, and declared that he would use every exertion to restore our horses. We now sent for the Cutnose, and after smoking for some time, took occasion to express to the two chiefs, our regret at seeing a misunderstanding between them. Neeshnepahkeeook told us that the Twistedhair was a bad old man, and wore two faces; for instead of taking care of our horses, he had suffered his young men to hunt with them, so that they had been very much injured, and that it was for this reason that the Brokenarm and himself had forbidden him to use them. The Twistedhair made no reply to this speech, after which we told Neeshnepahkeeook of our arrangement for to-morrow. He appeared very well satisfied, and said that he would himself go with us to the Brokenarm, who expected that we would see him, and who had "two bad horses for us," an expression by which was meant that he intended making us a present of two valuable horses. That chief, he also informed us, had been apprised of our want of provisions, and sent four young men to meet us with a supply; but having taken a different road, they had missed us. After this interview we retired to rest at a late hour.

*Friday.* In the morning, after sending out several hunters, we proceeded through a level rich country, similar to that of yesterday, for six miles, when we reached the house of the Twistedhair, situated near some larch trees, and a few bushes of balsam fir. It was built in the usual form, of sticks, mats, and dried hay, and although it contained no more than two fires and twelve persons, was provided with the customary appendage of a small hut, to which females in certain situations were to retreat. As soon as we halted at this place, we went with the Twistedhair to the spot where he had buried our saddles, and two other young Indians were despatched after the horses. Our hunters joined us with nothing but a few pheasants, the only deer which they killed being lost in the river. We therefore dined on soup, made of the roots of cows, which we purchased of the Indians. Late in the afternoon, the Twistedhair returned with about half the saddles we had left in the autumn, and some powder and lead which was buried at the same place. Soon after, the Indians brought us twenty-one of our horses, the greater part of whom were in excellent order, though some had not yet recovered from hard usage, and three had sore backs. We were however very glad to procure them in any condition. Several Indians came down from the village of Tunnache-mootoolt, and passed the night with us. The Cutnose and Twistedhair seem now perfectly reconciled, for they both slept in the house of the latter. The man who had imposed himself upon us as a brother of the Twistedhair, also came and renewed his advances, but we now found that he was an impertinent proud fellow, of no respectability in the nation, and we therefore felt no inclination to cultivate his intimacy. Our camp was in an open plain, and soon became very uncomfortable, for the wind was high and cold, and the rain and hail which began about seven o'clock, changed in about two hours

MAY 9TH

453

to a heavy fall of snow, which continued till after six o'clock the next morning, when it ceased, after covering the ground eight inches deep, and leaving the air keen and cold.

MAY 10TH   *Saturday*. We soon collected our horses, and after a scanty breakfast of roots, set out on a course S. 35° E. across the plains, the soil of which being covered with snow, we could only judge from observing that near the ravines, where it had melted, the mud was deep, black, and well supplied with quamash. The road was very slippery, and the snow stuck to the horses' feet and made them slip down very frequently. After going about sixteen miles, we came to the hills of Commearp creek, which are six hundred feet in height, but the tops of which only are covered with snow, the lower parts as well as the bottoms of the creek having had nothing but rain while it snowed in the high plains. On descending these hills to the creek, we reached about four o'clock, the house of Tunnachemootoolt, where was displayed the flag which we had given him, raised on a staff: under this we were received with due form, and then conducted a short distance to a good spot for an encampment, on Commearp creek.

We soon collected the men of consideration, and after smoking, explained how destitute we were of provisions. The chief spoke to the people, who immediately brought about two bushels of dried quamash roots, some cakes of the roots of cows, and a dried salmon trout: we thanked them for this supply, but observed that, not being accustomed to live on roots alone, we feared that such diet might make our men sick, and therefore proposed to exchange one of our good horses, which was rather poor, for one that was fatter, and which we might kill. The hospitality of the chief was offended at the idea of an exchange; he observed that his people had an abundance of young horses, and that if we were disposed to use that food, we might have as many as we wanted. Accordingly, they soon gave us two fat young horses, without asking any thing in return, an act of liberal hospitality much greater than any we have witnessed since crossing the Rocky mountains, if it be not in fact the only really hospitable treatment we have received in this part of the world. We killed one of the horses, and then telling the natives that we were fatigued and hungry, and that as soon as we were refreshed, we would communicate freely with them, began to prepare our repast.

During this time, a principal chief, called Hohastillpilp, came from his village about six miles distant, with a party of fifty men, for the purpose of visiting us. We invited him into our circle, and he alighted and smoked with us, while his retinue, who had five elegant horses, continued mounted at a short distance. While this was going on, the chief had a large leathern tent spread for us, and desired that we would make that our home whilst we remained at his village. We removed there, and having made a fire, and cooked a supper of horse-beef and roots, collected all the distinguished men present, and spent the evening in explaining who we were, the objects of our journey, and giving answers to their inquiries. To each of the chiefs, Tunnachemootoolt, and Hohastillpilp, we gave a small medal, explaining their use and importance, as honorary distinctions both among the whites and red men. Our men are delighted at once more having made a hearty meal. They have generally been in the habit of crowding the houses of the Indians, and endeavouring to purchase provisions on the best terms they

454

could; for the inhospitality of the country was such, that in the extreme of hunger they were often obliged to treat the natives with but little ceremony, but this the Twistedhair had told us was disagreeable. Finding that these people are so kind and liberal, we ordered our men to treat them with great respect and not to throng round their fires, so that they now agree perfectly well together. After our council, the Indians felt no disposition to retire, and our tent was crowded with them all night.

*Sunday.* The next morning we arose early and breakfasted again on horse- flesh. This village of Tunnachemootoolt, is in fact only a single house, one hundred and fifty feet long, built after the Chopunnish fashion, with sticks, straw, and dried grass. It contains twenty-four fires, about double that number of families, and might perhaps muster one hundred fighting men. The usual outhouse, or retiring hut for females, is not omitted. Their chief subsistence is roots, and the noise made by the women in pounding them, gives the hearer the idea of a nail factory. Yet, notwithstanding so many families are crowded together, the Chopunnish are much more cleanly in their persons and habitations, than any people we have met since we left the Ottoes on the river Platte.

In the course of the morning, a chief named Yoompahkatim, a stout good looking man, of about forty years of age, who had lost his left eye, arrived from his village on the south side of Lewis's river. We gave him a small medal, and finding that there were now present the principal chiefs of the Chopunnish nation, Tunnachemootoolt (the Brokenarm) Neeshnepahkeeook, Yoompahkatim, and Hohastilpilp, whose rank is in the order they are mentioned, we thought this a favourable moment to explain to them the intentions of our government. We therefore collected the chiefs and warriors, and having drawn a map of the relative situation of our country, on a mat, with a piece of coal, detailed the nature and power of the American nation, its desire to preserve harmony between all its red brethren, and its intention of establishing trading houses for their relief and support. It was not without difficulty, nor till after nearly half the day was spent, that we were able to convey all this information to the Chopunnish, much of which might have been lost or distorted, in its circuitous route through a variety of languages; for in the first place, we spoke in English to one of our men, who translated it into French to Chaboneau; he interpreted it to his wife in the Minnetaree language, and she then put it into Shoshonee, and the young Shoshonee prisoner explained it to the Chopunnish in their own dialect. At last we succeeded in communicating the impression they wished, and then adjourned the council; after which we amused them by showing the wonders of the compass, the spy-glass, the magnet, the watch and air-gun, each of which attracted its share of admiration. They said that after we had left the Minnetarees last autumn, three young Chopunnish had gone over to that nation, who had mentioned our visit and the extraordinary articles we had with us, but they placed no confidence in it until now. Among other persons present, was a youth, son of the Chopunnish chief, of much consideration, killed not long since by the Minnetarees of Fort de Prairie. As soon as the council was over, he brought a very fine mare with a colt, and begged us to accept them as a proof that he meant to pursue our advice, for he had opened his ears to our councils, which had made his heart glad.

We now resumed our medical labours, and had a number of patients afflicted with scrofula, rheumatism and sore eyes, to all which we administered very cheerfully as far as our skill and supplies of medicine would permit. We also visited a chief who has for three years past so completely lost the use of his limbs, that he lies like a perfect corpse in whatever position he is placed, yet he eats heartily, digests his food very well, has a regular pulse, and retains his flesh; in short, were he not somewhat pale from lying so long out of the sun, he might be mistaken for a man in perfect health. This disease does not seem to be common; indeed, we have seen only three cases of it among the Chopunnish, who alone are afflicted with it. The scrofulous disorders we may readily conjecture to originate in the long confinement to vegetable diet; which may perhaps also increase the soreness of the eyes; but this strange disorder baffles at once our curiosity and our skill.

MAY 12TH  *Monday.* Our assistance was again demanded early the next morning by a crowd of Indians, to whom we gave eye-water. Shortly after, the chiefs and warriors held a council among themselves, to decide on the answer to our speech; and the result was, as we were informed, that they confided in what we had told them, and resolved to follow our advice. This resolution once made the principal chief, Tunnachemootoolt, took a quantity of flour of the roots of cows, and going round to all the kettles and baskets, in which his people were cooking, thickened the soup into a kind of mush. He then began a harangue, making known the result of the deliberations among the chiefs, and after exhorting them to unanimity, concluded by an invitation to all who agreed to the proceedings of the council, to come and eat, while those who would not abide by the decision of the chiefs were requested to show their dissent by not partaking in the feast. During this animated harangue, the women, who were probably uneasy at the prospect of forming this new connection with strangers, tore their hair, and wrung their hands with the greatest appearance of distress. But the concluding appeal of the orator effectually stopped the mouths of every malcontent, and the proceedings were ratified, and the mush devoured with the most zealous unanimity.

The chiefs and warriors then came in a body to visit us, as we were seated near our tent, and at their instance, two young men, one of whom was the son of Tunnachemootoolt, and the other the youth whose father had been killed by the Pahkees, presented to each of us a fine horse. We caused the chiefs to be seated, and gave every one of them a flag, a pound of powder, and fifty balls, and a present of the same kind to the young men from whom we had received the horses. They then invited us into the tent, and told us that they now wished to answer what we had told them yesterday; but that many of their people were at that moment waiting in great pain for our medical assistance. It was therefore agreed that captain Clark, who is the favourite physician, should visit the sick, while captain Lewis would hold the council; which was accordingly opened by an old man, the father of Hohasstilpilp.

He began by declaring that the nation had listened with attention to our advice, and had only one heart and one tongue in declaring their determination to follow it. They knew well the advantages of peace, for they valued the lives of their young men too much to expose them to the dangers of war; and their desire to live quietly with their neighbours, had induced

456

them last summer to send three warriors with a pipe to the Shoshonees, in the plains of Columbia, south of Lewis's river. These ministers of peace had been killed by the Shoshonees, against whom the nation immediately took up arms. They had met them last winter, and killed forty-two men, with the loss of only three of their own party; so that having revenged their deceased brethren, they would no longer make war on the Shoshonees, but receive them as friends. As to going with us to the plains of the Missouri, they would be very willing to do so, for though the Blackfoot Indians and the Pahkees had shed much of their blood, they still wished to live in peace with them. But we had not yet seen either of these nations, and it would therefore be unsafe for them to venture, till they were assured of not being attacked by them. Still, however, some of their young men would accompany us across the mountains, and if they could effect a peace with their enemies, the whole nation would go over to the Missouri in the course of next summer. On our proposal that one of the chiefs should go with us to the country of the whites, they had not yet decided, but would let us know before we left them. But that, at all events, the whites might calculate on their attachment and their best services, for though poor, their hearts were good. The snow was, however, still so deep on the mountains, that we should perish in attempting the passage, but if we waited till after the next full moon, the snows would have sufficiently melted to enable our horses to subsist on the grass.

As soon as this speech was concluded, captain Lewis replied at some length: with this they appeared highly gratified, and after smoking the pipe, made us a present of another fat horse for food. We, in turn, gave the Brokenarm a vial of eye-water, with directions to wash the eyes of all who should apply for it; and as we promised to fill it again when it was exhausted, he seemed very much pleased with our liberality. To the Twistedhair, who had last night collected six more horses, we gave a gun, an hundred balls, and two pounds of powder, and told him he should have the same quantity when we received the remainder of our horses. In the course of the day three more of them were brought in, and a fresh exchange of small presents put the Indians in excellent humour. On our expressing a wish to cross the river, and form a camp, in order to hunt and fish till the snows had melted, they recommended a position a few miles distant, and promised to furnish us to-morrow with a canoe to cross. We invited the Twistedhair to settle near our camp, for he has several young sons, one of whom we hope to engage as a guide, and he promised to do so. Having now settled all their affairs, the Indians divided themselves into two parties, and began to play the game of hiding a bone, already described, as common to all the natives of this country, which they continued playing for beads and other ornaments.

TUESDAY, MAY 13TH, 1806   Our medical visits occupied us till a late hour, after which we collected our horses and proceeded for two miles in a south-eastern direction, crossing a branch from the right, at the distance of a mile. We then turned nearly north, and crossing an extensive open bottom, about a mile and a half wide, reached the bank of the Kooskooskee. Here we expected the canoe which they had promised; but although a man had been despatched with it at the appointed time, he did not arrive before sunset. We therefore encamped, with a number of Indians who had followed us from the village.

MAY 14TH

*Wednesday.* In the morning, after sending out some hunters, transported the baggage by means of the canoe, and then drove our horses into the river, over which they swam without accident, although it is one hundred and fifty yards wide, and the current very rapid. We then descended the river about half a mile, and formed our camp on the spot which the Indians had recommended. It was about forty paces from the river, and formerly an Indian habitation; but nothing remained at present but a circle thirty yards in diameter, sunk in the ground about four feet, with a wall round it of nearly three and a half feet in height. In this place we deposited our baggage, and round its edges formed our tents of sticks and grass. This situation is in many respects advantageous. It is an extensive level bottom, thinly covered with long-leafed pine, with a rich soil, affording excellent pasture, and supplied, as well as the high and broken hills on the east and northeast, with the best game in the neighbourhood; while its vicinity to the river makes it convenient for the salmon, which are now expected daily. As soon as we had encamped, Tunnachemootoolt and Hohastilpilp, with about twelve of their nation, came to the opposite side and began to sing, this being the usual token of friendship on similar occasions. We sent the canoe for them, and the two chiefs came over with several of the party, among whom were the two young men who had given us the two horses in behalf of the nation. After smoking some time, Hohastilpilp presented to captain Lewis an elegant gray gelding, which he had brought for the purpose, and was perfectly satisfied at receiving in return a handkerchief, two hundred balls, and four pounds of powder.

The hunters killed some pheasants, two squirrels, and a male and a female bear, the first of which was large and fat, and of a bay colour; the second meagre, grisly, and of smaller size. They were of the species common to the upper part of the Missouri, and might well be termed the variegated bear, for they are found occasionally of a black grisly brown or red colour. There is every reason to believe them to be of precisely the same species. Those of different colours are killed together, as in the case of these two, and as we found the white and bay associated together on the Missouri; and some nearly white were seen in this neighbourhood by the hunters. Indeed, it is not common to find any two bears of the same colour, and if the difference in colour were to constitute a distinction of species, the number would increase to almost twenty. Soon after they killed a female bear with two cubs. The mother was black, with a considerable intermixture of white hairs and a white spot on the breast. One of the cubs was jet black, and the other of a light reddish brown, or bay colour. The poil [hair] of these variegated bears is much finer, longer, and more abundant than that of the common black bear: but the most striking difference between them is, that the former are larger, have longer tusks, and longer as well as blunter talons; that they prey more on other animals; that they lie neither so long nor so closely in winter quarters, and never climb a tree, however closely pressed by the hunters. This variegated bear, though specifically the same with those we met on the Missouri, are by no means so ferocious, probably, because of the scarcity of game, and the habit of living on roots may have weaned them from the practices of attacking and devouring animals. Still, however, they are not so passive as the common black bear, which are also to be found here; for they have already fought with our hunters, though with less fury than those on the other side of the mountain.

A large part of the meat we gave to the Indians, to whom it was a real luxury, as they scarcely taste flesh once in a month. They immediately prepared a large fire of dried wood, on which were thrown a number of smooth stones from the river. As soon as the fire went down, and the stones were heated, they were laid next to each other, in a level position, and covered with a quantity of branches of pine, on which were placed flitches of the bear, and thus placing the boughs and flesh alternately for several courses, leaving a thick layer of pine on the top. On this heap was then poured a small quantity of water, and the whole covered with earth to the depth of four inches. After remaining in this state about three hours, the meat was taken off, and was really more tender than that which we had boiled or roasted, though the strong flavour of the pine, rendered it disagreeable to our palates. This repast gave them much satisfaction, for though they sometimes kill the black bear, yet they attack very reluctantly the furious variegated bear, and only when they can pursue him on horseback, through the plains, and shoot him with arrows.

The stone-horses we found so troublesome that we have endeavoured to exchange them for either mares or geldings; but although we offered two for one, they were unwilling to barter. It was therefore determined to castrate them; and being desirous of ascertaining the best method of performing this operation, two were gelded in the usual manner, while one of the natives tried the experiment in the Indian way, without tying the string of the stone (which he assured us was much the better plan) and carefully scraping the string clean and separating it from the adjoining veins before cutting it. All the horses recovered; but we afterwards found that those on which the Indian mode had been tried, although they bled more profusely at first, neither swell nor appear to suffer as much as the others, and recovered sooner, so that we are fully persuaded that the Indian method is preferable to our own.

As we shall now be compelled to pass some time in this neighbourhood, a     MAY 15TH
number of hunters were sent in different directions, and the rest were employed in completing the camp. From this labour we, however, exempted five of the men, two of whom are afflicted with colic, and the others complain of violent pains in the head, all which are occasioned, we presume, by the diet of roots, to which they have recently been confined. We secured the baggage with a shelter of grass, and made a kind of bower of the under part of an old sail, the leathern tent being now too rotten for use, while the men formed very comfortable huts in the shape of the awning of a wagon, by

459

means of willow poles and grass. Tunnachemootoolt and his young men left us this morning on their way home; and soon after we were visited by a party of fourteen Indians on horseback, armed with bows and arrows going on a hunting excursion. The chief game is the deer, and whenever the ground will permit, the favourite hunt is on horseback; but in the woodlands, where this is impracticable, they make use of a decoy. This consists of the skin of the head and upper part of the neck of a deer, kept in its natural shape by a frame of small sticks on the inside. As soon as the hunter perceives a deer he conceals himself, and with his hand moves the decoy so as to represent a real deer in the act of feeding, which is done so naturally that the game is seduced within reach of their arrows. We also exercised our horses by driving them together, so as to accustom them to each other, and incline them the less to separate.

MAY 16TH  *Friday.* The next morning, an Indian returned with one of them, which had strayed away in the night to a considerable distance, an instance of integrity and kindness by no means singular among the Chopunnish. Hohastilpilp, with the rest of the natives left us to-day. The hunters who have as yet come in, brought nothing, except a few pheasants, so that we still place our chief reliance on the mush made of roots (among these the cows and the quamash are the principal) with which we use a small onion, which grows in great abundance, and which corrects any bad effects they may have on the stomach. The cows and quamash, particularly, incline to produce flatulency, to obviate which we employ a kind of fennel, called by the Shoshonees, year-hah, resembling aniseed in flavour, and a very agreeable food.

In the course of the day two other hunters brought in a deer. The game they said was scarce; but they had wounded three bear as white as sheep. The last hunters who had left us yesterday, also came in to-night, with information, that at the distance of five or six miles, they attempted to cross Collins's creek, on the other side, where game is most abundant, but that they could not ford it with their horses, on account of its depth, and the rapidity of the current.

MAY 17TH  *Saturday.* It rained during the greater part of the night, and our flimsy covering being insufficient for our protection, we lay in the water most of the time. What was more unlucky, our chronometer became wet, and, in consequence, somewhat rusty, but by care we hope to restore it. The rain continued nearly the whole day, while on the high plains the snow is falling, and already two or three inches in depth. The bad weather confined us to the camp and kept the Indians from us, so that for the first time since we left the narrows of the Columbia, a day has passed without our being visited by any of the natives.

The country along the Rocky mountains for several hundred miles in length and about fifty wide, is a high level plain; in all its parts extremely fertile, and in many places covered with a growth of tall long-leafed pine. This plain is chiefly interrupted near the streams of water, where the hills are steep and lofty; but the soil is good, being unincumbered by much stone, and possesses more timber than the level country. Under shelter of these hills, the bottom lands skirt the margin of the rivers, and though narrow and confined, are still fertile and rarely inundated. Nearly the whole of this wide spread tract is covered with a profusion of grass and plants, which are at this time as high as the knee. Among these are a variety of esculent plants and roots, acquired without much difficulty, and yielding not only a nutritious, but a very agreeable food. The air is pure and dry, the climate quite as mild, if not milder, than the same parallels of latitude in the Atlantic states, and must be equally healthy, for all the disorders which we have witnessed, may fairly be imputed more to the nature of the diet than to any intemperance of climate. This general observation is of course to be qualified, since in the same tract of country, the degrees of the combination of heat and cold obey the influence of situation. Thus the rains of the low grounds near our camp, are snows in the high plains, and while the sun shines with intense heat in the confined bottoms, the plains enjoy a much colder air, and the vegetation is retarded at least fifteen days, while at the foot of the mountains the snows are still many feet in depth; so that within twenty miles of our camp we observe the rigours of winter cold, the cool air of spring, and the oppressive heat of midsummer. Even on the plains, however, where the snow has fallen, it seems to do but little injury to the grass and other plants, which, though apparently tender and susceptible, are still blooming, at the height of nearly eighteen inches through the snow. In short, this district affords many advantages to settlers, and if properly cultivated, would yield every object necessary for the subsistence and comfort of civilized man.

The Chopunnish themselves are in general stout, well formed, and active; they have high, and many of them aquiline noses, and the general appearance of the face is cheerful and agreeable, though without any indication of gaiety and mirth. Like most of the Indians they extract their beards; but the women only pluck the hair from the rest of the body. That of the men is very often suffered to grow, nor does there appear to be any natural deficiency in that respect; for we observe several men, who, if they had adopted the practice of shaving, would have been as well supplied as ourselves. The dress of both sexes resembles that of the Shoshonees, and consists of a long shirt reaching to the thigh, leggings as high as the waist, moccasins and robes, all of which are formed of skins.

Their ornaments are beads, shells, and pieces of brass attached to different parts of the dress, or tied round the arms, neck, wrists, and over the shoulders: to these are added pearls and beads, suspended from the ears, and a single shell of wampum through the nose. The head-dress of the men is a bandeau of fox or otter skin, either with or without the fur, and sometimes an ornament is tied to a plait of hair, falling from the crown of the head: that of the women is a cap without rim, formed of bear grass and cedar bark; while the hair itself, of both sexes, falls in two rows down the front of the body. Collars of bears' claws are also common. But the personal ornament most esteemed is a sort of breastplate, formed of a strip of otter skin, six inches wide, cut out of the whole length of the back of the animal, including the head; this being dressed with the hair on, a hole is made at the upper end, through which the head of the wearer is placed, and the skin hangs in front with the tail reaching below the knee, and ornamented with pieces of pearl, red cloth, and wampum; or, in short, any other fanciful decoration. Tippets also are occasionally worn. That of Hohastilpilp was formed of human scalps, and adorned with the thumbs and fingers of several men slain by him in battle.

461

The Chopunnish are among the most amiable men we have seen. Their character is placid and gentle, rarely moved into passion, yet not often enlivened by gaiety. Their amusements consist in running races, shooting with arrows at a target, and they partake of the great and prevailing vice of gambling. They are, however, by no means so much attached to baubles as the generality of Indians, but are anxious to obtain articles of utility, such as knives, tomahawks, kettles, blankets, and awls for moccasins. They have also suffered so much from the superiority of their enemies, that they are equally desirous of procuring arms and ammunition, which they are gradually acquiring, for the band of Tunnachemootoolt have already six guns, which they acquired from the Minnetarees.

The Chopunnish bury their dead in sepulchres, formed of boards, constructed like the roof of a house. The body is rolled in skins and laid one over another, separated by a board only, both above and below. We have sometimes seen their dead buried in wooden boxes, and rolled in skins in the manner above mentioned. They sacrifice their horses, canoes, and every other species of property to their dead; the bones of many horses are seen lying round their sepulchres.

Among the reptiles common to this country are the two species of innocent snakes already described, and the rattlesnake, which last is of the same species as that of the Missouri, and though abundant here, is the only poisonous snake we have seen between the Pacific and the Missouri. Besides these there are the common black lizard and horned lizard. Of frogs there are several kinds, such as the small green tree frog, the small frog common in the United States, which sings in the spring of the year, a species of frog frequenting the water, much larger than the bull-frog, and in shape between the delicate length of the bull-frog, and the shorter and less graceful form of the toad like; the last of which, however, its body is covered with little pustules, or lumps: we have never heard it make a noise of any kind. Neither the toad bull-frog; the moccasin-snake, nor the copperhead-snake are to be found here. Captain Lewis killed a snake near the camp three feet and eleven inches in length, and much the colour of the rattlesnake. There was no poisonous tooth to be found. It had two hundred and eighteen scuta on the abdomen, and fifty-nine squama or half-formed scuta on the tail. The eye was of a moderate size: the iris of a dark yellowish brown, and the pupil black. There was nothing remarkable in the form of the head, which was not so wide across the jaws as that of the poisonous class of snakes usually are.

There is a species of lizard, which we have called the horned lizard, about the size and much resembling in figure the ordinary black lizard. The belly is, notwithstanding, broader, the tail shorter, and the action much slower than the ordinary lizard. It crawls like the toad, is of a brown colour, and interspersed with yellowish brown spots; it is covered with minute shells [scales], interspersed with little horny projections like prickles on the upper part of the body. The belly and throat resemble the frogs, and are of a light yellowish brown. The edge of the belly is regularly beset with these horny projections, which give to those edges a serrate figure; the eye is small and of a dark colour. Above and behind the eyes are several projections of the bone, which being armed at the extremities with a firm black substance, having the appearance of horns sprouting from the head, has induced us to

INTERIOR OF A MANDAN HUT (Bodmer)

call it the horned lizard. These animals are found in great abundance in the sandy parts of the plains, and after a shower of rain are seen basking in the sun. For the greatest part of the time they are concealed in holes. They are found in great numbers on the banks of the Missouri, and in the plains through which we have passed above the Wollawollahs.

Most of the insects common to the United States are seen in this country: such as the butterfly, the common housefly, the blowingfly, the horsefly, except one species of it, the gold-coloured earfly, the place of which is supplied by a fly of a brown colour, which attaches itself to the same part of the horse, and is equally troublesome. There are likewise nearly all the varieties of beetles known in the Atlantic states, except the large cow beetle, and the black beetle, commonly called the tumblebug. Neither the hornet, the wasp, nor the yellowjacket inhabit this part of the country, but there is an insect resembling the last of these, though much larger, which is very numerous, particularly in the Rocky mountains and on the waters of the Columbia; the body and abdomen are yellow, with transverse circles of black, the head black, and the wings, which are four in number, of a dark brown colour: their nests are built in the ground, and resemble that of the hornet, with an outer covering to the comb. These insects are fierce, and sting very severely, so that we found them very troublesome in frightening our horses as we passed the mountains. The silkworm is also found here, as well as the humble-bee, though the honey-bee is not.

Twelve hunters set out this morning after the bear, which are now our chief dependence; but as they are now ferocious, the hunters henceforward never go except in pairs. Soon after they left us, a party of Chopunnish erected a hut on the opposite side of the river in order to watch the salmon, which is expected to arrive every day. For this purpose they have constructed with sticks, a kind of wharf, projecting about ten feet into the river, and three feet above its surface, on the extremity of which one of the fishermen exercised himself with a scooping net, similar to that used in our country; but  after several hours labour he was still unsuccessful. In the course of the morning three Indians called at our camp and told us that they had been hunting near the place where we met the Chopunnish last autumn, and which is called by them the quamash grounds, but after roaming about for several days had killed nothing. We gave them a small piece of meat, which they said they would keep for their small children, which they said were very hungry, and then, after smoking, took leave of us. Some of our hunters returned almost equally unsuccessful. They had gone over the whole country between Collins's creek and the Kooskooskee, to their junction, at the distance of ten miles, without seeing either a deer or bear, and at last brought in a single hawk and a salmon dropped by an eagle. This last was not in itself considerable, but gave us hopes of soon seeing that fish in the river, an event which we ardently desire, for though the rapid rise of the river denotes a great decrease of snow on the mountains, yet we shall not be able to leave our camp for some time.

*Monday.* After a cold rainy night, during a greater part of which we lay in the water, the weather became fair, and we then sent some men to a village above us, on the opposite side, to purchase some roots. They carried with

MAY 18TH

MAY 19TH

them for this purpose a small collection of awls, knitting pins, and arm-bands, with which they obtained several bushels of the root of cows, and some bread of the same material. They were followed too by a train of invalids from the village, who came to ask for our assistance. The men were generally afflicted with sore eyes, but the women had besides this a variety of other disorders, chiefly rheumatic, a violent pain and weakness in the loins, which is a common complaint among the females, and one of them seemed much dejected, and as we thought, from the account of her disease, hysterical. We gave her thirty drops of laudanum, and after administering eye-water and rubbing the rheumatic patients with volatile liniment, and giving cathartics to others, they all thought themselves much relieved, and returned highly satisfied to the village. We were fortunate enough to retake one of the horses on which we crossed the Rocky mountains in the autumn, and which had become almost wild since that time.

MAY 20TH    *Tuesday.* Again it rained during the night, and the greater part of this day. Our hunters were out in different directions, but though they saw a bear and a deer or two, they only killed one of the latter, which proved to be of the mule-deer species. The next day, *Wednesday 21st*, finding the rain still continue we left our ragged sail tent, and formed a hut with willow poles and grass. The rest of the men were occupied in building a canoe for present use, as the Indians promise to give us a horse for it when we leave them. We received nothing from our hunters except a single sandhill crane, which are very abundant in this neighbourhood, and consumed at dinner the last morsel of meat which we have. As there now seems but little probability of our procuring a stock of dried meat, and the fish is as yet an uncertain resource, we made a division of all our stock of merchandise, so as to enable the men to purchase a store of roots and bread for the mountains. We might ourselves collect those roots, but as there are several species of hemlock growing among the cows, and difficult to be distinguished from that plant, we are afraid to suffer the men to collect them, lest the party might be poisoned by mistaking them. On parcelling out the stores, the stock of each man was found to consist of only one awl and one knitting-pin, half an ounce of vermillion, two needles, a few skeins of thread, and about a yard of ribbon—a slender means of bartering for our subsistence; but the men have been now so much accustomed to privations, that neither the want of meat, nor the scanty funds of the party, excite the least anxiety among them.

MAY 22D    *Thursday.* We availed ourselves of the fair weather to dry our baggage and store of roots, and being still without meat, killed one of our colts, intending to reserve the other three for the mountains. In the afternoon we were amused by a large party of Indians, on the opposite side of the river, hunting on horseback. After riding at full speed down the steep hills, they at last drove the deer into the river, where we shot it, and two Indians immediately pursued it on a raft, and took it. Several hunters, who had gone to a considerable distance near the mountains, returned with five deer. They had purchased also two red salmon trout, which the Indians say remain in this river during the greater part of the winter, but are not good at this season, as it in fact appeared, for they were very meagre. The salmon, we understand, are now arrived at no great distance, in Lewis's river, but some days will yet elapse before they come up to this place. This, as well as the scarcity of game, made us wish to remove lower down; but on examination we found that there was no place in that direction calculated for a camp, and therefore resolved to remain in our present position. Some uneasiness has been excited by a report, that two nights ago a party of Shoshonees had surrounded a Chopunnish house, on the south side of Lewis's river, but the inhabitants having discovered their intentions, had escaped without injury.

*Friday.* The hunters were sent out to make a last effort to procure provi- MAY 23D sions, but after examining the whole country between Collins's creek and the Kooskooskee, they found nothing except a few pheasants of the dark brown kind. In the meantime we were visited by four Indians who had come from a village on Lewis's river, at the distance of two days' ride, who came for the purpose of procuring a little eye-water: the extent of our medical fame is not a little troublesome, but we rejoice at any circumstance which enables us to relieve these poor creatures, and therefore willingly washed their eyes, after which they returned home.

*Saturday.* This proved the warmest day we have had since our arrival here. MAY 24TH Some of our men visited the village of the Brokenarm, and exchanged some awls, which they had made of the links of a small chain belonging to one of their steel traps, for a plentiful supply of roots.

Besides administering medical relief to the Indians, we are obliged to devote much of our time to the care of our own invalids. The child of Sacajawea is very unwell; and with one of the men we have ventured an experiment of a very robust nature. He has been for some time sick, but has now recovered his flesh, eats heartily and digests well, but has so great a weakness in the loins that he cannot walk nor even sit upright without extreme pain. After we had in vain exhausted the resources of our art, one of the hunters mentioned that he had known persons in similar situations restored by violent sweats, and at the request of the patient, we permitted the remedy to be applied. For this purpose, a hole about four feet deep and three in diameter was dug in the earth, and heated well by a large fire in the bottom of it. The fire was then taken out, and an arch formed over the hole by means of willow poles, and covered with several blankets, so as to make a perfect awning. The patient being stripped naked, was seated under this on a bench, with a piece of board for his feet, and with a jug of water sprinkled the bottom and sides of the hole, so as to keep up as hot a steam as he could bear. After remaining twenty minutes in this situation, he was taken out, immediately plunged twice in cold water, and brought back to the hole, where he resumed the vapour bath. During all this time he drank copiously a strong infusion of horse-mint, which was used as a substitute for the seneca root, which our informant said he had seen employed on these occasions, but of which there is none in this country. At the end of three quarters of an hour, he was again withdrawn from the hole, carefully wrapped, and suffered to cool gradually. This operation was performed yesterday, and this morning he walked about, and is nearly free from pain. About eleven o'clock a canoe arrived with three Indians, one of whom was the poor creature who had lost the use of his limbs, and for whose recovery the natives seem very anxious, as he is a chief of considerable rank among them. His situation is beyond the reach of our skill. He complains of no pain in any peculiar limb, and we therefore think his disorder cannot be rheumatic, as his limbs would have been more diminished if his disease had been a paralytic affection. We had already ascribed it to his diet of roots, and had recommended his living on fish and flesh, and using the cold bath every morning, with a dose of cream of tartar, or flowers of sulphur, every third day. These prescriptions seem to have been of little avail, but as he thinks himself somewhat better for them, we concealed our ignorance by giving him a few drops of laudanum and a little portable soup, with a promise of sweating him, as we had done our own man.

MAY 25TH On attempting it however, in the morning, we found that he was too weak to sit up or be supported in the hole: we therefore told the Indians that we knew of no other remedy except frequent perspirations in their own sweat-houses, accompanied by drinking large quantities of the decoction of horse-mint, which we pointed out to them. Three hunters set out to hunt towards the Quamash flats if they could pass Collins's creek. Others crossed the river for the same purpose, and one of the men was sent to a village on the opposite side, about eight miles above us. Nearly all the inhabitants were either hunting, digging roots, or fishing in Lewis's river, from which they had brought several fine salmon. In the course of the day, some of our hunters wounded a female bear with two cubs, one of which was white and the other perfectly black.

The Indians who accompanied the sick chief are so anxious for his safety that they remained with us all night, and in the morning, when we gave him some cream of tartar, and portable soup, with directions how to treat him, they still lingered about us in hopes we might do something effectual, though we desired them to take him home.

The hunters sent out yesterday returned with Hohastilpilp, and a number of inferior chiefs and warriors. They had passed Commearp creek at the distance of one and a half miles, and a larger creek three miles beyond; they then went on till they were stopped by a large creek ten miles above our camp, and finding it too deep and rapid to pass, they returned home. On their way, they stopped at a village four miles up the second creek, which we have never visited, and where they purchased bread and roots on very moderate terms; an article of intelligence very pleasing at the present moment, when our stock of meat is again exhausted. We have however still agreeable prospects, for the river is rising fast, as the snows visibly diminish, and we saw a salmon in the river to-day. We also completed our canoe.

MAY 27TH *Tuesday.* The horse which the Indians gave us some time ago, had gone astray; but in our present dearth of provisions we searched for him and killed him. Observing that we were in want of food, Hohastilpilp informed us that most of the horses which we saw running at large belonged to him or his people, and requested that whenever we wished any meat we would make use of them without restraint. We have, indeed, on more than one occasion, had to admire the generosity of this Indian, whose conduct presents a model of what is due to strangers in distress. A party was sent to the village discovered yesterday, and returned with a large supply of bread and roots. Sergeant Ordway and two men were also despatched to Lewis's river, about half a day's ride to the south, where we expect to obtain salmon, which are said to be very abundant at that place. The three men who had attempted to go to the Quamash flats, returned with five deer; but although they had proceeded some distance up Collins's creek, it continued too deep for them to cross. The Indians who accompanied the chief, were so anxious to have the operation of sweating him performed under our inspection, that we determined to gratify them by making a second attempt. The hole was therefore enlarged, and the father of the chief, a very good looking old man, went in with him, and held him in a proper position. This strong evidence of feeling is directly opposite to the received opinions of the insensibility of savages, nor are we less struck by the kindness and attention paid to the sick man by those who are unconnected with him, which are the more surprising, as the long illness of three years might be supposed to exhaust their sympathy. We could not produce as complete a perspiration as we desired, and after he was taken out, he complained of suffering considerable pain, which we relieved with a few drops of laudanum, and he then rested well.

*Wednesday.* The next morning he was able to use his arms, and feels better than he has done for many months, and sat up during the greater part of the day. MAY 28TH

We sent to the village of Tunnachemootoolt for bread and roots, and a party of hunters set out to hunt up a creek, about eight miles above us. In the evening, another party, who had been so fortunate as to find a ford across Collins's creek, returned from the Quamash flats with eight deer, of which they saw great numbers, though there were but few bears. Having now a tolerable stock of meat, we were occupied during the following day, *Thursday*, in various engagements in the camp.

The Indian chief is still rapidly recovering, and for the first time during the last twelve months, had strength enough to wash his face. We had intended to repeat the sweating to-day, but as the weather was cloudy, with occasional rain, we declined it. This operation, though violent, seems highly efficacious; for our own man, on whom the experiment was first made, is recovering his strength very fast, and the restoration of the chief is wonderful. He continued to improve, and on the following day, after a very violent sweating, was able to move one of his legs and thighs, and some of his toes; the fingers and arms being almost entirely restored to their former strength. Parties were sent out as usual to hunt and trade with the Indians. Among others, two of the men who had not yet exchanged their stock of merchandise for roots, crossed the river for that purpose, in our boat. But as they reached the opposite shore, the violence of the current drove the boat broadside against some trees, and she immediately filled and went to the bottom. With difficulty one of the men was saved, but the boat itself, with three blankets, a blanket-coat, and their small pittance of merchandise, were irrevocably lost.

*Saturday.* Two men visited the Indian village, where they purchased a dressed bear skin, of a uniform pale reddish brown colour, which the Indians called yackah in contradistinction to hohhost, or the white bear. This remark induced us to inquire more particularly into their opinions as to the several species of bears; and we therefore produced all the skins of that ani- MAY 31ST

467

mal which we had killed at this place, and also one very nearly white, which we had purchased. The natives immediately classed the white, the deep and the pale grizzly red, the grizzly dark brown, in short, all those with the extremities of the hair of a white or frosty colour, without regard to the colour of the ground of the poil, under the name of hohhost. They assured us, that they were all of the same species with the white bear; that they associated together, had longer nails than the others, and never climbed trees. On the other hand, the black skins, those which were black, with a number of entire white hairs intermixed, or with a white breast, the uniform bay, the brown, and light reddish brown, were ranged under the class yackah, and were said to resemble each other in being smaller, and having shorter nails than the white bear, in climbing trees, and being so little vicious that they could be pursued with safety.

This distinction of the Indians seems to be well founded, and we are inclined to believe, first, that the white or grizzly bear of this neighbourhood form a distinct species, which moreover is the same with those of the same colour on the upper part of the Missouri, where the other species are not found; second, that the black and reddish brown, &c. is a second species, equally distinct from the white bear of this country, as from the black bear of the Atlantic and Pacific oceans, which two last seem to form only one species. The common black bear are indeed unknown in this country; for the bear of which we are speaking, though in most respects similar, differs from it in having much finer, thicker, and longer hair, with a greater proportion of fur mixed with it, and also in having a variety of colours, while the common black bear has no intermixture or change of colour, but is of a uniform black.

In the course of the day the natives brought us another of our original stock of horses, of which we have now recovered all except two, and those, we are informed, were taken back by our Shoshonee guide, when he returned home. They amount to sixty-five, and most of them fine strong active horses, in excellent order.

## Sunday, June 1st, 1806

Two of our men who had been up the river to trade with the Indians, returned quite unsuccessful. Nearly opposite to the village, their horse fell with his load, down a steep cliff, into the river, across which he swam. An Indian on the opposite side, drove him back to them, but in crossing most of the articles were lost, and the paint melted. Understanding their intentions, the Indians attempted to come over to them, but having no canoe, were obliged to use a raft, which struck on a rock, upset, and the whole store of roots and bread were destroyed. This failure completely exhausted our stock of merchandise; but the remembrance of what we suffered from cold and hunger during the passage of the Rocky mountains, makes us anxious to increase our means of subsistence and comfort when we again encounter the same inconvenience. We therefore created a new fund, by cutting off the buttons from our clothes, preparing some eye-water, and basilicon, to which were added some vials, and small tin boxes, in which we had once kept phosphorus.

*Monday.* With this cargo two men set out in the morning to trade, and brought home three bushels of roots and some bread, which, in our situation, was as important as the return of an East India ship. In the meantime, several hunters went across Collins's creek to hunt on the Quamash grounds, and the Indians informed us that there were great quantities of moose to the southeast of the east branch of Lewis's river, which they call the Tommanamah. We had lately heard that some Indians who reside at some distance, on the south side of the Kooskooskee, are in possession of two tomahawks, one of which was left at our camp at Musquitoe creek, the other had been stolen while we were encamped at the Chopunnish last autumn. This last we were anxious to obtain, in order to give to the relations of our unfortunate companion, sergeant Floyd, to whom it once belonged. We therefore sent Drewyer yesterday with Neeshnepahkeeook and Hohastilpilp, the two chiefs, to demand it. On their arrival, it seemed that the present owner, who had purchased it from the thief, was himself at the point of death; so that his relations were unwilling to give it up, as they meant to bury it in the grave with the deceased. But the influence of Neeshnepahkeeook at length succeeded; and they consented to surrender the tomahawk on receiving two strands of beads and a handkerchief, from Drewyer, and from each of the chiefs a horse, to be killed at the funeral of the deceased, according to the custom of the country.

Soon after their return, sergeant Ordway and his party, for whose safety we had now become extremely anxious, came home from Lewis's river, with some roots of cows and seventeen salmon. The distance, however, from which they were brought, was so great, that most of them were nearly spoiled; but such as continued sound, were extremely delicious, the flesh being of a fine rose colour, with a small mixture of yellow, and so fat that they were cooked very well without the addition of any oil or grease.

When they set out on the *27th* they had hoped to reach the salmon fishery in the course of that day, but the route by which the guides led them was so circuitous, that they rode seventy miles before they reached their place of destination, in the evening of the *29th*. After going for twenty miles up the Commearp creek, through an open plain, broken only by the hills and timber along the creek, they then entered a high, irregular, mountainous country, the soil of which was fertile, and well supplied with pine. Without stopping to hunt, although they saw great quantities of deer, and some of the bighorn, they hastened for thirty miles across this district to the Tommanamah, or east branch of Lewis's river; and not finding any salmon, descended that stream for twenty miles, to the fishery at a short distance below its junction with the south branch. Both these forks appear to come from or enter a mountainous country. The Tommanamah itself, they said, was about one hundred and fifty yards wide; its banks, for the most part, formed of solid perpendicular rocks, rising to a great height, and as they passed along some of its hills, they found that the snow had not yet disappeared, and the grass was just springing up. During its whole course it presented one continued rapid, till at the fishery itself, where the river widens to the space of two hundred yards, the rapid is nearly as considerable as at the great rapids of the Columbia. Here the Indians have erected a large house of split timber, one hundred and fifty feet long, and thirty-five wide, with a flat roof; and at this season is much resorted to by the men, while the women

469

are employed in collecting roots. After remaining a day, and purchasing some fish, they returned home.

JUNE 3D  *Tuesday.* Finding that the salmon has not yet appeared along the shores, as the Indians assured us they would in a few days, and that all the salmon which they themselves use, are obtained from Lewis's river, we begin to lose our hopes of subsisting on them. We are too poor, and at too great a distance from Lewis's river, to purchase fish at that place, and it is not probable that the river will fall sufficiently to take them before we leave this place. Our Indian friends sent an express to-day over the mountains to Traveller's-rest, in order to procure intelligence from the Ootlashoots, a band of Flatheads who have wintered on the east side of the mountains, and the same band which we first met on that river. As the route was deemed practicable for this express, we also proposed setting out, but the Indians dissuaded us from attempting it, as many of the creeks, they said, were still too deep to be forded; the roads very deep and slippery, and no grass as yet for our horses; but in twelve or fourteen days we shall no longer meet with the some obstacles: we therefore determined to set out in a few days for the Quamash flats, in order to lay in a store of provisions, so as to cross the mountains about the middle of the month.

For the two following days we continued hunting in our own neighbourhood, and by means of our own exertions, and trading with the Indians for trifling articles, succeeded in procuring as much bread and roots, besides other food, as will enable us to subsist during the passage of the mountains. The old chief in the meantime gradually recovered the use of his limbs, and our own man was nearly restored to his former health. The Indians who had been with us, now returned, and invited us to their village on the following day, *Friday, June 6th*, to give us their final answer to a number of proposals which we had made to them.

Neeshnepahkeeook then informed us, that they could not accompany us, as we wished, to the Missouri; but that in the latter end of the summer they meant to cross the mountain and spend the winter to the eastward. We had also requested some of their young men to go with us, so as to effect a reconciliation between them and the Pahkees, in case we should meet these last. He answered, that some of their young men would go with us, but they were not selected for that purpose, nor could they be until a general meeting of the whole nation, who were to meet in the plain on Lewis's river, at the head of Commearp. This meeting would take place in ten or twelve days, and if we set out before that time, the young men should follow us. We therefore depend but little on their assistance as guides, but hope to engage for that purpose, some of the Ootlashoots near Traveller's-rest creek. Soon after this communication, which was followed by a present of dried quamash, we were visited by Hohastilpilp and several others, among whom were the two young chiefs who had given us horses some time ago.

SATURDAY, JUNE 7TH, 1806   The two young chiefs returned after breakfast to their village on Commearp creek, accompanied by several of our men, who were sent to purchase ropes and bags for packing, in exchange for some parts of an old seine, bullets, old files, and pieces of iron. In the evening they returned with a few strings but no bags. Hohastilpilp crossed the river in the course of the day, and brought with him a horse, which he gave one of our men who had previously made him a present of a pair of Canadian shoes or shoepacks. We were all occupied in preparing packs and saddles for our journey; and as we intend to visit the Quamash flats on the tenth, in order to lay in a store of provisions for the journey over the mountains, we do not suffer the men to disturb the game in that neighbourhood.

*Sunday.* The Cutnose visited us this morning with ten or twelve warriors: among these were two belonging to a band of Chopunnish, which we had not yet seen, who call themselves Willetpos, and reside on the south side of Lewis's river. One of them gave a good horse, which he rode, in exchange for one of ours, which was unable to cross the mountain, on receiving a tomahawk in addition. We were also fortunate in exchanging two other horses of inferior value for others much better, without giving any thing else to the purchaser. After these important purchases, several foot races were run between our men and the Indians: the latter, who are very active, and fond of these races, proved themselves very expert, and one of them was as fleet as our swiftest runners. After the races were over, the men divided themselves into two parties and played prison base, an exercise which we are desirous of encouraging, before we begin the passage over the mountains, as several of them are becoming lazy from inaction. At night these games were concluded by a dance.

One of the Indians informed us that we could not pass the mountains before the next full moon, or about the first of July; because, if we attempted it before that time, the horses would be forced to travel without food three days on the top of the mountains. This intelligence was disagreeable, as it excited a doubt as to the most proper time for passing the mountains; but having no time to lose, we are determined to risk the hazards, and start as soon as the Indians generally consider it practicable, which is about the middle of this month.

*Monday.* Our success yesterday encouraged us to attempt to exchange some more of our horses, whose backs were unsound, but we could dispose of one only. Hohastilpilp, who visited us yesterday, left us with several Indians, for the plains near Lewis's river, where the whole nation are about to assemble. The Brokenarm too, with all his people, stopped on their way to the general rendezvous, at the same place. The Cutnose, or Neeshnepahkeeook, borrowed a horse, and rode down a few miles after some young eagles. He soon returned with two of the grey kind, nearly grown, which he meant to raise for the sake of the feathers. The young chief, who some time since made us a present of two horses, came with a party of his people, and passed the night with us.

The river, which is about one hundred and fifty yards wide, has been discharging vast bodies of water, but notwithstanding its depth, the water has been nearly transparent, and its temperature quite as cold as our best springs. For several days, however, the river has been falling, and is now six feet lower than it has been, a strong proof that the great body of snow has left the mountains. It is, indeed, nearly at the same height as when we arrived here; a circumstance which the Indians consider as indicating the time when the mountains may be crossed. We shall wait, however, a few days, because the roads must still be wet and slippery, and the grass on the mountains will be improved in a short time. The men are in high spirits at the prospect of setting out, and amused themselves during the afternoon with different games.

JUNE 10TH  *Tuesday.* After collecting our horses, which took much time, we set out at eleven o'clock for the Quamash flats. Our stock is now very abundant, each man being well mounted, with a small load on a second horse, and several supernumerary ones, in case of accident or want of food. We ascended the river hills, which are very high, and three miles in extent; our course being north 22° east, and then turned to north 15° west, for two miles till we reached Collins's creek. It is deep and difficult to cross, but we passed without any injury, except wetting some of our provisions, and then proceeded due north for five miles to the eastern edge of the Quamash flats, near where we first met the Chopunnish in the autumn. We encamped on the bank of a small stream, in a point of woods, bordering the extensive level and beautiful prairie which is intersected by several rivulets, and as the quamash is now in blossom, presents a perfect resemblance of lakes of clear water.

A party of Chopunnish, who had overtaken us a few miles above, halted for the night with us, and mentioned that they too had come down to hunt in the flats, though we fear they expect that we will provide for them during their stay.

The country through which we passed is generally free from stone, extremely fertile, and supplied with timber, consisting of several species of fir, long-leafed pine and larch. The undergrowth is chokecherry, near the water courses, and scattered through the country, black alder, a large species of red root now in bloom, a plant resembling the pawpaw in its leaf, and bearing a berry with five valves of a deep purple colour. There were also two species of sumac, the purple haw, seven bark, serviceberry, gooseberry, the honeysuckle, bearing a white berry, and a species of dwarf pine, ten or twelve feet high, which might be confounded with the young pine of the long-leafed species, except that the former bears a cone of a globular form, with small scales, and that its leaves are in fascicles of two resembling in length and appearance the common pitch pine. We also observed two species of wild rose, both quinquepetalous, both of a damask red colour, and similar in the stem; but one of them is as large as the common red rose of our gardens; its leaf too is somewhat larger than that of the other species of wild rose, and the apex, as we saw them last year, were more than three times the size of the common wild rose.

We saw many sandhill cranes, and some ducks in the marshes near our camp, and a greater number of burrowing squirrels, some of which we killed, and found them as tender and well flavoured as our grey squirrels.

JUNE 11TH  *Wednesday.* All our hunters set out by daylight; but on their return to dinner, had killed nothing except a black bear and two deer. Five of the Indians also began to hunt, but they were quite unsuccessful, and in the afternoon returned to their village. Finding that the game had become shy and scarce, the hunters set out after dinner with orders to stay out during the night, and hunt at a greater distance from the camp, in ground less frequented. But the next day they returned with nothing except two deer. They were therefore again sent out, and about noon the following day, seven of them came in with eight deer out of a number, as well as a bear, which they had wounded, but could not take. In the meantime we had sent two men forward about eight miles to a prairie on this side of Collins's creek, with orders to hunt till our arrival. Two other hunters returned towards night, but they had killed only one deer, which they had hung up in the morning, and it had been devoured by the buzzards. An Indian who had spent the last evening with us, exchanged a horse for one of ours, which being sick, we gave a small axe and a knife in addition. He seemed very much pleased, and set out immediately to his village, lest we should change our minds and give up the bargain, which is perfectly allowable in Indian traffic. The hunters resumed the chase in the morning, but the game is now so scarce that they killed only one deer. We therefore cut up and dried all the meat we had collected, packed up all our baggage, and hobbled our horses to be in readiness to set out.

*Sunday.* But in the morning they had straggled to such a distance that we     JUNE 15TH
could not collect them without great difficulty, and as it rained very hard, we waited till it should abate. It soon, however, showed every appearance of a settled rain, and we therefore set out at ten o'clock. We crossed the prairie at the distance of eight miles, where we had sent our hunters, and found two deer which they had hung up for us. Two and a half miles farther, we overtook the two men at Collins's creek. They had killed a third deer, and had seen one large and another white bear. After dining we proceeded up the creek about half a mile, then crossing through a high broken country for about ten miles, reached an eastern branch of the same creek, near which we encamped in the bottom, after a ride of twenty-two miles. The rains during the day made the roads very slippery, and joined to the quantity of fallen timber, rendered our progress slow and laborious to the horses, many of which fell through without suffering any injury. The country through which we passed has a thick growth of long-leafed pine, with some pitch-pine, larch, white-pine, white cedar or arbor vitae of large size, and a variety of firs. The undergrowth consists chiefly of reed root, from six to ten feet in height, with the other species already enumerated. The soil is in general good, and has somewhat of a red cast, like those near the southwest mountain in Virginia. We saw in the course of our ride the speckled woodpecker, the logcock or large woodpecker, the bee-martin, and found the nest of a humming bird, which had just began to lay its eggs.

*Monday.* We readily collected our horses, and having taken breakfast, pro-     JUNE 16TH
ceeded at six o'clock up the creek, through handsome meadows of fine grass, and a great abundance of quamash. At the distance of two miles we crossed the creek, and ascended a ridge in a direction towards the northeast. Fallen timber still obstructed our way so much, that it was eleven o'clock before we had made seven miles, to a small branch of Hungry creek. In the hollows

and on the north side of the hills large quantities of snow still remain, in some places to the depth of two or three feet. Vegetation too is proportionally retarded, the dog-tooth violet being just in bloom, and the honeysuckle, huckleberry, and a small species of white maple, beginning to put forth their leaves. These appearances in a part of the country comparatively low, are ill omens of the practicability of passing the mountains. But being determined to proceed, we halted merely to take a hasty meal, while the horses were grazing, and then resumed our march. The route was through thick woods and over high hills, intersected by deep ravines and obstructed by fallen timber. We found much difficulty also in following the road, the greater part of it being now covered with snow, which lies in great masses eight or ten feet deep, and would be impassable were it not so firm as to bear our horses. Early in the evening we reached Hungry creek, at the place where captain Clark had left a horse for us as we passed in September, and finding a small glade with some grass, though not enough for our horses, we thought it better to halt for the night, lest by going further we should find nothing for the horses to eat. Hungry creek is small at this place, but is deep, and discharges a torrent of water, perfectly transparent, and cold as ice. During the fifteen miles of our route to-day, the principal timber was the pitch-pine, white-pine, larch, and fir. The long-leafed pine extends but a small distance on this side of Collins's creek, and the white-cedar does not reach beyond the branch of Hungry creek on which we dined. In the early part of the day we saw the columbine, the bluebell, and the yellow flowering pea in bloom. There is also in these mountains a great quantity of angelica, stronger to the taste, and more highly scented than that common in the United States. The smell is very pleasant, and the natives, after drying and cutting them into small pieces, wear them in strings around their necks.

JUNE 17TH  *Tuesday.* We find lately that the air is pleasant in the course of the day, but notwithstanding the shortness of the night, becomes very cold before morning. At an early hour we collected our horses, and proceeded down the creek, which we crossed twice with much difficulty and danger, in consequence of its depth and rapidity. We avoided two other crossings of the same kind, by crossing over a steep and rocky hill. At the distance of seven miles, the road begins the ascent of the main ridges which divide the waters of the Chopunnish and Kooskooskee rivers. We followed it up a mountain for about three miles, when we found ourselves enveloped in snow, from twelve to fifteen feet in depth, even on the south side of the mountain, with the fullest exposure to the sun. The winter now presented itself in all its rigours, the air was keen and cold, no vestige of vegetation was to be seen, and our hands and feet were benumbed.

We halted at the sight of this new difficulty. We already knew, that to wait till the snows of the mountains had dissolved, so as to enable us to distinguish the road, would defeat our design of returning to the United States this season. We now found also that as the snow bore our horses very well, travelling was infinitely easier than it was last fall, when the rocks and fallen timber had so much obstructed our march. But it would require five days to reach the fish-weirs at the mouth of Colt creek, even if we were able to follow the proper ridges of the mountains; and the danger of missing our direction is exceedingly great, while every track is covered with snow. During these five days too we have no chance of finding either grass or under-wood for our horses, the snow being so deep. To proceed, therefore, under such circumstances, would be to hazard our being bewildered in the moun-tains, to insure the loss of our horses, and should we even be so fortunate as to escape with our lives, we might be obliged to abandon all our papers and collections. It was therefore decided not to venture any further; to deposit here all the baggage and provisions, for which we had no immediate use, and reserving only subsistence for a few days, return while our horses were yet strong, to some spot where we might live by hunting, till a guide could be procured to conduct us across the mountains. Our baggage was placed on scaffolds and carefully covered, as were also the instruments and papers, which we thought it safer to leave than to risk them over the roads and creeks by which we came.

Having completed this operation, we set out at one o'clock, and treading back our steps, reached Hungry creek, which we ascended for two miles, and finding some scanty grass, we encamped. The rain fell during the greater part of the evening, and as this was the first time that we have ever been compelled to make any retrograde movement, we feared that it might depress the spirits of the men; but though somewhat dejected at the circum-stance, the obvious necessity precluded all repining. During the night our horses straggled in search of food to a considerable distance among the thick timber on the hill sides, nor could we collect them till nine o'clock the next morning.

*Wednesday.* Two of them were however still missing, and we therefore di- rected two of the party to remain and hunt for them. At the same time, we despatched Drewyer and Shannon to the Chopunnish, in the plains beyond the Kooskooskee, in order to hasten the arrival of the Indians who had promised to accompany us; or at any rate, to procure a guide to conduct us to Traveller's-rest. For this purpose they took a rifle, as a reward to any one who would engage to conduct us, with directions to increase the reward, if necessary, by an offer of two other guns, to be given immediately, and ten horses, at the falls of the Missouri.

We then resumed our route. In crossing Hungry creek, one of the horses fell, and rolling over with the rider, was driven for a considerable dis-tance among the rocks; but he fortunately escaped without losing his gun or suffering any injury. Another of the men was cut very badly, in a vein in the inner side of the leg, and we had great difficulty in stopping the blood. About one o'clock we halted for dinner at the glade, on a branch of Hungry creek, where we had dined on the *16th*. Observing much track of deer, we left two men at this place to hunt, and then proceeded to Collins's creek, where we encamped in a pleasant situation, at the upper end of the meadows two miles above our encampment of the *15th* inst. The hunters were im-mediately sent out, but they returned without having killed any thing, though they saw some few tracks of deer, very great appearance of bear, and what is of more importance, a number of what they thought were salmon-trout, in the creek. We therefore hope, by means of these fish and other game to subsist at this place without returning to the Quamash flats, which we are unwilling to do, since there are in these meadows great abundance of good food for our horses.

JUNE 19TH     *Thursday.* The hunters renewed the chase at a very early hour, but they brought only a single fish at noon. The fishermen were more unsuccessful, for they caught no fish, and broke their two Indian gigs. We, however, mended them with a sharp piece of iron, and towards evening they took a single fish, but instead of finding it the salmon of this spring's arrival, which would of course have been fine, it proved to be a salmon-trout of the red kind, which remain all winter in the upper parts of the rivers and creeks, and are generally poor at this season. In the afternoon, the two men who were left behind, in search of the horses, returned without being able to find them, and the other two hunters arrived from Hungry creek with a couple of deer. Several large morels were brought in to-day, and eaten, as we were now obliged to use them without either salt, pepper or grease, and seemed a very tasteless insipid food. Our stock of salt is now wholly exhausted, except two quarts, which we left on the mountain. The mosquitoes have become very troublesome since we arrived here, particularly in the evening.

JUNE 20TH     *Friday.* The scantiness of our subsistence was now such that we were determined to make one effort to ascertain if it be possible to remain here. The hunters therefore set out very early. On their return in the evening, they brought one deer, and a brown bear of the species called by the Chopunnish yahhar, the talons of which were remarkably short, broad at the base, and sharply pointed. It was in bad order, and the flesh of bear in this situation is much inferior to lean venison or elk. We also caught seven trout. But the hunters now reported that game was so scarce, and so difficult to be approached, in consequence of thick underbrush and fallen timber, that with their utmost exertions, they could not procure us subsistence for more than one or two days longer. We determined, therefore, to set out in the morning for the Quamash flats, where we should hear sooner from the Chopunnish on the subject of our guide, and also renew our stock of food, which is now nearly exhausted.

Determined, as we now are, to reach the United States, if possible, this winter, it would be destructive to wait till the snows have melted from the road. The snows have formed a hard coarse bed without crust, on which the horses walk safely without slipping; the chief difficulty, therefore, is to find the road. In this we may be assisted by the circumstance, that, although, generally ten feet in depth, the snow has been thrown off by the thick and spreading branches of the trees, and from round the trunk: the warmth of the trunk itself, acquired by the reflection of the sun, or communicated by natural heat of the earth, which is never frozen under these masses, has dissolved the snow so much, that immediately at the roots, its depth is not more than one or two feet. We therefore hope, that the marks of the baggage rubbing against the trees, may still be perceived, and we have decided, in case the guide cannot be procured, that one of us will take three or four of our most expert woodsmen, and with several of our best horses, and an ample supply of provisions, go on two days' journey in advance, and, endeavour to trace the route by the marks of the Indian baggage on the trees, which they would then mark more distinctly, with a tomahawk. When they should have reached two days' journey beyond Hungry creek, two of the men were to be sent back, to apprise the rest of their success, and if necessary, cause them to delay there, lest, by advancing too soon, they should be forced to halt where no food could be obtained for the horses. If the trace of the baggage is too indistinct, the whole party is to return to Hungry creek, and we will then attempt the passage by ascending the main southwest branch of Lewis's river through the country of the Shoshonees, over to Madison or Gallatin rivers. On that route, the Chopunnish inform us, there is a passage not obstructed by snow at this period of the year. That there is such a passage, we learnt from the Shoshonees, whom we first met on the east fork of Lewis's river; but they also represented it as much more difficult than that by which we came, being obstructed by high steep rugged mountains, followed by an extensive plain, without either wood or game. We are, indeed, inclined to prefer the account of the Shoshonees, because they would have certainly recommended that route had it been better than the one we have taken; and because there is a war between the Chopunnish and the Shoshonees, who live on that route, the former are less able to give accurate information of the state of the country. This route too, is so circuitous, that it would require a month to perform it, and we therefore consider it as the extreme resource.

*Saturday.* In hopes of soon procuring a guide to lead us over a more practicable route, we collected our horses at an early hour in the morning, and proceeded towards the flats. The mortification of being obliged to tread back our steps, rendered still more tedious a route always so obstructed by brush and fallen timber, that it could not be passed without difficulty and even danger to our horses. One of these poor creatures wounded himself so badly in jumping over fallen logs that he was rendered unfit for use, and sickness has deprived us of the service of a second. At the pass of Collins's creek we met two Indians, who returned with us about half a mile, to the spot where we had formerly slept in September, and where we now halted to dine and let our horses graze. These Indians had four supernumerary horses, and were on their way to cross the mountains. They had seen Drewyer and Shannon, who they said would not return for two days. We pressed them to remain with us till that time, in order to conduct us over the mountains, to which they consented, and deposited their stores of roots and bread in the bushes at a little distance. After dinner we left three men to hunt till our return, and then proceeded; but we had not gone further than two miles when the Indians halted in a small prairie, where they promised to remain at least two nights, if we did not overtake them sooner. We left them, and about seven in the evening found ourselves at the old encampment on the flats; and were glad to find that four of our hunters had killed a deer for supper.

*Sunday.* At daylight all the hunters set out, and having chased through the whole country, were much more successful than we even hoped, for they brought in eight deer and three bear. Hearing too that the salmon was now abundant in the Kooskooskee, we despatched a man to our old encampment above Collins's creek, for the purpose of purchasing some with a few beads, which were found accidentally in one of our waistcoat pockets. He did not return in the evening, nor had we heard from Drewyer and Shannon, who we begin to fear have had much difficulty in engaging a guide, and we were equally apprehensive that the two Indians might set out to-morrow for the mountains.

JUNE 21ST

JUNE 22D

477

JUNE 23D  *Monday*. Early in the morning, therefore, we despatched two hunters to prevail on them, if possible, to remain a day or two longer, and if they persisted in going on, they were to accompany them with the three men at Collins's creek, and mark the route, as far as Traveller's rest, where they were to remain till we joined them by pursuing the same road.

Our fears for the safety of Drewyer, Shannon, and Whitehouse, were fortunately relieved by their return in the afternoon. The former brought three Indians, who promised to go with us to the falls of the Missouri, for the compensation of two guns. One of them is the brother of the Cutnose, and the other two had each given us a horse, at the house of the Brokenarm, and as they are men of good character, and respected in the nation, we have the best prospect of being well served. We therefore secured our horses near the camp, and at an early hour next morning, set out on a second attempt to cross the mountains. On reaching Collins's creek, we found only one of our men, who informed us that a short time before he arrived there yesterday, the two Indians, tired of waiting, had set out, and the other four of our men had accompanied them as they were directed. After halting, we went on to Fish creek, the branch of Hungry creek, where we had slept on the nineteenth instant. Here we overtook two of the party who had gone on with the Indians, and had now been fortunate enough to persuade them to wait for us. During their stay at Collins's creek, they had killed a single deer only, and of this they had been very liberal to the Indians, whom they were prevailing upon to remain, so that they were without provisions, and two of them had set out for another branch of Hungry creek, where we shall meet them to-morrow.

In the evening the Indians, in order as they said to bring fair weather for our journey, set fire to the woods. As these consist chiefly of tall fir trees, with very numerous dried branches, the blaze was almost instantaneous, and as the flame mounted to the tops of the highest trees, resembled a splendid display of fire-works.

JUNE 25TH  *Wednesday*. In the morning, one of our guides complained of being sick, a symptom by no means pleasant, for sickness is generally with an Indian the pretext for abandoning an enterprise which he dislikes. He promised, however, to overtake us, and we therefore left him with his two companions, and set out at an early hour. At eleven o'clock we halted for dinner at the branch of Hungry creek, where we found our two men, who had killed nothing. Here too we were joined, rather unexpectedly by our guides, who now appeared disposed to be faithful to their engagements. The Indian was indeed really sick, and having no other covering except a pair of moccasins and an elk skin dressed without the hair, we supplied him with a buffalo robe. In the evening we arrived at Hungry creek, and halted for the night about a mile and a half below our encampment of the sixteenth.

JUNE 26TH  *Thursday*. Having collected our horses, and taken breakfast, we set out at six o'clock, and pursuing our former route, at length began to ascend, for the second time, the ridge of mountains. Near the snowy region we killed two of the small black pheasants, and one of the speckled pheasant. These birds generally inhabit the higher parts of the mountains, where they feed on the leaves of pines and firs; but both of them seem solitary and silent

478

birds, for we have never heard either of them make a noise in any situation, and the Indians inform us that they do not in flying drum or produce a whirring sound with their wings. On reaching the top of the mountain, we found our deposit perfectly untouched. The snow in the neighbourhood has melted nearly four feet since the seventeenth. By measuring it accurately, and comparing it by a mark which we then made, the general depth we discover to have been ten feet ten inches, though in some places still greater; but at this time it is about seven feet.

It required two hours to arrange our baggage and to prepare a hasty meal, after which the guides urged us to set off, as we had a long ride to make before reaching a spot where there was grass for our horses. We mounted, and following their steps, sometimes crossed abruptly steep hills, and then wound along their sides, near tremendous precipices, where, had our horses slipped, we should have been lost irrecoverably. Our route lay on the ridgy mountains which separate the waters of the Kooskooskee and Chopunnish, and above the heads of all the streams, so that we met no running water. The whole country was completely covered with snow, except that occasionally we saw a few square feet of earth at the roots of some trees, round which the snow had dissolved. We passed our camp of September 18, and late in the evening reached the deserted spot, and encamped near a good spring of water. It was on the steep side of a mountain, with no wood and a fair southern aspect, from which the snow seems to have melted for about ten days, and given place to an abundant growth of young grass, resembling the green sward. There is also another species of grass, not unlike a flag, with a broad succulent leaf which is confined to the upper parts of the highest mountains. It is a favourite food of the horses, but at present is either covered with snow, or just making its appearance. There is a third plant peculiar to the same regions, and is a species of whortleberry. There are also large quantities of a species of bear-grass, which, though it grows luxuriantly over all these mountains, and preserves its verdure during the whole winter, is never eaten by horses.

In the night there came to the camp a Chopunnish, who had pursued us with a view of accompanying us to the falls of the Missouri. We now learnt that the two young Indians whom we had met on the twenty-first, and detained several days, were going merely on a party of pleasure to the Ootla-shoots, or as they call them, Shallees, a band of Tushepahs, who live on Clark's river, near Traveller's-rest.

*Friday.* Early the next morning, we resumed our route over the heights and JUNE 27TH steep hills of the same great ridge. At eight miles distance we reached an eminence where the Indians have raised a conic mound of stone, six or eight feet high, on which is fixed a pole made of pine, about fifteen feet. Here we halted and smoked for some time at the request of the Indians, who told us, that in passing the mountains with their families, some men are usually sent on foot from this place to fish at the entrance of Colt creek, whence they rejoin the main party at the Quamash glade on the head of the Kooskooskee. From this elevated spot we have a commanding view of the surrounding mountains, which so completely enclose us, that although we have once passed them, we almost despair of ever escaping from them without the assistance of the Indians. The marks on the trees, which had been our chief dependence, are much fewer and more difficult to be distinguished than we had supposed; but our guides traverse this trackless region with a kind of instinctive sagacity; they never hesitate, they are never embarrassed; yet so undeviating is their step, that wherever the snow has disappeared, for even a hundred paces, we find the summer road. With their aid the snow is scarcely a disadvantage, for although we are often obliged to slip down, yet the fallen timber and the rocks, which are now covered, were much more troublesome when we passed in the autumn. The travelling road is indeed comparatively pleasant, as well as more rapid, the snow being hard and coarse, without a crust, and perfectly hard enough to prevent the horses sinking more than two or three inches. After the sun has been on it for some hours it becomes softer than early in the morning, yet they are almost always able to get a sure foothold.

After some time we resumed our route, and at the distance of three miles descended a steep mountain, then crossing two branches of the Chopunnish river, just above their forks, began to mount a second ridge. Along this we proceeded for some time, and then, at the distance of seven miles, reached our camp of the sixteenth of September. Near this place we crossed three small branches of the Chopunnish, and then ascended a second dividing ridge, along which we continued for nine miles, when the ridge became somewhat lower, and we halted for the night on a position similar to that of our encampment last evening.

We had now travelled twenty-eight miles without taking the loads from our horses or giving them any thing to eat, and as the snow where we halted has not much dissolved, there was still but little grass. Among the vegetation we observed great quantities of the white lily, with reflected petals, which are now in bloom, and in the same forwardness as they were in the plains on the tenth of May. As for ourselves, the whole stock of meat being gone, we distributed to each mess a pint of bear's oil, which, with boiled roots, made an agreeable dish. We saw several black-tailed or mule-deer, but could not get a shot at them, and were informed that there is an abundance of elk in the valley, near the fishery, on the Kooskooskee. The Indians also assert that on the mountains to our right are large numbers of what they call white buffalo or mountain sheep.

Our horses strayed to some distance to look for food, and in the morning, when they were brought up, exhibited rather a gaunt appearance. The Indians, however, promised that we should reach some good grass at noon, and we therefore set out after an early breakfast. Our route lay along the dividing ridge, and across a very deep hollow, till at the distance of six miles we passed our camp of the fifteenth of September. A mile and a half further we passed the road from the right, immediately on the dividing ridge, leading by the fishery. We went on as we had done during the former part of the route over deep snows, when having made thirteen miles we reached the side of a mountain, just above the fishery, which having no timber, and a southern exposure, the snow had disappeared, leaving an abundance of fine grass. Our horses were very hungry as well as fatigued, and as there was no other spot within our reach this evening, where we could find any food for them, we determined to encamp, though it was not yet midday. But as there was no water in the neighbourhood, we melted snow for cooking.

*Sunday.* Early in the morning we continued along the ridge which we have been following for several days, till at the end of five miles it terminated; and now bidding adieu to the snows in which we have been imprisoned, we descended to the main branch of the Kooskooskee. On reaching the water side, we found a deer which had been left for us by two hunters who had been despatched at an early hour to the warm springs, and which proved a very seasonable addition to our food; for having neither meat nor oil, we were reduced to a diet of roots, without salt or any other addition. At this place, about a mile and a half from the spot where Quamash creek falls in from the northeast, the Kooskooskee is about thirty yards wide, and runs with great velocity over a bed, which, like those of all the mountain streams, is composed of pebbles. We forded the river, and ascended for two miles the steep acclivities of a mountain, and at its summit found coming in from the right the old road which we had passed on our route last autumn. It was now much plainer and more beaten, which the Indians told us was owing to the frequent visits of the Ootlashoots, from the valley of Clark's river to the fishery; though there was no appearance of their having been here this spring. Twelve miles from our camp we halted to graze our horses on the Quamash flats, on the creek of the same name. This is a handsome plain of fifty acres in extent, covered with an abundance of quamash, and seems to form a principal stage or encampment for the Indians in passing the mountains. We saw here several young pheasants, and killed one of the small black kind, which is the first we have observed below the region of snow. In the neighbourhood were also seen the tracks of two barefoot Indians, which our companions supposed to be Ootlashoots, who had fled in distress from the Pahkees. Here we discovered that two of the horses were missing. We therefore sent two men in quest of them, and then went on seven miles further to the warm springs, where we arrived early in the afternoon. The two hunters who had been sent forward in the morning had collected no game, nor were several others, who went out after our arrival, more successful. We therefore had a prospect of continuing our usual diet of roots, when late in the afternoon the men returned with the stray horses and a deer for supper.

These warm springs are situated at the foot of a hill, on the north side of Traveller's-rest creek, which is ten yards wide at this place. They issue from the bottoms, and through the interstices of a grey freestone rock, which rises in irregular masses round their lower side. The principal spring, which the Indians have formed into a bath by stopping the run with stone and pebbles, is about the same temperature as the warmest bath used at the hot springs in Virginia. On trying, captain Lewis could with difficulty remain in it nineteen minutes, and then was affected with a profuse perspiration. The two other springs are much hotter, the temperature being equal to that of the warmest of the hot springs in Virginia. Our men as well as the Indians amused themselves with going into the bath; the latter, according to their universal custom, going first into the hot bath, where they remain as long as they can bear the heat, then plunging into the creek, which is now of an icy coldness, and repeating this operation several times, but always ending with the warm bath.

MONDAY, JUNE 30TH, 1806  We despatched some hunters ahead, and were about setting out, when a deer came to lick at the springs; we killed it, and being now provided with meat for dinner, proceeded along the north side of the creek, sometimes in the bottoms, and over the steep sides of the ridge, till at the distance of thirteen miles, we halted at the entrance of a small stream where we had stopped on the *12th of September*. Here we observed a road to the right, which the Indians inform us leads to a fine extensive valley on Clark's river, where the Shallees or Ootlashoots occasionally reside. After permitting our horses to graze, we went on along a road much better than any we have seen since entering the mountains, so that before sunset we made nineteen miles, and reached our old encampment on the south side of the creek near its entrance into Clark's river. In the course of the day we killed six deer, of which there are great numbers, as well as bighorn and elk, in this neighbourhood. We also obtained a small grey squirrel like that on the coast of the Pacific, except that its belly was white. Among the plants was a kind of lady's slipper, or moccasin flower, resembling that common in the United States, but with a white corolla, marked with longitudinal veins of a pale red colour on the inner side.

## Tuesday, July 1st, 1806

We had now made one hundred and fifty-six miles from the Quamash flats, to the mouth of Traveller's-rest creek. This being the point where we proposed to separate, it was resolved to remain a day or two in order to refresh ourselves, and the horses, which have borne the journey extremely well, and are still in fine order, but require some little rest. We had hoped to meet here some of the Ootlashoots, but no tracks of them can be discovered. Our Indian companions express much anxiety lest they should have been cut off by the Pahkees during the winter, and mention the tracks of the two barefooted persons as a proof how much the fugitives must have been distressed.

We now formed the following plan of operations. Captain Lewis with nine men, are to pursue the most direct route to the falls of the Missouri, where three of his party are to be left to prepare carriages for transporting the baggage and canoes across the portage. With the remaining six he will ascend Maria's river, to explore the country and ascertain whether any branch of it reaches as far north as the latitude of fifty degrees, after which he will descend that river to its mouth. The rest of the men will accompany captain Clark to the head of Jefferson river, which sergeant Ordway and a party of nine men will descend with the canoes and other articles deposited there. Captain Clark's party, which will then be reduced to ten, will proceed to the Yellowstone at its nearest approach to the three forks of the Missouri. There he will build canoes, and go down that river with seven of his party, and wait at its mouth till the rest of the party join him. Sergeant Pryor, with two others, will then take the horses by land to the Mandans. From that nation he is to go to the British posts on the Assiniboin with a letter to Mr. Henry, to procure his endeavours to prevail on some of the Sioux chiefs to accompany him to the city of Washington.

Having made these arrangements, this and the following day were employed in hunting and repairing our arms. We were successful in procuring a number of fine large deer, the flesh of which was exposed to dry. Among other animals in this neighbourhood, are the dove, black wood-pecker, lark woodpecker, logcock, prairie lark, sandhill crane, prairie hen, with the short and pointed tail; the robin, a species of brown plover, a few curlews, small blackbirds [cowbirds], ravens, hawks, and a variety of sparrows, as well as the bee martin, and several species of corvus. The mosquitoes too have been excessively troublesome since our arrival here. The Indians assert also, that there are great numbers of the white buffalo or mountain sheep, on the snowy heights of the mountains, west of Clark's river. They generally inhabit the rocky and most inaccessible parts of the mountains, but as they are not fleet, are easily killed by the hunters.

The plants which most abound in this valley are the wild rose, the honeysuckle, with a white berry, the sevenbark, serviceberry, the elder, aspen and alder, the chokecherry, and both the narrow and broad-leafed willow. The principal timber consists of long-leafed pine, which grows as well in the river bottoms as on the hills; the firs and larch are confined to the higher parts of the hills, while on the river itself, is a growth of cottonwood, with a wider leaf than that of the upper part of the Missouri, though narrower than that which grows lower down that river. There are also two species of clover in this valley; one with a very narrow small leaf, and a pale red flower; the other with a white flower, and nearly as luxuriant in its growth as our red clover.

The Indians who had accompanied us, intended leaving us in order to seek their friends, the Ootlashoots; but we prevailed on them to accompany captain Lewis a part of his route, so as to show him the shortest road to the Missouri, and in the meantime amused them with conversation and running races, both on foot and with horses, in both of which they proved themselves hardy, athletic and active. To the chief, captain Lewis gave a small medal and a gun, as a reward for having guided us across the mountains; in return, the customary civility of exchanging names passed between them, by which the former acquired the title of Yomekollick, or white bear-skin unfolded. The Chopunnish who had overtaken us on the *26th*, made us a present of an excellent horse, for the good advice we gave him, and as a proof of his attachment to the whites, as well as of his desire to be at peace with the Pahkees.

*Thursday.* The next morning, all our preparations being completed, we saddled our horses, and the two parties who had been so long companions, now separated with an anxious hope of soon meeting, after each had accomplished the purpose of his destination. JULY 3D

The nine men and five Indians who accompanied captain Lewis, proceeded in a direction due north, down the west side of Clark's river. Half a mile from the camp we forded Traveller's-rest creek, and two and a half miles further, passed a western branch of the river; a mile beyond this, was a small creek on the eastern side, and a mile lower down, the entrance of the eastern branch of the river. This stream is from ninety to one hundred and twenty yards wide, and its water, which is discharged through two channels, is more turbid than that of the main river. The latter is one hundred and fifty yards in width, and waters an extensive level plain and prairie, which on its lower parts are ornamented with long-leafed pine, and cottonwood, while the tops of the hills are covered with pine, larch, and fir. We proceeded two miles further to a place where the Indians advised us to cross, but having no boats, and timber being scarce, four hours were spent in collecting timber to make three small rafts; on which, with some difficulty and danger, we passed the river. We then drove our horses into the water and they swam to the opposite shore, but the Indians crossed on horseback, drawing at the same time their baggage alongside of them in small basins of deer skins. The whole party being now reassembled, we continued for three miles, and encamped about sunset at a small creek. The Indians now showed us a road at no great distance, which they said would lead up the eastern branch of Clark's river, and another river called Coka-lahishkit, or the *river of the road to buffalo*, thence to Medicine river and the falls of the Missouri. They added, that not far from the dividing ridge of the waters of Clark's river and the Missouri, the roads forked, and though both led to the falls, the left hand route was the best. The route was so well beaten that we could no longer mistake it, and having now shown us the way, they were anxious to go on in quest of their friends, the Shahlees, besides which, they feared, by venturing further with us, to encounter the Pahkees, for we had this afternoon seen a fresh track of a horse, which they supposed to be a Shahlee scout. We could not insist on their remaining longer with us; but as they had so kindly conducted us across the mountains, we were desirous of giving them a supply of provisions, and therefore distributed to them half of three deer, and the hunters were ordered to go out early in the morning, in hopes of adding to the stock.

The horses suffer so dreadfully from the mosquitoes, that we are obliged to kindle large fires and place the poor animals in the midst of the smoke. Fortunately, however, it became cold after dark, and the mosquitoes disappeared.

JULY 4TH  *Friday*. The hunters accordingly set out, but returned unsuccessful about eleven o'clock. In the meantime we were joined by a young man of the Pal-loatpallah tribe, who had set out a few days after us, and had followed us alone across the mountains, the same who had attempted to pass the mountains in June, while we were on the Kooskooskee, but was obliged to return. We now smoked a farewell pipe with our estimable companions, who expressed every emotion of regret at parting with us, which they felt the more, because they did not conceal their fears of our being cut off by the Pahkees. We also gave them a shirt, a handkerchief, and a small quantity of ammunition. The meat which they received from us was dried and left at this place as a store during the homeward journey. This circumstance confirms our belief, that there is no route along Clark's river to the Columbian plains, so near or so good as that by which we came; for, although these people mean to go for several days' journey down that river, to look for the Shahlees, yet they intend returning home by the same pass of the mountain through which they conducted us. This route is also used by all the nations whom we know west of the mountains who are in the habit of visiting the plains of the Missouri; while on the other side all the war paths of the Pahkees, which fall into this valley of Clark's river, concentre at Traveller's-rest, beyond which these people have never ventured to the west.

Having taken leave of the Indians, we mounted our horses, and proceeded up the eastern branch of Clark's river through the level plain in which we were encamped. At the distance of five miles we had crossed a small creek fifteen yards wide, and now entered the mountains. The river is here closely confined within the hills for two miles, when the bottom widens into an extensive prairie, and the river is one hundred and ten yards in width. We went three miles further, over a high plain succeeded by a low and level prairie, to the entrance of the Cokalahishkit. This river empties itself from the northeast, is deep, rapid, and about sixty yards wide, with banks, which though not high, are sufficiently bold to prevent the water from overflowing. The eastern branch of Clark's river is ninety yards wide above the junction, but below it spreads to one hundred. The waters of both are turbid, though the Cokalahishkit is the clearer of the two; the beds of both are composed of sand and gravel, but neither of them is navigable on account of the rapids and shoals which obstruct their currents. Before the junction of these streams, the country had been bare of trees, but as we turned up the north branch of the Cokalahishkit, we found a woody country, though the hills were high and the low grounds narrow and poor. At the distance of eight miles in a due east course, we encamped in a bottom, where there was an abundance of excellent grass. The evening proved fine and pleasant, and we were no longer annoyed by mosquitoes. Our only game were two squirrels, one of the kind common to the Rocky mountains, the second a ground squirrel of a species we had not seen before. Near the place where we crossed Clark's river, we saw at a distance, some wild horses, which are said, indeed, to be very numerous on this river as well as on the heads of the Yellowstone.

*Saturday.* Early in the morning we proceeded on for three and a half miles, in a direction north 75° east, then inclining to the south, crossed an extensive, beautiful, and well watered valley, nearly twelve miles in length, at the extremity of which we halted for dinner. Here we obtained a great quantity of quamash, and shot an antelope from a gang of females, who at this season herd together, apart from the bucks. After dinner we followed the course of the river eastwardly for six miles, to the mouth of a creek thirty-five yards wide, which we called Werner's creek. It comes in from the north, and waters a high extensive prairie, the hills near which are low, and supplied with the long-leafed pine, larch, and some fir. The road then led north 22° west, for four miles, soon after which it again turned north 73° east, for two and a half miles, over a handsome plain, watered by Werner's creek, to the river, which we followed on its eastern direction, through a high prairie, rendered very unequal by a vast number of little hillocks and sinkholes, and at three miles distance encamped near the entrance of a large creek, twenty yards wide, to which we gave the name of Seaman's creek. We had seen no Indians, although near the camp were the concealed fires of a war party, who had passed about two months ago.

*Sunday.* At sunrise we continued our course eastward along the river. At seven miles distance we passed the north fork of the Cokalahishkit, a deep and rapid stream, forty-five yards in width, and like the main branch itself somewhat turbid, though the other streams of this country are clear. Seven miles further the river enters the mountains, and here end those extensive

485

prairies on this side, though they widen in their course towards the south-east, and form an Indian route to Dearborn's river, and thence to the Missouri. From the multitude of knobs irregularly scattered through them, captain Lewis called this country the Prairie of the Knobs. They abound in game, as we saw goats, deer, great numbers of the burrowing squirrels, some curlews, bee martins, woodpeckers, plover, robins, doves, ravens, hawks, ducks, a variety of sparrows, and yesterday observed swans on Werner's creek. Among the plants we observed the southern wood, and two other species of shrubs, of which we preserved specimens.

On entering the high grounds we followed the course of the river through the narrow bottoms, thickly timbered with pine and cottonwood intermixed, and variegated with the boisrouge [redwood], which is now in bloom, the common small blue flag and pepper-grass; and at the distance of three and a half miles, reached the two forks of the river mentioned by the Indians. They are nearly equal in width, and the road itself here forks and follows each of them. We followed that which led us in a direction north 75° east, over a steep high hill, thence along a wide bottom to a thickly wooded side of a hill, where the low grounds are narrow, till we reached a large creek, eight miles from the forks and twenty-five from our last encampment. Here we halted for the night. In the course of the day the track of the Indians, whom we supposed to be the Pahkees, continued to grow fresher, and we passed a number of old lodges and encampments.

JULY 7TH    *Monday.* At seven o'clock the next morning, we proceeded through a beautiful plain on the north side of the river, which seems here to abound in beaver. The low grounds possess much timber, and the hills are covered chiefly with pitch pine, that of the long-leafed kind having disappeared since we left the Prairie of the Knobs. At the distance of twelve miles we left the river or rather the creek, and having for four miles crossed, in a direction north 15° east, two ridges, again struck to the right, which we followed through a narrow bottom, covered with low willows and grass, and abundantly supplied with both deer and beaver. After seven miles we reached the foot of a ridge, which we ascended in a direction north 45° east, through a low gap of easy ascent from the westward, and on descending it were delighted at discovering that this was the dividing ridge between the waters of the Columbia and those of the Missouri. From this gap the Fort mountain is about twenty miles in a northeastern direction. We now wound through the hills and hollows of the mountains, passing several rivulets, which run to the right, and at the distance of nine miles from the gap encamped, after making thirty-two miles. We procured some beaver, and this morning saw some signs and tracks of buffalo, from which it seems those animals do sometimes penetrate to a short distance within the mountains.

JULY 8TH    *Tuesday.* At three miles from our camp we reached a stream, issuing from the mountains to the southwest, though it only contains water for a width of thirty feet, yet its bed is more than three times that width, and from the appearance of the roots and trees in the neighbouring bottom, must sometimes run with great violence; we called it Dearborn's river. Half a mile further we observed from a height the Shishequaw mountain, a high insulated mountain of a conic form, standing several miles in advance of the eastern

486

range of the Rocky mountains, and now about eight miles from us, and immediately on our road, which was in a northwest direction. But as our object was to strike Medicine river, and hunt down to its mouth in order to procure skins for the food and gear necessary for the three men who are to be left at the falls, none of whom are hunters, we determined to leave the road, and therefore proceeded due north, through an open plain, till we reached Shishequaw creek, a stream about twenty yards wide, with a considerable quantity of timber in its low grounds. Here we halted and dined, and now felt, by the luxury of our food, that we were approaching once more the plains of the Missouri, so rich in game. We saw a great number of deer, goats, wolves, and some barking squirrels, and for the first time caught a distant prospect of two buffalo. After dinner we followed the Shishequaw for six and a half miles, to its entrance into Medicine river, and along the banks of this river for eight miles, when we encamped on a large island. The bottoms continued low, level, and extensive; the plains too are level; but the soil of neither is fertile, as it consists of a light coloured earth, intermixed with a large proportion of gravel; the grass in both is generally about nine inches high. Captain Lewis here shot a large and remarkably white wolf. We had now made twenty-eight miles.

*Wednesday.* We set out early the next morning, but the air soon became very cold, and it began to rain. We halted for a few minutes in some old Indian lodges, but finding that the rain continued we proceeded on, though we were all wet to the skin, and halted for dinner at the distance of eight miles. The rain, however, continued, and we determined to go no further. The river is about eighty yards wide, with banks which, though low, are seldom overflowed; the bed is composed of loose gravel and pebbles, the water clear and rapid, but not so much as to impede the navigation. The bottoms are handsome, wide, and level, and supplied with a considerable quantity of narrow-leafed cottonwood. During our short ride we killed two deer and a buffalo, and saw a number of wolves and antelopes.

JULY 9TH

*Thursday.* The next morning early we set out and continued through a country similar to that of yesterday, with bottoms of wide-leafed cottonwood occasionally along the borders, though for the most part the low grounds are without timber. In the plains are great quantities of two species of prickly pear, now in bloom. Gooseberries of the common red kind are in abundance and just beginning to ripen, but there are no currants. The river has now widened to an hundred yards; is deep, crowded with islands, and in many parts rapid. At the distance of seventeen miles, the timber disappears totally from the river bottoms. About this part of the river, the wind, which had blown on our backs, and constantly put the elk on their guard, shifted round, and we then shot three of them, and a brown bear. Captain Lewis halted to skin them, while two of the men took the pack-horses forward to seek for an encampment. It was nine o'clock before he overtook them, at the distance of seven miles in the first grove of cottonwood. They had been pursued as they came along by a very large bear, on which they were afraid to fire, lest their horses being unaccustomed to the gun, might take fright and throw them. This circumstance reminds us of the ferocity of these animals, when we were last near this place, and admonishes us to be very cautious.

JULY 10TH

487

We saw vast numbers of buffalo below us, which kept a dreadful bellowing during the night. With all our exertions we were unable to advance more than twenty-four miles, owing to the mire, through which we are obliged to travel, in consequence of the rain.

JULY 11TH   *Friday.* The next morning, however, was fair, and enlivened by great numbers of birds, who sang delightfully in the clusters of cottonwood. The hunters were sent down Medicine river to hunt elk, while captain Lewis crossed the high plain, in a direction 75° east, to the Whitebear island, a distance of eight miles, where the hunters joined him. They had seen elk; but in this neighbourhood the buffalo are in such numbers, that on a moderate computation, there could not have been fewer than ten thousand within a circuit of two miles. At this season, they are bellowing in every direction, so as to form an almost continued roar, which at first alarmed our horses, who being from the west of the mountains, are unused to the noise and appearance of these animals. Among the smaller game are the brown thrush, pigeons, doves, and a beautiful bird called a buffalo-pecker [cowbird].

Immediately on our arrival we began to hunt, and by three in the afternoon had collected a stock of food and hides enough for our purpose. We then made two canoes, one in the form of a basin, like those used by the Mandans, the other consisting of two skins, in a form of our own invention. They were completed the next morning, but the wind continued so high that it was not till towards night that we could cross the river in them, and make our horses swim. In the meantime, nearly the whole day was consumed in search after our horses, which had disappeared last night, and seven of which were not recovered at dark, while Drewyer was still in quest of them. The river is somewhat higher than it was last summer, the present season being much more moist than the preceding one, as may be seen in the greater luxuriance of the grass.

JULY 13TH   *Sunday.* We formed our camp this morning at our old station, near the head of the Whitebear islands, and immediately went to work in making gear. On opening the cache, we found the bear skins entirely destroyed by the water, which, in a flood of the river, had penetrated to them. All the specimens of plants were unfortunately lost; the chart of the Missouri, however, still remained unhurt, and several articles contained in trunks and boxes had suffered but little injury; but a vial of laudanum had lost its stopper, and ran into a drawer of medicines, which it spoiled beyond recovery. The mosquitoes have been so troublesome that it was impossible even to write without the assistance of a mosquito bier. The buffalo are leaving us fast on their way to the southeast.

JULY 14TH   *Monday.* We continued making preparations for transporting our articles, and as the old deposit was too damp, we secured the trunks on a high scaffold, covered with skins, among the thick brush on a large island: a precaution against any visit from the Indians, should they arrive before the main party arrives here. The carriage wheels were in good order, and the iron frame of the boat had not suffered materially. The buffalo have now nearly disappeared, leaving behind them a number of large wolves who are now prowling about us.

*Tuesday.* To our great joy Drewyer returned to-day from a long search after the horses; for we had concluded, from his long stay, that he had probably met with a bear, and with his usual intrepidity attacked the animal, in which case, if by any accident he should be separated from his horse, his death would be almost inevitable. Under this impression, we resolved to set out to-morrow in quest of him, when his return relieved us from our apprehensions. He had searched for two days before he discovered that the horses had crossed Dearborn's river, near a spot where was an Indian encampment, which seemed to have been abandoned about the time the horses were stolen, and which was so closely concealed that no trace of a horse could be seen within the distance of a quarter of a mile. He crossed the river and pursued the track of these Indians westward, till his horse became so much fatigued that he despaired of overtaking them, and then returned. These Indians we suppose to be a party of Tushepaws, who have ventured out of the mountains to hunt buffalo. During the day we were engaged in drying meat and dressing skins.

At night M'Neal, who had been sent in the morning to examine the cache at the lower end of the portage, returned; but had been prevented from reaching that place by a singular adventure. Just as he arrived near Willow run, he approached a thicket of brush, in which was a white bear, which he did not discover till he was within ten feet of him: his horse started, and wheeling suddenly round, threw M'Neal almost immediately under the bear, who started up instantly, and finding the bear raising himself on his hind feet to attack him, struck him on the head with the butt end of his musket; the blow was so violent that it broke the breech of the musket and knocked the bear to the ground, and before he recovered, M'Neal seeing a willow tree close by, sprang up, and there remained while the bear closely guarded the foot of the tree until late in the afternoon. He then went off, and M'Neal being released came down, and having found his horse, which had strayed off to the distance of two miles, returned to camp. These animals are, indeed, of a most extraordinary ferocity, and it is matter of wonder, that in all our encounters we have had the good fortune to escape. We are now troubled with another enemy, not quite so dangerous, though even more disagreeable: these are the mosquitoes, who now infest us in such myriads, that we frequently get them into our throats when breathing, and the dog even howls with the torture they occasion.

Having now accomplished the object of our stay, captain Lewis determined to leave sergeant Gass with two men and four horses to assist the party who are expected to carry our effects over the portage, whilst he, with Drewyer, and the two Fields, with six horses, proceeded to the sources of Maria's river. Accordingly, early in the morning, captain Lewis descended in a skin canoe to the lower side of Medicine river, where the horses had previously been sent, and then rode with his party to the fall of forty-seven feet, where he halted for two hours to dine, and took a sketch of the fall. In the afternoon they proceeded to the great falls, near which they slept under a shelving rock, with a happy exemption from mosquitoes. These falls have lost much of their grandeur since we saw them, the river being much lower now than at that time, though they still form a most sublime spectacle. As we came along, we met several white bear, but they did not venture to attack us.

There were but few buffalo, however, the large having principally passed the river, directed their course downwards. There are, as usual, great numbers of goats and antelopes dispersed through the plains, and large flocks of geese, which raise their young about the entrance of Medicine river. We observe here also the cuckoo, or as it is sometimes called, the raincraw, a bird which is not known either within or west of the Rocky mountains.

JULY 17TH *Thursday.* After taking a second draught of the falls, captain Lewis directed his course N. 10° W. with an intention of striking Maria's river at the point to which he had ascended it in 1805. The country is here spread into wide and level plains, swelling like the ocean, in which the view is uninterrupted by a single tree or shrub, and is diversified only by the moving herds of buffalo. The soil consists of a light-coloured earth, intermixed with a large proportion of coarse gravel without sand, and is by no means so fertile as either the plains of the Columbia, or those lower down the Missouri. When dry it cracks, and is hard and thirsty while in its wet state: it is as soft and slimy as soap. The grass is naturally short, and at this time is still more so from the recent passage of the buffalo.

Among the birds which we met was the parti-coloured plover [avocet], with the head and neck of a brick red, a bird which frequents the little ponds scattered over the plains. After travelling twenty miles we reached Tansy river, and as we could not go as far as Maria's river this evening, and perhaps not find either wood or water before we arrived there, we determined to encamp. As we approached the river, we saw the fresh track of a bleeding buffalo, a circumstance by no means pleasant, as it indicated the Indians had been hunting, and were not far from us. The tribes who principally frequent this country, are the Minnetarees of Fort de Prairie, and the Blackfoot Indians, both of whom are vicious and profligate rovers, and we have therefore every thing to fear, not only from their stealing our horses, but even our arms and baggage, if they are sufficiently strong. In order therefore to avoid, if possible, an interview with them, we hurried across the river to a thick wood, and having turned out the horses to graze, Drewyer went in quest of the buffalo to kill it, and ascertain whether the wound was given by the Indians, while the rest reconnoitred the whole country. In about three hours they all returned without having seen the buffalo or any Indians in the plains. We then dined, and two of the party resumed their search, but could see no signs of Indians, and we therefore slept in safety. Tansy river is here about fifty yards wide, though its water occupies only thirty-five feet, and is not more than three in depth. It most probably rises within the first range of the Rocky mountains, and its general course is from east to west, and as far as we are able to trace it through wide bottoms, well supplied with both the long and broad-leafed cottonwood. The hills on its banks, are from one hundred to one hundred and fifty feet in height, and possess bluffs of earth, like the lower part of the Missouri: the bed is formed of small gravel and mud; the water turbid, and of a whitish tint; the banks low, but never overflowed; in short, except in depth and velocity, it is a perfect miniature of the Missouri.

*Friday.* A little before sunrise we continued on a course N. 25° W. for six miles, when we reached the top of a high plain, which divides the waters of Maria and Tansy rivers, and a mile further reached a creek of the former, about twenty-five yards wide, though with no water except in occasional pools in the bed. Down this creek we proceeded for twelve miles through thick groves of timber on its banks, passing such immense quantities of buffalo, that the whole seemed to be a single herd. Accompanying them were great numbers of wolves, besides which we saw some antelopes and hares. After dinner we left the creek which we called Buffalo creek, and crossing the plain for six miles, came to Maria's river and encamped in a grove of cottonwood, on its western side, keeping watch through the night lest we should be surprised by the Indians.

*Saturday.* Captain Lewis was now convinced that he was above the point to which he had formerly ascended, and fearing that some branch might come in on the north, between that point and our present position, he early in the morning despatched two hunters, who descended the river in a direction north 80° east, till they came to our former position, at the distance of six miles, without seeing any stream except Buffalo creek. Having completed an observation of the sun's meridian altitude, captain Lewis proceeded along the north side of Maria's river. The bottoms are in general about half a mile wide, and possess considerable quantities of cottonwood timber, and an underbrush, consisting of honeysuckle, rose bushes, narrow-leafed willow, and the plant called by the engagées, buffalo grease. The plains are level and beautiful, but the soil is thin and overrun with prickly pears. It consists of a sort of white or whitish-blue clay, which after being trodden, when wet, by the buffalo, stands up in sharp hard points, which are as painful to the horses as the great quantity of small gravel, which is every where scattered over the ground, is in other parts of the plains. The bluffs of the river are high, steep, and irregular, and composed of a sort of earth which easily dissolves and slips into the water, though with occasional strata of freestone near the tops. The bluffs of the Missouri above Maria's river, differ from these, in consisting of a firm red or yellow clay, which does not yield to water, and a large proportion of rock. The buffalo are not so abundant as they were yesterday; but there are still antelopes, wolves, geese, pigeons, doves, hawks, ravens, crows, larks, and sparrows, though the curlew has disappeared.

At the distance of eight miles a large creek falls in on the south side, and seven miles beyond it, another thirty yards wide, which seem to issue from three mountains, stretching from east to west, in a direction north 10° west from its mouth, and which, from their loose, irregular, and rugged appearance, we called the Broken mountains. That in the centre terminates in a conic spire, for which reason we called it the Tower mountain. After making twenty miles we halted for the night.

*Sunday.* The next morning we continued our route up the river, through a country resembling that which we passed yesterday, except that the plains are more broken, and the appearances of mineral salts, common to the Missouri plains, are more abundant than usual; these are discerned in all the pools, which indeed at present contain the only water to be found throughout the plains, and are so strongly impregnated as to be unfit for any use, except that of the buffalo, who seem to prefer it to even the water of the river. The low grounds are well timbered, and contain also silk-grass, sand-rush, wild liquorice, and sunflowers, the barb of which are now in bloom. Besides the geese, ducks, and other birds common to the country, we have seen fewer buffalo to-day than yesterday though elk, wolves, and antelopes continue in equal numbers. There is also much appearance of beaver, though none of otter. At the distance of six miles we passed a creek from the south; eighteen miles further one from the north; four miles beyond which we encamped. The river is here one hundred and twenty yards wide, and its water is but little diminished as we ascend. Its general course is very straight. From the apparent descent of the country to the north and above the Broken mountains, it seems probable that the south branch of the Saskashawan receives some of its waters from these plains, and that one of its streams must, in descending from the Rocky mountains, pass not far from Maria's river, to the northeast of the Broken mountains. We slept in peace, without being annoyed by the mosquitoes, whom we have not seen since we left the Whitebear islands.

MONDAY, JULY 21ST, 1806 At sunrise we proceeded along the northern side of the river for a short distance, when finding the ravines too steep, we crossed to the south; but after continuing for three miles, returned to the north and took our course through the plains, at some distance from the river. After making fifteen miles, we came to the forks of the river, the largest branch of which bears south 75° west to the mountains, while the course of the other is north 40° west. We halted for dinner, and believing, on examination, that the northern branch came from the mountains, and would probably lead us to the most northern extent of Maria's river, we proceeded along, though at a distance over the plains, till we struck it eight miles from the junction. The river is about thirty yards wide, the water clear, but shallow, rapid, and unfit for navigation. It is closely confined between cliffs of freestone, and the adjacent country broken and poor. We crossed to the south side, and proceeded for five miles, till we encamped under a cliff, where not seeing any timber, we made a fire of buffalo dung, and passed the night.

*Tuesday.* The next day we went on; but as the ground was now steep and unequal, and the horses' feet very sore, we were obliged to proceed slowly. The river is still confirmed by freestone cliffs, till at the distance of seven miles the country opens, is less covered with gravel, and has some bottoms, though destitute of timber or underbrush. The river here makes a considerable bend to the northwest, so that we crossed the plains for eleven miles when we again crossed the river. Here we halted for dinner, and having no wood, made a fire of the dung of buffalo, with which we cooked the last of our meat, except a piece of spoiled buffalo. Our course then lay across a level beautiful plain, with wide bottoms near the bank of the river. The banks are about three or four feet high, but are not overflowed. After crossing for ten miles a bend of the river towards the south, we saw, for the first time during the day, a clump of cottonwood trees in an extensive bottom, and halted there for the night.

This place is about ten miles below the foot of the Rocky mountains; and being now able to trace distinctly that the point at which the river issued from those mountains, was to the south of west, we concluded that we had reached its most northern point, and as we have ceased to hope that any branches of Maria's river extend as far north as the fiftieth degree of latitude, we deem it useless to proceed further, and rely chiefly on Milk and Whiteearth rivers for the desired boundary. We therefore determined to remain here two days, for the purpose of making the necessary observations, and resting our horses.

*Wednesday.* The next morning, Drewyer was sent to examine the bearings of the river, till its entrance into the mountains, which he found to be at the distance of ten miles, and in a direction south 50° west; he had seen also the remains of a camp of eleven leathern lodges, recently abandoned, which induced us to suppose that the Minnetarees of Fort de Prairie are somewhere in this neighbourhood; a suspicion which was confirmed by the return of the hunters, who had seen no game of any kind. As these Indians have probably followed the buffalo towards the main branch of Maria's river, we shall not strike it above the north branch.

The course of the mountains still continues from southeast to northwest; in which last direction from us, the front range appears to terminate abruptly at the distance of thirty-five miles. Those which are to the southwest, and more distinctly in view, are of an irregular form, composed chiefly of clay, with a very small mixture of rock, without timber, and although low are yet partially covered with snow to their bases. The river itself has nearly double the volume of water which it possessed when we first saw it below, a circumstance to be ascribed, no doubt, to the great evaporation and absorption of the water in its passage through these open plains. The rock in this neighbourhood is of a white colour, and a fine grit, and lies in horizontal strata in the bluffs of the river. We attempted to take some fish, but could procure only a single trout. We had, therefore, nothing to eat, except the grease which we pressed from our tainted meat, and formed a mush of cows, reserving one meal more of the same kind for to-morrow. We have seen near this place a number of the whistling squirrel, common in the country watered by the Columbia, but which we observed here for the first time in the plains of the Missouri. The cottonwood too, of this place, is similar to that of the Columbia. Our observations this evening were prevented by clouds.

JULY 24TH  *Thursday.* The weather was clear for a short time in the morning, but the sky soon clouded over, and it rained during the rest of the day. We were therefore obliged to remain one day longer for the purpose of completing our observations. Our situation now became unpleasant from the rain, the coldness of the air, and the total absence of all game; for the hunters could find nothing of a large kind, and we were obliged to subsist on a few pigeons and a kettle of mush made of the remainder of our bread of cows. This supplied us with one more meal in the morning, when finding that the cold and rainy weather would still detain us here, two of the men were despatched to hunt. They returned in the evening with a fine buck, on which we fared sumptuously. In their excursion they had gone as far as the main branch of Maria's river, at the distance of ten miles, through an open extensive valley, in which were scattered a great number of lodges lately evacuated.

JULY 26TH  *Saturday.* The next morning the weather was still cloudy, so that no observation could be made, and what added to our disappointment, captain Lewis's chronometer stopped yesterday from some unknown cause, though when set in motion again it went as usual. We now despaired of taking the longitude of this place; and as our staying any longer might endanger our return to the United States during the present season, we, therefore, waited till nine o'clock, in hopes of a change of weather; but seeing no prospect of that kind, we mounted our horses, and leaving with reluctance our position, which we now named Camp Disappointment, directed our course across the open plains, in a direction nearly southeast. At twelve miles distance we reached a branch of Maria's river, about sixty-five yards wide, which we crossed, and continued along its southern side for two miles, where it is joined by another branch, nearly equal in size from the southwest, and far more clear than the north branch, which is turbid, though the beds of both are composed of pebbles. We now decided on pursuing this river to its junction with the fork of Maria's river, which we had ascended, and then cross

BLACKFOOT INDIAN (Bodmer)

the country obliquely to Tansy river, and descend that stream to its confluence with Maria's river. We, therefore, crossed and descended the river, and at one mile below the junction, halted to let the horses graze in a fertile bottom, in which were some Indian lodges, that appear to have been inhabited during the last winter. We here discern more timber than the country in general possesses; for besides an undergrowth of rose, honeysuckle, and redberry bushes, and a small quantity of willow timber, the three species of cottonwood, the narrow-leafed, the broad-leafed, and the species known to the Columbia, though here seen for the first time on the Missouri, are all united at this place. Game too, appears in greater abundance. We saw a few antelopes and wolves, and killed a buck, besides which we saw also two of the small burrowing foxes of the plains, about the size of the common domestic cat, and of a reddish brown colour, except the tail, which is black.

At the distance of three miles, we ascended the hills close to the river side, while Drewyer pursued the valley of the river on the opposite side. But scarcely had captain Lewis reached the high plain, when he saw about a mile on his left, a collection of about thirty horses. He immediately halted, and by the aid of his spy-glass discovered that one half of the horses were saddled, and that on the eminence above the horses, several Indians were looking down towards the river, probably at Drewyer. This was a most unwelcome sight. Their probable numbers rendered any contest with them of doubtful issue; to attempt to escape would only invite pursuit, and our horses were so bad that we must certainly be overtaken; besides which, Drewyer could not yet be aware that the Indians were near, and if we ran he would most probably be sacrificed. We therefore determined to make the best of our situation, and advance towards them in a friendly manner. The flag which we had brought in case of any such accident was therefore displayed, and we continued slowly our march towards them. Their whole attention was so engaged by Drewyer, that they did not immediately discover us. As soon as they did see us, they appeared to be much alarmed and ran about in confusion, and some of them came down the hill and drove their horses within gunshot of the eminence, to which they then returned, as if to wait our arrival. When we came within a quarter of a mile, one of the Indians mounted and rode at full speed to receive us; but when within a hundred paces of us, he halted, and captain Lewis who had alighted to receive him, held out his hand, and beckoned to him to approach, he only looked at us for some time, and then, without saying a word, returned to his companions with as much haste as he had advanced. The whole party now descended the hill and rode towards us. As yet we saw only eight, but presumed that there must be more behind us, as there were several horses saddled. We however advanced, and captain Lewis now told his two men that he believed these were the Minnetarees of Fort de Prairie, who, from their infamous character, would in all probability attempt to rob them; but being determined to die, rather than lose his papers and instruments, he intended to resist to the last extremity, and advised them to do the same, and to be on the alert should there be any disposition to attack us. When the two parties came within a hundred yards of each other, all the Indians, except one, halted; captain Lewis therefore ordered his two men to halt while he advanced, and after shaking hands with the Indian, went on and did the same with the others in the rear, while the Indian himself shook hands with the two men. They all now came up, and after alighting, the Indians asked to smoke with us. Captain Lewis, who was very anxious for Drewyer's safety, told them that the man who had gone down the river had the pipe, and requested that as they had seen him one of them would accompany R. Fields to bring him back. To this they assented, and Fields went with a young man in search of Drewyer.

Captain Lewis now asked them by signs if they were the Minnetarees of the north, and was sorry to learn by their answer that his suspicion was too true. He then inquired if there was any chief among them. They pointed out three; but though he did not believe them, yet it was thought best to please them, and he therefore gave to one a flag, to another a medal, and to a third a handkerchief. They appeared to be well satisfied with these presents, and now recovered from the agitation into which our first interview had thrown them, for they were really more alarmed than ourselves at the meeting. In our turn, however, we became equally satisfied on finding that they were not joined by any more of their companions, for we consider ourselves quite a match for eight Indians, particularly as these have but two guns, the rest being armed with only eye-dogs and bows and arrows. As it was growing late captain Lewis proposed that they should encamp together near the river; for he was glad to see them and had a great deal to say to them. They assented; and being soon joined by Drewyer, we proceeded towards the river, and after descending a very steep bluff, two hundred and fifty feet high, encamped in a small bottom.

Here the Indians formed a large semicircular tent of dressed buffalo skins, in which the two parties assembled, and by the means of Drewyer, the evening was spent in conversation with the Indians. They informed us that they were a part of a large band which at present lay encamped on the main branch of Maria's river, near the foot of the Rocky mountains, and at the distance of a day and a half's journey from this place. Another large band were hunting buffalo near the Broken mountains, from which they would proceed in a few days to the north of Maria's river. With the first of these there was a white man. They added, that from this place to the establishment on the Saskashawan, at which they trade, is only six days' easy march; that is, such a day's journey as can be made with their women and children, so that we computed the distance at one hundred and fifty miles. There they carry the skins of wolves and some beavers, and exchange them for guns, ammunition, blankets, spirituous liquors, and the other articles of Indian traffic. Captain Lewis in turn informed them that he had come from a great distance up the large river which runs towards the rising sun; that he had been as far as the great lake where the sun sets; that he had seen many nations, the greater part of whom were at war with each other, but by his mediation were restored to peace; and all had been invited to come and trade with him west of the mountains; he was now on his way home, but had left his companions at the falls, and come in search of the Minnetarees, in hopes of inducing them to live at peace with their neighbours, and to visit the trading houses which would be formed at the entrance of Maria's river. They said that they were anxious of being at peace with the Tushepaws, but those people had lately killed a number of their relations, as they proved by showing several of the party who had their hair cut as a sign of mourning. They were equally willing, they added, to come down and trade with us. Captain Lewis therefore proposed that they should send some of their young men to invite all their band to meet us at the mouth of Maria's river, and the rest of the party to go with us to that place, where he hoped to find his men, offering them ten horses and some tobacco in case they would accompany us. To this they made no reply. Finding them very fond of the pipe, captain Lewis, who was desirous of keeping a constant watch during the night, smoked with them until a late hour, and as soon as they were all asleep, he woke R. Fields, and ordering him to rouse us all in case any Indian left the camp, as they would probably attempt to steal our horses, he lay down by the side of Drewyer in the tent with all the Indians, while the Fields were stretched near the fire at the mouth of it.

*Captain Lewis shoots an Indian for just cause (from Sergeant Gass's journal).*

*Sunday.* At sunrise the Indians got up and crowded round the fire near which J. Fields, who was then on watch, had carelessly left his rifle, near the head of his brother, who was still asleep. One of the Indians slipped behind him, and unperceived, took his brother's and his own rifle, while at the same time, two others seized those of Drewyer and captain Lewis. As soon as Fields turned round, he saw the Indian running off with the rifles, and instantly calling his brother, they pursued him for fifty or sixty yards, and just as they overtook him, in the scuffle for the rifles, R. Fields stabbed him through the heart with his knife; the Indian ran about fifteen steps and fell dead. They now ran back with their rifles to the camp. The moment the fellow touched his gun, Drewyer, who was awake, jumped up and wrested her from him. The noise awoke captain Lewis, who instantly started from the ground and reached to seize his gun, but finding her gone, drew a pistol from his belt and turning about saw the Indian running off with her. He followed him and ordered him to lay her down, which he was doing just as the Fields came up, and were taking aim to shoot him, when captain Lewis ordered them not to fire, as the Indian did not appear to intend any mischief. He dropped the gun and was going slowly off as Drewyer came out and asked permission to kill him, but this captain Lewis forbid as he had not yet attempted to shoot us. But finding that the Indians were now endeavouring to drive off all the horses, he ordered three of them to follow the main party who were chasing the horses up the river, and fire instantly upon the thieves; while he, without taking time to run for his shot-pouch, pursued the fellow who had stolen his gun and another Indian, who were driving away the horses on the left of the camp. He pressed them so closely that they left twelve of their horses, but continued to drive off one of our own. At the distance of three hundred paces they entered a steep niche in the river bluffs, when captain Lewis, being too much out of breath to pursue them any further, called out, as he did several times before, that unless they gave up the horse he would shoot them. As he raised his gun one of the Indians jumped behind a rock and spoke to the other, who stopped at the distance of thirty paces, as captain Lewis shot him in the belly. He fell on his knees and right elbow, but raising himself a little, fired, and then crawled behind a rock. The shot had nearly been fatal, for captain Lewis, who was bareheaded, felt the wind of the ball very distinctly. Not having his shot-pouch, he could not reload his rifle, and having only a single load also for his pistol, he thought it most prudent not to attack the Indians, and therefore retired slowly to the camp. He was met by Drewyer, who hearing the report of the guns, had come to his assistance, leaving the Fields to pursue the Indians. Captain Lewis ordered him to call out to them to desist from the pursuit, as we could take the horses of the Indians in place of our own, but they were at too great a distance to hear him. He therefore returned to the camp, and whilst he was saddling the horses, the Fields returned with four of our own, having followed the Indians until two of them swam the river, two others ascended the hills, so that the horses became dispersed.

We, however, were rather gainers by this contest, for we took four of the Indian horses, and lost only one of our own. Besides which, we found in the camp four shields, two bows with quivers, and one of the guns which we took with us, and also the flag which we had presented to them, but left the medal round the neck of the dead man, in order that they might be informed who we were. The rest of their baggage, except some buffalo meat, we left; and as there was no time to be lost, we mounted our horses, and after ascending the river hills, took our course through the beautiful level plains, in a direction a little to the south of east. We had no doubt but that we should be immediately pursued by a much larger party, and that as soon as intelligence was given to the band near the Broken mountains, they would hasten to the mouth of Maria's river to intercept us. We hope, however, to be there before them, so as to form a junction with our friends. We therefore pushed our horses as fast as we possibly could; and fortunately for us, the Indian horses were very good, the plains perfectly level, and without many stones or prickly pears, and in fine order for travelling after the late rains. At eight miles from our camp we passed a stream forty yards wide, to which, from the occurrence of the morning, we gave the name of Battle river. At three o'clock we reached Rose river, five miles above where we had formerly passed it, and having now come by estimate sixty-three miles, halted for an hour and a half to refresh our horses; then pursued our journey seventeen miles further, when, as the night came on, we killed a buffalo, and again stopped for two hours. The sky was now overclouded, but as the moon gave light enough to show us the route, we continued along through immense herds of buffalo for twenty miles, and then almost exhausted with fatigue, halted at two in the morning to rest ourselves and the horses.

*Monday*. At daylight we awoke sore and scarcely able to stand; but as our own lives as well as those of our companions depended on our pressing forward, we mounted our horses and set out. The men were desirous of crossing the Missouri, at the Grog spring, where Rose river approaches so near the river, and passing down the southwest side of it, and thus avoid the country at the junction of the two rivers, through which the enemy would most probably pursue us. But as this circuitous route would consume the whole day, and the Indians might in the meantime attack the canoes at the point, captain Lewis told his party it was now their duty to risk their lives for their friends and companions; that he would proceed immediately to the point, to give the alarm to the canoes, and if they had not yet arrived, he would raft the Missouri, and after hiding the baggage, ascend the river on foot through the woods till he met them. He told them also that it was his determination, in case they were attacked in crossing the plains, to tie the bridles of the horses and stand together till they had either routed their enemies, or sold their lives as dearly as possible.

To this they all assented, and we therefore continued our route to the eastward, till at the distance of twelve miles we came near the Missouri, when we heard a noise which seemed like the report of a gun. We therefore quickened our pace for eight miles further, and about five miles from the Grog spring, now heard distinctly the noise of several rifles, from the river. We hurried to the bank, and saw with exquisite satisfaction our friends coming down the river. They landed to greet us, and after turning our horses loose, we embarked with our baggage, and went down to the spot where we had made a deposit. This, after reconnoitering the adjacent country, we opened; but unfortunately the cache had caved in, and most of the articles were injured. We took whatever was still worth preserving, and immediately proceeded to the point, where we found our deposits in good order.

By a singular good fortune we were here joined by sergeant Gass and Willard from the falls, who had been ordered to bring the horses here to assist in collecting meat for the voyage, as it had been calculated that the canoes would reach this place much sooner than captain Lewis's party. After a very heavy shower of rain and hail, attended with violent thunder and lightning, we left the point, and giving a final discharge to our horses, went over to the island where we had left our red periogue, which however we found so much decayed that we had no means of repairing her: we, therefore, took all the iron work out of her, and proceeded down the river fifteen miles, and encamped near some cottonwood trees, one of which was of the narrow-leafed species, and the first of that species we had remarked as we ascended the river.

Sergeant Ordway's party, which had left the mouth of Madison river on the *13th*, had descended in safety to the Whitebear islands, where he arrived on the *19th*, and after collecting the baggage, left the falls on the *27th* in the white periogue, and five canoes, while sergeant Gass and Willard set out at the same time by land with the horses, and thus fortunately met together.

*Tuesday*. A violent storm of rain and hail came on last night, and as we had no means of making a shelter, we lay in the rain, and during the whole day continued so exposed. The two small canoes were sent ahead in order to hunt elk and buffalo, which are in immense quantities, so as to provide shelter as well as food for the party. We then proceeded very rapidly with the aid of a strong current, and after passing at one o'clock the Natural walls, encamped late in the evening at our former encampment of the *29th of May, 1805*. The river is now as high as it has been during the present season, and every little rivulet discharges torrents of water, which bring down such quantities of mud and sand, that we can scarcely drink the water of the Missouri. The buffalo continue to be very numerous, but the elk are few. The bighorns, however, are in great numbers along the steep cliffs of the river, and being now in fine order, their flesh is extremely tender, delicate, and well flavoured, and resembles in colour and flavour our mutton, though it is not so strong. The brown curlew has disappeared, and has probably gone to some other climate after rearing its young in these plains.

JULY 30TH    *Wednesday.* The rain still prevented us from stopping to dry our baggage, and we therefore proceeded with a strong current, which joined to our oars, enabled us to advance at the rate of seven miles an hour. We went on shore several times for the purpose of hunting, and procured several bighorns, two buffalo, a beaver, an elk, and a female brown bear, whose talons were six and a quarter inches in length. In the evening we encamped on an island two miles above Goodrich's island, and early in the morning continued our route in the rain, passing, during the greater part of the day, through high pine hills, succeeded by low grounds abounding in timber and game. The buffalo are scarce; but we procured fifteen elk, fourteen deer, two bighorns, and a beaver. The elk are in fine order, particularly the males, who now herd together in small parties. Their horns have reached their full growth, but ill retain the velvet or skin which covers them. Through the bottoms are scattered a number of lodges, some of which seem to have been built last winter, and were probably occupied by the Minnetarees of Fort de Prairie. The river is still rising, and more muddy than we have ever seen it.

## *Friday, August 1st, 1806*

Late last night we took shelter from the rain in some old Indian lodges, about eight miles below the entrance of North-mountain creek, and then set out at an early hour. We passed the Muscleshell river at eleven o'clock, and fifteen miles further landed at some Indian lodges, where we determined to pass the night, for the rain still continued, and we feared that the skins of the bighorn would spoil by being constantly wet. Having made fires, therefore, and exposed them to dry, we proceeded to hunt. The next day was fair and warm, and we availed ourselves of this occasion to dry all our baggage in the sun. Such is the immediate effect of fair weather, that since last evening the river has fallen eighteen inches. Two men were sent forward in a canoe to hunt; and now, having reloaded our canoes, we resolved to go on as fast as possible, and accordingly set out at an early hour, and without stopping as usual to cook a dinner, encamped in the evening two miles above our camp of *May 12, 1805.* We were here joined by the two hunters, who had killed twenty-nine deer since they left us. These animals are in great abundance in the river bottoms, and very gentle. We passed also a great number of elk, wolves, some bear, beaver, geese, a few ducks, the parti-coloured corvus, a calumet eagle, some bald eagles, and red-headed woodpeckers, but very few buffalo.

*Monday*. By four o'clock next morning we were again in motion. At eleven we passed the Bigdry river, which has now a bold, even, but shallow current, sixty yards in width, and halted for a few minutes at the mouth of Milk river. This stream is at present full of water, resembling in colour that of the Missouri, and as it possesses quite as much water as Maria's river, we have no doubt that it extends to a considerable distance towards the north. We here killed a very large rattlesnake. Soon after we passed several herds of buffalo and elk, and encamped at night, two miles below the gulf, on the northeast side of the river. For the first time this season we were saluted with the cry of the whippoorwill, or goatsucker of the Missouri.

*Tuesday*. We waited until noon in hopes of being overtaken by two of the men, who had gone ahead in a canoe to hunt two days ago, but who were at a distance from the river, as we passed them. As they did not arrive by that time, we concluded that they had passed us in the night, and therefore proceeded until late, when we encamped about ten miles below Littledry river. We again saw great numbers of buffalo, elk, deer, antelope, and wolves; also eagles, and other birds, among which were geese and a solitary pelican, neither of whom can fly at present, as they are now shedding the feathers of their wings. We also saw several bear, one of them the largest, except one, we had ever seen, for he measured nine feet from the nose to the extremity of the tail.

During the night a violent storm came on from the northeast with such torrents of rain that we had scarcely time to unload the canoes before they filled with water. Having no shelter, we ourselves were completely wet to the skin, and the wind and cold air made our situation very unpleasant. We left it early, *Wednesday, 6th;* but after we had passed Porcupine river, were, by the high wind, obliged to lie by until four o'clock, when the wind abating we continued, and at night encamped five miles below our camp of the *1st of May, 1805*. Here we were again drenched by the rain, which lasted all the next morning; but being resolved, if possible, to reach the Yellowstone, a distance of eighty-three miles, in the course of the day, we set out early, and being favoured by the rapid current and good oarsmen, proceeded with great speed.

In passing Martha's river, we observed that its mouth is at present a quarter of a mile lower than it was last year. Here we find for the first time the appearance of coal-burnt hills and pumicestone, which seem always to accompany each other. At this place also are the first elms and dwarf cedars in the bluffs of the river. The ash first makes its appearance in one solitary tree at the Ash rapid, but is seen occasionally scattered through the low grounds at the Elk rapid, and thence downwards, though it is generally small. The whole country on the northeast side, between Martha and Milk rivers, is a beautiful level plain, with a soil much more fertile than that higher up the river. The buffalo, elk, and other animals still continue numerous; as are also the bear, who lie in wait at the crossing places, where they

501

seize elk and the weaker cattle, and then stay by the carcase in order to keep off the wolves, till the whole is devoured. At four o'clock we reached the mouth of Yellowstone, where we found a note from captain Clark, informing us of his intention of waiting for us a few miles below. We therefore left a memorandum for our two huntsmen, whom we now supposed must be behind us, and then pursued our course till night came on, and not being able to overtake captain Clark, we encamped.

AUGUST 8TH    *Friday.* In the morning we set out in hopes of overtaking captain Clark; but after descending to nearly the entrance of White-earth river without being able to see him, we were at a loss what to conjecture. In this situation we landed, and began to caulk and repair the canoes, as well as prepare some skins for clothing, for since we left the Rocky mountains we have had no leisure to make clothes, so that the greater part of the men are almost naked. In these occupations we passed this and the following day, without any interruption except from the mosquitoes, which are very troublesome, and then having completed the repairs of the canoes, we embarked, *Sunday, 10th*, at five in the afternoon; but the wind and rain prevented us going further than near the entrance of White-earth river.

AUGUST 11TH    *Monday.* The next day, being anxious to reach the Burnt hills by noon, in order to ascertain the latitude, we went forward with great rapidity; but by the time we reached that place, it was twenty minutes too late to take the meridian altitude.

Having lost the observation, captain Lewis observed on the opposite side of the river, a herd of elk on a thick sandbar of willows, and landed with Cruzatte to hunt them. Each of them fired and shot an elk. They then reloaded and took different routes in pursuit of the game, when just as captain Lewis was taking aim at an elk, a ball struck him in the left thigh, about an inch below the joint of the hip, and missing the bone, went through the left thigh and grazed the right to the depth of the ball. It instantly occurred to him that Cruzatte must have shot him by mistake for an elk, as he was dressed in brown leather, and Cruzatte had not a very good eye-sight. He therefore called out that he was shot, and looked towards the place from which the ball came; but seeing nothing, he called on Cruzatte by name several times, but received no answer. He now thought that as Cruzatte was out of hearing, and the shot did not seem to come from more than forty paces distance, it must have been fired by an Indian; and not knowing how many might be concealed in the bushes, he made towards the periogue, calling out to Cruzatte to retreat as there were Indians in the willows. As soon as he reached the periogue, he ordered the men to arms, and mentioning that he was wounded, though he hoped not mortally by the Indians, bade them follow him to relieve Cruzatte. They instantly followed for an hundred paces, when his wound became so painful, and his thigh stiffened in such a manner, that he could go no further. He therefore ordered the men to proceed, and if overpowered by numbers, retreat towards the boats, keeping up a fire; then limping back to the periogue, he prepared himself with his rifle, a pistol, and the air-gun, to sell his life dearly in case the men should be overcome. In this state of anxiety and suspense he remained for about twenty minutes, when the party returned with Cruzatte, and reported that no Indians could be seen in the neighbourhood. Cruzatte was now much alarmed and declared that he had shot an elk after captain Lewis left him, but disclaimed every idea of having intentionally wounded his officer. There was no doubt but that he was the person who gave the wound, yet as it seemed to be perfectly accidental, and Cruzatte had always conducted himself with propriety, no further notice was taken of it. The wound was now dressed, and patent lint put into the holes; but though it bled considerably, yet as the ball had touched neither a bone nor an artery, we hope that it may not prove fatal. As it was, however, impossible for him to make the observation of the latitude of the Burnt hills, which is chiefly desirable, as being the most northern parts of the Missouri, he declined remaining till to-morrow, and proceeded on till evening. Captain Lewis could not now be removed without great pain, as he had a high fever.

He therefore remained on board during the night, and early the next morning, proceeded with as much expedition as possible, and soon afterwards we put ashore to visit a camp, which we found to be that of Dickson and Hancock, the two Illinois traders, who told us that they had seen captain Clark yesterday. As we stopped with them, we were overtaken by our two hunters, Colter and Collins, who had been missing since the third, and whose absence excited much uneasiness. They informed us, that after following us the first day, they concluded that we must be behind, and waited for us during several days, when they were convinced of their mistake, and had then come on as rapidly as they could. We made some presents to the two traders, and then proceeded till at one o'clock we joined our friends and companions under captain Clark.   AUGUST 12TH

*Rivers and trails in the area where the expedition re-crossed the Continental Divide (the top of this sketch-map is toward the south).*

THURSDAY, JULY 3D, 1806  On taking leave of captain Lewis and the Indians, the other division, consisting of captain Clark with fifteen men and fifty horses, set out through the valley of Clark's river, along the western side of which they rode in a southern direction. The valley is from ten to fifteen miles in width, tolerably level, and partially covered with the long-leafed and the pitch pine, with some cottonwood, birch, and sweet willow on the borders of the streams. Among the herbage are two species of clover, one the white clover common to the western parts of the United States, the other much smaller both in its leaf and blossom than either the red or white clover, and particularly relished by the horses. After crossing eight different streams of water, four of which were small, we halted at the distance of eighteen miles on the upper side of a large creek, where we let our horses graze, and after dinner resumed our journey in the same direction we had pursued during the morning, till at the distance of eighteen miles further, we encamped on the north side of a large creek. The valley became more beautiful as we proceeded, and was diversified by a number of small open plains, abounding with grass, and a variety of sweet-scented plants, and watered by ten streams which rush from the western mountains with considerable velocity. The mountains themselves are covered with snow about one-fifth from the top, and some snow is still to be seen on the high points and in the hollows of the mountains to the eastward. In the course of our ride we saw a great number of deer, a single bear, and some of the burrowing squirrels common about the Quamash flats. The mosquitoes too were very troublesome.

*Friday.* Early in the morning three hunters were sent out, and the rest of the party having collected the horses and breakfasted, we proceeded at seven o'clock up the valley, which is now contracted to the width of from eight to ten miles, with a good proportion of pitch pine, though its low lands, as well as the bottoms of the creeks, are strewed with large stones. We crossed five creeks of different sizes, but of great depth, and so rapid, that in passing the last, several of the horses were driven down the stream and some of our baggage wet. Near this river we saw the tracks of two Indians, whom we supposed to be Shoshonees. Having made sixteen miles, we halted at an early hour for the purpose of doing honour to the birth-day of our country's independence. The festival was not very splendid, for it consisted of a mush made of cows and a saddle of venison, nor had we any thing to tempt us to prolong it. We therefore went on till at the distance of a mile we came to a very large creek, which, like all those in the valley, had an immense rapidity of descent; and we therefore proceeded up for some distance, in order to select the most convenient spot for fording. Even there, however, such was the violence of the current, that although the water was not higher than the bellies of the horses, the resistance they made in passing, caused the stream to rise over their backs and loads. After passing the creek we inclined to the left, and soon after struck the road which we had descended last year, near the spot where we dined on the *7th of September*. Along this road we continued on the west side of Clark's river, till at the distance of thirteen miles, during which we passed three more deep large creeks, we reached its western branch, where we encamped, and having sent out two hunters, des-

JULY 4TH

505

patched some men to examine the best ford across the river. The game of to-day consisted of four deer; though we also saw a herd of ibex, or bighorn.

JULY 5TH    *Saturday*. By daylight the next morning we again examined the fords, and having discovered what we conceived to be the best, began the passage at a place where the river is divided by small islands into six different channels. We, however, crossed them all without any damage, except wetting some of our provisions and merchandise; and at the distance of a mile came to the eastern branch, up which we proceeded about a mile, till we came into the old road we had descended in the autumn. It soon led us across the river, which we found had fallen to the same depth at which we found it last autumn, and along its eastern bank to the foot of the mountain nearly opposite Flower creek. Here we halted to let our horses graze, near a spot where there was still a fire burning and the tracks of two horses, which we presumed to be Shoshonees; and having dried all our provisions, proceeded at about four o'clock, across the mountain into the valley where we had first seen the Flat-heads.

We then crossed the river, which we now perceived took its rise from a high peaked mountain at about twenty miles to the northeast of the valley, and then passed up it for two miles, and encamped after a ride of twenty miles during the day. As soon as we halted several men were despatched in different directions to examine the road, and from their report, concluded that the best path would be one about three miles up the creek. This is the road travelled by the Ootlashoots, and will certainly shorten our route two days at least, besides being much better, as we had been informed by the Indians, than by that we came last fall.

JULY 6TH    *Sunday*. The night was very cold, succeeded by frost in the morning; and as the horses were much scattered, we were not able to set out before nine o'clock. We then went along the creek for three miles, and leaving to the right the path by which we came last fall, pursued the road taken by the Ootlashoots, up a gentle ascent to the dividing mountain which separates the waters of the middle fork of Clark's river, from those of Wisdom and Lewis's rivers. On reaching the other side, we came to Glade creek, down which we proceeded, crossing it frequently into the glades on each side, where the timber is small, and in many places destroyed by fire; where are great quantities of quamash now in bloom. Throughout the glades are great numbers of holes made by the whistling or burrowing squirrel; and we killed a hare of the large mountain species. Along these roads there are also appearances of old buffalo paths, and some old heads of buffaloes; and as these animals have wonderful sagacity in the choice of their routes, the coincidence of a buffalo with an Indian road, was the strongest assurance that it was the best.

In the afternoon we passed along the hill-side, north of the creek, till, in the course of six miles, we entered an extensive level plain. Here the tracks of the Indians scattered so much that we could no longer pursue it, but Sacajawea recognised the plain immediately. She had travelled it often during her childhood, and informed us that it was the great resort of the Shoshonees, who came for the purpose of gathering quamash and cows, and of taking beaver, with which the plain abounded, and that Glade creek was a branch of Wisdom river, and that on reaching the higher part of the plain, we should see a gap in the mountains, on the course to our canoes, and from that gap a high point of mountain covered with snow. At the distance of a mile we crossed a large creek from the right, rising, as well as Fish creek, in a snowy mountain, over which there is a gap. Soon after, on ascending a rising ground, the country spreads itself into a beautiful plain, extending north and south about fifteen miles wide and thirty in length, and surrounded on all sides by high points of mountains covered with snow, among which was the gap pointed out by the squaw, bearing S. 56° E. We had not gone two miles from the last creek when we were overtaken by a violent storm of wind, accompanied with hard rain, which lasted an hour and a half. Having no shelter, we formed a solid column to protect ourselves from the gust, and then went on five miles to a small creek, where finding some small timber, we encamped for the night, and dried ourselves. We here observed some fresh signs of Indians, who had been gathering quamash. Our distance was twenty-six miles.

*Monday.* In the morning our horses were so much scattered, that although we sent out hunters in every direction, to range the country for six or eight miles, nine of them could not be recovered. They were the most valuable of all our horses, and so much attached to some of their companions, that it was difficult to separate them in the day-time. We therefore presumed that they must have been stolen by some roving Indians, and accordingly left a party of five men to continue the pursuit, while the rest went on to the spot where the canoes had been deposited. Accordingly we set out at ten o'clock, and pursued a course S. 56° E. across the valley which we found to be watered by four large creeks, with extensive low and miry bottoms; and then reached Wisdom river, along the northeast side of which we continued, till at the distance of sixteen miles we came to the three branches. Near that place we stopped for dinner at a hot spring situated in the open plain. The bed of the spring is about fifteen yards in circumference, and composed of loose, hard, gritty stones, through which the water boils in great quantities. It is slightly impregnated with sulphur, and so hot that a piece of meat about the size of three fingers, was completely done in twenty-five minutes. After dinner we proceeded across the eastern branch, and along the north side of the middle branch for nine miles, when we reached the gap in the mountains, and took our last leave of this extensive valley, which we called the Hotspring valley. It is indeed a beautiful country; though enclosed by mountains covered with snow, the soil is exceedingly fertile and well supplied with esculent plants; while its numerous creeks furnish immense quantities of beaver. Another valley less extensive and more rugged opened itself to our view as we passed through the gap; but as we had made twenty-five miles, and the night was advancing, we halted near some handsome springs, which fall into Willard's creek.

*Tuesday.* After a cold night, during which our horses separated and could not be collected till eight o'clock in the morning, we crossed the valley along the southwest side of Willard's creek for twelve miles, when it entered the mountains, and then turning S. 20° E. came to the Shoshonee cove, after riding seven miles; whence we proceeded down the west branch of Jefferson river, and at the distance of nine miles, reached its forks, where we had deposited our merchandise in the month of August. Most of the men were in the habit of chewing tobacco; and such was their eagerness to procure it after so long a privation, that they scarcely took the saddles from their horses before they ran to the cave, and were delighted at being able to resume this fascinating indulgence. This was one of the severest privations which we have encountered. Some of the men, whose tomahawks were so constructed as to answer the purposes of pipes, broke the handles of these instruments, and after cutting them into small fragments, chewed them; the wood having, by frequent smoking, become strongly impregnated with the taste of that plant. We found every thing safe, though some of the goods were a little damp, and one of the canoes had a hole. The ride of this day was twenty-seven miles in length, and through a country diversified by low marshy grounds, and high, open, and stony plains, terminated by high mountains, on the tops and along the northern sides of which the snow still remained. Over the whole were scattered great quantities of hyssop and the different species of shrubs, common to the plains of the Missouri.

We had now crossed the whole distance from Traveller's-rest creek to the head of Jefferson's river, which seems to form the best and shortest route over the mountains, during almost the whole distance of one hundred and sixty-four miles. It is, in fact, a very excellent road, and by cutting a few trees, might be rendered a good route for wagons, with the exception of about four miles over one of the mountains, which would require some levelling.

JULY 9TH    *Wednesday.* We were all occupied in raising and repairing the canoes, and making the necessary preparations for resuming our journey to-morrow. The day proved cold and windy, so that the canoes were soon dried. We were here overtaken by sergeant Ordway and his party, who had discovered our horses near the head of the creek on which we encamped, and although they were very much scattered, and endeavoured to escape as fast as they could, he brought them back. The squaw found to-day a plant which grows in the moist lands, the root of which is eaten by the Indians. The stem and leaf, as well as the root of this plant, resemble the common carrot, in form, size and taste, though the colour is of somewhat a paler yellow. The night continued very cold.

JULY 10TH    *Thursday.* In the morning a white frost covered the ground; the grass was frozen, and the ice three quarters of an inch thick in a basin of water. The boats were now loaded, and captain Clark divided his men into two bands, one to descend the river with the baggage, while he, with the other, proceeded on horseback to the Rochejaune [Yellowstone river].

After breakfast the two parties set out, those on shore skirting the eastern side of Jefferson river, through Service valley, and over the Rattlesnake mountain, into a beautiful and extensive country, known among the Indians by the name of Hahnahappapchah, or Beaverhead valley, from the number of those animals to be found in it, and also from a point of land resembling the head of a beaver. It extends from the Rattlesnake mountain as low as Frazier's creek, and is about fifty miles in length, in a direct line, while its width varies from ten to fifteen miles, being watered in its whole

course by the Jefferson and six different creeks. The valley is open and fertile, and besides the innumerable quantities of beaver and otter, with which
its creeks are supplied, the bushes of the low grounds are a favourite resort
for deer, while on the higher parts of the valley are seen scattered groups of
antelopes, and still further, on the steep sides of the mountains, we observed
many of the bighorn, which take refuge there from the wolves and bears. At
the distance of fifteen miles the two parties stopped to dine, when captain
Clark finding that the river became wider and deeper, and that the canoes
could advance more rapidly than the horses, determined to go himself by
water, leaving sergeant Pryor with six men, to bring on the horses. In this
way they resumed their journey after dinner, and encamped on the eastern
side of the river, opposite the head of the Three-thousand-mile island. The
beaver were basking in great numbers along the shore; they saw also some
young wild geese and ducks. The mosquitoes were very troublesome during
the day, but after sunset the weather became cool and they disappeared.

*Friday.* The next morning captain Clark sent four men ahead to hunt, and
after an early breakfast proceeded down a very narrow channel, which was
rendered more difficult by a high southwest wind, which blew from the high
snowy mountains in that quarter, and met them in the face at every bend of
the river, which was now become very crooked. At noon they passed the
high point of land on the left, to which Beaverhead valley owes its name, and
at six o'clock reached Philanthropy river, which was at present very low.
The wind now shifted to the northeast, and though high, was much warmer
than before. At seven o'clock they reached their encampment at the entrance
of Wisdom river on the sixth of August. They found the river very high, but
falling. Here too, they overtook the hunters, who had killed a buck and some
young geese. Besides these they had seen a great number of geese and sandhill cranes, and some deer. The beaver too were in great quantities along the
banks of the rivers, and through the night were flapping their tails in the
water round the boats.

*Saturday.* Having found the canoe which had been left here as they ascended, they employed themselves, till eight o'clock in drawing out the nails
and making paddles of the sides of it. Then leaving one of their canoes here,
they set out after breakfast. Immediately below the forks the current became stronger than above, and the course of the river straighter, as far as
Panther creek, after which it became much more crooked. A high wind now
arose from the snowy mountains to the northwest, so that it was with much
difficulty and some danger they reached, at three o'clock, the entrance of
Fields's creek. After dining at that place, they pursued their course and
stopped for the night below their encampment of the *31st of July* last.
Beaver, young geese, and deer continued to be their game, and they saw
some old signs of buffalo. The mosquitoes also were still very troublesome.

*Sunday.* Early in the morning they set out, and at noon reached the entrance
of Madison river, where sergeant Pryor had arrived with the horses about
an hour before. The horses were then driven across Madison and Gallatin
rivers, and the whole party halted to dine and unload the canoes below the
mouth of the latter. Here the two parties separated; sergeant Ordway with

nine men set out in six canoes to descend the river, while captain Clark with the remaining ten, and the wife and child of Chaboneau, were to proceed by land, with fifty horses, to Yellowstone river. They set out at five in the afternoon from the forks of the Missouri, in a direction nearly eastward; but as many of the horses had sore feet, they were obliged to move slowly, and after going four miles, halted for the night on the bank of Gallatin's river.

This is a beautiful stream, and though the current is rapid and obstructed by islands near its mouth, is navigable for canoes. On its lower side the land rises gradually to the foot of a mountain, running almost parallel to it; but the country below it and Madison's river is a level plain, covered at present with low grass, the soil being poor, and injured by stones and strata of hard white rock along the hill sides. Throughout the whole, game was very abundant. They procured deer in the low grounds; beaver and otter were seen in Gallatin's river, and elk, wolves, eagles, hawks, crows, and geese, were seen at different parts of the route. The plain was intersected by several great roads, leading to a gap in the mountain, about twenty miles distant, in a direction E. N. E. but the Indian woman, who was acquainted with the country, recommended a gap more to the southward.

JULY 14TH *Monday.* This course captain Clark determined to pursue; and therefore at an early hour in the morning, crossed Gallatin's river in a direction south 78° east, and passing over a level plain, reached the Jefferson at the distance of six miles. That river is here divided into many channels, which spread themselves for several miles through the low grounds, and are dammed up by the beaver in such a manner, that after attempting in vain to reach the opposite side, they were obliged to turn short about to the right, till with some difficulty they reached a low but firm island, extending nearly in the course they desired to follow. The squaw now assured captain Clark that the large road from Medicine river to the gap we were seeking, crossed the upper part of this plain. He therefore proceeded four miles up the plain and reached the main channel of the river, which is still navigable for canoes, though much divided and dammed up by multitudes of beaver. Having forded the river, they passed through a little skirt of cottonwood timber to a low open plain, where they dined. They saw elk, deer, and antelopes, and in every direction the roads made by the buffalo; as well as some old signs of them. The squaw informed them, that but a few years ago these animals were numerous, not only here but even to the sources of Jefferson's river; but of late they have disappeared, for the Shoshonees being fearful of going west of the mountains, have hunted this country with more activity, and of course driven the buffalo from their usual haunts. After dinner they continued inclining to the south of east, through an open level plain, till at the distance of twelve miles they reached the three forks of Gallatin's river. On crossing the southerly branch, they fell into the buffalo road, described by the squaw, which led them up the middle branch for two miles; this branch is provided with immense quantities of beaver, but is sufficiently navigable for small canoes, by unlading at the worst dams. After crossing, they went on a mile further, and encamped at the beginning of the gap in the mountain, which here forms a kind of semicircle, through which the three branches of the river pass. Several roads come in from the right and left, all tending to the gap. A little snow still remains on a naked mountain to the

510

eastward, but in every other direction the mountains are covered with great quantities.

*Tuesday*. After an early breakfast they pursued the buffalo road over a low gap in the mountain to the heads of the eastern fork of Gallatin's river, near which they had encamped last evening, and at the distance of six miles reached the top of the dividing ridge, which separates the waters of the Missouri and the Yellowstone; and on descending the ridge, they struck one of the streams of the latter river. They followed its course through an open country, with high mountains on each side, partially covered with pine, and watered by several streams, crowded as usual with beaver dams. Nine miles from the top of the ridge they reached the Yellowstone itself, about a mile and a half below where it issues from the Rocky mountains.

It now appeared that the communication between the two rivers was short and easy. From the head of the Missouri at its three forks to this place is a distance of forty-eight miles, the greater part of which is through a level plain; indeed, from the forks of the eastern branch of Gallatin's river, which is there navigable for small canoes, to this part of the Yellowstone, the distance is no more than eighteen miles, with an excellent road over a high, dry country, with hills of inconsiderable height and no difficulty in passing. They halted three hours to rest their horses, and then pursued the buffalo road along the bank of the river.

Although just leaving a high snowy mountain, the Yellowstone is already a bold, rapid, and deep stream, one hundred and twenty yards in width. The bottoms of the river are narrow within the mountains, but widen to the extent of nearly two miles in the valley below, where they are occasionally overflowed, and the soil gives nourishment to cottonwood, rose bushes, honeysuckle, rushes, common coarse grass, a species of rye, and such productions of moist lands. On each side these low grounds are bounded by dry plains of coarse gravel and sand, stretching back to the foot of the mountains, and supplied with a very short grass. The mountains on the east side of the river are rough and rocky, and still retain great quantities of snow, and two other high snowy mountains may be distinguished, one bearing north fifteen or twenty miles, the other nearly east. They have no covering except a few scattered pine, nor indeed was any timber fit for even a small canoe to be seen. At the distance of nine miles from the mountain, a river discharges itself into the Yellowstone, from the northwest, under a high rocky cliff. It rises from the snowy mountains in that direction; is about thirty-five yards wide; has a bold, deep current; is skirted by some cottonwood and willow trees, and like the Yellowstone itself, seems to abound in beaver. They gave it the name of Shields's river, after one of the party. Immediately below is a very good buffalo road, which obviously leads from its head through a gap in the mountain, over to the waters of the Missouri. They passed Shields's river, and at three miles further, after crossing a high rocky hill, encamped in a low bottom, near the entrance of a small creek. As they came through the mountains they had seen two black bear and a number of antelopes, as well as several herds of elk, of between two and three hundred in number, but they were able to kill only a single elk.

JULY 16TH    *Wednesday*. The next morning, therefore, a hunter was despatched ahead, while the party collected the straggling horses. They then proceeded down the river, which is very straight, and has several islands covered with cottonwood and willow; but they could not procure a single tree large enough for a canoe, and being unwilling to trust altogether to skin canoes, captain Clark preferred going on until they found some timber. The feet of the horses were now nearly worn to the quick, particularly the hind feet, so that they were obliged to make a sort of moccasin of green buffalo skin, which relieved them very much in crossing the plains. After passing a bold creek from the south, of twenty yards in width, they halted for dinner on an island, then went on till at night they encamped near the entrance of another small stream, having made twenty-six miles during the day. They saw some bear and great numbers of antelopes and elks; but the soreness of their horses' feet rendered it difficult to chase them. One of the men caught a fish which they had not seen before; it was eight inches long, and resembled a trout in form, but its mouth was like that of the sturgeon, and it had a red streak passing on each side from the gills to the tail. In the plains were but few plants except the silk-grass, the wild indigo, and the sunflower, which are now all in bloom. The high grounds on the river are faced with a deep freestone rock, of a hard, sharp grit, which may also be seen in perpendicular strata throughout the plain.

JULY 17TH    *Thursday*. It rained during the night, and as the party had no covering but a buffalo skin, they rose drenched with water; and pursuing their journey at an early hour, over the point of a ridge, and through an open low bottom, reached at the distance of six and a half miles, a part of the river, where two large creeks enter immediately opposite to each other; one from the northwest, the other from the south of southwest. These captain Clark called

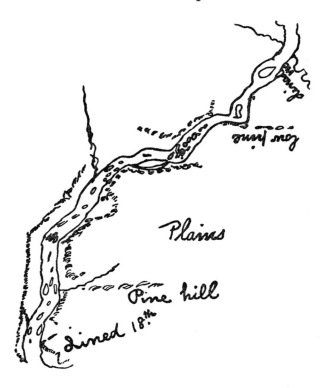

*Sketch-map of a stretch on the Yellowstone River, from Captain Clark's journal.*

512

Rivers-across. Ten miles and a half further they halted for dinner below the entrance of a large creek on the northeast side, about thirty yards in width, which they named Otter river. Nearly opposite to this is another, to which they gave the name of Beaver river. The waters of both are of a milky colour, and the banks well supplied with small timber. The river is now becoming more divided by islands, and a number of small creeks fall in on both sides. The largest of these is about seven miles from the Beaver river, and enters on the right: they called it Bratton's river, from one of the men. The highlands too approach the river more nearly than before, but although their sides are partially supplied with pine and cedar, the growth is still too small for canoes. The buffalo is beginning to be more abundant, and to-day, for the first time on this river, they saw a pelican; but deer and elk are now more scarce than before. In one of the low bottoms of the river was an Indian fort, which seems to have been built during the last summer. It was built in the form of a circle, about fifty feet in diameter, five feet high, and formed of logs, lapping over each other, and covered on the outside with bark set up on end. The entrance also was guarded by a work on each side of it, facing the river. These entrenchments, the squaw informs us, are frequently made by the Minnetarees and other Indians at war with the Shoshonees, when pursued by their enemies on horseback. After making thirty-three miles, they encamped near a point of woods in the narrow bottom of the river.

*Friday*. Before setting out they killed two buffalo, which ventured near the camp, and then pursued their route over the ridges of the highlands, so as to avoid the bends of the river, which now washes the feet of the hills. The face of the country is rough and stony, and covered with immense quantities of the prickly pear. The river is nearly two hundred yards wide, rapid as usual, and with a bed of coarse gravel and round stones. The same materials are the basis of the soil in the high bottoms, with a mixture of dark brown earth. The river hills are about two hundred feet high, and still faced with a dark freestone rock; and the country back of them broken into open waving plains. Pine is the only growth of importance; but among the smaller plants were distinguished the purple, yellow, and black currants, which are now ripe, and of an excellent flavour.

JULY 18TH

About eleven o'clock a smoke was descried to the S. S. E. towards the termination of the Rocky mountains, intended most probably, as a signal by the Crow Indians, who have mistaken us for their enemies, or as friends to trade with them. They could not however stop to ascertain the truth of this conjecture, but rode on, and after passing another old Indian fort, similar to that seen yesterday, halted for the night on a small island, twenty-six miles from their camp of last evening.

One of the hunters in attempting to mount his horse, after shooting a deer, fell on a small piece of timber, which ran nearly two inches into the muscular part of his thigh. The wound was very painful; and were it not for their great anxiety to reach the United States this season, the party would have remained till he was cured: but the time was too precious to wait. The gentlest and strongest horse was therefore selected, and a sort of litter formed in such a manner as to enable the sick man to lie nearly at full length. They then proceeded gently, and at the distance of two miles passed a river entering from the southeast side, about forty yards wide, and called by the Indians Itchkeppearja, or Rose river, a name which it deserves, as well from its beauty as from the roses which we saw budding on its borders. Soon after they passed another Indian fort on an island, and after making nine miles, halted to let the horses graze, and sent out a hunter to look for timber to make a canoe, and procure, if possible, some wild ginger to make a poultice for Gibson's thigh, which was now exceedingly painful, in consequence of his constrained position. He returned, however, without being able to find either; but brought back two bucks, and had had a contest with two white bears who had chased him; but being on horseback he escaped, after wounding both of them. There are great quantities of currants in the plains, but almost every blade of grass for many miles have been destroyed by immense swarms of grasshoppers, who appear to be ascending the river. After taking some refreshment they proceeded, and found that the hills became lower on both sides; those on the right overhanging the river in cliffs of a darkish yellow earth, and the bottoms widening to several miles in extent. The timber too, although chiefly cottonwood, is coming large.

They had not gone far when Gibson's wound became so violently painful that he could no longer remain on horseback. He was therefore left with two men under the shade of a tree, while captain Clark went on to seek for timber. At the distance of eighteen miles from his camp of last night he halted near a thick grove of trees, some of which were large enough for small canoes, and then searched all the adjacent country till evening, when Gibson was brought on to the camp. The game of to-day consisted of six deer, seven elk, and an antelope. The smoke which had been seen on the *17th*, was again distinguished this afternoon, and one of the party reported that he had observed an Indian on the highlands on the opposite side of the river.

JULY 20TH *Sunday*. The next morning at daylight, two good judges of timber were sent down the river in quest of lumber, but returned without being able to find any trees larger than those near the camp, nor could they procure any for axe-handles except chokecherry. Captain Clark determined therefore to make two canoes, which being lashed together, might be sufficient to convey the party down the river, while a few men might lead the horses to the Mandan nation. Three axes were now sharpened with a file, and some of the men proceeded to cut down two of the largest trees, on which they worked till night. The rest of the party were occupied in dressing skins for clothes, or in hunting, in which they were so fortunate as to procure a deer, two buffalo and an elk. The horses being much fatigued, they were turned out to rest for a few days; but in the morning, twenty-four of them were missing. Three hunters were sent in different directions to look for them; but all returned unsuccessful, and it now seemed probable that the Indians who had made the smoke a few days since, had stolen the horses. In the meantime the men worked so diligently on the canoes that one of them was nearly completed. Late in the evening, a very black cloud accompanied with thunder and lightning rose from the southeast, and rendered the weather extremely warm and disagreeable. The wind too was very high, but shifted towards morning to the northeast, and became moderately cool.

*Tuesday.* Three men were now despatched in quest of the horses, but they came back without being able to discover even a track, the plains being so hard and dry that the foot makes no impression. This confirms the suspicion of their being stolen by the Indians, who would probably take them across the plains, to avoid being pursued by their traces; besides, the improbability of their voluntarily leaving rushes and grass of the river bottoms to go on the plains, where they could find nothing but a short dry grass. Four men were again sent out with orders to encircle the camp for a great distance round, but they too returned with no better success than those who had preceded them.

*Wednesday.* The search was resumed in the morning, and a piece of a robe, and a moccasin, were discovered not far from the camp. The moccasin was worn out in the sole, and yet wet, and had every appearance of having been left but a few hours before. This sign was conclusive that the Indians had taken our horses, and were still prowling about for the remainder, who fortunately escaped last night, by being in a small prairie, surrounded by thick timber. At length Labiche, who is one of the best trackers, returned from a very wide circuit, and informed captain Clark that he had traced the tracks of the horses, which were bending their course rather down the river towards the open plains, and from the track, going very rapidly. All hopes of recovering them were now abandoned. The Indians are not the only plunderers who surround the camp, for last night the wolves or dogs stole the greater part of the dried meat from the scaffold. The wolves, which constantly attend the buffalo, are here in great numbers, for this seems to be the commencement of the buffalo country. Besides them, are seen antelopes, pigeons, doves, hawks, ravens, crows, larks, sparrows, eagles, bank-martins, &c. &c., great numbers of geese too, which raise their young on this river, have passed the camp. The country itself consists of beautiful level plains, but the soil is thin and stony, and both plains and low grounds are covered with great quantities of prickly pear.

At noon the two canoes were finished. They are twenty-eight feet long, sixteen or eighteen inches deep, and from sixteen to twenty-four inches wide, and being lashed together, every thing was prepared for setting out to-morrow; Gibson having now recovered. Sergeant Pryor was now directed with Shannon and Windsor, to take our horses to the Mandans, and if he found that Mr. Henry was on the Assiniboin river, to go thither and deliver him a letter, the object of which was to prevail on the most distinguished chiefs of the Sioux to accompany him to Washington.

THURSDAY, JULY 24TH, 1806  The canoes were loaded, and sergeant Pryor and his party set out with orders to proceed down to the entrance of the Bighorn river, which was supposed to be at no great distance, and where they should be taken in the boats across the Yellowstone. At eight o'clock captain Clark embarked in the little flotilla, and proceeded on very steadily down the river, which continues to be about two hundred yards wide, and contains a number of islands, some of which are supplied with a small growth of timber. At the distance of a mile from the camp, the river passes under a high bluff for about twenty-three miles, when the bottoms widen on both sides. At the distance of twenty-nine miles, a river falls in from the south. This was the river supposed to be the Bighorn; but afterwards, when the Bighorn was found, the name of Clark's fork was given to this stream. It is a bold river, one hundred and fifty yards wide at the entrance, but a short distance above, is contracted to a hundred yards. The water is of a light muddy colour, and much colder than that of the Yellowstone, and its general course is south and east of the Rocky mountains. There is a small island situated immediately at the entrance; and this or the adjoining main land would form a very good position for a fort. The country most frequented by the beaver begins here, and that which lies between this river and the Yellowstone is, perhaps, the best district for the hunters of that animal. About a mile before reaching this river, there is a ripple in the Yellowstone, on passing which the canoes took in some water. The party therefore landed to bail the boats, and then proceeded six miles further to a large island, where they halted for the purpose of waiting for sergeant Pryor.

It is a beautiful spot with a rich soil, covered with wild rye, and a species of grass like the blue-grass, and some of another kind, which the Indians wear in plaits round the neck, on account of a strong scent resembling that of the vanilla. There is also a thin growth of cottonwood scattered over the island. In the centre is a large Indian lodge which seems to have been built during the last summer. It is in the form of a cone, sixty feet in diameter at the base, composed of twenty poles, each forty-five feet long, and two and a half in circumference, and the whole structure covered with bushes. The interior was curiously ornamented. On the tops of the poles were feathers of eagles, and circular pieces of wood, with sticks across them in the form of a girdle: from the centre was suspended a stuffed buffalo skin: on the side fronting the door was hung a cedar bush: on one side of the lodge a buffalo's head; on the other several pieces of wood stuck in the ground. From its whole appearance, it was more like a lodge for holding councils, than an ordinary dwelling house.

Sergeant Pryor not having yet arrived, they went on about fifteen and a half miles further to a small creek on the right, to which they gave the name of Horse creek, and just below it overtook sergeant Pryor with the horses. He had found it almost impossible, with two men, to drive on the remaining horses, for as soon as they discovered a herd of buffalo the loose horses, having been trained by the Indians to hunt, immediately set off in pursuit of them, and surrounded the buffalo herd with almost as much skill as their riders could have done. At last he was obliged to send one horseman forward, and drive all the buffalo from the route. The horses were here driven across, and sergeant Pryor again proceeded with an additional man to his party. The river is now much more deep and navigable, and the current more regular than above Clark's fork, and although much divided by well-wooded islands, when collected, the stream is between two and three hundred feet in width. Along its banks are some beaver, and an immense number of deer, elk, and buffalo. Towards night they passed a creek from the southeast, thirty-five yards wide, which they called Pryor's creek; half a mile below which they encamped, after making sixty-nine and a half miles during the day.

*Friday.* At sunrise the next morning they resumed their voyage, and passed a number of islands and small streams, and occasionally high bluffs, composed of a yellow gritty stone. A storm of rain and high southwest wind soon overtook them, and obliged them to land and form a sort of log hut, covered with deer skins. As soon as it ceased they proceeded, and about four o'clock, after having made forty-nine miles, captain Clark landed to examine a very remarkable rock situated in an extensive bottom on the right, about two hundred and fifty paces from the shore. It is nearly four hundred paces in circumference, two hundred feet high, and accessible only from the northeast, the other sides being a perpendicular cliff of a light coloured gritty rock. The soil of the top is five or six feet deep, of a good quality, and covered with short grass. The Indians have carved the figures of animals and other objects on the sides of the rock, and on the top are raised two piles of stones.

From this height the eye ranged over a large extent of variegated country: On the southwest the Rocky mountains covered with snow; a low mountain, about forty miles distant, bearing south 15° east, and in a direction north 55° west; and at the distance of thirty-five miles, the southern extremity of what are called the Littlewolf mountains. The low grounds of the river extend nearly six miles to the southward, when they rise into plains reaching to the mountains, and watered with a large creek, while at some distance below a range of highland, covered with pine, stretches on both sides of the river, in a direction north and south. The north side of the river, for some distance, is surrounded by jutting romantic cliffs; these are succeeded by rugged hills, beyond which the plains are again open and extensive; and the whole country is enlivened by herds of buffalo, elk and wolves.

After enjoying the prospect from this rock, to which captain Clark gave the name of Pompey's pillar, he descended, and continued his course. At the distance of six or seven miles, he stopped to get two bighorns, which were shot from the boat; and while on shore, saw in the face of the cliff on the left, about twenty feet above the water, the fragment of a rib of a fish, three feet long, and nearly three inches round, incrusted in the rock itself, and though neither decayed nor petrified is very rotten. After making fifty-eight miles they reached the entrance of a stream on the right, about twenty-two yards wide, and which discharges a great quantity of muddy water. Here they encamped rather earlier than usual, on account of a heavy squall, accompanied with some rain.

*Saturday.* Early next morning they proceeded. The river is now much di- vided by stony islands and bars; but the current, though swift, is regular, and there are many handsome islands covered with cottonwood. On the left shore the bottoms are very extensive; the right bank is formed of high cliffs of a whitish gritty stone; and beyond these, the country on both sides is diversified with waving plains, covered with pine. At the distance of ten miles is a large creek on the right, about forty yards in width, but containing very little water; and in the course of the day, two smaller streams on the left, and a fourth on the right. At length, after coming sixty-two miles, they landed at the entrance of the Bighorn river; but finding the point between the two composed of soft mud and sand, and liable to be overflowed, they ascended the Bighorn for half a mile, then crossed and formed a camp on its lower side. Captain Clark then walked up the river.

At the distance of seven miles, a creek, twenty yards wide, which from the colour of the water he called Muddy creek, falls in on the northeast, and a few miles further, the river bends to the east of south. The bottoms of the river are extensive, and supplied chiefly with cottonwood trees, variegated with great quantities of rosebushes. The current is regular and rapid; and like the Missouri, constantly changes so as to wash away the banks on one side, leaving sandbars on the other. Its bed contains much less of the large gravel than that of the Yellowstone, and its water is more muddy, and of a brownish colour, while the Yellowstone has a lighter tint. At the junction, the two rivers are nearly equal in breadth, extending from two hundred to two hundred and twenty yards, but the Yellowstone contains much more water, being ten or twelve feet deep, while the depth of the Bighorn varies from five to seven feet. This is the river which had been described by the Indians as rising in the Rocky mountains, near the Yellowstone, and the sources of the river Platte, and then finds its way through the Côte Noir, and the eastern range of the Rocky mountains. In its long course it receives two large rivers, one from the north and the other from the south, and being unobstructed by falls, is navigable in canoes for a great distance, through a fine rich open country, supplied with a great quantity of timber, and inhabited by beaver, and by numerous species of animals, among which are those from which it derives the name of Bighorn. There are no permanent settlements near it; but the whole country which it waters, is occasionally visited by roving bands of hunters from the Crow tribe, the Paunch, a band of Crows, and the Castahana, a small band of Snake Indians.

JULY 27TH   *Sunday.* They again set out very early, and on leaving the Bighorn, took a last look at the Rocky mountains, which had been constantly in view from the first of May. The river now widens to the extent of from four to six hundred yards; is much divided by islands and sandbars; its banks generally low and falling in, and resembles the Missouri in many particulars; but its islands are more numerous, its waters less muddy, and the current more rapid. The water too is of a yellowish-white, and the round stones, which form the bars above the Bighorn, have given place to gravel. On the left side the river runs under cliffs of light, soft, gritty stone, varying in height from seventy to an hundred feet, behind which are level and extensive plains. On the right side of the river are low extensive bottoms, bordered with cottonwood, various species of willow, rosebushes, grape-vines, the redberry or buffalo-grease bushes, and a species of sumac; to these succeed high grounds, supplied with pine, and still further on are level plains. Throughout the country are vast quantities of buffalo, which, as this is the running season, keep a continued bellowing. Large herds of elk also are lying in every point, and are so gentle that they may be approached within twenty paces without being alarmed. Several beaver were seen in the course of the day; indeed, there is a greater appearance of those animals than there was above the Bighorn. Deer, however, are by no means abundant, and the antelopes, as well as the bighorns, are scarce.

Fifteen miles from the Bighorn river they passed a large dry creek on the left, to which they gave the name of Elk creek, and halted for breakfast about three miles further, at the entrance of Windsor's river, a stream from the left, which though fifty yards wide, contains scarcely any water. Forty-eight miles from the Bighorn is a large bed of a stream sixty yards wide, but with very little water. They called it Labiche's river. Several other smaller streams, or rather beds of creeks, were passed in the course of the day, and after coming eighty and a half miles, they encamped on a large island.

*Monday.* At daylight the next morning they proceeded down the smooth JULY 28TH gentle current, passing by a number of islands and several creeks, which are now dry. These are, indeed, more like torrents, and like the dry brooks of the Missouri, merely serve to carry off the vast quantities of water which fall in the plains, and bring them also a great deal of mud, which contributes to the muddiness of the Yellowstone. The most distinguished of these are at the distance of six miles, a creek of eighty yards in width, from the northwest, and called by the Indians, Littlewolf river: twenty-nine miles lower another on the left, seventy yards in width, which they call Table creek, from several mounds in the plains to the northwest, the tops of which resemble a table. Four miles further a stream of more importance enters behind an island from the south. It is about one hundred yards in width, with a bold current of muddy water, and is probably the river called by the Indians the Little Bighorn; and another stream on the right, twenty-five yards wide, the Indian name of which is Mashaskap. Nearly opposite to this creek they encamped after making seventy-three miles. The river during part of the route is confined by cliffs, which on the right are of a soft, yellowish, gritty rock, while those on the left are harder, and of a lighter colour. In some of these cliffs were several stratas of coal of different thickness and heights above the water; but like that of the Missouri, is of an inferior quality.

*Tuesday.* During the night there was a storm of thunder and lightning, JULY 29TH with some rain, a high northeast wind, which continued during the morning, and prevented the party from making more than forty-one miles. The country resembles that passed yesterday; the dry beds of rivers continue, and large quantities of coal are seen in the sides of the cliffs. The river itself is now between five hundred yards and half a mile in width, and has more sand and bars of gravel than above. The beaver are in great numbers; and in the course of the day some catfish and a soft-shelled turtle were procured. In the evening they encamped on the left, opposite to the entrance of a stream, called by the Indians Lazeka, or Tongue river. This stream rises in the Côte Noir, and is formed of two branches, one having its sources with the heads of the Chayenne, the other with one of the branches of the Bighorn. It has a very wide bed, and a channel of water a hundred and fifty yards wide, but the water is of a light brown colour, very muddy, and nearly milk-warm. It is shallow, and its rapid current throws out great quantities of mud and some coarse gravel. Near the mouth is a large proportion of timber, but the warmth of the water would seem to indicate that the country through which it passed was open and without shade.

JULY 30TH    *Wednesday.* They set out at an early hour, and after passing, at the distance of twelve miles, the bed of a river one hundred yards wide, but nearly dry at present, reached two miles below it a succession of bad shoals, interspersed with a hard, dark brown, gritty rock, extending for six miles, the last of which stretches nearly across the river, and has a descent of about three feet. At this place they were obliged to let the canoes down with the hand, for fear of their splitting on a concealed rock; though when the shoals are known a large canoe could with safety pass through the worst of them. This is the most difficult part of the whole Yellowstone river, and was called the Buffalo shoals, from the circumstance of one of those animals being found in them. The neighbouring cliffs on the right are about one hundred feet high; on the left the country is low, but gradually rises, and at some distance from the shore present the first appearance of burnt hills which have been seen on the Yellowstone. Below the Buffalo shoals the river is contracted to the width of three or four hundred yards, the islands less numerous, and a few scattering trees only are seen either on its banks or on the highlands: twenty miles from those shoals is a rapid, caused by a number of rocks strewed over the river; but though the waves are high, there is a very good channel on the left, which renders the passage secure. There was a bear standing on one of these rocks, which occasioned the name of the Bear rapid. As they were descending this rapid a violent storm from the northwest obliged them to take refuge in an old Indian lodge near the mouth of a river on the left, which has lately been very high, has widened to the distance of a quarter of a mile, but though its present channel is eighty-eight yards wide, there is not more water in it than would easily pass through a hole of an inch in diameter. It was called York's dry river.

    As soon as the rain and wind had abated, they resumed their journey, and at seven miles encamped under a spreading cottonwood tree on the left side, after making forty-eight miles. A mile and a half above on the opposite side is a river containing one hundred yards width of water, though the bed itself is much wider. The water is very muddy, and like its banks of a dark brown colour. Its current throws out great quantities of red stones; and this circumstance, with the appearance of the distant hills, induced captain Clark to call it the Redstone, which he afterwards found to be the meaning of its Indian name, Wahasah.

JULY 31ST    *Thursday.* During the whole night the buffalo were prowling about the camp, and excited much alarm, lest in crossing the river they should tread on the boats and split them to pieces. They set out as usual, and at the distance of two miles passed a rapid of no great danger, which they called Wolf rapid, from seeing a wolf in them. At this place commences a range of highlands. These highlands have no timber, and are composed of earth of different colours, without much rock, but supplied throughout with great quantities of coal, or carbonated wood. After passing these hills the country again opens into extensive plains, like those passed yesterday, and the river is diversified with islands, and partially supplied with water by a great number of wide, but nearly dry brooks. Thus eighteen miles below the camp is a shallow, muddy stream on the left, one hundred yards wide, and supposed to be that known among the Indians by the name of Saasha, or Littlewolf river: five miles below on the right side is another river, forty yards wide, and four feet in depth, which, from the steep coal banks on each side, they called Oaktaroup, or Coal river; and at eighteen miles further a third stream of sixty yards in width, to which they gave the name of Gibson's river. Having made sixty-six miles, they halted for the night, and just as they landed, saw the largest white bear that any of the party had ever before seen, devouring a dead buffalo on a sandbar. They fired two balls into him, and he then swam to the main land and walked along the shore. Captain Clark pursued him, and lodged two more balls in his body; but though he bled profusely he made his escape, as night prevented them from following him.

## Friday, August 1st, 1806

The next day a high wind from ahead made the water rough, and retarded their progress, and as it rained during the whole day, their situation in the open boats was very disagreeable. The country bears in every respect the same appearance as that of yesterday, though there is some ash timber in the bottom, and low pine and cedar on the sides of the hills. The current of the river is less rapid, has more soft mud, and is more obstructed by sandbars, and the rain has given an unusual quantity of water to the brooks. The buffalo now appear in vast numbers. A herd happened to be on their way across the river. Such was the multitude of these animals, that although the river, including an island, over which they passed was a mile in length, the herd stretched as thick as they could swim, completely from one side to the other, and the party was obliged to stop for an hour. They consoled themselves for the delay by killing four of the herd, and then proceeded till at the distance of forty-five miles on an island, below which two other herds of buffalo, as numerous as the first, soon after crossed the river.

*Saturday.* The river is now about a mile wide, less rapid, and more divided by islands and bars of sand and mud than hitherto: the low grounds too are more extensive, and contain a greater quantity of cottonwood, ash, and willow trees. On the northwest is a low, level plain; on the southeast some rugged hills, on which we saw, without being able to approach, some of the bighorns. The buffalo and elk, as well as the pursuers of both, the wolves, are in great numbers. On each side of the river are several dry brooks; but the only stream of any size is that they called Ibex river, on the right, about thirty yards wide, and sixteen miles from the camp. The bear which gave so much trouble on the head of the Missouri, are equally fierce in this quarter. This morning one of them, which was on a sandbar as the boat passed, raised himself on his hind feet, and after looking at the party, plunged in and swam towards them. He was received with three balls in the body; he then turned round and made for the shore. Towards evening another entered the water to swim across. Captain Clark ordered the boat towards the shore, and just as the bear landed, shot the animal in the head. It proved to be the largest female they had ever seen, and so old that its tusks were worn quite smooth. The boats escaped with difficulty between two herds of buffalo, which were crossing the river, and would probably have again detained the party. Among the elk of this neighbourhood are an unusual number of males, while higher up the river the numerous herds consist of females chiefly. After making eighty-four miles, they encamped among some ash and elm trees on the right. They, however, rather passed the night than slept there, for the mosquitoes were so troublesome, that scarcely any of the party could close their eyes during the greater part of the time.

AUGUST 3D *Sunday*. They therefore set out early in the morning to avoid the persecution of those insects. At the distance of two miles they passed Fields's creek, a stream thirty-five yards wide, which enters on the right, immediately above a high bluff, which is rapidly sinking into the river. Here captain Clark went ashore in pursuit of some bighorns, but the mosquitoes were so numerous, that he was unable to shoot with certainty. He therefore returned to the canoes: and soon after observing a ram of the same animals, sent one of the hunters, who shot it, and it was preserved entire as a specimen. About two o'clock they reached, eight miles below Fields's creek, the junction of the Yellowstone with the Missouri, and formed a camp on the point where they had encamped on the *26th of April, 1805*. The canoes were now unloaded, and the baggage exposed to dry, as many of the articles were wet, and some of them spoiled.

The Rochejaune, or Yellowstone river, according to Indian information, has its remote sources in the Rocky mountains, near the peaks of the Rio del Norde, on the confines of New Mexico, to which country there is a good road during the whole distance along the banks of the Yellowstone. Its western waters are probably connected with those of Lewis's river, while the eastern branches approach the heads of Clark's river, the Bighorn, and the Platte; so that it waters the middle portion of the Rocky mountains for several hundred miles from northwest to southeast. During its whole course from the point at which captain Clark reached it to the Missouri, a distance which he computed at eight hundred and thirty-seven miles, this river is large and navigable for periogues, and even batteaux, there being none of the moving sandbars which impede the navigation of the Missouri, and only a single ledge of rocks, which, however, is not difficult to pass. Even its tributary waters, the Bighorn, Clark's fork, and Tongue river, may be ascended in boats for a considerable distance. The banks of the river are low, but bold, and nowhere subject to be overflowed, except for a short distance below the mountains. The predominating colour of the river is a yellowish-brown; that of the Missouri, which possesses more mud, is of a deep drab colour; the bed of the former being chiefly composed of loose pebble; which, however, diminish in size in descending the river, till after passing the Lazeka, the pebble cease as the river widens, and the mud and sand continue to form the greater part of the bottom. Over these the water flows with a velocity constantly and almost equally decreasing in proportion to its distance from the mountains. From the mountains to Clark's fork, the current may be estimated at four and a half miles per hour; thence as low as the Bighorn, at three and a half miles; between that and the Lazeka at three miles; and from that river to the Wolf rapid, at two and three quarter miles; from which to its entrance, the general rapidity is two miles per hour. The appearance and character of the country present nearly similar varieties of fertile, rich, open lands. Above Clark's fork, it consists of high waving plains bordered by stony hills, partially supplied with pine; the middle portion, as low as the Buffalo shoals, contains less timber, and the number diminishes still lower, where the river widens, and the country spreads itself into extensive plains.

Like all the branches of the Missouri which penetrate the Rocky mountains, the Yellowstone and its streams, within that district of country beyond Clark's fork, abound in beaver and otter; a circumstance which strongly recommends the entrance of the latter river as a judicious position for the purposes of trade. To an establishment at that place, the Shoshonees, both within and westward of the Rocky mountains, would willingly resort, as they would be farther from the reach of the Blackfoot Indians, and the Minnetarees of Fort de Prairie, than they could be in trading with any factories on the Missouri. The same motive of personal safety, would most probably induce many of the tribes on the Columbia and Lewis's river to prefer this place to the entrance of Maria's river, at least for some years; and as the Crow and Paunch Indians, the Castahanahs, and the Indians residing south of Clark's fork, would also be induced to visit it, the mouth of that river might be considered as one of the most important establishments for the western fur trade. This too may be the more easily effected, as the adjacent country possesses a sufficiency of timber for the purpose, an advantage which is not found on any spot between Clark's fork and the Rocky mountains.

*Monday.* The camp became absolutely uninhabitable, in consequence of the multitude of mosquitoes; the men could not work in preparing skins for clothing, nor hunt in the timbered low grounds; in short, there was no mode of escape, except by going on the sandbars in the river; where, if the wind should blow, the insects do not venture; but when there is no wind, and particularly at night, when the men have no covering except their worn-out blankets, the pain they suffer is scarcely to be endured. There was also a want of meat, for the buffalo were not to be found; and though the elk are very abundant, yet their fat and flesh is more difficult to dry in the sun, and is also much more easily spoiled than the meat or fat of either deer or buffalo. Captain Clark therefore determined to go on to some spot which should be free from mosquitoes, and furnish more game. After having written a note to captain Lewis, to inform him of his intention, and stuck it on a pole, at the confluence of the two rivers, he loaded the canoes at five in the afternoon, and proceeded down the river to the second point and encamped on a sandbar; but here the mosquitoes seemed to be even more numerous than above. The face of the Indian child is considerably puffed up and swollen with the bites of these animals, nor could the men procure scarcely any sleep during the night, and they continued to harass them the next morning as they proceeded.

AUGUST 4TH

*Tuesday.* On one occasion captain Clark went on shore and ascended a hill after one of the bighorns; but the mosquitoes were in such multitudes that he could not keep them from the barrel of his rifle long enough to take aim.

AUGUST 5TH

About ten o'clock, however, a light breeze sprung up from the northwest, and dispersed them in some degree. Captain Clark then landed on a sandbar, intending to wait for captain Lewis, and went out to hunt. But not finding any buffalo, he again proceeded in the afternoon, and having killed a large white bear, encamped under a high bluff exposed to a light breeze from the southwest, which blew away the mosquitoes. About eleven o'clock, however, the wind became very high and a storm of rain came on, which lasted for two hours, accompanied with sharp lightning and loud peals of thunder.

AUGUST 6TH  *Wednesday*. They therefore rose, very wet, and proceeded to a sandbar below the entrance of Whiteearth river. Just above this place, the Indians had, apparently within seven or eight days past, been digging a root which they employ in making a kind of soup. Having fixed their tents, the men were employed in dressing skins and hunting. They shot a number of deer; but only two of them were fat, owing probably to the great quantities of mosquitoes who annoy them whilst feeding. The next day, after some severe rain, they proceeded at eleven o'clock, through intervals of rain and high wind till six in the evening, when they encamped on a sandbar. Here they had a very violent wind, for two hours, which left the air clear and cold, so that the mosquitoes completely disappeared.

AUGUST 8TH  *Friday*. On the following morning, sergeant Pryor, accompanied by Shannon, Hall, and Windsor, arrived, but without the horses. They reported that on the second day after they left captain Clark, they halted to let the horses graze near the bed of a large creek, which contained no running water; but soon after a shower of rain fell, and the creek swelled so suddenly, that several horses which had straggled across the dry bed of the creek, were obliged to swim back. They now determined to form their camp; but the next morning were astonished at not being able to find a single one of their horses. They immediately examined the neighbourhood, and soon finding the track of the Indians who had stolen the horses, pursued them for five miles, where the fugitives divided into two parties. They now followed the largest party five miles further, till they lost all hopes of overtaking the Indians, and returned to the camp; and packing the baggage on their backs, pursued a northeast course towards the Yellowstone. On the following night a wolf bit sergeant Pryor through the hand as he lay asleep, and made an attempt to seize Windsor, when Shannon discovered and shot him. They passed over a broken open country, and having reached the Yellowstone near Pompey's pillar, they determined to descend the river, and for this purpose made two skin canoes, such as they had seen among the Mandans and Ricaras. They are made in the following manner:—Two sticks of an inch and a quarter in diameter are tied together so as to form a round hoop, which serves for the brim, while a second hoop, for the bottom of the boat, is made in the same way, and both secured by sticks of the same size from the sides of the hoops, fastened by thongs at the edges of the hoops and at the interstices of the sticks: over this frame the skin is drawn closely and tied with thongs, so as to form a perfect basin, seven feet and three inches in diameter, sixteen inches deep, and with sixteen ribs or cross-sticks, and capable of carrying six or eight men with their loads. Being unacquainted with the river, they thought it most prudent to divide their guns and ammunition, so that in case of accident all might not be lost, and therefore built two canoes. In these frail vessels they embarked, and were surprised at the perfect security in which they passed through the most difficult shoals and rapids of the river, without ever taking in water, even during the highest winds.

In passing the confluence of the Yellowstone and Missouri, he took down the note from the pole, supposing that captain Lewis had passed; and now learning where the party was, pressed on in the skin canoes to join them. The day was spent in hunting, so as to procure a number of skins to trade with the Mandans; for having now neither horses nor merchandise, our only resort in order to obtain corn and beans, is a stock of skins, which those Indians very much admire.

*Saturday.* A heavy dew fell this morning. Captain Clark now proceeded slowly down the river, hunting through the low grounds in the neighbourhood after the deer and elk, till late in the afternoon he encamped on the southeast side. Here they remained during the next day, *Sunday, 10th*, attempting to dry the meat, while the hunters were all abroad; but they could obtain nothing except an antelope and one black-tailed deer; those animals being very scarce on this part of the river. In the low grounds of the river captain Clark found to-day a species of cherry which he had never seen before, and which seems peculiar to this small district of country, though even there it is not very abundant.

The men also dug up quantities of a large and very insipid root, called by the Indians hankee, and by the engagées, the white apple. It is used by them in a dry and pounded state, so as to mix with their soup; but our men boiled it and eat it with meat. In descending the river yesterday, the squaw brought in a large well-flavoured gooseberry, of a rich crimson colour; and a deep purple berry of a species of currant, common on this river as low as the Mandans, and called by the engagées, the Indian currant.

*Monday.* The next morning captain Clark set out early, and landed on a sandbar about ten o'clock for the purpose of taking breakfast and drying the meat. At noon they proceeded on about two miles, when they observed a canoe near the shore. They immediately landed, and were equally surprised and pleased at discovering two men by the names of Dickson and Hancock, who had come from the Illinois on a hunting excursion up the Yellowstone. They had left the Illinois in the summer of 1804, and had spent the last winter with the Tetons, in company with a Mr. Ceautoin, who had come there as a trader, but whom they had robbed, or rather they had taken all his merchandise and given him a few robes in exchange. These men had met the boat which we had despatched from fort Mandan, on board of which they were told there was a Ricara chief on his way to Washington; and also another party of Yankton chiefs, accompanying Mr. Durion on a visit of the same kind. We were sorry to learn that the Mandans and Minnetarees were at war with the Ricaras, and had killed two of them. The Assiniboins too, are at war with the Mandans. They have, in consequence, prohibited the Northwestern company from trading to the Missouri, and even killed two of their traders near the Mouse river, and are now lying in wait for Mr. M'Kenzie of the Northwestern company, who had been for a long time

525

among the Minnetarees. These appearances are rather unfavourable to the project of carrying some of the chiefs to the United States; but we still hope, that by effecting a peace between the Mandans, Minnetarees, and Ricaras, the views of our government may be accomplished.

After leaving these trappers, captain Clark went on and encamped nearly opposite the entrance of Goatpen creek, where the party were again assailed by their old enemies, the mosquitoes.

TUESDAY, AUGUST 12TH, 1806   The party continued slowly to descend the river. One of the skin canoes was by accident pierced with a small hole, and they halted for the purpose of mending it with a piece of elk skin, and also to wait for two of the party who were behind. Whilst there, they were overjoyed at seeing captain Lewis's boats heave in sight about noon. But this feeling was changed into alarm on seeing the boats reach the shore without captain Lewis, who they then learnt had been wounded the day before, and was then lying in the periogue. After giving to his wound all the attention in our power, we remained here some time, during which we were overtaken by our two men, accompanied by Dickson and Hancock, who wished to go with us as far as the Mandans. The whole party being now happily reunited, we left the two skin canoes, and all embarked together, about 3 o'clock, in the boats. The wind was however very high from the southwest, accompanied with rain, so that we did not go far before we halted for the night on a sandbar. Captain Lewis's wound was now sore and somewhat painful.

*Wednesday.* The next day they set out by sunrise, and having a very strong breeze from the northwest, proceeded on rapidly. At eight o'clock we passed the mouth of the Little Missouri. Some Indians were seen at a distance below in a skin canoe, and were probably some of the Minnetarees on their return from a hunting excursion, as we passed one of their camps on the southwest side, where they had left a canoe. Two other Indians were seen far off on one of the hills, and we shall therefore soon meet with our old acquaintances the Mandans. At sunset we arrived at the entrance of Miry river, and encamped on the northeast side, having come by the assistance of the wind and our oars, a distance of eighty-six miles. The air was cool, and the mosquitoes ceased to trouble us as they had done.   AUGUST 13TH

*Thursday.* We again set out at sunrise, and at length approached the grand village of the Minnetarees, where the natives had collected to view us as we passed. We fired the blunderbuss several times by way of salute, and soon after landed at the bank near the village of the Mahahas, or Shoe Indians, and were received by a crowd of people, who came to welcome our return. Among these were the principal chief of the Mahahas, and the chief of the Little Minnetaree village, both of whom expressed great pleasure at seeing us again; but the latter wept most bitterly. On inquiry, it appeared that his tears were excited because the sight of us reminded him of his son, who had been lately killed by the Blackfoot Indians.   AUGUST 14TH

After remaining there a few minutes, we crossed to the Mandan village of the Blackcat, where all the inhabitants seemed very much pleased at seeing us. We immediately sent Chaboneau with an invitation for the Minnetarees to visit us, and despatched Drewyer to the lower village of the Mandans to bring Jesseaume as an interpreter. Captain Clark, in the meantime, walked up to the village of the Blackcat, and smoked and eat with the chief. This village has been rebuilt since our departure, and was now much smaller; a quarrel having arisen among the Indians, in consequence of which a number of families had removed to the opposite side of the river. On the arrival of Jesseaume, captain Clark addressed the chiefs. We spoke to them now, he said, in the same language we had done before; and repeated his invitation to accompany him to the United States, to hear in person the counsels of their great father, who can at all times protect those who open their ears to his counsels, and punish his enemies. The Blackcat [Poscopsahe] in reply, declared that he wished to visit the United States, and see his great father, but was afraid of the Sioux, who had killed several of the Mandans since our departure, and who were now on the river below, and would intercept him if he attempted to go. Captain Clark endeavoured to quiet his apprehensions by assuring him that he would not suffer the Sioux to injure one of our red children who should accompany us, and that they should return loaded with presents, and protected at the expense of the United States.

The council was then broken up, after which we crossed and formed our camp on the other side of the river, where we should be sheltered from the rain. Soon after the chief of the Mahahas informed us, that if we would send to his village, we should have some corn. Three men were therefore despatched, and soon after returned loaded with as much as they could carry; and were soon followed by the chief and his wife, to whom we presented a few needles and other articles fit for women.

In a short time the Borgne (the great chief of all the Minnetarees) came down, attended by several other chiefs, to whom, after smoking a pipe, captain Clark now made a harangue, renewing his assurances of friendship and the invitation to go with us to Washington. He was answered by the Borgne, who began by declaring that he much desired to visit his great father, but that the Sioux would certainly kill any of the Mandans who should attempt to go down the river. They were bad people, and would not listen to any advice. When he saw us last, we had told him that we had made peace with all the nations below, yet the Sioux had since killed eight of his tribe, and stolen a number of their horses. The Ricaras too had stolen their horses, and in the contest his people had killed two of the Ricaras. Yet in spite of these dispositions he had always had his ears open to our counsels, and had actually made a peace with the Chayennes and the Indians of the Rocky mountains. He concluded by saying, that however disposed they were to visit the United States, the fear of the Sioux would prevent them from going with us. The council was then finished, and soon afterwards an invitation was received from the Blackcat, who, on captain Clark's arrival at his village, presented him with a dozen bushels of corn, which he said was a large proportion of what his people owned; and after smoking a pipe, declared that his people were too apprehensive of the Sioux to venture with us.

Captain Clark then spoke to the chiefs and warriors of the village. He told them of his anxiety that some of them should see their great father, and hear his good words and receive his gifts, and requested them to fix on some confidential chief who might accompany us. To this they made the same objections as before, till at length a young man offered to go, and the warriors all assented to it. But the character of this man was known to be bad, and one of the party with captain Clark informed him that at the moment he had in his possession a knife which he had stolen. Captain Clark therefore told the chief of this theft, and ordered the knife to be given up. This was done with a poor apology for having it in his possession, and captain Clark then reproached the chiefs for wishing to send such a fellow to see and hear so distinguished a person as their great father. They all hung down their heads for some time, till the Blackcat apologised by saying, that the danger was such that they were afraid of sending any of their chiefs, as they considered his loss almost inevitable. Captain Clark remained some time with them, smoking and relating various particulars of his journey, and then left them to visit the second chief of the Mandans (or the Black-crow) [Kagohami, or Little Raven], who had expressed some disposition to accompany us. He seemed well inclined to the journey, but was unwilling to decide till he had called a council of his people, which he intended to do in the afternoon. On returning to the camp, he found the chief of the Mahahas, and also the chief of the Little Minnetaree village, who brought a present of corn on their mules, of which they possess several, and which they procure from the Crow Indians, who either buy or steal them on the frontiers of the Spanish settlements. A great number of the Indians visited us for the purpose of renewing their acquaintance, or of exchanging robes or other articles for the skins brought by the men.

In the evening we were applied to by one of our men, Colter, who was desirous of joining the two trappers who had accompanied us, and who now proposed an expedition up the river, in which they were to find traps and give him a share of the profits. The offer was a very advantageous one, and as he had always performed his duty, and his services might be dispensed with, we agreed that he might go, provided none of the rest would ask or expect a similar indulgence. To this they cheerfully answered, that they wished Colter every success, and would not apply for liberty to separate before we reached St. Louis. We, therefore, supplied him, as did his comrades also, with powder and lead, and a variety of articles which might be useful to him, and he left us the next day. The example of this man shows how easily men may be weaned from the habits of a civilised life to the ruder, but scarcely less fascinating manners of the woods. This hunter has been now absent for many years from the frontiers, and might naturally be presumed to have some anxiety, or some curiosity at least to return to his friends and his country; yet just at the moment when he is approaching the frontiers, he is tempted by a hunting scheme, to give up those delightful prospects, and go back without the least reluctance to the solitude of the woods.

In the evening Chaboneau, who had been mingling with the Indians, and had learned what had taken place during our absence, informed us, that as soon as we had left the Minnetarees, they sent out a war party against the Shoshonees, whom they attacked and routed, though in the engagement they lost two men, one of whom was the son of the chief of the Little Minnetaree village. Another war party had gone against the Ricaras, two of whom they killed. A misunderstanding too had taken place between the Mandans and Minnetarees, in consequence of a dispute about a woman, which had nearly occasioned a war; but at length a pipe was presented by the Minnetarees, and a reconciliation took place.

*Saturday.* The Mandans had offered to give us corn, and on sending this morning, we found a greater quantity collected for our use than all our canoes would contain. We therefore thanked the chief and took only six loads. At ten o'clock the chiefs of the different villages came down to smoke with us. We therefore took this opportunity of endeavouring to engage the Borgne in our interests by a present of the swivel, which is no longer serviceable, as it cannot be discharged from our largest periogue. It was now loaded, and the chiefs being formed into a circle round it, captain Clark addressed them with great ceremony. He said that he had listened with much attention to what had yesterday been declared by the Borgne, whom he believed to be sincere, and then reproached them with their disregard of our counsels, and their wars on the Shoshonees and Ricaras. Littlecherry, the old Minnetaree chief, answered that they had long stayed at home and listened to our advice, but at last went to war against the Sioux because their horses had been stolen, and their companions killed; and that in an expedition against those people, they had met the Ricaras, who were on their way to strike them, and a battle ensued. But in future he said they would attend to our words and live at peace. The Borgne added, that his ears too would always be open to the words of his good father, and shut against bad counsel. Captain Clark then presented to the Borgne the swivel, which he told him had announced the words of his great father to all the nations we had seen, and which, whenever it was fired, should recall those which we had delivered to him. The gun was then discharged, and the Borgne had it conveyed in great pomp to his village. The council was then adjourned.

In the afternoon captain Clark walked up to the village of the Littlecrow, taking a flag, which he intended to present to him, but was surprised on being told by him, that he had given over all intention of accompanying us, and refused the flag. He found that this was occasioned by a jealousy between him and the principal chief, Bigwhite [Sheheke]; on the interference, however, of Jesseaume, the two chiefs were reconciled, and it was agreed that the Bigwhite himself should accompany us with his wife and son.

AUGUST 17TH  *Sunday.* The principal chiefs of the Minnetarees came down to bid us farewell, as none of them could be prevailed on to go with us. This circumstance induced our interpreter, Chaboneau, with his wife and child, to remain here, as he could be no longer useful; and notwithstanding our offers of taking him with us to the United States, he said that he had there no acquaintance, and no chance of making a livelihood, and preferred remaining among the Indians. This man has been very serviceable to us, and his wife particularly useful among the Shoshonees. Indeed, she has borne with a patience truly admirable, the fatigues of so long a route, incumbered with the charge of an infant, who is even now only nineteen months old. We therefore paid him his wages, amounting to five hundred dollars and thirty-three cents, including the price of a horse and a lodge purchased of him; and soon afterwards dropped down to the village of the Bigwhite, attended on shore by all the Indian chiefs who went to take leave of him.

We found him surrounded by his friends, who sat in a circle smoking, while the women were crying. He immediately sent his wife and son, with their baggage, on board, accompanied by the interpreter and his wife, and two children; and then after distributing among his friends some powder and ball, which we had given to him, and smoking a pipe with us, went with us to the river side. The whole village crowded about us, and many of the people wept aloud at the departure of the chief. As captain Clark was shaking hands with the principal chiefs of all the villages, they requested that he would sit with them one moment longer. Being willing to gratify them, he stopped and ordered a pipe, after smoking which, they informed

530

HUNTING THE BISON (Bodmer)

him that when they first saw us, they did not believe all that we then told them; but having now seen that our words were all true, they would carefully remember them, and follow our advice; that he might tell their great father that the young men should remain at home and not make war on any people except in defence of themselves. They requested him to tell the Ricaras to come and visit them without fear, as they meant that nation no harm, but were desirous of peace with them. On the Sioux, however, they had no dependence, and must kill them whenever they made war parties against their country.

Captain Clark, in reply, informed them that we had never insisted on their not defending themselves, but requested only that they would not strike those whom we had taken by the hand; that we would apprise the Ricaras of their friendly intentions, and that, although we had not seen those of the Sioux with whom they were at war, we should relate their conduct to their great father, who would take measures for producing a general peace among all his red children. The Borgne now requested that we would take good care of this chief, who would report whatever their great father should say; and the council being then broken up, we took leave with a salute from a gun, and then proceeded.

On reaching fort Mandan, we found a few pickets standing on the river side, but all the houses except one, had been burnt by an accidental fire. At the distance of eighteen miles we reached the old Ricara village, where we encamped on the southwest side, the wind being too violent, and the waves too high to permit us to go any further. The same cause prevented us from setting out before eight o'clock the next day.

*Monday.* Soon after we embarked, an Indian came running down to the beach, who appeared very anxious to speak to us. We went ashore, and found it was the brother of the Bigwhite, who was encamped at no great distance, and hearing of our departure, came to take leave of the chief. The Bigwhite gave him a pair of leggings, and they separated in a most affectionate manner; and we then continued though the wind and waves were still high. The Indian chief seems quite satisfied with his treatment, and during the whole of his time was employed in pointing out the ancient monuments of the Mandans, or in relating their traditions. At length, after making forty miles, we encamped on the northeast side, opposite an old Mandan village, and below the mouth of Chesshetah river.

*Tuesday.* The wind was so violent that we were not able to proceed until four in the afternoon, during which time the hunters killed four elk and twelve deer. We then went on for ten miles, and came to on a sandbar. The rain and wind continued through the night, and during the whole of the next day, the waves were so high, that one man was constantly occupied in bailing the boats. We passed at noon, Cannonball river; and at three in the afternoon, the entrance of the river Wardepon, the boundary of the country claimed by the Sioux; and after coming eighty-one miles, passed the night on a sandbar. The plains are beginning to change their appearance, the grass becoming of a yellow colour. We have seen great numbers of wolves to-day, and some buffalo and elk, though these are by no means so abundant as on the Yellowstone.

531

Since we passed in 1804, a very obvious change has taken place in the current and appearance of the Missouri. In places where at that time there were sandbars, the current of the river now passes, and the former channel of the river is in turn a bank of sand. Sandbars then naked, are covered with willows several feet high: the entrance of some of the creeks and rivers changed in consequence of the quantity of mud thrown into them; and in some of the bottoms are layers of mud eight inches in depth.

AUGUST 21ST  *Thursday.* We rose after a night of broken rest, owing to the mosquitoes, and having put our arms in order, so as to be prepared for an attack, continued our course. We soon met three traders, two of whom had wintered with us among the Mandans in 1804, and who were now on their way there. They had exhausted all their powder and lead; we therefore supplied them with both. They informed us that seven hundred Sioux had passed the Ricara towns on their way to make war against the Mandans and Minnetarees, leaving their women and children encamped near the Big-bend of the Missouri, and that the Ricaras all remained at home, without taking any part in the war. They also told us that the Pawnee, or Ricara chief, who went to the United States in the spring of 1805, died on his return near Sioux river.

We then left them, and soon afterwards arrived opposite to the upper Ricara villages. We saluted them with the discharge of four guns, which they answered in the same manner; and on our landing we were met by the greater part of the inhabitants of each village, and also by a band of Chayennes, who were encamped on a hill in the neighbourhood.

As soon as captain Clark stepped on shore, he was greeted by the two chiefs to whom we had given medals on our last visit, and as they, as well as the rest, appeared much rejoiced at our return, and desirous of hearing from the Mandans, he sat down on the bank, while the Ricaras and Chayennes formed a circle round him; and after smoking, he informed them, as he had already done the Minnetarees, of the various tribes we had visited, and our anxiety to promote peace among our red brethren. He then expressed his regret at their having attacked the Mandans, who had listened to our counsels, and had sent on a chief to smoke with them, and to assure them that they might now hunt in the plains, and visit the Mandan villages in safety, and concluded by inviting some of the chiefs to accompany us to Washington. The man whom we had acknowledged as the principal chief when we ascended, now presented another, who he said was a greater chief than himself, and to him, therefore, he had surrendered the flag and medal with which we had honoured him. This chief, who was absent at our last visit, is a man of thirty-five years of age, a stout, well-looking man, and called by the Indians, Grayeyes.

He now made a very animated reply. He declared that the Ricaras were willing to follow the counsels we had given them, but a few of their bad young men would not live in peace, but had joined the Sioux, and thus embroiled them with the Mandans. These young men had, however, been driven out of the villages, and as the Ricaras were now separated from the Sioux, who were a bad people, and the cause of all their misfortunes, they now desired to be at peace with the Mandans, and would receive them with kindness and friendship. Several of the chiefs he said were desirous of visiting their great father, but as the chief who went to the United States last summer had not returned, and they had some fears for his safety, on account of the Sioux, they did not wish to leave home until they heard of him. With regard to himself, he would continue with his nation, to see that they followed our advice.

The sun being now very hot, the chief of the Chayennes invited us to his lodge, which was at no great distance from the river. We followed him, and found a very large lodge, made of twenty buffalo skins, surrounded by eighteen or twenty lodges, nearly equal in size. The rest of the nation are expected to-morrow, and will make the number of one hundred and thirty or fifty lodges, containing from three hundred and fifty to four hundred men, at which the men of the nation may be computed. These Chayennes are a fine looking people, of a large stature, straight limbs, high cheek-bones and noses, and of a complexion similar to that of the Ricaras. Their ears are cut at the lower part, but few wear ornaments in them, the hair is generally cut over the eyebrows and small ornaments fall down the cheeks, the remainder being either twisted with horse or buffalo hair, and divided over each shoulder, or else flowing loosely behind. Their decorations consist chiefly of blue beads, shells, red paint, brass rings, bears' claws, and strips of otter skins, of which last they, as well as the Ricaras, are very fond. The women are coarse in their features, with wide mouths, and ugly. Their dress consists of a habit falling to the midleg, and made of two equal pieces of leather, sewed from the bottom with arm holes, with a flap hanging nearly half way down the body, both before and behind. These are burnt in various figures by means of a hot stick, and adorned with beads, shells, and elks' tusks, which all Indians admire. The other ornaments are blue beads in the ears, but the hair is plain and flows down the back. The summer dress of the men is a simple buffalo robe, a cloth round the waist, moccasins, and occasionally leggings. Living remote from the whites, they are shy and cautious, but are peaceably disposed, and profess to make war against no people except the Sioux, with whom they have been engaged in contests immemorially. In their excursions they are accompanied by their dogs and horses, which they possess in great numbers, the former serving to carry almost all their light baggage.

After smoking for some time, captain Clark gave a small medal to the Chayenne chief, and explained at the same time the meaning of it. He seemed alarmed at this present, and sent for a robe and a quantity of buffalo meat, which he gave to captain Clark, and requested him to take back the medal, for he knew that all white people were medicine, and he was afraid of the medal, or of any thing else which the white people gave to the Indians. Captain Clark then repeated his intention in giving the medal, which was the medicine his great father had directed him to deliver to all chiefs who listened to his word and followed his counsels; and that as he had done so, the medal was given as a proof that we believed him sincere. He now appeared satisfied and received the medal, in return for which he gave double the quantity of buffalo meat he had offered before. He seemed now quite reconciled to the whites, and requested that some traders might be sent among the Chayennes, who lived he said, in a country full of beaver, but did not understand well how to catch them, and were discouraged from it by having no sale for them when caught. Captain Clark promised that they should be soon supplied with goods, and taught the best mode of catching beaver.

The Bigwhite, chief of the Mandans, now addressed them at some length, explaining the pacific intentions of his nation; and the Chayenne observed that both the Ricaras and Mandans seemed to be in fault; but at the end of the council the Mandan chief was treated with great civility, and the greatest harmony prevailed among them. The great chief, however, informed us, that none of the Ricaras could be prevailed on to go with us till the return of the other chief, and that the Chayennes were a wild people, and afraid to go. He invited captain Clark to his house, and gave him two carrots of tobacco, two beaver skins, and a trencher of boiled corn and beans. It is the custom of all the nations on the Missouri, to offer to every white man food and refreshment when he first enters their tents.

Captain Clark returned to the boats, where he found the chief of the lower village, who had cut off part of his hair, and disfigured himself in such a manner that we did not recognise him at first, until he explained that he was in mourning for his nephew, who had been killed by the Sioux. He proceeded with us to the village on the island, where we were met by all the inhabitants. The second chief, on seeing the Mandan, began to speak to him in a loud and threatening tone, till captain Clark declared that the Mandans had listened to our counsels, and that if any injury was done to the chief, we should defend him against every nation. He then invited the Mandan to his lodge, and after a very ceremonious smoking, assured captain Clark that the Mandan was as safe as at home, for the Ricaras had opened their ears to our counsels, as well as the Mandans. This was repeated by the great chief, and the Mandan and Ricara chiefs now smoked and conversed in great apparent harmony; after which we returned to the boats. The whole distance to-day was twenty-nine miles.

AUGUST 22D    *Friday*. It rained all night, so that we all rose this morning quite wet, and were about proceeding, when captain Clark was requested to visit the chiefs. They now made several speeches, in which they said that they were unwilling to go with us, until the return of their countryman; and that, although they disliked the Sioux as the origin of all their troubles, yet as they had more horses than they wanted, and were in want of guns and powder, they would be obliged to trade once more with them for those articles, after which they would break off all connection with them. He now returned to the boats, and after taking leave of the people, who seemed to regret our departure, and firing a salute of two guns, proceeded seventeen miles, and encamped below Grouse island. We made only seventeen miles to-day, for we were obliged to land near Wetarhoo river to dry our baggage, besides which the sandbars are now unusually numerous as the river widens below the Ricara villages. Captain Lewis is now so far recovered that he was able to walk a little to-day for the first time. While here we had occasion to notice that the Mandans as well as the Minnetarees and Ricaras keep their horses in the same lodges with themselves.

AUGUST 23D    *Saturday*. We set out early, but the wind was so high, that soon after passing the Sahwacanah, we were obliged to go on shore, and remain till three o'clock, when a heavy shower of rain fell and the wind lulled. We then continued our route, and after a day's journey of forty miles encamped. Whilst on shore we killed three deer and as many elk. Along the river are great quantities of grapes and chokecherries, and also a species of currant which we have never seen before: it is black, with a leaf much larger than that of the other currants, and inferior in flavour to all of them.

*Sunday.* We set out at sunrise, and at eight o'clock passed Lahoocat's is- AUGUST 24TH land, opposite to the lower point of which we landed to examine a stratum of stone, near the top of a bluff of remarkably black clay. It is soft, white, and contains a very fine grit; and on being dried in the sun will crumble to pieces. The wind soon after became so high that we were obliged to land for several hours, but proceeded at five o'clock. After making forty-three miles, we encamped at the gorge of the Lookout bend of the Missouri. The Sioux have lately passed in this quarter, and there is now very little game, and that so wild, that we were unable to shoot any thing. Five of the hunters were therefore sent ahead before daylight next morning to hunt in the Pawnee island, and we followed them soon after.

*Monday.* At eight o'clock we reached the entrance of the Chayenne, where AUGUST 25TH we remained till noon, in order to take a meridian observation. At three o'clock we passed the old Pawnee village, near which we had met the Tetons in 1804, and encamped in a large bottom on the northeast side, a little below the mouth of Notimber creek. Just above our camp the Ricaras had formerly a large village on each side of the river, and there are still seen the remains of five villages on the southwest side, below the Chayenne, and one also on Lahoocat's island; but these have all been destroyed by the Sioux. The weather was clear and calm, but by means of our oars we made forty-eight miles. Our hunters procured nothing except a few deer.

The skirt of timber in the bend above the Chayenne is inconsiderable, and scattered from four to sixteen miles on the southwest side of the river, and the thickest part is from the distance of from ten to six miles of the Chayenne. A narrow bottom of small cottonwood trees is also on the northeast point, at the distance of four miles above the river. A few large trees, and a small undergrowth of willows on the lower side bottom on the Missouri half a mile, and extend a quarter of a mile up the Chayenne: there is a bottom of cotton timber in the part above the Chayenne. The Chayenne discharges but a little water at its mouth, which resembles that of the Missouri.

*Tuesday.* After a heavy dew we set out, and at nine o'clock reached the en- AUGUST 26TH trance of Teton river, below which were a raft and a skin canoe, which induced us to suspect that the Tetons were in the neighbourhood. The arms were therefore put in perfect order, and every thing prepared to revenge the slightest insult from those people, to whom it is necessary to show an example of salutary rigour. We, however, went on without seeing any of them, although we were obliged to land near Smoke creek for two hours, to stop a leak in the periogue. Here we saw great quantities of plums and grapes, but not yet ripe. At five o'clock we passed Louisville's fort, on Cedar island, twelve miles below which we encamped, having been able to row sixty miles, with the wind ahead during the greater part of the day.

*The Big White (Sheheke), a subordinate Mandan chief whom the explorers took back east with them (from a crayon portrait by St. Memin).*

AUGUST 27TH   *Wednesday.* Before sunrise we set out with a stiff eastern breeze in our faces, and at the distance of a few miles landed on a sandbar near Tylor's river, and sent out the hunters, as this was the most favourable spot to recruit our stock of meat, which was now completely exhausted. But after a hunt of three hours, they reported that no game was to be found in the bottoms, the grass having been laid flat by the immense number of buffaloes which had recently passed over it; and that they saw only a few buffalo bulls, which they did not kill, as they were quite unfit for use. Near this place we observed, however, the first signs of the wild turkey; and not long after landed in the Bigbend, and killed a fine fat elk, on which we feasted.

536

Towards night we heard the bellowing of the buffalo bulls, on the lower is-island of the Bigbend. We pursued this agreeable sound, and after killing some of the cows, encamped on the island, forty-five miles from the camp of last night.

*Thursday.* We proceeded at an early hour, having previously despatched some hunters ahead, with orders to join us at our old camp a little above Corvus creek, where we intended remaining one day, in order to procure the skins and skeletons of some animals, such as the mule-deer, the antelope, the barking squirrel, and the magpie, which we were desirous of carrying to the United States, and which we had seen in great abundance. After rowing thirty-two miles we landed at twelve, and formed a camp in a high bottom, thinly timbered and covered with grass, and not crowded with mosquitoes. Soon after we arrived the squaws and several of the men went to the bushes near the river, and brought great quantities of large well flavoured plums of three different species.

The hunters returned in the afternoon, without being able to pro-cure any of the game we wished, except the barking squirrel, though they killed four common deer, and had seen large herds of buffalo, of which they brought in two.

*Friday.* They resumed their hunt in the morning, and the rest of the party were employed in dressing skins, except two, who were sent to the village of the barking squirrels, but could not see one of them out of their holes. At ten o'clock the skins were dressed, and we proceeded; and soon passed the en-trance of White river, the water of which is at this time nearly the colour of milk. The day was spent in hunting along the river, so that we did not ad-vance more than twenty miles; but with all our efforts we were unable to kill either a mule-deer or an antelope, though we procured the common deer, a porcupine, and some buffalo. These last animals are now so numerous that from an eminence we discovered more than we had ever seen before, at one time; and if it be not impossible to calculate the moving multitude, which darkened the whole plains, we are convinced that twenty thousand would be no exaggerated number. With regard to game in general, we observe that the greatest quantity of wild animals are usually found in the country lying between two nations at war.

*Saturday.* We set out at the usual hour, but after going some distance were obliged to stop for two hours, in order to wait for one of the hunters. During this time we made an excursion to a large orchard of delicious plums, where we were so fortunate as to kill two buck elks. We then proceeded down the river, and were about landing at a place where we had agreed to meet all the hunters, when several persons appeared on the high hills to the northeast, whom, by the help of the spy-glass, we distinguished to be Indians. We landed on the southwest side of the river, and immediately after saw, on a height opposite to us, about twenty persons, one of whom, from his blanket great-coat, and a handkerchief round his head, we supposed to be a French-man. At the same time, eighty or ninety more Indians, armed with guns and bows and arrows, came out of a wood some distance below them, and fired a salute, which we returned. From their hostile appearance, we were apprehensive that they might be Tetons; but as from the country through which they were roving, it was possible that they were Yanktons, Pawnees, or Mahas, and therefore less suspicious, we did not know in what way to receive them.

In order, however, to ascertain who they were, without risk to the party, captain Clark crossed, with three persons who could speak different Indian languages, to a sandbar near the opposite side, in hopes of conversing with them. Eight young men soon met him on the sandbar, but none of them could understand either the Pawnee or Maha interpreter. They were then addressed in the Sioux language, and answered that they were Tetons, of the band headed by the Black-buffalo, Tahtackasabah. This was the same who had attempted to stop us in 1804; and being now less anxious about offending so mischievous a tribe, captain Clark told them that they had been deaf to our counsels, had ill treated us two years ago, and had abused all the whites who had since visited them. He believed them, he added, to be bad people and they must therefore return to their companions, for if they crossed over to our camp we would put them to death. They asked for some corn, which captain Clark refused; they then requested permission to come and visit our camp, but he ordered them back to their own people. He then returned, and all the arms were prepared in case of an attack; but when the Indians reached their comrades, and had informed their chiefs of our intention, they all set out on their way to their own camp; but some of them halted on a rising ground, and abused us very copiously, threatening to kill us if we came across. We took no notice of this for some time, till the return of three of our hunters, whom we were afraid the Indians might have met; but as soon as they joined us, we embarked; and to see what the Indians would attempt, steered near the side of their river. At this the party on the hill seemed agitated, some set out for their camp, others walked about, and one man walked towards the boats and invited us to land. As he came near, we recognised him to be the same who had accompanied us for two days in 1804, and who is considered as the friend of the whites. Unwilling, however, to have any interview with these people, we declined his invitation; upon which he returned to the hill, and struck the earth three times with his gun, a great oath among the Indians, who consider swearing by the earth as one of the most sacred forms of imprecation.

At the distance of six miles we stopped on a bleak sandbar; where, however, we thought ourselves safe from attack during the night, and also free from mosquitoes. We had now made only twenty-two miles; but in the course of the day had procured a mule-deer, which we much desired. About eleven in the evening the wind shifted to the northwest, and it began to rain, accompanied with hard claps of thunder and lightning; after which the wind changed to southwest, and blew with such violence that we were obliged to hold the canoes for fear of their being driven from the sandbar; the cables of two of them however broke, and two others were blown quite across the river, nor was it till two o'clock that the whole party was reassembled, waiting in the rain for daylight.

SUNDAY, AUGUST 31ST, 1806  We examined our arms, and proceeded with the wind in our favour. For some time we saw several Indians on the hills, but soon lost sight of them. In passing the dome, and the first village of barking squirrels, we stopped and killed two fox squirrels, an animal which we have not seen on the river higher than this place. At night we encamped on the northeast side, after a journey of seventy miles. We had seen no game, as usual, on the river; but in the evening the mosquitoes soon discovered us.

## Monday, September 1st, 1806

We set out early, but were shortly compelled to put to shore, for half an hour, till a thick fog disappeared. At nine o'clock we passed the entrance of the Quicurre, which presents the same appearance as when we ascended, the water rapid and of a milky-white colour. Two miles below several Indians ran down to the bank, and beckoned to us to land; but as they appeared to be Tetons, and of a war party, we paid no attention to them, except to inquire to what tribe they belonged; but as the Sioux interpreter did not understand much of the language, they probably mistook his question. As one of our canoes was behind, we were afraid of an attack on the men, and therefore landed on an open commanding situation, out of the view of the Indians, in order to wait for them.

      We had not been in this position fifteen minutes, when we heard several guns, which we immediately concluded were fired at the three hunters; and being now determined to protect them against any number of Indians, captain Clark with fifteen men ran up the river, whilst captain Lewis hobbled up the bank, and formed the rest of the party in such a manner as would best enable them to protect the boats. On turning a point of the river, captain Clark was agreeably surprised at seeing the Indians remaining in the place where we left them, and our canoe at the distance of a mile. He now went on a sandbar, and when the Indians crossed, gave them his hand, and was informed that they had been amusing themselves with shooting at an old keg, which we had thrown into the river, and was floating down. We now found them to be part of a band of eighty lodges of Yanktons, on Plum creek, and therefore invited them down to the camp, and after smoking several pipes, told them that we had mistaken them for Tetons, and had intended putting every one of them to death, if they had fired at our canoe; but finding them Yanktons, who were good men, we were glad to take them by the hand as faithful children, who had opened their ears to our counsels. They saluted the Mandan with great cordiality, and one of them declared that their ears had indeed been opened, and that they had followed our advice since we gave a medal to their great chief, and should continue to do so. We now tied a piece of ribbon to the hair of each Indian, and gave them some corn. We made a present of a pair of leggings to the principal chief, and then took our leave, being previously overtaken by our canoe.

      At two o'clock we landed to hunt on Bonhomme island, but obtained a single elk only. The bottom on the northeast side is very rich, and so thickly overgrown with pea-vines and grass, interwoven with grape-vines, that some of the party who attempted to hunt there, were obliged to leave it and ascend the plain, where they found the grass nearly as high as their heads. These plains are much richer below than above the Quicurre, and the whole country is now very beautiful. After making fifty-two miles against a head wind, we stopped for the night on a sandbar, opposite to the Calumet bluff, where we had encamped on the first of September, 1804, and where our flag-staff was still standing. We suffered very much from the mosquitoes, till the wind became so high as to blow them all away.

SEPTEMBER 2D  *Tuesday.* At eight o'clock we passed the river Jacques, but soon after were compelled to land, in consequence of the high wind from the northeast, and remain till sunset: after which we went on to a sandbar twenty-two miles from our camp of last evening. Whilst we were on shore we killed three buffaloes, and four prairie fowls, which are the first we have seen in descending. Two turkeys were also killed, and were very much admired by the Indians, who had never seen that animal before. The plains continue level and fertile, and in the low grounds there is much white oak, and some white ash in the ravines and high bottoms, with lyn and slippery elm occasionally. During the night the wind shifted to the southwest and blew the sand over us in such a manner, that our situation was very unpleasant. It lulled, however, towards daylight, and we then proceeded.

SEPTEMBER 3D  *Wednesday.* At eleven o'clock we passed the Redstone. The river is now crowded with sandbars, which are very differently situated now from what they were when we ascended. But notwithstanding these and the head wind, we made sixty miles before night, when we saw two boats and several men on shore. We landed, and found a Mr. James Airs, a partner of a house at Prairie de Chien, who had come from Mackinau by the way of Prairie de Chien and St. Louis with a license to trade among the Sioux for one year. He had brought two canoes loaded with merchandise, but lost many of his most useful articles in a squall some time since. After so long an interval, the sight of any one who could give us information of our country, was peculiarly delightful, and much of the night was spent in making inquiries into what had occurred during our absence. We found Mr. Airs a very friendly and liberal gentleman, and when we proposed to him to purchase a small quantity of tobacco, to be paid for in St. Louis, he very readily furnished every man of the party with as much as he could use during the rest of the voyage, and insisted on our accepting a barrel of flour. This last we found very agreeable, although we have still a little flour which we had deposited at the mouth of Maria's river. We could give in return only about six bushels of corn, which was all that we could spare.

SEPTEMBER 4TH  *Thursday.* The next morning we left Mr. Airs about eight o'clock, and after passing the Big Sioux river, stopped at noon near Floyd's bluff. On ascending the hill we found that the grave of Floyd had been opened, and was now half uncovered. We filled it up, and then continued down to our old camp near the Maha village, where all our baggage, which had been wet by the rain of last night, was exposed to dry. There is no game on the river except wild geese and pelicans. Near Floyd's grave are some flourishing black walnut trees, which are the first we have seen on our return.

At night we heard the report of several guns in a direction towards the Maha village, and supposed it to be the signal of the arrival of some trader. But not meeting him when we set out, the next morning, *Friday*, we concluded that the firing was merely to announce the return of the Mahas to the village, this being the season at which they return home from buffalo hunting, to take care of their corn, beans and pumpkins. The river is now more crooked, the current more rapid, and crowded with snags and sawyers, and the bottoms on both sides well supplied with timber. At three o'clock we passed the Bluestone bluff, where the river leaves the highlands and meanders through a low rich bottom, and at night encamped, after making seventy-three miles.

SEPTEMBER 6TH

*Saturday*. The wind continued ahead, but the mosquitoes were so tormenting that to remain was more unpleasant than even to advance, however slowly, and we therefore proceeded. Near the Little Sioux river we met a trading boat belonging to Mr. Augustus Chateau, of St. Louis, with several men, on their way to trade with the Yanktons at the river Jacques. We obtained from them a gallon of whiskey, and gave each of the party a dram, which is the first spirituous liquor any of them have tasted since the fourth of July, 1805. After remaining with them for some time we went on to a sandbar, thirty miles from our last encampment, where we passed the night in expectation of being joined by two of the hunters. But as they did not come on, we set out next morning, *Sunday*, leaving a canoe with five men, to wait for them, but had not gone more than eight miles, when we overtook them; we therefore fired a gun, which was a signal for the men behind, which, as the distance in a direct line was about a mile, they readily heard and soon joined us. A little above the Soldier's river we stopped to dine on elk, of which we killed three, and at night, after making forty-four miles, encamped on a sandbar, where we hoped in vain to escape from the mosquitoes.

SEPTEMBER 8TH

*Monday*. We therefore set out early the next morning and stopped for a short time at the Council bluffs, to examine the situation of the place, and were confirmed in our belief that it would be a very eligible spot for a trading establishment. Being anxious to reach the Platte, we plied our oars so well, that by night we had made seventy-eight miles, and landed at our old encampment at White-catfish camp, twelve miles above that river. We had here occasion to remark the wonderful evaporation from the Missouri, which does not appear to contain more water, nor is its channel wider than at the distance of one thousand miles nearer its source, although within that space it receives about twenty rivers, some of them of considerable width, and a great number of creeks. This evaporation seems, in fact, to be greater now than when we ascended the river, for we are obliged to replenish the inkstand every day with fresh ink, nine-tenths of which must escape by evaporation.

SEPTEMBER 9TH

*Tuesday*. By eight o'clock we passed the river Platte, which is lower than it was, and its waters almost clear, though the channel is turbulent as usual. The sandbars which obstructed the Missouri are, however, washed away, and nothing is to be seen except a few remains of the bar. Below the Platte, the current of the Missouri becomes evidently more rapid, and the obstructions from fallen timber increased. The river bottoms are extensive, rich, and covered with tall, large timber, which is still more abundant in the hollows of the ravines, where may be seen, oak, ash, elm, interspersed with some walnut and hickory. The mosquitoes also, though still numerous, seem to lose some of their vigour. As we advance so rapidly, the change of climate is very perceptible, the air is more sultry than we have experienced for a long time before, and the nights so warm that a thin blanket is now sufficient, although a few days ago two were not burdensome. Late in the afternoon we encamped opposite to the Baldpated prairie, after a journey of seventy-three miles.

SEPTEMBER 10TH  *Wednesday*. We again set out early and the wind being moderate, though still ahead, we came sixty-five miles to a sandbar, a short distance above the grand Nemaha. In the course of the day we met a trader, with three men, on his way to the Pawnee Loups or Wolf Pawnees, on the Platte. Soon after another boat passed us with seven men from St. Louis, bound to the Mahas. With both of these trading parties we had some conversation, but our anxiety to go on would not suffer us to remain long with them. The Indians, and particularly the squaws and children are weary of the long journey, and we are not less desirous of seeing our country and friends. We saw on the shore, deer, raccoons, and turkeys.

SEPTEMBER 11TH  *Thursday*. A high wind from the northwest detained us till after sunrise, when we proceeded slowly; for as the river is rapid and narrow, as well as more crowded with sandbars and timber than above, much caution is necessary in avoiding these obstacles, particularly in the present low state of the water. The Nemaha seems less wide than when we saw it before, and Wolf river has scarcely any water. In the afternoon we halted above the Nadowa to hunt, and killed two deer, after which we went on to a small island, forty miles from our last night's encampment. Here we were no longer annoyed by mosquitoes, which do not seem to frequent this part of the river; and after having been persecuted with these insects during the whole route from the falls, it is a most agreeable exemption. Their noise was very agreeably changed for that of the common wolves, which were howling in different directions, and the prairie wolves, whose barking resembles precisely that of the common cur dog.

SEPTEMBER 12TH  *Friday*. After a thick fog and a heavy dew we set out by sunrise, and at the distance of seven miles met two periogues, one of them bound to the Platte, for the purpose of trading with the Pawnees, the other on a trapping expedition to the neighbourhood of the Mahas. Soon after we met the trading party under Mr. M'Clellan; and with them was Mr. Gravelines, the interpreter, whom we had sent with a Ricara chief to the United States. The chief had unfortunately died at Washington, and Gravelines was now on his way to the Ricaras, with a speech from the president, and the presents which had been made to the chief. He had also directions to instruct the Ricaras in agriculture. He was accompanied on this mission by old Mr. Durion, our former Sioux interpreter, whose object was to procure by his influence, a safe passage for the Ricara presents through the bands of Sioux, and also to engage some of the Sioux chiefs, not exceeding six, to visit Washington.

Both of them were instructed to inquire particularly after the fate of our party, no intelligence having been received from us during a long time. We authorised Mr. Durion to invite ten or twelve Sioux chiefs to accompany him, particularly the Yanktons, whom we had found well disposed towards our country. The afternoon being wet, we determined to remain with Mr. M'Clellan during the night; and therefore, after sending on five hunters ahead, spent the evening in inquiries after occurrences in the United States during our absence; and by eight o'clock next morning overtook the hunters; but they had killed nothing.

*Saturday.* The wind being now too high to proceed safely through timber stuck in every part of the channel, we landed, and sent the small canoes ahead to hunt. Towards evening we overtook them, and encamped, not being able to advance more than eighteen miles. The weather was very warm, and the rushes in the bottoms so high and thick that we could scarcely hunt, but were fortunate enough to obtain four deer and a turkey, which, with the hooting owl, the common buzzard, crow, and hawk, were the only game we saw. Among the timber is the cottonwood, sycamore, ash, mulberry, papaw, walnut, hickory, prickly ash, several species of elm, intermixed with great quantities of grape-vines, and three kinds of peas.

*Sunday.* We resumed our journey, and this being a part of the river to which the Kanzas resort, in order to rob the boats of traders, we held ourselves in readiness to fire upon any Indians who should offer us the slightest indignity, as we no longer needed their friendship, and found that a tone of firmness and decision is the best possible method of making proper impression on these freebooters. We, however, did not encounter any of them; but just below the old Kanzas village met three trading boats from St. Louis, on their way to the Yanktons and Mahas. After leaving them we saw a number of deer, of which we killed five, and encamped on an island, fifty-three miles from our encampment of last evening.

*Monday.* A strong breeze ahead prevented us from advancing more than forty-nine miles to the neighbourhood of Haycabin creek. The river Kanzas is very low at this time. About a mile below it we landed to view the situation of a high hill, which has many advantages for a trading house or fort; while on the shore we gathered great quantities of papaws, and shot an elk. The low grounds are now delightful, and the whole country exhibits a rich appearance; but the weather is oppressively warm, and descending as rapidly as we do from a cool open country, between the latitude of 46 and 49°, in which we have been for nearly two years, to the wooded plains in 38 and 39°, the heat would be almost insufferable were it not for the constant winds from the south and southeast.

*Tuesday.* We set out at an early hour, but the weather soon became so warm that the men rowed but little. In the course of the day we met two trading parties, on their way to the Pawnees and Mahas, and after making fifty-two miles, remained on an island till next morning, *Wednesday*, when we passed in safety the island of the Little Osage village. This place is considered by the navigators of the Missouri, as the most dangerous part of it, the whole water being compressed, for two miles, within a narrow channel, crowded with timber, into which the violence of the current is constantly washing the banks. At the distance of thirty miles we met a captain M'Clellan, lately of the United States army, with whom we encamped. He informed us that the general opinion in the United States was that we were lost; the last accounts which had been heard of us being from the Mandan villages. Captain M'Clellan is on his way to attempt a new trade with the Indians. His plan is to establish himself on the Platte, and after trading with the Pawnees and Ottoes, prevail on some of their chiefs to accompany him to Santa Fee, where he hopes to obtain permission to exchange his merchandise for gold and silver, which is there in abundance. If this be granted, he can transport his goods on mules and horses from the Platte to some part of Louisiana, convenient to the Spanish settlements, where he may be met by the traders from New Mexico.

SEPTEMBER 18TH  *Thursday.* We parted with captain M'Clellan, and within a few miles passed the Grand river, below which we overtook the hunters, who had been sent forward yesterday afternoon. They had not been able to kill any thing, nor did we see any game except one bear and three turkeys, so that our whole stock of provisions is one biscuit for each person; but as there is an abundance of papaws, the men are perfectly contented. The current of the river is more gentle than it was when we ascended, the water being lower though still rapid in places where it is confined. We continued to pass through a very fine country, for fifty-two miles, when we encamped nearly opposite to Mine river.

SEPTEMBER 19TH  *Friday.* We worked our oars all day, without taking time to hunt, or even landing, except once to gather papaws; and at eight o'clock reached the entrance of the Osage river, a distance of seventy-two miles. Several of the party have been for a day or two attacked with a soreness in the eyes; the eye-ball being very much swelled and the lid appearing as if burnt by the sun, and extremely painful, particularly when exposed to the light. Three of the men are so much affected by it, as to be unable to row. We therefore turned one of the boats adrift, and distributed the men among the other canoes, when we set out a little before daybreak.

SEPTEMBER 20TH  *Saturday.* The Osage is at this time low, and discharges but a very small quantity of water. Near the mouth of Gasconade, where we arrived at noon, we met five Frenchmen on their way to the Great Osage village. As we moved along rapidly, we saw on the banks some cows feeding, and the whole party almost involuntarily raised a shout of joy at seeing this image of civilisation and domestic life.

Soon after we reached the little French village of Lacharette, which we saluted with a discharge of four guns, and three hearty cheers. We then landed, and were received with kindness by the inhabitants, as well as some traders from Canada, who were going to traffic with the Osages and Ottoes. They were all equally surprised and pleased at our arrival, for they had long since abandoned all hopes of ever seeing us return.

These Canadians have boats prepared for the navigation of the Missouri, which seem better calculated for the purpose than those in any other form. They are in the shape of batteaux, about thirty feet long, and eight wide; the bow and stern pointed, the bottom flat, and carrying six oars only, and their chief advantage is their width and flatness, which saves them from the danger of rolling sands.

Having come sixty-eight miles, and the weather threatening to be bad, we remained at La Charette till the next morning, *Sunday*, when we proceeded, and as several settlements have been made during our absence, were refreshed with the sight of men and cattle along the banks. We also passed twelve canoes of Kickapoo Indians, going on a hunting excursion. At length, after coming forty-eight miles, we saluted, with heartfelt satisfaction, the village of St. Charles, and on landing were treated with the greatest hospitality and kindness by all the inhabitants of that place. Their civility detained us till ten o'clock the next morning.

*Monday.* The rain having ceased, we set out for Coldwater creek, about three miles from the mouth of the Missouri, where we found a cantonment of troops of the United States, with whom we passed the day, and then, *Tuesday, 23d*, descended to the Mississippi, and round to St. Louis, where we arrived at twelve o'clock, and having fired a salute went on shore and received the heartiest and most hospitable welcome from the whole village.

SEPTEMBER 22D

**By the last Mails.**

*MARYLAND.*  BALTIMORE, OCT. 29, 1806.

A LETTER from *St. Louis* (*Upper Louisiana*), dated *Sept.* 23, 1806, announces the arrival of Captains LEWIS and CLARK, from their expedition into the interior.—They went to the *Pacific Ocean*; have brought some of the natives and curiosities of the countries through which they passed, and only lost one man. They left the *Pacific Ocean* 23d March, 1806, where they arrived in November, 1805;—and where some American vessels had been just before.—They state the Indians to be as numerous on the *Columbia* river, which empties into the *Pacific*, as the whites in any part of the U. S. They brought a family of the *Mandan* indians with them. The winter was very mild on the *Pacific*.—They have kept an ample journal of their tour; which will be published, and must afford much intelligence.

*The expedition's return, as reported in "The Columbian Centinel," Boston, on November 5, 1806.*

# ACKNOWLEDGMENTS

For their constant cooperation in providing research material used in preparing this edition, the publishers express their gratitude to Gerald D. McDonald, Chief of the American History Division of the New York Public Library, and to his staff. The material included the following books:

Patrick Gass's *Journal of the Voyages and Travels of a Corps of Discovery* . . . (Pittsburgh, 1807)

Prince Maximilian of Wied-Neuwied's *Travels in the Interior of North America* . . . (3 volumes, London, 1843)

Elliott Coues' *History of the Expedition* . . . (a revised version of the Biddle edition in 4 volumes, Harper, 1893)

Olin D. Wheeler's *The Trail of Lewis and Clark* (2 volumes, Putnam, 1904)

Reuben Gold Thwaites' *The Original Journals of the Lewis and Clark Expedition* (8 volumes, Dodd, Mead, 1904–1905)

*Publications* of the State Historical Society of Wisconsin

Carl Bodmer's water-colors were made while he was accompanying Prince Maximilian of Wied-Neuwied on an epochal tour of North America in 1833–1834, and engravings of them first appeared in the "Atlas" volume of Maximilian's account. Several of our Bodmer reproductions are made from specimens kindly loaned by Harry Shaw Newman of The Old Print Shop, Inc., New York. The others, together with the paintings by George Bird King (made *ca.* 1837), are from *The Indian Journals* of Lewis Henry Morgan, by arrangement with the publisher, The University of Michigan Press, Ann Arbor.

The original William Clark map is in the Coe Collection of Western Americana at Yale University Library, New Haven, which has granted permission for our facsimile.

The Peale portraits (*ca.* 1807) of Meriwether Lewis and William Clark in Volume One appear by courtesy of Independence Hall, Philadelphia; those of Lewis and Clark in Volume Two by courtesy of the Missouri Historical Society, St. Louis (the Lewis is from an engraving by Strickland of a water-color by Charles de St.-Memin; the head of Clark was painted *ca.* 1820 by Chester Harding, but the figure is attributed to a local scenery painter). St.-Memin's crayon portrait of She-He-Ke ("Big White") is in the collection of the American Philosophical Society, Philadelphia.

We also gratefully acknowledge the assistance of Frederick J. Dockstader, Director of the Museum of the American Indian (Heye Foundation), New York, and that of Robert M. Metzdorf at the Yale University Library.

*This edition of*

THE LEWIS AND CLARK

JOURNALS

*has been made to the*

*typographic plan of*

Eugene Ettenberg.

*The two volumes have been designed*

*in the form of an explorer's journal, and the text has been set in the*

MONTICELLO *type. Though of recent design, Monticello is based on the*

*first successful American typeface. The parent face, cast by* Archibald

Binny *at Philadelphia in 1789, was the most popular native typeface of*

Jefferson's *time.*